MW00613041

Astri, My Astri:
Norwegian Heritage Stories

Deb Nelson Gourley

Norwegian translations by Vigdis Sundsvold (14 stories)
English translations by James Skurdall (2 stories)

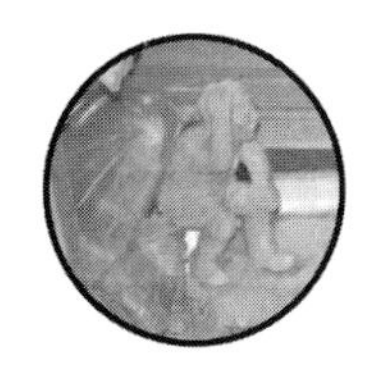
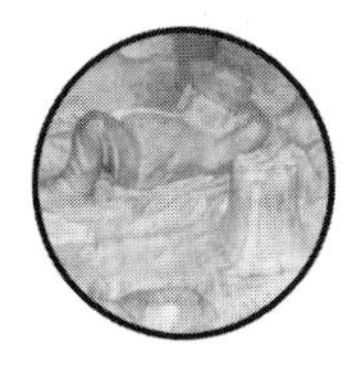
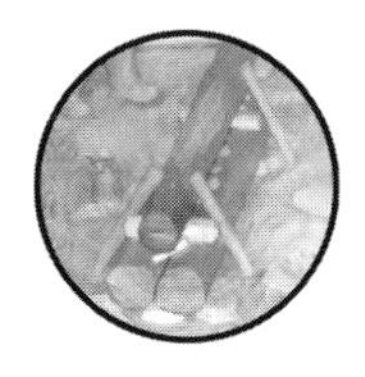
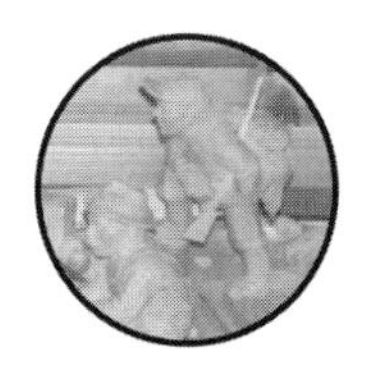

Library of Congress Control Number: 2004095831

ISBN 0-9760541-0-8

Published by:
Deb Nelson Gourley
602 3rd Ave SW
Waukon, IA 52172-2113 USA
Phone: 563-568-6229
Fax: 563-568-5377

Printed by:
Anundsen Publishing Company, Decorah, Iowa

Cover picture designed by Deb Nelson Gourley from a woodcarving by Hans Sorken at the *Norsk Skogmuseum* (Norwegian Forest Museum) Elverum, Norway. Cover layout by Chris Shelton.

Foreword/Forord

The 'great immigration' of Norwegians to North America in the 1800s may seem like ancient history as we enter the 21st century. Furthermore, that saga, it would seem, has already been told. Norwegian and Norwegian-American writers published those stories a century ago, when they were fresh—when the Norwegian language was still largely intact in their midst.

But here comes a new collection, for and about Norwegians and Norwegian-Americans, that adds to that body of stories. With the dedication of an indefatigable detective, author Deb Nelson Gourley displays her abilities as both researcher and storyteller. Her highly readable stories are simultaneously deeply personal yet universal.

An old trunk, a handwritten note, cemetery and courthouse records—these become the skeletal framework which the author then clothes with flesh, blood, and bunads. There is something here for the newcomer to Norwegian-American immigrant literature as well as for the old hand.

• • • • •

Den store norske innvandringa til Nord-Amerika på 1800-tallet fortoner seg som fjern fortid for oss som nå er på vei inn i det 21. århundret. På sett og vis er også historia om den alt fortalt. Norske og norskamerikanske forfattere ga ut sine tekster om innvandringa for hundre år siden, da den ennå pågikk, og da innvandrerne ennå brukte norsk som språk seg imellom i Midtvesten.

Men her kommer en ny samling med fortellinger, for og om nordmenn og norskamerikanere. Det er et tilskudd til den litteraturen vi alt har. Deb Nelson Gourley er som en utrøttelig detektiv i sitt arbeid både som ættegransker og forteller. Hennes fortellinger er personlige samtidig som de angår oss alle.

Ei gammel kiste, et handskrevet lite brev, kirkegårdsregistre og lokale arkiv, alt dette utgjør rammene for historiene som fortelleren levendegjør. Hun forteller så vi ser de gamle for oss, i sine bunadsklær. Her er det stoff av interesse for den som nettopp har begynt å lese norskamerikansk litteratur og for den som kan en god del fra før.

Harley Refsal
Associate Professor
Scandinavian Folk Art
Scandinavian Studies
Luther College, Decorah, Iowa

Foreword/Forord

Astri, My Astri: Norwegian Heritage Stories is a delightful bilingual account of a search for Norwegian roots embellished with stories that have inspired the author and informed her about her heritage. The personal markers, beginning with the discovery of an immigrant trunk, and the selected narratives will all serve as an inspiration to anyone exploring the legacy of their own immigrant past.

Astri, My Astri: Norwegian Heritage Stories tegner et fengslende bilde av en personlig leting etter norske røtter som vil inspirere lesere på begge sider av Atlanterhavet. Den tospråklige teksten tar sitt utgangspunkt i immigrantkisten som fulgte forfatterens forfedre til den nye verden og blir så utvidet til å inkludere et utvalg av artikler som belyser en åndelig og kulturell norsk arv overført til Amerika.

Odd S. Lovoll
King Olav V Professor of Scandinavian-American Studies
St. Olaf College, Northfield, Minnesota (Retired)
Professor II of History
University of Oslo, Oslo, Norway

• • • • •

Deb Nelson Gourley's book will attract readers outside her own family circle. Like most Norwegian-American stories of the Midwest, her stories begin in a culture of farms and farming. She tells about the Indian rebellion of 1862, about epidemics, about letters and packages and visits to Norway after years of Nazi occupation. Her family and its history are thereby linked to a larger historical framework.

Boka har interesse ut over fortellerens egen slekt. Som de fleste norskamerikanske fortellingene i Midtvesten, begynner hennes historie i en jordbrukskultur. Boka er satt sammen av mange historier. Hun forteller om indianeropprøret i 1862, om epidemier, om brev og pakker og besøk etter verdenskrigen. I disse tekstene knyttes familien til et større historisk bilde.

Øyvind T. Gulliksen
Associate Professor
American Literature and Culture
Telemark University College, Norway

Contents/Innhold

(Each chapter is written in both English and Norwegian)

Preface/Forord

Astri, My Astri: Norwegian Heritage Stories is a collection of sixteen Norwegian heritage stories published in both English and Norwegian. Although based on my own 7/8 Norwegian ancestry, the stories touch anyone who has an interest in Norwegian heritage, culture, genealogy, or bilingual studies.

The stories take one on a journey from immigrating in the 1840s to the discovery of an immigrant trunk more than one hundred years later and the subsequent unraveling of a rich family history. Among the topics included are the Last Sioux Uprising of 1862, the great flu epidemic of 1918, hiking above the Arctic Circle, the heavy water assault during World War II, Norwegian *rosemaling* and *bunader*, *Syttende Mai*, stave churches, founding of a Norwegian Lutheran church in America, and the life of Snowshoe Thompson.

First published as feature stories in Minnesota's *Fillmore County Journal*, the expanded stories now include Norwegian translations and countless pictures. The immigrant trunk bilingual story was featured in the *Decorah Public Opinion* in Decorah, Iowa, appearing in both English and Norwegian on the front page just as it would have appeared years ago. The Norwegian version of the story also appeared in the *Hallingdølen* paper from Hallingdal, Norway.

Inspiration for the stories are my twenty-seven Norwegian ancestors, who began emigrating as early as 1845 from various areas of Norway, including Hallingdal, Numedal, Telemark, Voss, Sognefjord, Valdres, and Selbu near Trondheim. They consist of one great-grandparent, ten great-great-grandparents, fifteen great-great-great-grandparents, and one great-great-great-great-grandparent. During the 1840s and 1850s they first settled in Luther Valley and Koshkonong, Wisconsin, and then moved onward to Norwegian settlements in Fillmore, Houston, and Jackson Counties in Minnesota and Winneshiek County in Iowa.

I was raised on the family 150-year-old Norwegian ancestral farm in Amherst, near Canton, in southeastern Minnesota. I received my Bachelor of Science and Master of Science degrees from the University of Minnesota and worked on staff for both the University of Minnesota and University of Wisconsin. I was also the Quality Control Specialist at Tri-State Breeders Cooperative in Westby, Wisconsin, and the President/CEO/majority owner of Elite Genetics, Inc., in Waukon, Iowa. Having previously worked as a copy/layout editor at the *Fillmore County Journal*, I have self-published this book.

I dedicate *Astri, My Astri: Norwegian Heritage Stories* to my mother, Char Nelson, for all her assistance with genealogy research over the years. It was a daunting task since most of my ancestors had immigrated in the 1840s and 1850s. In 1976, over 125 years later, I was the first descendant in my family to return to Norway. Furthermore, no genealogy records had been kept over the years and all we had to begin our research with were the Americanized names Knudson, Larson, Bendickson, Thompson, and Nelson.

I also dedicate this book to my sons, Alex and Ben Huntrods, for their encouragement and support during the long process of turning a database with thousands of names and file cabinets full of research into a book. My hope is that the book will inspire other youth, as it has Alex and Ben, to learn about their heritage.

In addition to the persons already mentioned elsewhere in the book, I extend my sincere thanks and appreciation to Vigdis Sundsvold, Oslo, Norway, for her tremendous job of translating into Norwegian, when I many times added further research. And to Alice Stangeland Kirn, Teresa (Nelson) O'Connor, and Brittany O'Connor, I extend my heartfelt thanks for their many helpful comments and suggestions.

To Professor Odd S. Lovoll, Associate Professor Øyvind T. Gulliksen, and Associate Professor Harley Refsal, I am most grateful for their previewing my book and writing helpful, encouraging reviews. To James Skurdall, I extend my appreciation for his translation of the chapters *Hallingdal Rosemaling* and *Hesteslepp i Sikkilsdalen* into English and for his comments and suggestions.

To Chris Shelton, who has designed many of my international catalog covers over the years, my special thanks for his assistance with the layout of the book's cover and the colored insert. To Don and Corey Shelton at JaDecc's Computer Center, Waukon, Iowa my sincere appreciation for the technical support during my years of desktop publishing. To Eaton Cote, Photographic Arts, Waukon, Iowa, my thanks for photographing the bunads, trunks, and woodcarvings. And to John and Pat Torgrimson at the *Fillmore County Journal*, my special thanks for not only encouraging me to write my stories, but also for featuring them in the Journal.

I designed the book's cover picture from a photo taken by my son Alex of a woodcarving by Hans Sorken at the *Norsk Skogmuseum* (Norwegian Forest Museum) Elverum, Norway. It has been a thrill to research, write, and self-publish *Astri, My Astri: Norwegian Heritage Stories*. I hope my readers will enjoy the book as much as I have enjoyed producing it.

By Deb Nelson Gourley

• • • • •

Astri My Astri: Norwegian Heritage Stories er en samling med seksten slektshistorier som utgis både på engelsk og på norsk. Selv om de er knyttet til min 7/8 norske herkomst, har historiene noe å si til alle som har interesse for norsk arv, kultur, slektsforskning eller tospråklighet.

Historiene tar deg med på en reise fra immigrasjonen i 1840-årene fram til oppdagelsen av en immigrantkiste mer enn hundre år senere, og til den påfølgende oppklaringen av en rik familiehistorie. Blant de tema som berøres, er det siste siouxopprøret i 1862, den store influensaepidemien i 1918, en haiketur nord for polarsirkelen, kampen om tungtvannet under andre verdenskrig, norsk rosemaling og bunader, 17. mai, stavkirker, etableringen av en norsk-luthersk kirke i Amerika samt Snowshoe Thompsons liv.

Historiene ble først trykket i Minnesotas *Fillmore County Journal*, og framstår nå i utvidet form med norske oversettelser og utallige bilder. Den tospråklige historien om immigrantkisten ble slått opp på førstesiden i *Decorah Public Opinion* i Decorah, Iowa, akkurat som man ville ha gjort det for mange år siden, på både engelsk og norsk. Den norske versjonen av historien stod også på trykk i *Hallingdølen* i Hallingdal i Norge.

Utgangspunktet for historiene er mine tjuesju norske aner. De første immigrerte så tidlig som i 1845 fra forskjellige steder i Norge, fra Hallingdal, Numedal, Telemark, Voss, Sognefjord, Valdres og Selbu i nærheten av Trondheim. De bestod av en oldefar, ti tipp-oldeforeldre, femten tipp-tipp-oldeforeldre samt en tipp-tipp-tipp-oldeforelder. I løpet av 1840- og 1850-årene slo de første seg ned i Luther

Valley og Koshkonong i Wisconsin, og flyttet videre til norske bebyggelser i Fillmore, Houston og Jackson Counties i Minnesota, og til Winnishiek County i Iowa.

Jeg vokste opp på familiens 150 år gamle slektsgård i Amherst, i nærheten av Canton i det sørøstlige Minnesota. Jeg tok gradene Bachelor of Science og Master of Science ved University of Minnesota, og har arbeidet i staben både ved University of Minnesota og University of Wisconsin. Jeg har også vært kvalitetskontrollør ved Tri-State Breeders Cooperative i Westby, Wisconsin, og president/CEO/hovedaksjonær i Elite Genetics, Inc., i Waukon, Iowa. Da jeg tidligere har arbeidet som kopi/layoutredaktør ved *Fillmore County Journal*, har jeg selv gitt ut boken.

Jeg tilegner *Astri, My Astri: Norwegian Heritage Stories* til min mor, Char Nelson, med takk for mange års hjelp med slektsforskningen. Det var en avskrekkende oppgave siden mange av mine aner hadde immigrert i 1840- og 1850-årene. I 1976, mer enn 125 år senere, var jeg den første etterkommeren som returnerte til Norge. Da det heller ikke har vært ført noen slektstavler i familien, måtte vi begynne arbeidet med de amerikaniserte navnene: Knudson, Larson, Bendickson, Thompson og Nelson.

Jeg tilegner også denne boken til mine sønner, Alex og Ben Huntrods, med takk for all den oppmuntring og støtte de har gitt meg i arbeidet med å forvandle de tusener av navn og opplysninger jeg hadde lagret på datamaskinen til en bok. Det er mitt håp at boken vil inspirere andre unge, slik den har inspirert Alex og Ben til å lære om sin arv.

I tillegg til de personer jeg ellers har nevnt andre steder i boken, vil jeg rette en oppriktig takk til Vigdis Sundsvold, Oslo, Norge, for den krevende jobben med å oversette til norsk - og oversette om igjen når jeg mer enn en gang har tilført nye opplysninger. Og til Alice Stangeland Kirn, Teresa (Nelson) O'Connor, og til Brittany O'Connor; jeg er dypt takknemlig for de mange nyttige kommentarer og forslag.

Til professor Odd S. Lovoll, Associate Professor Øyvind T. Gulliksen og Associate Professor Harley Refsal; jeg er svært takknemlig for deres hjelpsomme og oppmuntrende gjennomlesing og forhåndsomtaler. Jeg retter også min takk til James Skurdall for hans oversettelse til engelsk av kapitlene *Hallingdal rosemaling* og *Hesteslepp i Sikkilsdalen*, og for hans kommentarer og forslag.

Til Chris Shelton, som gjennom årene har designet mange av mine internasjonale katalogomslag, retter jeg en spesiell takk for hjelpen med fargeinnlegg og utforming av bokomslaget. Til Don og Corey Shelton ved JaDecc's Computer Center, Waukon, Iowa, vil jeg takke for teknisk support gjennom år med hjemmepublikasjoner. Til Eaten Cote, Photographic Arts, Wakon, Iowa, takker jeg for fotograferingen av bunader, kister og treskjæringer. Jeg takker også John og Pat Torgrimson ved *Fillmore County Journal* både for oppmuntringene til å skrive mine historier, og for at de ga dem hovedoppslag i avisen.

Jeg har utformet omslagsbildet med utgangspunkt i et foto min sønn Alex har tatt av en treskjæring av Hans Sorken ved *Norsk Skogmuseum* i Elverum, Norge. Det har vært et sant eventyr å gjøre grunnarbeidet, skrive og selv gi ut *Astri, Mi Astri: Norwegian Heritage Stories*. Jeg håper mine lesere vil ha like stor glede av boken som jeg har hatt mens jeg laget den.

Av Deb Nelson Gourley

Oversatt av Vigdis Sundsvold

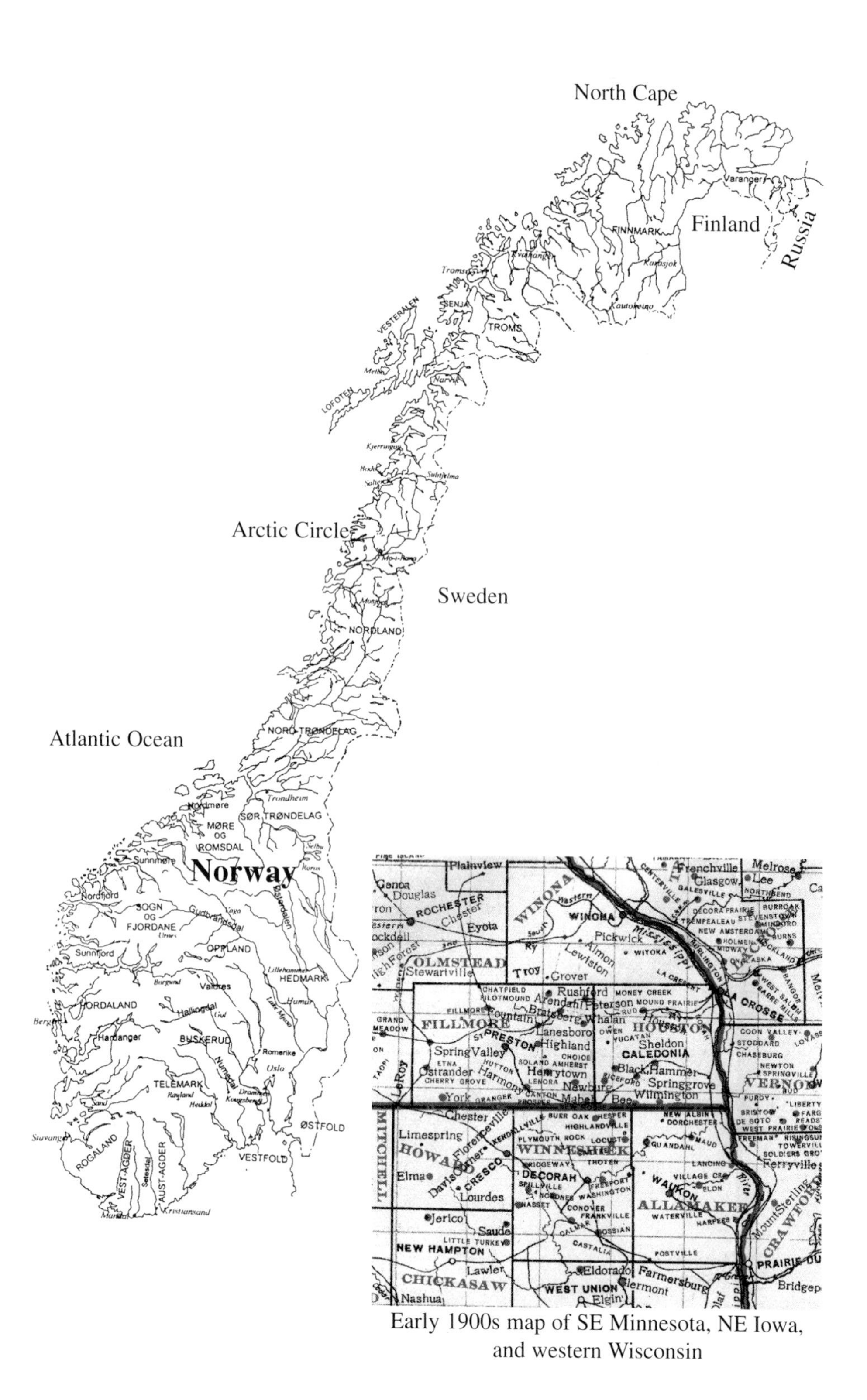

Early 1900s map of SE Minnesota, NE Iowa, and western Wisconsin

Deb Nelson Gourley

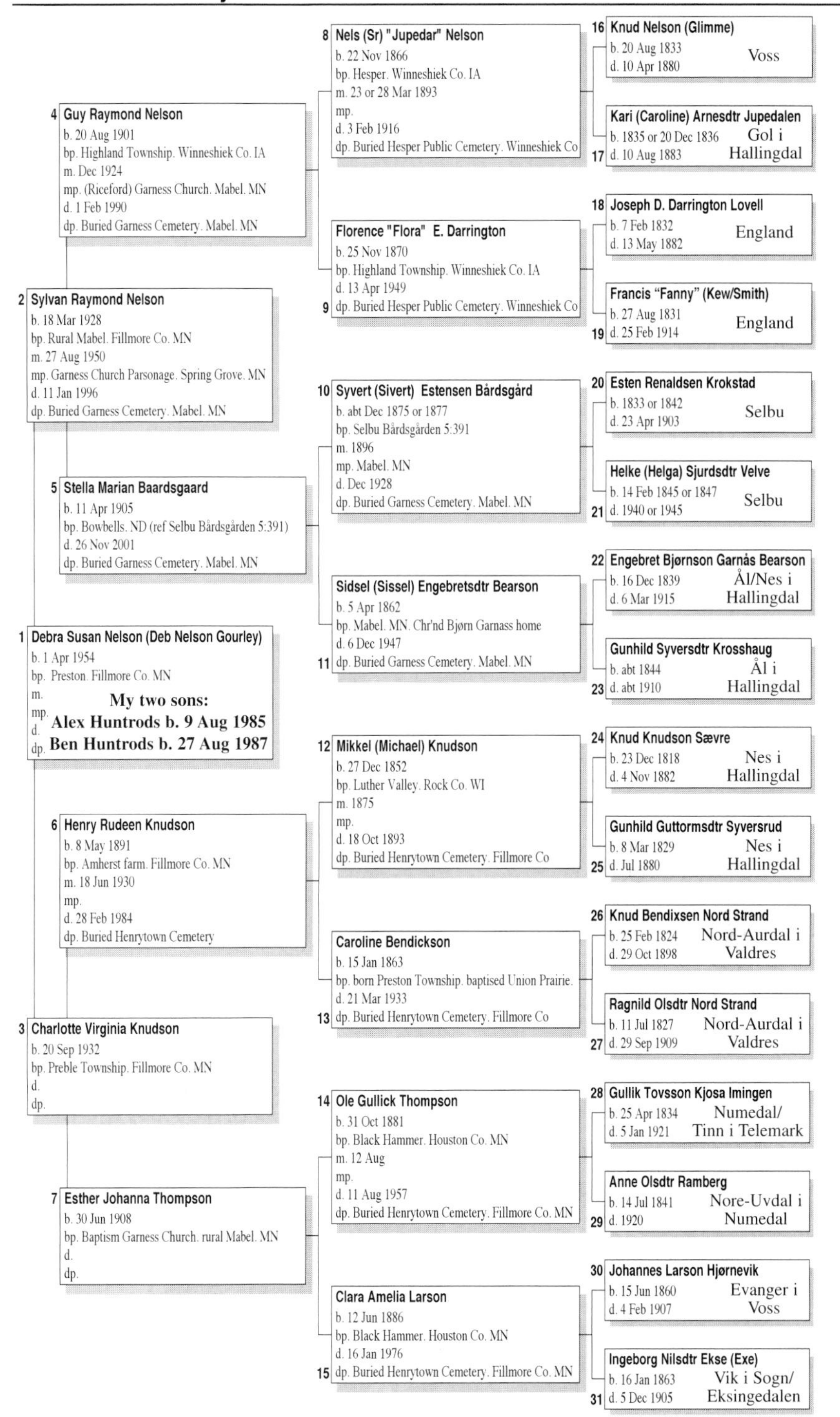

Debbie Nelson
November 1976

1

Astri Herbrandsdatter 1812

Tracing the history of my Norwegian trunk - Opening a family history

The wagon was fully loaded for the burn pile when I spotted amongst the scrap lumber the old painted trunk. I was an eight-year-old at the time and yelled above the tractor noise: *"Where did it come from?" "Why does it have 1812 on it?"* and *"Can I keep it?"*

It was 1962, and my family was in the process of moving four miles down the road from a farm near Lenora to the Knudson ancestral farm in Amherst. Both farms are located in southeastern Minnesota's Fillmore County, a part of the United States that at one time had more Norwegians than any other place in America.

My mom said I could store the trunk in the basement of our newly constructed home if I cleaned it up, so off the wagon came my newfound treasure and out came the garden hose. The wooden trunk was three feet long, two feet wide, two feet tall, and because of the substantial amount of metalwork weighed about one hundred pounds. As I sprayed off years of dust, I could see blue and white flowers painted on an orange-red colored background, along with the chrome-yellow lettering, *"Arstri Her Brans Datter 1812."*

Little did I know that finding this trunk would lead to studying Norwegian, traveling throughout Norway, and researching archives to discover the identity of Astri Herbrandsdatter.

Knud and Gunhild immigration

Because Grandpa Henry's father, Mikkel Knudson, died when Henry was only a two-year-old, very little was

known about my mother's Knudson genealogy or the trunk. My grandparents knew only that the trunk had been used to store seed oats in the granary. This at least explained why there was a little mouse hole in the corner where the bottom and sideboards joined.

My first genealogical find was in the Knudson family's aged cloth-and-leather-covered book, *History of Fillmore County*, 1882. Documentation on the inside cover indicates that Knud S. Knudson, my great-great-grandfather, purchased the book for ten dollars on the 24th day of August, 1882. The Amherst Township section, on page 457, tells of Knud and Gunhild's immigrant life and their severe hardships: *Knud S. Knudson was born in Norway on the 23d of December, 1818. He immigrated to America, and settled in Rock County, Wisconsin, in 1846. In the spring of* [1851], *he married Miss Gune Gutumsdatter. They came to this place* [1853] *and took one hundred and sixty acres of land, upon which he erected a log-home, 12x14 feet, which is still standing. He has added to his farm, and now owns six hundred acres. His wife died in July 1880, leaving six children, five having died before her.*

On page 369 of Hjalmar Rued Holand's 1908 book, *De Norske Settlementers Historie* (History of the Norwegian Settlements), a translation from Norwegian further tells about my great-great-grandfather: *Northeast from Harmony lies the Henrytown neighborhood. A Halling* [someone from Hallingdal valley in Norway] *with the name of Knut Knutson was the first man in Amherst Township, and he settled in Stringtown* [old name for Amherst] *in 1853.*

Vesterheim Museum

The Vesterheim Norwegian-American Museum, in Decorah, Iowa, has an incredible collection of trunks from Norway. As far back as the Viking Era and perhaps before that, there had been a tradition of keeping textiles in trunks. Ornamental iron was used for the trunk's handles, key, locks, hinges, and bands, which would reinforce areas of exceptional wear or stress. The richly decorated pieces of furniture, often made as dowry chests, were ideal for carrying the emigrants' belongings from Norway.

The floral designs, painted on the outside and sometimes the inside of the trunk, are called *rosemaling* or literally, rose painting. The secret of the paint's durability was the grinding of the pigment and mixing it with oil. Hallingdal and Telemark had the most prolific painters. Famous individuals were recognized by their unique style, as the majority of the pieces were unsigned. Highly prized tools of the trade were the *rosemalers* recipes for colors or varnish.

The writing on my trunk, *Astri Herbrandsdatter 1812*, meant Astri was Herbrand's daughter, and she was most likely given her trunk in 1812. Marriage records show she was married in 1813. It was customary for a girl to collect linens and household items and store them in a trunk for marriage. Inside most trunks, including mine, there is a *leddik* or small compartment for a hymnal and other precious articles. Emigrants carried bedding, food, spinning wheels, and tools in their trunks. On board the ship the trunks served as tables and chairs.

Returning to Norway

In 1972, I enrolled in the College of Agriculture at the University of Minnesota, where I also took Norwegian language classes to further my genealogy research. Four years later, the day after I graduated with an Animal Science degree, I left for Norway not only to continue my studies but also to learn about my heritage. I was the first family member to return to Norway in 130 years.

Shortly before departing on my six-month Norway adventure, I learned that an International Exchange Student from Norway, Thomas Gaustad, had recently studied at the University's St. Paul campus. I contacted his parents, Veterinarian Mads and Anna Gaustad from Hamar, and was most graciously welcomed to stay with them on their family farm. Since my relatives had lost all contact with our ancestors in Norway, I was most fortunate to find such a loving host family to live with when I was not traveling or studying in Oslo.

Traveling from the north to the south of Norway is the same distance as going from Minneapolis, Minnesota to New Orleans, Louisiana. Nearly half of Norway's length lies north of the Arctic Circle. In the summer of 1976, I traveled over 7,000 miles in Norway, hitchhiking with my backpack, speaking only Norwegian, and researching genealogy.

While in Norway, I received numerous helpful letters from the now deceased Gerhard B. Naeseth, a well-known genealogist from the Vesterheim Genealogical Center in Madison, Wisconsin. I was also getting lots of valuable ancestral leads from my mom back in Amherst, who was searching almost every Norwegian Lutheran cemetery in southeast Minnesota and northeast Iowa. After much research I found I was 7/8 Norwegian with ancestors coming from Hallingdal, Numedal, Telemark, Voss, Sognefjord, Valdres, and Selbu near Trondheim.

In one of mom's countless letters, she explained that she had found the tombstones of my Knudson great-great-grandparents in the Elstad Lutheran

Church Cemetery near Highland, a few miles from the home farm. Both tombstones had been broken in half, but were cemented back together and still standing. Mom suggested that the name on my trunk, *Astri Herbrandsdatter*, might be connected to the names on the tombstones, since the trunk was found on their home farm:

• *Knud Knudson Sævre, født* [born] *23 Dec 1818, død* [died] *8 Nov 1882*
• *Gunild* [the rest was unreadable]

With my mom's discovery of Knud and Gunhild's tombstones, Gerhard Naeseth was able to match my great-great-grandparents' names to his immigrant records. In a July 9, 1976, letter sent to me while I was in Norway, he wrote: *My card file reveals that Knud Knudson Sævre, born December 22, 1818, emigrated in 1846 from Nes in Buskerud. Apparently, he came alone. He was married at Luther Valley in Rock County, Wisconsin, March 30, 1851 to Gunhild Guttormsdatter Myhre, born March 8, 1829. She emigrated in 1848, also from Nes in Buskerud, arriving on the ship "Drafna." I have not located Knud on a passenger list. There were at least two children born at Luther Valley: Carl Gustav, November 21, 1851; Mikkel* [my great-grandfather]*, December 27, 1852. Gunhild also came alone. If you should learn the names of the parents of Knud and Gunhild, I would appreciate having that information.*

The next step was now up to me. I knew from Gerhard Naeseth's letter that I would need to research the *Nes i Hallingdal*, Buskerud church records. Luckily for me, I was assisted by Professor Ingrid Semmingsen, who was visiting her brother, Veterinarian Mads Gaustad. I learned that the one and only Sæve farm (Knud's last name) was located in *Nes i Hallingdal*; however, the Nes church records I needed were archived in Oslo.

Knud Knudson Sævre

Gunild

1976 letter from Gerhard B. Naeseth

4909 Sherwood Road
Madison,Wis.,53711
July 9, 1976

Miss Debra S. Nelson
c/o Mads Gaustad
Nøttestad
2312 Ottestad, Norway

Dear Miss Nelson:

Thank you for your letter of July 5, which arrived today. You are visiting an excellent part of Norway. When I last was there, I was a dinner guest at the home of Gustav Gjestvang, owner of the large Ottestad gaard. Beautiful, very old, home, very close to a church. I have an old horseshoe from that home, as a remembrance. An extra coincidence: Doing a little research on my own family, I discovered that my great-grand-grandmother was born on the Ottestad farm, as the daughter of a husmann.

If you see Professor Semmingsen again -- as I am sure you will -- please give her our greetings. My wife and I plan to come to Norway in October for a brief visit, especially to be present for the 50th birthday party of the Norwegian Genealogical Society in Oslo. Our present plans are to spend our twelve days or so in Oslo.

But now to your questions. I can offer a little help. My card file reveals that Knud Knudsen Sevre (Sævre?), born December 22, 1818, emigrated in 1846 from Nes in Buskerud. Apparently, he came alone. He was married at Luther Valley in Rock county,Wisconsin,March 30,1851,to Gunhild Guttormsdatter Myhre, born March 8, 1829. She emigrated in 1848, also from Nes in Buskerud, arriving on the ship "Drafna". (I have not located Knud on a passenger list) There were at least two children born at Luther Valley: Carl Gustav,November 21,1851; Mikkel,December 27,1852. Gunhild also came alone. If you should learn the names of the parents of Knud and Gunhild, I would appreciate having that information.

Now about Lars G. Jornevik. Martin Ulvestad in his "Nordmændene i Amerika," volume 1, page 99, devotes a page to the history of the Norwegians in Jackson county,Minnesota. Among those killed by Indians, August 24,1862,were Lars Larsen Førenes,from Strilelandet,born 1834,and his wife, Anna Larsen,also born 1834. Hjalmar Rued Holand in his "De Norske Settlementers Historie," pages 520-521, makes reference, also in a chapter on Jackson county, to Lars L. Furunes, from Bergenstift, as coming to Jackson county from Winneshiek county,Iowa. And to the death of him and his wife. I do not see them in the 1860 census for Winneshiek county. American county histories often make a mess of Norwegian names.

Looking further at your chart, I find indication that Bjørn Garnaas also came from Nes in Hallingdal (Buskerud) Some Rambergs came from Flesberg,Nummedal. Some Exe persons (Ekse) came from Evanger, Voss.

On Monday I will see what the University Library will reveal concerning the Jornevik (Førenes or Furunes) family, if anything. If I find something, I will write again. If as you dig,you believe that I can help, try me again.

Yours very sincerely,

Gerhard B. Naeseth

Gerhard B. Naeseth

Oslo Statsarkivet

Since I was a college student, I was able to receive an extended visa from the Norwegian Consulate to stay in Norway for half a year. Along with my genealogy interest, I was working on my Reproductive Physiology Master's Degree sheep insemination internship at the University of Oslo, Norway. I studied with Drs. Aamdal and Fougner at the Norges Veterinærhøgskole, Institutt for Reproduksjonsfysiologi og Patologi.

With the information obtained from Gerhard Naeseth and my mom in hand, I headed into downtown Oslo to the Statsarkivet (National Archives), to try to locate Knud and Gunhild's ancestry. I began my search in the enormous Nes i Hallingdal church books, turning the fragile pages one by one ever so carefully. On page 152, #24, I located Knud's birth and baptismal records along with his parents' names, Corporal Knud Knudson Haraldsæt and Kjerste Knudsdatter Jørgenmoen Garnås. And then I found Gunhild. Fourteen years after discovering my trunk, it was there, right before my eyes on page 264, #108. Astri Herbrandsdatter's identity was finally revealed to me in the birth records of her daughter: *Gunhild Guttormsdatter, born 8 March 1829, father Corporal Guttorm Jensen Gulbrandsrud and mother Astri Herbrandsdatter Børtnes Syversrud.*

Gunhild Guttormsdatter (Guttorm's daughter) had presumably emigrated from Norway with the trunk that belonged to her mother, Astri Herbrandsdatter. I was indeed the proud owner of my great-great-great-grandmother's trunk. Overjoyed, I immediately called my parents, Sylvan and Char Nelson, in Amherst, only to find they had trouble understanding my English, which by then had taken on a very heavy Norwegian accent.

Emigrant Ship "Drafna"

On the website, *100 Years of Emigrant Ships from Norway*, Gunild Guttormsdatter is listed as passenger #70, age 19, female, on the ship *Drafna* in 1848. A story there tells of the passengers' journey from Norway to Wisconsin: *Leaving Drammen, Norway early in June 1848, a party of Norwegians embarked for the United States . . . They arrived in New York, August 31, 1848 after spending ten weeks on a stormy sea aboard the ship Drafna. Upon arriving in New York the travelers had to take physical examinations and many of them were sick from the poor water and food . . . The party made the trip by boat from New York to Milwaukee (via the Erie Canal). Friends from Karskeland (Koshkonong) met them in Milwaukee with ox-teams and kubberuller* [wagons with log wheels] . . . *The small children, old people, and baggage was carried in those wagons, while the rest of the party followed on foot. Their destination, Karskeland, was reached on September 12, 1848.*

1700's Trunk

In the summer of 2001, my family and I returned to Norway with detailed pictures of my *Astri Herbrandsdatter 1812* trunk. I visited the Hallingdal Folk Museum in Nes to learn more about my heirloom, with a heart located below each hinge. Although I still do not know the name of the person who did the *rosemaling* on my trunk, I did learn about its ornamental iron. The three reinforcement bands across the curved lid dated it to the 1700's.

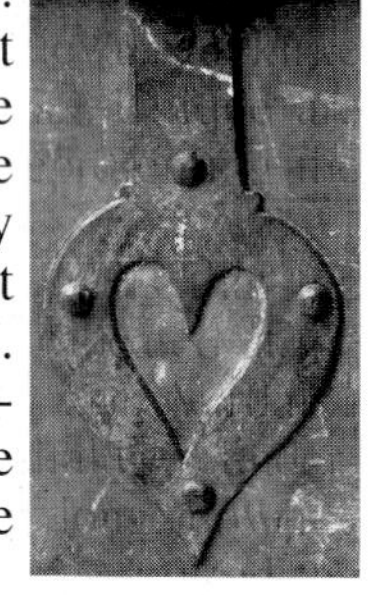

Norwegian emigration to America began in 1825 with the voyage of the single-masted sloop *Restauration*. My trunk could quite possibly be one of the older Norwegian trunks in America. It's been over 40 years since I rescued my *Astri Herbrandsdatter 1812* trunk from the burn pile, and it's still as much a treasure as the day I found it.

Astri Herbrandsdatter 1812

Historien om en norsk kiste avslørte familiens fortid

Vogna var fullastet og klar for å kjøres til bålet ute i skogen, da jeg fikk øye på den gamle, malte kisten mellom skrapveden som var båret ut fra vedskjulet. Jeg var åtte år på den tiden og skrek for å overdøve bråket fra traktoren: *"Hvor kommer den fra?" "Hvorfor står det 1812 på den?"* og *"Kan jeg få beholde den?"*

Det var i 1962, og min familie var i ferd med å flytte fra en gård som lå seks og en halv kilometer nærmere Lenora, til Knudson-familiens gård i Amherst. Begge gårdene lå i Fillmore County i det sørøstlige Minnesota, en del av USA som en tid hadde flere nordmenn enn noe annet sted i Amerika.

Min mor sa at jeg kunne sette kisten i kjelleren i det nybygde huset hvis jeg rengjorde den, så ned fra vogna kom den nyoppdagede skatten, og ut kom hageslangen. Trekisten var 92 cm lang, 61 cm bred og 61 cm høy, og veide 45 kilo. Etterhvert som jeg spylte vekk år med støv, kunne jeg se at det var malt blå og hvite blomster på en rødoransje bunn sammen med den gule skriften *"Arstri Her Brans Datter 1812."*

Lite visste jeg da at funnet skulle bringe meg over i norskstudier, og at jeg ville reise overalt i Norge og søke i arkivene for å avsløre Astri Herbrandsdatters identitet.

Immigrantene Knud og Gunhild

Fordi min bestefar Henrys far, Mikkel Knudson, døde da Henry var bare to år gammel, visste vi svært lite både om min mors Knudson-slekt og kisten. Mine besteforeldre visste bare at kisten hadde vært brukt til å lagre korn i på låven. Det forklarte i det minste hvorfor det var et lite musehull der

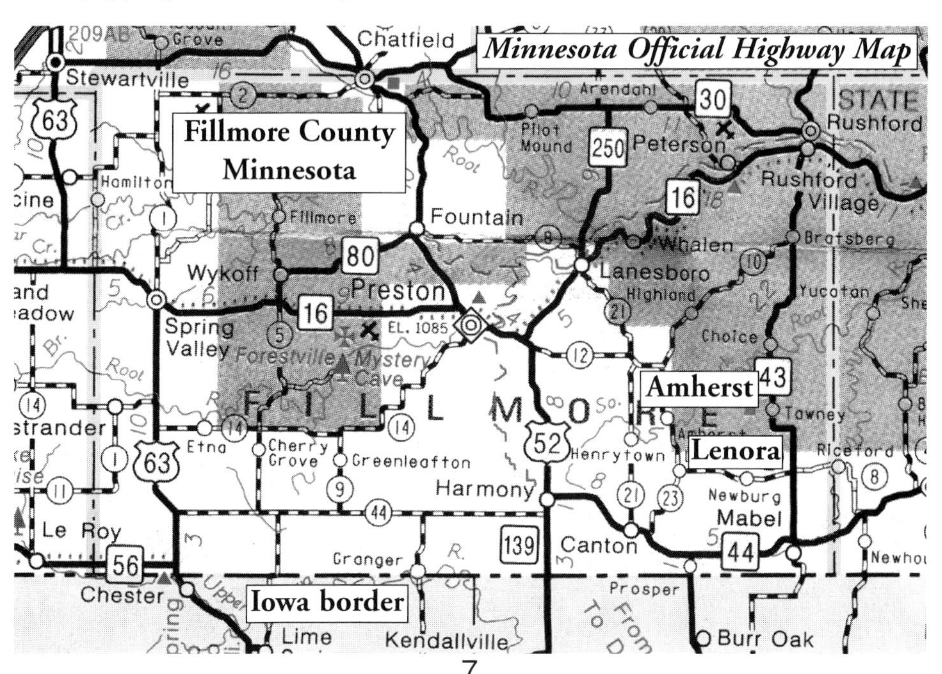

bunnen møtte sidebordene i det ene hjørnet.

Mitt første slektshistoriske funn var i Knudson-familiens *History of Fillmore County*, 1882, en gammel bok innbundet i lerret og lær. På innsideomslaget stod det skrevet at min tippoldefar, Knud S. Knudson, kjøpte boken for ti dollar den 24. august 1882. I kapittelet om Amherst Township, på side 457, forteller den om Knuds og Gunhilds liv som immigranter og om deres tunge strev: *Knud S. Knudson var født i Norge 23. desember 1818. Han immigrerte til Amerika og slo seg ned i Rock County, Wisconsin, i 1846. Våren* [1851] *giftet han seg med Frøken Gune Gutumsdatter. De kom til stedet* [1853] *og tok 648 dekar med jord, hvor han bygde et tømmerhus, 3,7 x 4,3 meter, som fortsatt står. Han bygde ut gården, som nå består av 2428 dekar. Hans kone døde i juli 1880, og etterlot seg seks barn, fem hadde dødd før henne.*

På side 369 i Hjalmar Rued Holands bok *De norske settlementers historie* fra 1908 (History of the Norwegian Settlements) forteller en oversettelse fra norsk mer om min tippoldefar: *Nordøst fra Harmony ligger Henrytown Menighed. En Halling ved Navn Knut Knutson var første Mand i Amherst Township og bosatte sig ved Stringtown* [det gamle navnet for Amherst] *i 1853.*

Nordøst fra Harmony ligger Henrytown Menighed. En Halling ved Navn Knut Knutson var første Mand i Amherst Township og bosatte sig ved Stringtown i 1853. Men ingen flere Hal-

Vesterheim Museum

Vesterheim Norwegian-American Museum i Decorah, Iowa, har en utrolig samling med kister fra Norge. Så langt tilbake som til vikingtiden og kanskje før det, har det vært vanlig å oppbevare tekstiler i kister. Jernornamentikk ble brukt som håndtak, nøkkel, lokk, hengsler og bånd på kistene, som på denne måten også ble forsterket slik at de tålte ekstra tyngde og press. De rikt dekorerte kistene, som tjente som møbler og ofte ble laget som brudekister, egnet seg godt til å bringe emigrantenes eiendeler med fra Norge.

Blomsterdekorasjonene som er malt på utsiden og noen ganger også på innsiden, kaller vi *rosemaling*. Hemmeligheten med malingens holdbarhet lå i måten man knuste pigmentene på og blandet dem med olje. Hallingdal og Telemark hadde de frodigste malerne. Enkeltmalere ble gjenkjent gjennom sin spesielle stil, ettersom det meste de laget ikke ble signert. Høyt verdsatt var rosemalernes oppskrifter på farger og ferniss.

Skriften på min kiste, *Astri Herbrandsdatter 1812*, betydde at Astri var Herbrands datter, og at hun sannsynligvis hadde fått kisten i 1812. Kirkebøkene viser at hun giftet seg i 1813. Det var vanlig at jentene samlet lintøy og husholdningssaker og oppbevarte dem i en kiste med tanke på ekteskap. Inni de fleste kistene, også min, finnes det en *leddik* eller et lite rom for salmebok og andre kostbare saker. Emigrantene bar med seg sengetøy, mat, spinnehjul og verktøy i kistene. Om bord på skipet tjente kistene som bord og stol.

Tilbake til Norge

I 1972 skrev jeg meg inn på College of Agriculture ved Universitetet i Minnesota, hvor jeg også tok norske språkkurs for å kunne gå videre med slektsforskningen. Fire år senere, dagen etter at jeg hadde oppnådd min Animal Science degree, dro jeg til Norge, ikke bare for å fortsette studiene, men også for å finne ut mer om arven min. Jeg var det første familiemedlemmet som besøkte Norge på 130 år.

Kort tid før jeg la ut på mitt seks måneder lange Norgeseventyr, fikk jeg vite at en utvekslingsstudent fra Norge, Thomas Gaustad, nylig hadde studert ved universitetet i St. Paul. Jeg kontaktet foreldrene hans, veterinærene Mads og Anna Gaustad fra Hamar, og ble

Mikkel Knudson - son of Knud and Gunhild

Caroline Bendickson - wife of Mikkel Knudson

imøtekommende ønsket velkommen til å bo hos dem på familiegården. Siden mine slektninger hadde mistet all kontakt med slekten vår i Norge, var jeg heldig som fant en så godhjertet familie å bo hos når jeg ikke var ute og reiste eller studerte i Oslo.

Hvis du reiser fra nord til sør i Norge, så er det samme distanse som om du reiser fra Minneapolis, Minnesota, til New Orleans, Louisiana. Nesten halve Norges lengde ligger nord for Polarsirkelen. Sommeren 1976 reiste jeg mer enn 11000 kilometer i Norge, jeg haiket med ryggsekk, snakket bare norsk, og søkte etter slekten.

Mens jeg var i Norge, fikk jeg utallige hjelpsomme brev fra den nå avdøde Gerhard B. Naeseth, en velkjent slektsforsker ved Vesterheim Genealogical Center i Madison, Wisconsin. Jeg fikk også mange verdifulle ledetråder knyttet til slekten fra min mor der hjemme i Amherst, som gjennomsøkte nær sagt hver eneste norsk-lutherske kirkegård i sørøstlige Minnesota og nordøstlige Iowa. Etter mye strev fant jeg ut at jeg var 7/8 norsk med aner fra Hallingdal, Numedal, Telemark, Voss, Sognefjord, Valdres, og fra Selbu i nærheten av Trondheim.

I ett av mors utallige brev forklarte hun hvordan hun hadde funnet mine tippoldeforeldres gravsteiner på den lutherske kirkegården i Elstad like ved Highland, noen få kilometer fra hjemgården. Begge gravstøttene hadde vært brukket i to, men var støpt sammen igjen og stod fortsatt. Mor antok at navnet på kisten min, *Astri Herbrandsdatter*, kunne forbindes med navnene på gravsteinene, ettersom kisten ble funnet på gården hvor de hadde bodd:

• *Knud Knudson Sævre, født 23. desember 1818, død 8. november 1882*
• *Gunild* [resten kunne ikke leses]

På grunn av mors oppdagelse av Knuds og Gunhilds gravstøtter, var Gerhard Naeseth i stand til å finne mine tipp-oldeforeldres navn i sitt immigrantarkiv. I et brev fra 9. juli 1976 som han sendte til meg mens jeg var i Norge, skrev han: *Mitt kartotek avslører at Knud Knudson Sævre, født 22. desember 1818, emigrerte i 1846 fra Nes i*

Buskerud. Tilsynelatende kom han alene. Han giftet seg 30. mars 1851 i Luther Valley i Rock County, Wisconsin, med Gunhild Guttormsdatter Myhre, født 8. mars 1829. Hun emigrerte i 1848, også fra Nes i Buskerud, og ankom med skipet "Drafna". Jeg har ikke funnet Knud på noen passasjer-liste. Det ble født minst to barn i Luther Valley: Carl Gustav, 15. november 1851; Mikkel [min oldefar], *27.desember 1852. Gunhild kom også alene. Hvis du skulle finne navnene til Knud og Gunhilds foreldre, så ville jeg sette pris på å få den informasjonen.*

Det neste steget var nå mitt. Jeg visste fra Gerhard Naeseths brev at jeg måtte søke i kirkebøkene fra Nes i Hallingdal, i Buskerud. Jeg var heldig og fikk hjelp av professor Ingrid Semmingsen, som besøkte sin bror, veterinæren Mads Gaustad. Jeg fant ut at den eneste gården med navnet Sæve (Knuds etternavn) lå i Nes i Hallingdal; kirkebøkene fra Nes som jeg trengte, var likevel arkivert i Oslo.

Statsarkivet i Oslo

Ettersom jeg var student, greide jeg gjennom det norske konsulatet å få utvidet min oppholdstillatelse i Norge, slik at jeg kunne være i Norge et halvt år. Ved siden av mine interesser for genealogi, arbeidet jeg på mastergraden i reproduksjonsfysiologi ved Universitetet i Oslo, med inseminasjon av sauer som spesialfelt. Jeg studerte under doktorene Aamdal og Fougner ved Norges veterinærhøgskole, Institutt for reproduksjonsfysiologi og patologi.

Med Gerhard Naeseths og min mors informasjon i hånden satte jeg kursen mot Statsarkivet i Oslo sentrum for å prøve å finne Knud og Gunhilds forfedre. Jeg begynte med å lete i de enorme kirkebøkene fra Nes i Hallingdal, forsiktig vendte jeg de

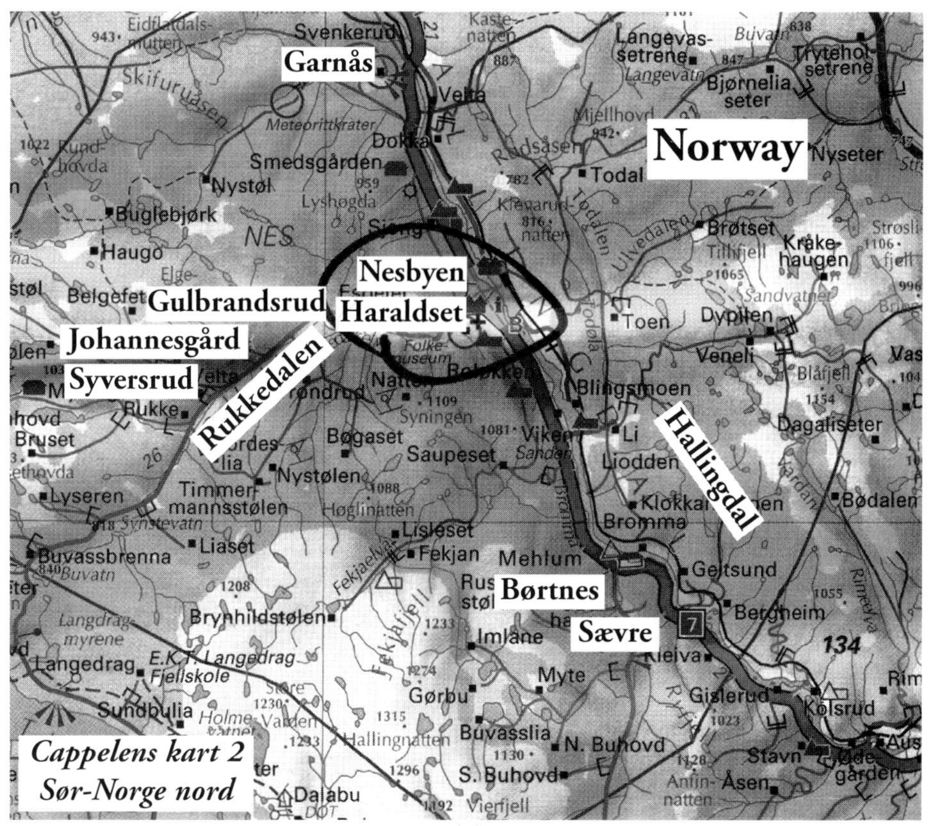

Cappelens kart 2
Sør-Norge nord

Knud Knudson Sævre

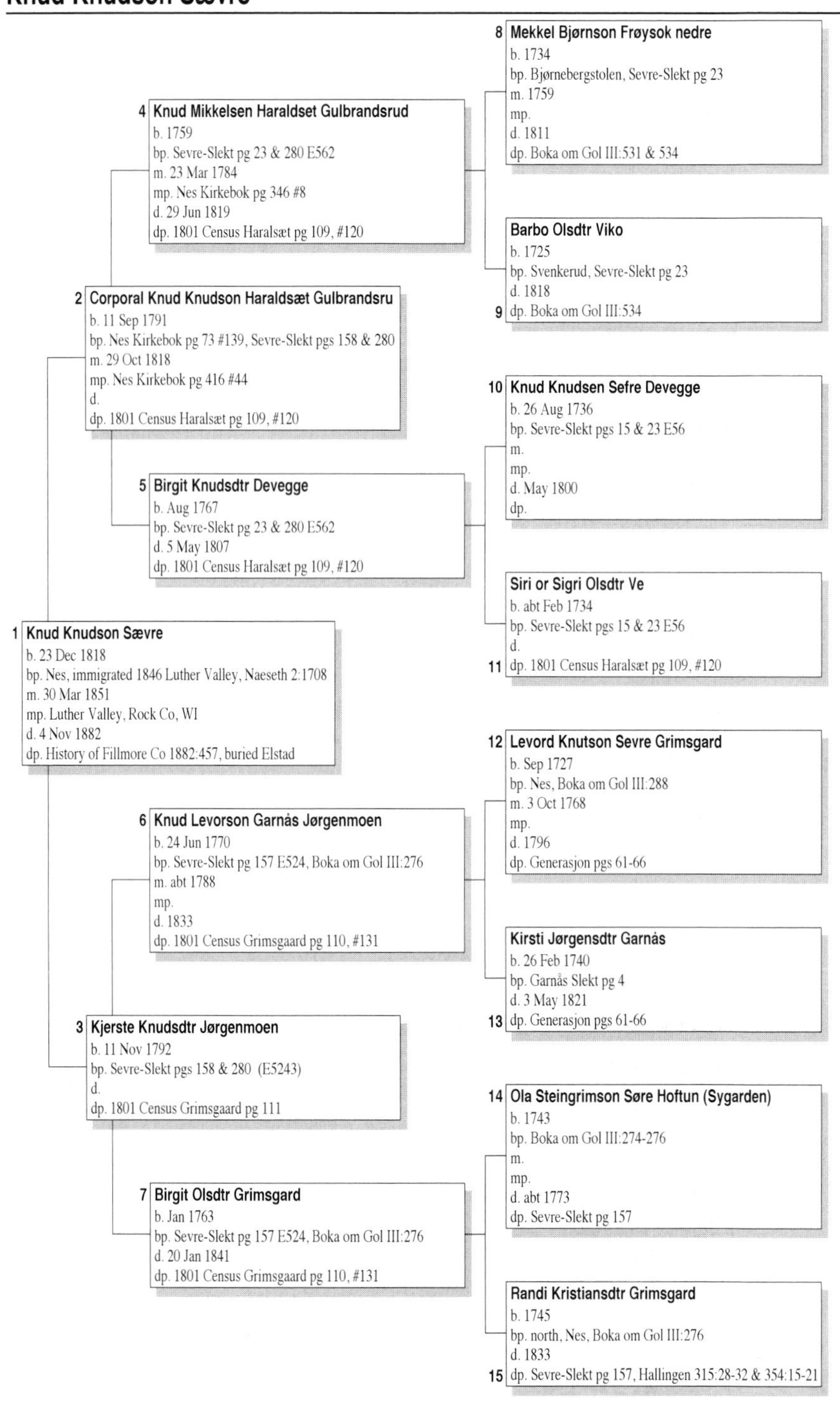

Gunhild Guttormsdtr Syversrud Myhre

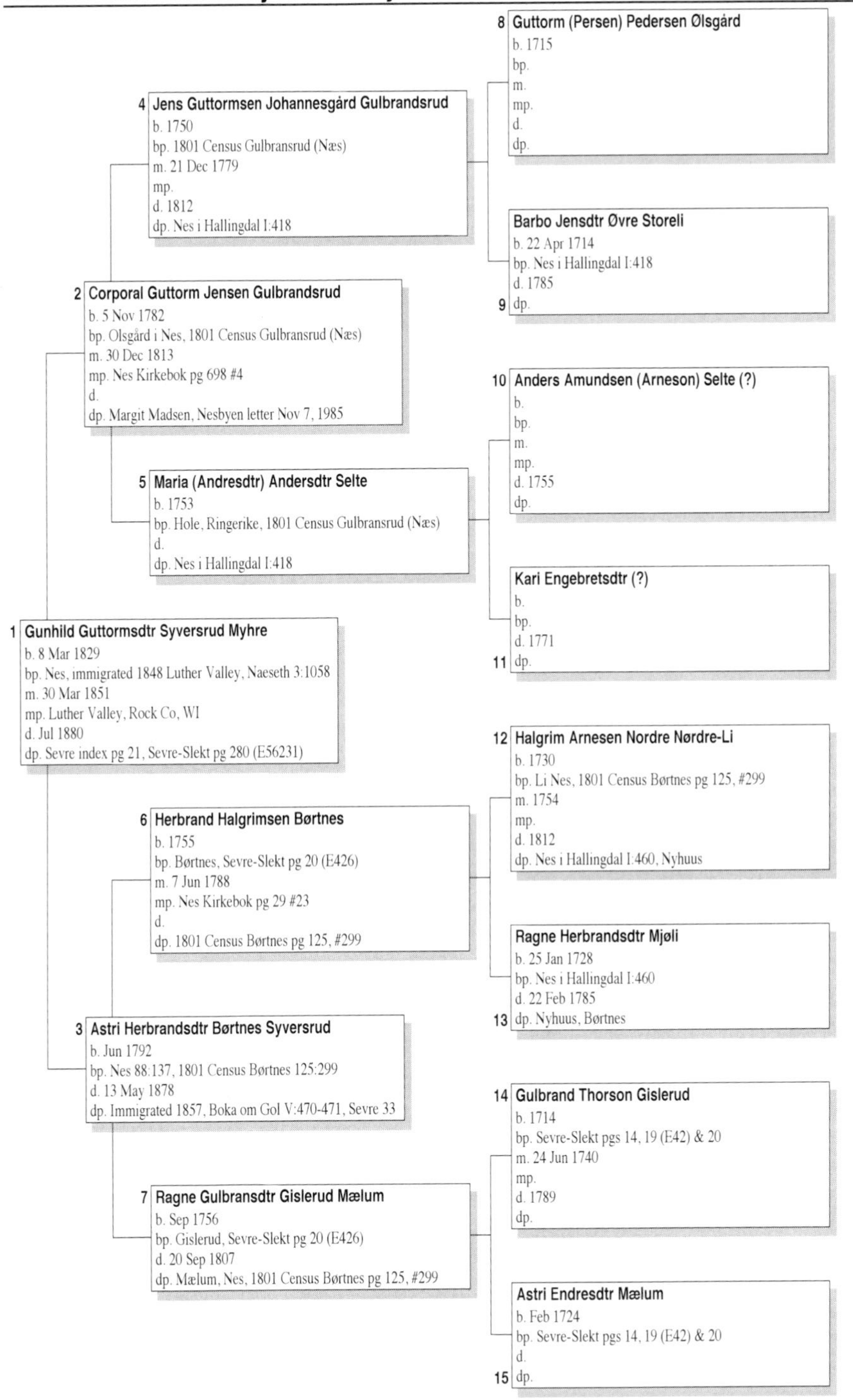

tynne sidene en etter en. På side 152, #24, fant jeg Knuds fødsels-og dåpsdato sammen med foreldrenes navn, korporal Knud Knudson Haraldsæt og Kjersti Knudsdatter Jørgenmoen Garnås. Og så fant jeg Gunhild. Fjorten år etter at jeg oppdaget kisten stod det der rett foran øynene mine på side 264, #108. Astri Herbrandsdatters identitet ble endelig avslørt for meg gjennom datterens fødselsdata: *Gunhild Guttormsdatter, født 8. mars 1829, far korporal Guttorm Jensen Gulbrandsrud og mor Astri Herbrandsdatter Børtnes Syversrud.*

Gunhild Guttormsdatter hadde formodentlig emigrert fra Norge med kisten som hadde tilhørt moren, Astri Herbrandsdatter. Jeg var virkelig den stolte eier av min tipp-tipp-oldemors kiste. Overlykkelig ringte jeg øyeblikkelig foreldrene mine, Sylvan og Char Nelson i Amherst, bare for å oppdage at de hadde problemer med å forstå engelsken min, som da hadde fått en kraftig norsk aksent.

Emigrantskipet "*Drafna*"

På websiden *100 Years of Emigrant Ships from Norway*, står *Gunild Guttormsdatter* oppført som passasjer # 70, alder 19, kvinne, på skipet *Drafna* i 1848. En historie forteller om passasjerenes reise fra Norge til Wisconsin: *Et selskap forlot Drammen, Norge, tidlig i juni 1848 med kurs for De forente stater... De ankom New York 31. august 1848 etter ti stormfulle uker om bord på skipet Drafna. Da de reisende ankom New York, måtte de undersøkes av lege, og mange av dem var syke av det dårlige vannet og maten...Selskapet reiste med båt fra New York til Milwaukee (via Erie-kanalen). Venner fra Karskeland (Koshkonong) møtte dem i Milwaukee med trekkokser og kubberuller* [vogner med tømmerhjul] ... *De små barna, de gamle og bagasjen ble fraktet på disse vognene, mens resten av selskapet fulgte til fots. De nådde bestemmelsesstedet, Karskeland, 12. september 1848.*

1700-tallskisten

Sommeren 2001 returnerte min familie og jeg til Norge med detaljerte bilder av Astri Herbrandsdatter 1812-kisten. Jeg besøkte Hallingdal Folkemuseum i Nes for å finne ut mer om arvestykket, som hadde et hjerte under hver hengsel. Selv om jeg ennå ikke vet navnet på personen som utførte rosemalingen på kisten min, så fikk jeg vite noe om jernornamentikken. De tre forsterkningsbåndene over det buede lokket daterte den til 1700-tallet.

Den norske emigrasjonen til Amerika begynte i 1825 med den enmastede sluppen *Restauration.* Min kiste kunne med stor sannsynlighet være en av de eldre norske kistene i Amerika. Det er gått over 40 år nå siden jeg reddet min *Astri Herbrandsdatter 1812*-kiste fra bålet, og den er en like stor skatt i dag som da jeg fant den.

2

"You are a Hjørnevik, but who are you?"

Delivering tragic immigrant news about the 1862 Sioux Indian Uprising 114 years later

There were no roads leading to Jørnevik, so it meant taking a train to the station between the two mountain tunnels. But when I finally found the Hjørnevik farm near *Evanger i Voss*, in the Bergen area of Norway in 1976, I felt as if I had come home.

It was customary for Norwegians to use their farm name in Norway as their last name in America. Knowing only that my great-great-great-grandparents' last name was Hjørnevik, it was possible to locate the one and only Hjørnevik farm.

I climbed up the steep mountainside path until I came to a quaint white and blue house with a breathtaking view of the valley and Evangervatn, a lake-like passage that leads to the fjord. Two Hjørnevik sisters, Torbjørg, 88, and Maria, 83, answered the door. Never having seen me before, they took one look at me and asked in Norwegian, *You are a Hjørnevik, but who are you?*

At that moment, a great sense of pride came over me, as I realized that I was probably the first person in my family to return to Hjørnevik from America. Torbjørg and Maria, speaking

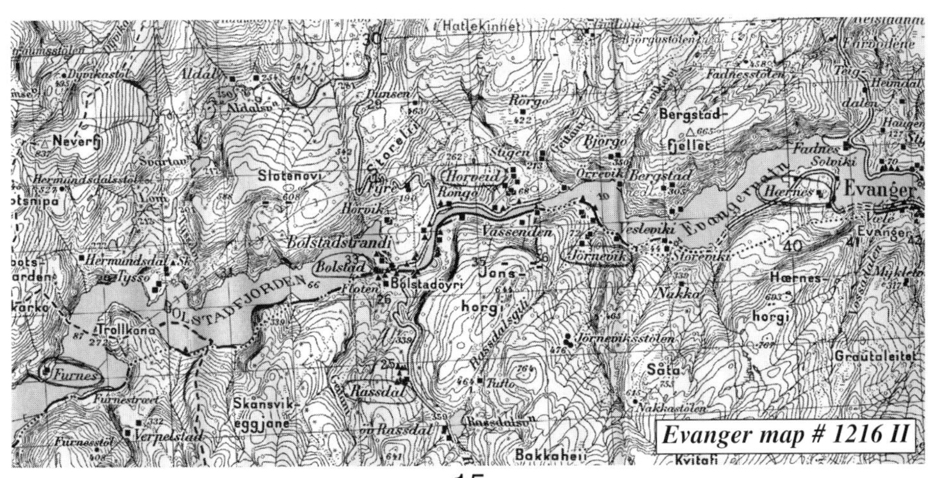

Evanger map # 1216 II

in their local dialect, began asking questions faster than I could translate.

I quickly dug out my genealogy chart from my backpack and began delivering the tragic news from America, 114 years after the events had occurred. It was the story of my family emigrating from Hjørnevik in about 1860 and the parents being brutally murdered during the Belmont Massacre of the 1862 Sioux Indian Uprising near Jackson, Minnesota.

The next day I visited Torbjørg's and Maria's brother, Salamon, 90, the Hjørnevik family genealogist. He was so excited he kept repeating, *slekt, slekt,* (relative, relative) over and over again. Salamon remembered being told my family had gone to America and that they were never heard from again. Salamon, whose genealogy records dated back to 1654, said my great-great-great-grandfather was a cousin of his grandfather.

According to *Norske Gaardnavne* (Norwegian Farm Names) by Oluf Rygh, the name Jørnevik appears in a Norwegian diploma in the form Joronnarviik as early as 1340, with the name Jorunn being a woman's name. The spelling Hjørnevik is a result of folk etymology.

Immigration to America

Lars G. Hjørnevik and Mrs. Lars G. Hjørnevik, my great-great-great-grandparents, whose ancestry is still unknown, left for America prior to 1861. Their son, Johannes Larson

A 1976 visit to Hjørnevik by the author, Deb.

(Hjørnevik), my great-great-grandfather, was born June 15, 1860.

It is thought that the Hjørneviks traveled with the Fyre, Langeland, and Mestad families, who are recorded in the Big Canoe Lutheran Church records, Winneshiek County, in northeast Iowa and then pushed on westward to Jackson County in southwest Minnesota. In 1860 or 1861, they settled in Belmont, a Norwegian community along the upper Des Moines River, north of the present site of Jackson, Minnesota.

Sioux Indian country

According to *Inkpaduta and the Sioux Indians*, 1998, by J.W. Parsons and S. Kennedy, there were several causes for the Sioux Indian Uprising of 1862. The Sioux land had been reduced to one-half its size by a treaty in return for promised monetary and material compensation. Problems arose due to the high concentration of the Indians, a food shortage, and exorbitant prices. Unsympathetic Indian agents, with ample supplies and food, refused to give food to the Indians until the annuity money had arrived from Washington, D.C. The Indians had given up their hunting grounds, deeded their lands, and now were near starvation.

The Norwegian settlers who arrived in the early 1860s understood and spoke very little English. Their interests were centered in their homes, and they had few dealings with the outside world. They had settled on the exposed frontier, almost in the heart of the Indian country, yet they knew nothing of the Indian customs or Indian warfare. Nearly all able-bodied men were absent, fighting their adopted country's Civil War battles. Jackson County had a reputation for patriotism equaled by few communities; however, this left the frontier settlement vulnerable to attack.

Great Sioux Uprising

Frustrated and provoked by years of broken treaty promises, government lies, and forced cultural change, the previously peaceful Sioux began a spontaneous bloody revolt in which over 800 settlers and soldiers were slain in less than one week during August 1862. More than forty thousand people fled their homes, depopulating twenty-three southwestern Minnesota counties. The tragic episode marked the outbreak of a series of Indian wars that did not end until nearly thirty years later at the Battle of Wounded Knee in South Dakota.

The Belmont Massacre in Jackson County was a part of the Great Sioux Uprising. Thirteen Belmont settlers were murdered in cold blood by a band of about fifty Indians, led by White Lodge, who went swiftly from cabin-to-cabin. When it was all over, the surviving panic-stricken Norwegians fled back, mainly to Winneshiek County, Iowa and Houston County, Minnesota.

Belmont Massacre August 24, 1862

(Author's note: See Norwegian settlement 1860-1862 listing for further details of the individuals below. For identification purposes, the text below contains Norwegian spellings instead of the Americanized surnames.)

The following account is taken from the *History of Jackson County*, pages 101-109:

"The attack on the Norwegian settlement of Jackson County occurred on Sunday, August 24, 1862 [about 10 o'clock in the morning] . . . Thirteen whites were murdered, a few others were wounded, and many narrowly escaped with their lives. So early as June reports reached the Belmont settlers that there was likely to be trouble with the Indians . . . Nights they gathered at the different cabins that seemed to offer better protection or where the firearms and ammunition were kept . . . and generally they returned to their homes in the morning to attend to the farm work.

"At the Ole Fyre home, on the northwest quarter of section 22, Belmont, several families had gathered

. . . When the Indians were seen approaching, Mrs. Fyre, Mrs. Hjørnevik, and Mrs. Ekse with the eight small children went into the cellar, the trap door was closed, and Ole Olson Fyre, 11-year-old son of Ole Fyre, piled clothing, boxes and trunks over it. The others remained upstairs.

"The Indians approached the cabin from the east and burst in the east door. All who were in the cabin, except the boy, were instantly killed . . . Johannes Ekse was evidently pounded to death, as no bullet wounds were found on his body. Lars Furnes and Lars G. Hjørnevik, my great-great-great-grandfather, were shot.

'I understand my time has come; I must go up again. Your children are smaller than mine and they keep quiet; if I stay here the Indians will find us.'

"Ole Olson Fyre, the boy, who was standing guard at the west door, bolted out that door and ran down a trail that led to a spring . . . saw an Indian taking aim at him . . . the bullet struck him, tearing away the tip of his right elbow . . . The Indian's love of 'firewater' saved a life. One of the first acts of the savages was to search the wagons, which had been brought from Mankato the day before, loaded with provisions and just as the Indian was about to discover the boy in the brush, the others at the cabin found a jug of whisky. Ole [who later took the name Ole F. Forde] ran . . . to notify the other settlers of their danger.

"The anxiety of the fugitives in the cellar while the murders were being committed over their heads cannot be described; so still were they, they scarcely breathed. Their fears were made worse by the crying of the two-year-old babe [Johannes, my great-great-grandfather] of Mrs. Lars G. Hjørnevik. That lady, with heroism seldom equaled in the annals of Indian warfare, knowing that the painted demons surrounded the house, deliberately came out of the cellar to accept her fate. To the other ladies she said: 'I understand my time has come; I must go up again. Your children are smaller than mine and they keep quiet; if I stay here the Indians will find us.' She came up from the cellar with the child and was killed, her body being horribly mutilated.

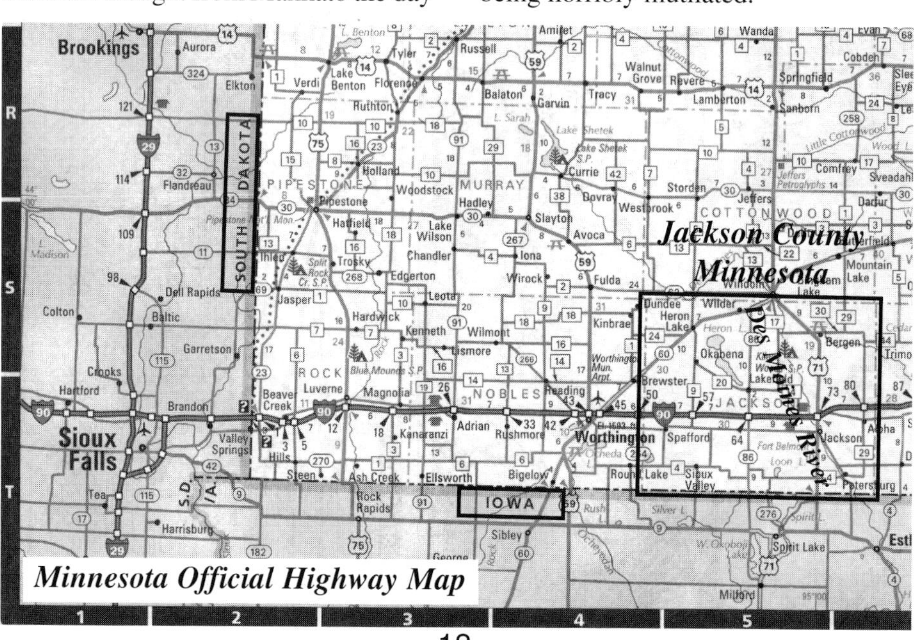

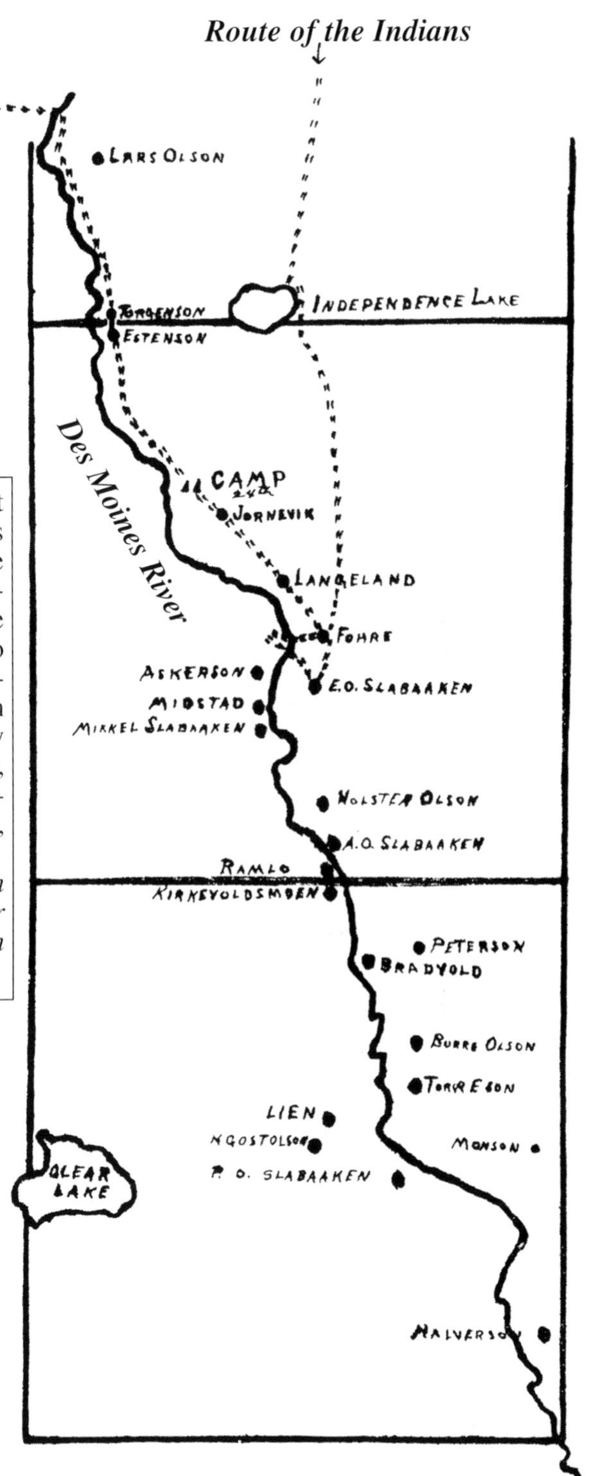

The Norwegian Settlement map showing the locations of the cabins and the route the Sioux Indians used during the Belmont Massacre on August 24, 1862. Due to the entire area being considered Jackson Township in the 1860s, the present day townships of Des Moines, Belmont, and part of Christiania in Jackson County, Minnesota are depicted. *Source: History of Jackson County Minnesota by Arthur P. Rose, 1910, map between pages 104 & 105.*

"Fortunately the Indians were busy with their whisky and did not learn from whence Mrs. Hjørnevik had come. The child [Johannes] was un-harmed, but soon it began to cry. The door of the cabin had been left open, and the baby was frightened at the hogs, which came into the cabin. One of the ladies came up, found the child in its mother's blood, and took it back into the cellar and cared for it.

"Close to the Fyre home, Mikkel Olson Slaabakken was killed and his nephew, Anders Olson Slaabakken, the thirteen year old son of Englebret Olson Slaabakken, was seriously wounded and left for dead. The Englebret Olson Slaabakken home was half a mile south of the Fyre home. West of the Ole Fyre home, the Indians came upon Knud Mestad and his wife Brita and murdered them. These unfortunate people lived on the west side of the river, and were on their way to Ole Fyre's when they were ambushed on the trail.

"Mrs. Fyre and Mrs. Ekse decided to seek another place of concealment. Accordingly they came forth with the children and hid in a cornfield. The savages, returning from their visit to the Slaabakken home . . . found that refugees had been hidden in the cellar at the time of the first attack but had now escaped, they were very angry and spent considerable time searching for them. After the murderers had gone the second time the women started out with the children for the south and spent Sunday night in a blacksmith shop on the Slaabakken farm . . . and then started out on foot for Spirit Lake.

"After the second visit to the house of Ole Fyre . . . the band proceeded up the river to the home of Knud Langeland. Mr. Langeland was down by the river rounding up his cattle at the time of the attack and so escaped. At the house his wife, Anna Langeland, and four children, Anna [child], Aagaata, Nicolai Johan, and Knud [child] Langeland, were murdered.

Martha Langeland escaped the fate of the rest of the family by hiding in a cornfield. He [Mr. Langeland] thought he witnessed signs of life in two of his children. Gathering them in his arms, he carried them all the way to Spirit Lake [26 miles]. One of the children died soon after his arrival; the other [Julia] recovered.

"From the Langeland home the Sioux proceeded on their way up the river to the homes of Ole Estenson and Ole Torgenson, where they arrived in the evening about dark. Theses men were the only ones in the settlement to make any effort to save their lives except in flight; they had the old Berserker blood in them and put up a good fight . . . They had guns and ammunition and the knowledge and disposition to use them . . . The white men ordered their families to lie down and returned the fire of the enemy so successfully that they fought off every attack. Volley after volley was poured into the house, and the bullets penetrated the walls and roof . . . The white men loaded their army muskets with slugs, and, as it had become dark, they fired only at the flashes of the Indians' guns. No one within the cabin was hit, and the attackers finally departed."

One of the children in the cellar, John Mestad, recalling what he had

Lars Gjornevik (Hjørnevik) and wife, the author's great-great-great-grandparents, were among those listed on the monument as massacred by the Sioux Indians on August 24th, 1862. The monument is located in Ashley Park, Jackson, Minnesota. *(Photo by Steve Raska)*

Johannes Larson Hjørnevik (seated left), the author's great-great-grandfather, was the two-year-old Hjørnevik baby that survived the Belmont Massacre during the Sioux Indian Uprising in 1862. He is shown with his wife Ingeborg, and two children, great-grandmother Clara (middle) and Louis (standing right).
(Photo courtesy Esther Johanna (Thompson) Knudson)

been told by his mother, Mrs. Ekse, provided the *Decorah Public Opinion*, September 13, 1944, with the following information:

"Through the wide cracks among the floor boards, the frightened women could see much of what took place . . . From the damp darkness of the cellar, the women watched the moccasin feet moving stealthily about the cabin rooms overhead." As to how the Hjørnevik baby survived, the following explanation was given: "'Leave him!' the redskin leader commanded as some of the warriors made ready to dispose of the baby . . . the Indians left the cabin . . . leaving the child [Johannes] to play in his mother's blood."

The journey of Mrs. Fyre, Mrs. Ekse, and the children is further described in a later account (Historical Data Project, Bismarck, ND) by the 11-year-old boy, Ole F. Forde:

"Four of the children were not big enough to walk . . . a younger [Fyre] boy, age 9, transported two of the children while the other two women each carried one. To carry these two children, he would take one in his arms, run ahead some 25 to 50 rods [425.5 to 825 feet], put the child down, and then run back and get the other child. The boy, Ole, who had been given up for dead, joined the group a week after the massacre."

A great-granddaughter of Mrs. Ekse, Odis Erickson (Byron) Vatland, Mabel, Minnesota, documented in the *Fillmore County History*, 1984, pages 160-161, the group's journey by foot and wagon. Brytteva was the mother to five of the children who had hidden in the cellar during the attack: Breta, 10 (grandmother to Odis); Knute, 9; Storre Nels, 7; John, 4; and Vesle Nels, 1. The children all lived to be adults and went by their mother's maiden name Mestad.

"At the first sound of the war whoops of the returning Indians, Brytteva took her five small children and the orphaned baby, the other woman took her small children and 12-year-old girl [possibly Martha Langeland who had arrived at the Fyre cabin] and they ran into the cornfield and scattered like quails between the rows.

"We remained in hiding until night. When darkness came, we started on our flight. Brytteva knew that somewhere to the south was a frontier town and in that direction we laid our course. Through the tangled underbrush of the wilderness, over fallen trees and across damp, boggy forest swamps we crept slowly on. We knew not at what moment a lusty savage might appear in our path. At times we saw the lurid light of burning cabins fired by Indians, and heard their savage yells of death and victory as we stole along through the ghastly gloom.

"At dawn, we hid again in a field of corn. Half naked, hungry and utterly exhausted, the children began to cry for food and water. There were springs near the river, but we dared not venture that way, for we knew the red man's haunts lay along the watercourse. When our cries became too piteous, Brytteva tore a sleeve from her dress and with it mopped up the dew on the grass and leaves of corn. Into a little pan that a frenzied child had carried with her all the way, the drops were thus gathered one by one; and before the sun had dissipated the morning dew, our thirst was in a measure appeased.

"For three days and three nights we continued the flight from our plundered homes. On Wednesday morning we were discovered by a small detachment of United States cavalry sent out to gather in survivors of the massacre. On its approach to the edge of a prairie opening, we darted into the underbrush like hunted fowl, thinking they were Indians. After a time, however, we were rounded up, and soon realized that it was a rescue by whites and not a capture by the red foe.

"In due time, we were placed in

great army wagons and taken overland, at government expense, back to our former homes in Winneshiek County . . . It was a long, long trip through central Minnesota and across the prairies of Iowa, but the soldiers were kind and fed us well on their coarse fare of beans, brown bread, and milk."

Monument in Jackson, Minnesota

A monument is located in Ashley Park, Jackson, Minnesota, in memory of those who died in both the 1857 and 1862 Indian massacres. Among those listed are the Hjørneviks, my great-great-great-grandparents. The inscription reads: *Erected by the State of Minnesota in the year 1909, to the memory of the pioneer settlers of Jackson County, whose names are inscribed below, massacred by the Sioux Indians on March 28th, 1857, and August 24th, 1862.*

- 1857 Massacre: William Wood, Ceurce Wood, Joshua Stewart, Two children of Joshua Stewart, Willie Thomas
- 1862 Massacre: Ole Fyre, Johanes Ekse, Mikkel Olson (Slaabakken), Lars Furnes, Mrs. Anna Langeland, Anna (child) Langeland, Aagaata Langeland, Nicolai Johan Langeland, Knud (child) Langeland, Knud Mestad and wife (Brita), Lars G. Hjørnevik and wife

Rattlesnake hunter

After Mrs. Ekse and Mrs. Fyre rescued the Hjørnevik baby, Johannes Larson (my great-great-grandfather), he was taken to Black Hammer Township, Houston County, Minnesota. According to Spring Grove/Black Hammer genealogists Gordon Eddy and Georgia Rosendahl, my great-great grandfather was raised by Lars Nilsson Ekse (first cousin to Johannes Ekse) and his wife, Anne Eriksdatter Berdal.

In 1882, Johannes married a niece to Lars Nilsson Ekse, Ingeborg Nielsdatter Ekse, in Houston County. Ingeborg was the daughter of Nils Nilsson Ekse and Kari Hermundsdatter Nese (see genealogy charts in 1918 Influenza story). Johannes and Ingeborg had two children: Louis in 1883 and my great-grandmother Clara, in 1886. Johannes and Ingeborg Larson are both buried in the Black Hammer Cemetery, in Houston County, Minnesota.

Johannes farmed near Black Hammer and was a rattlesnake hunter. Although bitten three times, he died of natural causes at age 47. Clara, growing up in the Black Hammer area, spent a great deal of time in the woods, and she was never afraid of snakes.

Clara married Ole Thompson, and they spent their married life living in the Big Woods in Fillmore County, Minnesota. He died in 1957. I stayed with my great-grandmother when I was a child, and we would go picking gooseberries and blackcaps in the woods. She had a pet squirrel named Chippy that would bite anyone but her.

Clara's daughter, Esther Johanna, married Henry Knudson of Amherst, Minnesota, and they had two daughters: my mother, Charlotte (Nelson), and Harriet (Shattuck). I always listened to Clara and Esther talking in Norwegian and have since learned that they were speaking the same dialect as Torbjørg, Maria, and Salamon Hjørnevik spoke in Norway.

It was difficult for me to return to Hjørnevik in the summer of 2001, knowing that Torbjørg, Maria, and Salamon had all died. It made it easier being greeted with open arms by a younger generation of relatives. Although it had been twenty-five years since my first visit in 1976, I still felt as if I were really home.

• • • • •

• To purchase a copy of the History of Jackson County, 1910, by Arthur P. Rose contact:

Jackson County Historical Society
307 N Hwy 86, PO Box 238
Lakefield, MN 56150-0238
Phone: 507-662-5505

Du er en Hjørnevik, men hvem er du?

Tragiske immigrantnyheter om siouxindianernes 1862-opprør overbrakt 114 år senere

Ingen veier førte til Jørnevik, så jeg måtte ta toget til en stasjon som lå mellom to fjelltunneler. Men da jeg i 1976 endelig fant Hjørnevik-gården i nærheten av Evanger i Voss, i Bergensområdet i Norge, kjente jeg det som om jeg var kommet hjem.

Det var vanlig at nordmenn brukte gårdsnavnet som etternavn i Amerika. Selv om jeg ikke visste annet enn at mine tipp-tipp-oldeforeldres etternavn var Hjørnevik, var det mulig å lokalisere den ene Hjørnevik-gården som fantes.

Jeg klatret opp den bratte fjellstien inntil jeg kom til et gammeldags hvitt og blått hus med en svimlende utsikt over dalen og Evangervatn, en innsjølignende passasje som fører til fjorden. To Hjørnevik-søstre, Torbjørg, 88, og Maria, 83, åpnet døra. De hadde aldri sett meg før, men tok en titt på meg, og sa på norsk: *Du er en Hjørnevik, men hvem er du?*

The author, Deb, visiting with Maria (left) and Torbjørg (right) Hjørnevik in their home during 1976.

I det øyeblikket kjente jeg en sterk stolthet komme over meg, for jeg forstod at jeg trolig var den første personen i min familie som vendte tilbake til Hjørnevik fra Amerika. Torbjørg og Maria, som snakket den lokale dialekten, begynte å stille spørsmål så raskt at jeg hadde problemer med å forstå hva de sa.

Jeg grov raskt fram slektskartet mitt fra ryggsekken, og begynte å overbringe de tragiske nyhetene fra Amerika, 114 år etter at begivenhetene hadde skjedd. Det var historien om min families emigrasjon fra Hjørnevik i 1860, og om foreldre som var blitt brutalt myrdet i Belmont-massakeren under siouxindianernes opprør i 1862, i nærheten av Jackson i Minnesota.

Neste dag besøkte jeg Torbjørgs og Marias bror, Salamon, 90, Hjørnevik-familiens slektsforsker. Han var så oppglødd at han ble ved å repetere *"slekt, slekt"* om og om igjen. Salamon husket at han var blitt fortalt at min familie hadde dratt til Amerika, og at ingen hadde hørt noe fra dem mer. I Salamons slektstavle, som gikk tilbake til 1654, sporet han opp at min tipp-tipp-oldefar var et søskenbarn av hans bestefar.

I følge *Norske Gaardnavne* av Oluf Rygh, dukker navnet Jørnevik opp i en norsk diploma under formen Joronnarvik, etter kvinnenavnet Jorunn, så tidlig som i 1340. Den skrevne

formen Hjørnevik ble så skapt av folkets uttale.

Immigrasjonen til Amerika, 1860

Lars G. Hjørnevik og fru Lars G. Hjørnevik, mine tipp-tipp-oldeforeldre, som vi fortsatt ikke kjenner opphavet til, dro til Amerika før 1861. Deres sønn, Johannes Larson (Hjørnevik), min tipp-oldefar, var født 15. juni 1860.

Det antas at familien Hjørnevik reiste sammen med familiene Fyre, Langeland og Mestad, som alle er innskrevet i kirkeboken til "Big Canoe" lutherske kirke i Winneshiek County i det nordøstlige Iowa, og som dro vestover til Jackson County i det sørvestlige Minnesota. I 1860 eller 1861 slo de seg ned i Belmont, et norsk samfunn ved øvre Des Moines-elva, nord for det sted hvor Jackson, Minnesota, nå ligger.

Siouxindianernes land

I følge *Inkpaduta and the Sioux Indians*, 1998, av J.W. Parson og S. Kennedy, var det mange årsaker til siouxindianernes opprør i 1862. Siouxenes land var redusert til halvparten av sin størrelse gjennom avtaler som lovet dem økonomisk og materiell kompensasjon. Problemene dukket opp på grunn av den tette konsentrasjonen av indianerne, matmangel og ublue priser. Usympatiske indianeragenter med rikelige forsyninger nektet å gi mat til indianerne før livrenten var ankommet fra Washington, D.C. Indianerne hadde gitt opp sine jaktmarker, fraskrevet seg sitt land, og var nå nær sultegrensen.

De norske settlerne som ankom tidlig på 1860-tallet, forstod og snakket svært lite engelsk. Deres interesser var sentrert om egne hjem, og de hadde lite kontakt med omverdenen. De hadde bosatt seg i et ubeskyttet grenseland, nærmest i hjertet av indianernes land, uten å vite noe om indianernes skikker og indiansk krigføring. Nesten alle arbeidsføre menn var fraværende, idet de kjempet i sitt nye lands borgerkrig. Jackson County var kjent for å være sjeldent patriotisk, noe som imidlertid gjorde grensegårdene sårbare for angrep.

Det store siouxopprøret

Frustrerte og provoserte av år med brutte løfter, regjeringens løgner og av påtvungne kulturelle forandringer, startet de tidligere så fredelige siouxene et spontant og blodig opprør, der mer enn 800 nybyggere og soldater ble slått på mindre enn en uke i løpet av august 1862. Mer enn førti tusen mennesker flyktet fra hjemmene sine, noe som avfolket tjuetre fylker i det sørvestlige Minnesota. Den tragiske episoden markerte utbruddet av en serie indianerkriger som ikke tok slutt før slaget ved Wounded Knee i Sør-Dakota, nesten tretti år senere.

Belmont-massakeren i Jackson County var en del av det store siouxopprøret. Tretten Belmont-settlere ble myrdet med kaldt blod av en gruppe på omtrent femti indianere som beveget seg raskt fra hytte til hytte, anført av White Lodge. Da alt var over, flyktet de skrekkslagne nordmennene som hadde overlevd, tilbake til hovedsakelig Winneshiek County, Iowa, og Houston County, Minnesota.

Belmont-massakeren, 24. august 1862

(Forfatterens anmerkning: Se Norwegian settlement 1860-1862, som gir nærmere detaljer om enkeltpersonene under. For å lette identifikasjon, er de amerikanske familienavnene skrevet slik de skrives på norsk.)

Den følgende beretningen er tatt fra *History of Jackson County*, side 101-109:

"Angrepet på det norske settlementet i Jackson County skjedde søndag 24. august 1862 [omtrent klokken 10 om morgenen]...Tretten hvite ble myrdet, noen få andre ble såret, og mange greide så vidt å flykte med livet i behold. Så tidlig som i juni hadde nybyggerne fått rapporter om at de måtte forvente trøbbel med indianerne...Om nettene samlet de seg i forskjellige hytter som de mente kunne gi bedre beskyttelse, eller hvor det var lagret våpen og ammunisjon...og vanligvis dro de hjem om morgenen for å ta seg av gårdsarbeidet.

"Hjemme hos Ole Fyre, i den nordvestlige delen av seksjon 22, Belmont, hadde flere familier samlet seg...Da de så indianerne nærme seg, søkte fru Fyre, fru Hjørnevik og fru Ekse tilflukt i kjelleren sammen med åtte små barn, kjellerluken ble stengt og Ole Olson Fyre, Ole Fyres 11 år gammel sønn, stablet klær, bokser og kister over den. De andre ble igjen oppe.

"Indianerne nærmet seg hytta fra øst og brast inn gjennom østdøra. Alle som var i hytta, unntatt gutten, ble øyeblikkelig drept...Johannes Ekse ble tydeligvis slått i hjel, ettersom det ikke ble funnet noen sår etter kuler på kroppen hans. Lars Furness og Lars G. Hjørnevik, min tipp-tipp-oldefar, ble skutt.

"Ole Olson Fyre, gutten som stod vakt ved vestdøra, stakk av gjennom den og løp ned en sti som ledet til en kilde...så en indianer som siktet mot ham...kulen traff ham og slet bort tuppen av den høyre albuen...Indianernes forkjærlighet for 'ildvann' reddet et liv. Noe av det første indianerne gjorde var å gjennomsøke vognene, som lastet med forsyninger var brakt fra Mankato dagen før, og akkurat da indianeren holdt på å oppdage gutten i buskaset, fant de andre i hytta en kanne whisky. Ole [som senere tok navnet Ole F. Forde] løp...for å advare de andre nybyggerne.

"Frykten blant de som hadde gjemt seg i kjelleren mens drapene skjedde over hodene deres, kan ikke beskrives; så stille var de at de nesten ikke pustet. Redselen ble bare verre av skrikene fra det to år gamle barnet til fru Lars G. Hjornevik [Johannes, min tipp-oldefar]. Kvinnen, som med et mot vi sjelden møter i beretningene om indianernes krigføring, visste at de malte demonene omringet huset, og hun kom frivillig ut av kjelleren for å møte sin skjebne. Til de andre kvinnene sa hun: 'Jeg forstår at min time er kommet; jeg må gå opp igjen. Deres barn er mindre enn mine og de holder seg stille; hvis jeg blir her vil indianerne finne oss.' Hun gikk opp fra kjelleren med barnet, og ble drept. Kroppen ble fryktelig lemlestet.

"Heldigvis var indianerne opptatt med whiskyen og skjønte ikke hvor fru Hjørnevik hadde kommet fra. Barnet [Johannes] var uskadd, men begynte snart å gråte. Hyttedøra var forlatt åpen, og barnet ble skremt av rånene som kom inn i hytta. En av kvinnene gikk opp, fant barnet der det var etterlatt i morens blod, og tok det med tilbake til kjelleren og tok seg av det.

"Ikke langt fra Fyres hjem ble Mikkel Olson Slaabakken drept, og hans nevø, Anders Olson Slaabakken, den tretten år gamle sønnen til Engebret Olson Slaabakken, ble alvorlig såret og etterlatt for å dø. Hjemstedet til Engebret Olson Slaabakken lå nesten sju kilometer lenger sør enn Fyres hjem. Vest for Ole Fyres hjem kom indianerne over Knud Mestad og hans kone, Brita, og drepte dem. Disse uheldige menneskene bodde på vestsiden av elva, og var på vei til Ole Fyre da de ble overfalt på stien.

"Fru Fyre og fru Ekse bestemte seg for å søke skjul et annet sted. Derfor kom de fram med barna, og gjemte seg i en kornåker. Villmennene som kom tilbake fra besøket hos Slaabakken ...fant ut at flyktningene hadde gjemt seg i kjelleren under det første angrepet, men at de nå hadde flyktet, de var svært sinte og brukte mye tid på å lete etter dem. Etter at drapsmennene hadde dratt for andre gang, la kvinnene ut mot sør med barna, og de tilbrakte søndagsnatten i en smie på Slaabakken-gården ...og bega seg så til fots mot Spirit Lake.

"Etter det andre besøket hos Ole Fyre...fortsatte banden oppover elva til de kom til Knud Langeland. Herr Langeland var nede ved elva for å samle sammen buskapen da angrepet skjedde, og det gjorde at han unnslapp. Ved huset ble hans kone Anna Langeland, og fire barn, Anna [barn], Aagaata, Nicolai John og Knud [barn] Langeland, drept. Martha Langeland unngikk den øvrige familiens skjebne ved å gjemme seg i en kornåker. Han [herr Langeland] trodde han så tegn til liv i to av sine barn. Han tok dem i armene og bar dem hele veien til Spirit Lake [mer enn fire mil]. Ett av barna døde rett etter at de kom fram dit; det andre [Julia] kom seg.

"Fra Langelands hjem beveget siuxindianerne seg videre oppover langs elva til der hvor Ole Estenson og Ole Torgerson bodde, og de kom dit da mørket falt på om kvelden. Disse mennene var de eneste av nybyggerne som gjorde et forsøk på å redde livet på annen måte enn ved å flykte; de hadde berserkenes blod i seg og la an til

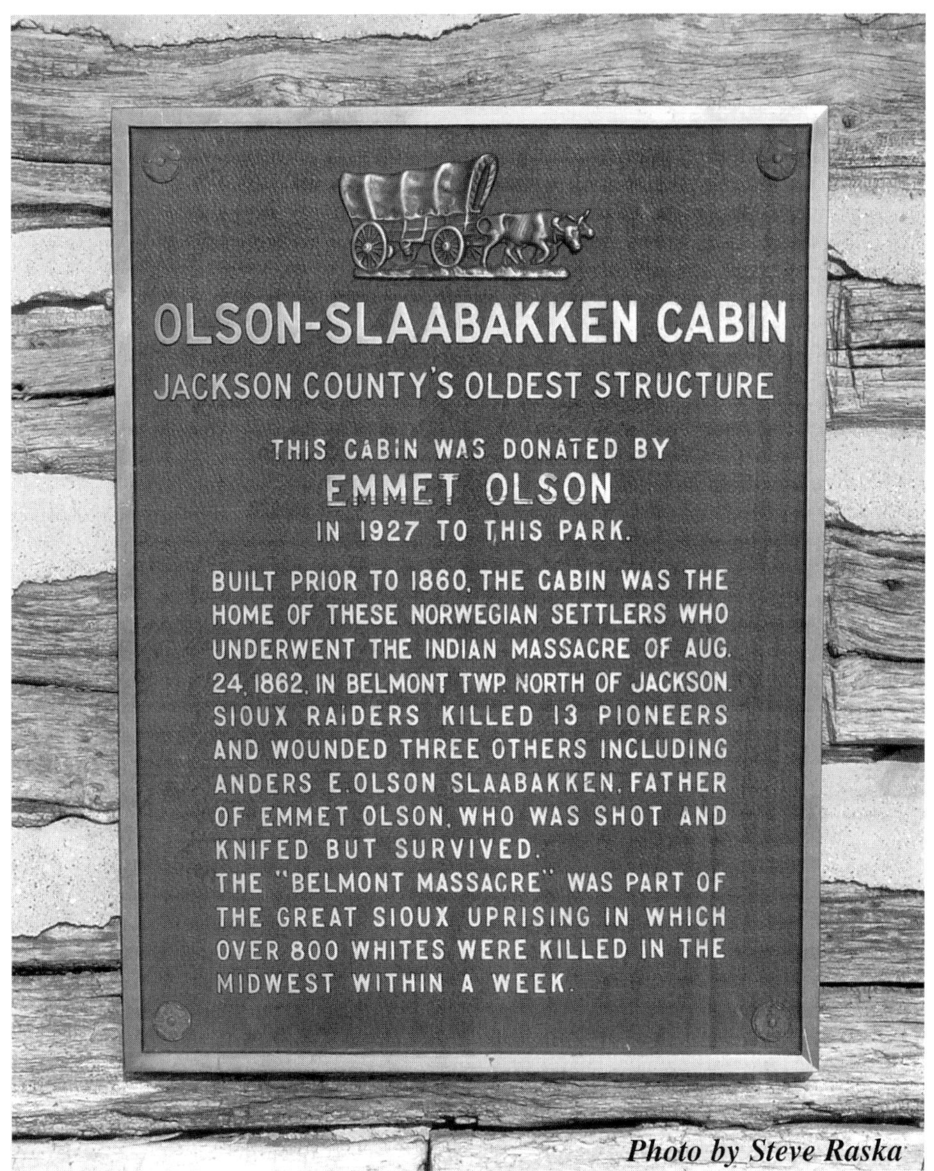

Photo by Steve Raska

Langeland Memorial

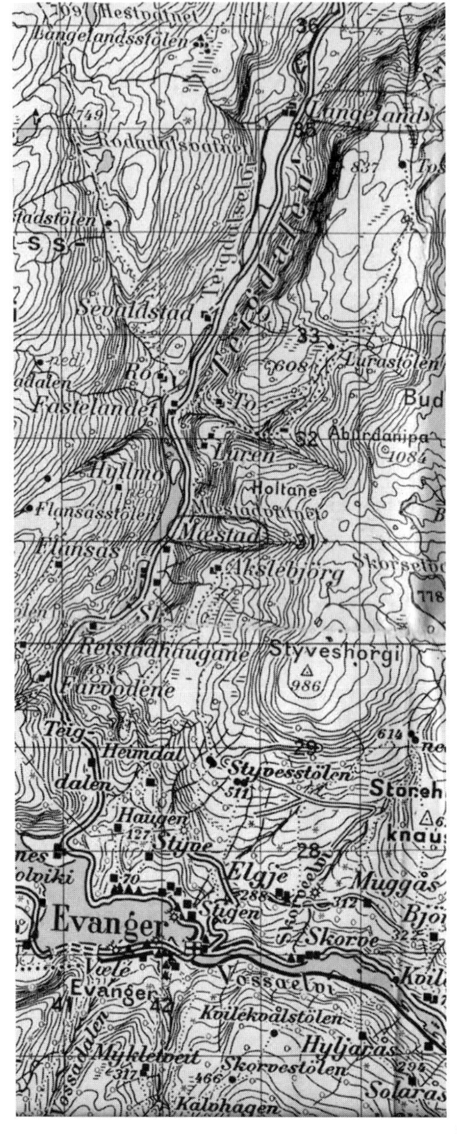

skikkelig motstand...De hadde geværer og ammunisjon, og både kunnskap og legning for å bruke dem...De hvite mennene bad familiene om å legge seg ned, og møtte skytingen fra fienden så godt at de stod mot alle angrep. Salve etter salve traff huset, og kulene trengte gjennom vegger og tak...De hvite mennene ladet de militære muskedundrene sine med kuler, og etter mørkets frambrudd skjøt de bare mot lysglimtene fra indianernes våpen. Ingen av de som var i hytta ble truffet, og angriperne dro til slutt sin vei."

Ett av barna i kjelleren, John Mestad, brakte i utgaven av *Decorah Public Opinion* den 13. september 1944, videre morens, fru Ekses, minner:

"Gjennom de brede sprekkene mellom gulvbordene kunne de skremte kvinnene se mye av det som skjedde ...Fra det tette mørket i kjelleren betraktet kvinnene mokkasinføttene som beveget seg stille gjennom hytterommene over hodene deres." Når det gjaldt måten Hjørnevik-babyen overlevde på, så ble følgende forklaring gitt: "'La ham være!' kommanderte rødhudenes leder da noen av krigerne gjorde seg klar til å kvitte seg med babyen....indianerne forlot hytta...og lot barnet [Johannes] tumle omkring i morens blod."

I en senere beretning hentet fra *Historical Data Project*, Bismarck, ND, er reisen til fru Fyre, fru Ekse og barna nærmere beskrevet av den elleve år gamle gutten, Ole F. Forde:

"Fire av barna var ikke gamle nok til å gå...en yngre gutt [Fyre], ni år gammel, bar to av barna, mens de andre to kvinnene bar ett barn hver. For å bære disse to barna måtte han ta ett i armene, løpe om lag 25-50 roder [130 til 250 meter], sette ned barnet, for så å løpe tilbake og hente det andre. Gutten, Ole, som man trodde var død, føyde seg til gruppen en uke etter massakeren."

En oldedatter av fru Ekse, Odis Erickson (Byron) Vatland, Mabel, Minnesota, berettet i *Fillmore County*

History, 1984, side 160-161, om gruppens reise til fots og med vogn. Brytteva var mor til fem av barna som hadde gjemt seg kjelleren under angrepet: Breta, 10 (bestemor til Odis); Knute, 9; Store Nels, 7; John, 4; og Vetle Nels,1. Barna levde alle til de ble voksne, og gikk under morens pikenavn Mestad.

"Ved første lyd av krigsrop fra indianerne, som vendte tilbake, tok Brytteva sine fem små barn og det foreldreløse barnet, den andre kvinnen tok de små barna og en 12 år gammel jente [muligens Martha Langeland som hadde ankommet Fyres hytte] og de løp inn i kornåkeren og spredte seg som vaktler mellom radene.

"Vi gjemte oss der til det ble natt. Da mørket kom, begynte vi på flukten. Brytteva visste at det et sted i sør fantes en grenseby, og vi satte kursen i den retningen. Gjennom den kronglete bunnen i villmarka, over nedfalne trær og over fuktige, bløte skogsmyrer, krøp vi sakte framover. Vi ventet at det hvert øyeblikk skulle dukke opp en svær villmann på veien. Noen ganger så vi det flammende lyset fra brennende hytter som var påtent av indianerne, og hørte de ville ropene deres om død og seier, mens vi stjal oss gjennom det uhyggelige mørket.

"I morgengryet gjemte vi oss igjen i en kornåker. Halvnakne, sultne og totalt utmattede begynte barna å gråte etter mat og vann. Det fantes kilder nær elva, men vi våget oss ikke den veien, for vi visste at den røde mannens skremsler lå langs vannveiene. Da våre skrik ble for hjerteskjærende, slet Brytteva av en arm fra kjolen sin og trakk opp duggen fra gras og korn. I en liten gryte som et vettskremt barn hadde båret med seg hele veien, ble dråpene samlet sammen en etter en; og før solen hadde tørket opp morgenduggen var tørsten vår på et vis slukket.

"I tre dager og tre netter fortsatte vi flukten fra våre utplyndrede hjem. Onsdags morgen oppdaget vi en liten avdeling fra United States' kavaleri som var sendt ut for å samle sammen de overlevende etter massakren. Idet de nærmet seg i præriens utkant, kastet vi oss skremt ned i underskogen som jagede fugler, for vi trodde de var indianere. Etter en stund ble vi likevel omringet, og forstod fort at vi var reddet av hvite og ikke tatt til fange av den røde fienden.

"Til avtalt tid ble vi plassert på store militære vogner og brakt landeveien tilbake til våre tidligere hjem i Winneshiek County, på regjeringens kostnad...Det var en lang, lang reise gjennom sentrale Minnesota og over Iowas prærier, men soldatene var snille og fødde oss godt på sin grove kost av bønner, brunt brød og melk."

Monumentet i Jackson, MN

Det står et monument i Ashley Park, Jackson, Minnesota, til minne om de som døde i indianermassakrene i 1857 og 1862. Blant de nevnte er mine tipp-tipp-oldeforeldre fra Hjørnevik. Inskripsjonen sier: *Reist av Staten Minnesota i året 1909, til minne om nybyggerpionerene i Jackson County, hvis navn er innskrevet nedenfor, massakrert av siouxindianerne 28. mars 1857 og 24. august 1862.*

- 1857-massakeren: William Wood, Ceurce Wood, Joshua Stewart, Joshua Stewarts to barn, Willie, Thomas
- 1862-massakren: Ole Fyre, Johannes Ekse, Mikkel Olson (Slaabakken), Lars Furnes, fru Anna Langeland, Anna (barn) Langeland, Aagaata Langeland, Nicolai Johan Langeland, Knud (barn) Langeland, Knud Mestad og hustru (Brita), Lars G. Hjørnevik og hustru.

Klapperslangejegeren

Etter at fru Ekse og fru Fyre hadde reddet Hjørnevik-babyen, Johannes Larson (min tipp-oldefar), ble han tatt med til Black Hammer Township i Houston County, Minnesota. I følge slektsforskerne, Gordon Eddy og Georgia Rosendahl, fra Spring Grove/Black Hammer, vokste Johannes opp i familien til Lars Nilsson Ekse (et søskenbarn av Johannes Ekse) og hans kone, Anne Eriksdatter Berdal.

I 1882 giftet Johannes seg i Houston County med Lars Nilsson Ekses niese, Ingeborg Nielsdatter Ekse. Ingeborg var datter av Nils Nilson Ekse og Kari Hermundsdatter Nese (se slektskart i historien om influensaen i 1918). Johannes og Ingeborg hadde to barn: Louis, i 1883, og min oldemor, Clara, i 1886. Johannes og Ingeborg Larson er begge gravlagt på kirkegården i Black Hammer i Houston County, Minnesota.

Johannes drev gården i nærheten av Black Hammer og var klapperslangejeger. Til tross for at han ble bitt tre ganger, døde han av naturlige årsaker i en alder av 47. Clara, som vokste opp i Black Hammer-området, tilbrakte mye tid i skogen, og hun var aldri redd for slanger.

Clara giftet seg med Ole Thompson, og de tilbrakte sitt liv som ektefolk i Big Woods i Fillmore County, Minnesota. Han døde i 1957. Når jeg var hos min oldemor da jeg var barn, brukte vi å plukke stikkelsbær og bjørnebær i skogen. Hun hadde et tamt ekorn som het Chippy og som prøvde å bite alle andre enn henne.

Claras datter, Ester Johanna, giftet seg med Henry Knudson fra Amherst, Minnesota, og de hadde to døtre: min mor, Charlotte (Nelson), og Harriet (Shattuck). Jeg hørte alltid på når Clara og Esther snakket norsk, og jeg har etter hvert forstått at de snakket den samme dialekten som Thorbjørg, Maria og Salamon Hjørnevik gjorde i Norge.

Det var vanskelig for meg å komme tilbake til Hjørnevik sommeren 2001, vel vitende om at Thorbjørg, Maria og Salamon alle var døde. Det gjorde det lettere at jeg ble møtt med åpne armer av yngre generasjoner med slektninger. Selv om det var tjuefem år siden mitt første besøk i 1976, så følte jeg det som om jeg var virkelig hjemme da jeg kom tilbake til Hjørnevik.

• • • • •

Genealogy tips

• To locate farms in Norway use Oluf Rygh's *Norske Gaardnavne* (Norwegian Farm Names), 17 volumes series, http://www.dokpro.uio.no/rygh_ng/rygh_form.html (i.e. Farm names – Ekse, Fyre, Jørnevik, Langeland, and Mæstad are all in the Parish-Ævanger, Muncipality-Ævanger, of County-Søndre Bergenhus amt, the older county name used in the database)

• To research rural communities in Norway use *Bygdebøker* (local history books) and *Gards og Ættesoge* (farms and family sagas)

Slektsforskningstips

• For å lokalisere gårder i Norge, bruk Oluf Ryghs *Norske Gaardnavne*, 17-bindsserien, http://www.dokpro.uio.no/rygh_ng/rygh_form.html (i.e. Gårdsnavn - Ekse, Fyre, Jørnevik, Langeland og Mæstad er alle i Ævanger sogn, Ævanger kommune, Søndre Bergenhus amt, det gamle fylkesnavnet er brukt i databasen)

• For slektsforskning i landkommuner i Norge: bruk bygdebøker (lokale historiebøker) og *Gards- og Ættesoge*

Gravestone of Johannes (Hjørnevik baby) and Ingeborg Larson in the Black Hammer Cemetery, Houston County, Minnesota.

3

Above the Arctic Circle

A 1976 visit to Kautokeino, home to 2500 indigenous Sami people and 70,000 reindeer

"We have nine months of winter and three months of poor skiing conditions."

Having graduated from the University of Minnesota and flown to Norway the very next day, I was a young student open to adventure. On July 12, 1976, when I accepted an invitation to visit a family in Tromsø (Wilhelm and Aud Schreuder), I had no idea they lived among the indigenous Sami people (formerly called Lapps) above the Arctic Circle of Norway. Speaking in Norwegian, I had visited only briefly with my new acquaintances during a train ride from Sandefjord to Drammen, near Oslo, in southern Norway. Impulsively, I said yes to their invitation, without knowing or even asking where Tromsø was.

Meeting me at the Drammen train station was my best friend, Marit Waaler, whom I had met earlier that spring on the steps of the University of Minnesota. Back at her parents' strawberry and tomato farm at *Egge i Lier*, I told them about my chat on the train and my upcoming plans to go to Tromsø, wherever that was. Marit and her sister, Bjørg, showed me the map and laughed as they said, *"Well then you'll need a bigger backpack to get there."* It was only with Marit and Bjørg's crash course on traveling alone in Norway and the Norwegian survival words taught to me by their father, Sigmund, that I reached Tromsø.

As the crow flies, it's a distance of 1,089 miles from southern to northern Norway. Traveling by car, train, bus, ferry, and coastal steamer, on my way to Tromsø, the *"Paris of the North,"* I saw some of the most incredible scenery in the world. I was in the *"Land of the Midnight Sun"* and *"Northern Lights."* This was only a prelude of what lay ahead as I ventured still farther north and then inland to Kautokeino, where during the winter months there are 2,500 indigenous Sami people and 70,000 reindeer.

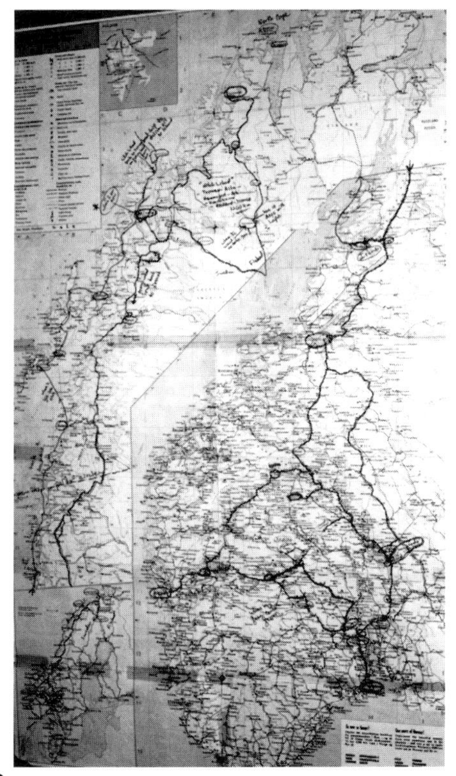

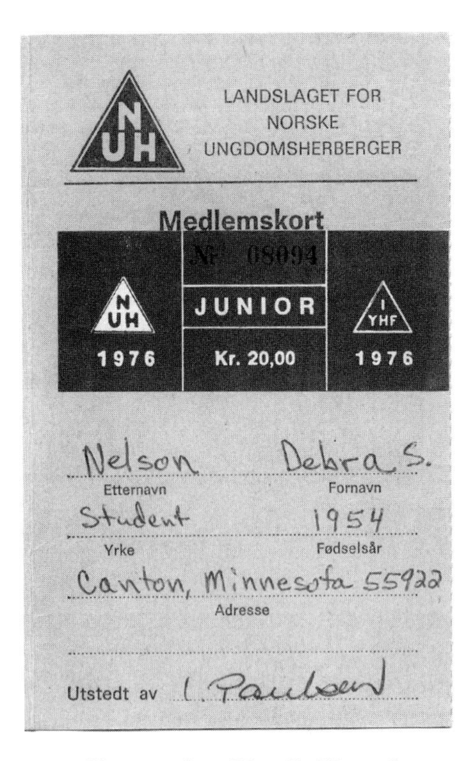

LANDSLAGET FOR
NORSKE
UNGDOMSHERBERGER

Medlemskort

Nr 08094

JUNIOR

1976 | Kr. 20,00 | 1976

Nelson Debra S.
Etternavn Fornavn

Student 1954
Yrke Fødselsår

Canton, Minnesota 55922
Adresse

Utstedt av I. Paulsen

Norwegian Youth Hostel

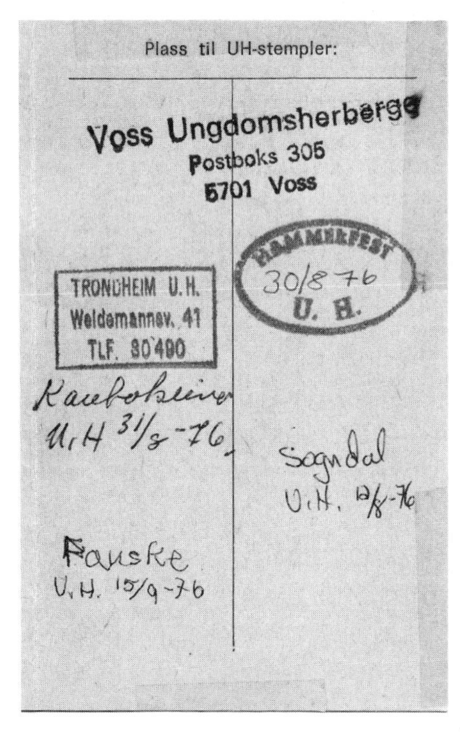

Plass til UH-stempler:

Voss Ungdomsherberge
Postboks 305
5701 Voss

HAMMERFEST
30/8 76
U. H.

TRONDHEIM U.H.
Weidemannsv. 41
TLF. 30490

Kautokeino
U.H 31/8-76

Sogndal
U.H. 12/8-76

Fauske
U.H. 15/9-76

I was immersed in a unique culture based on the Samis' close relationship with nature. Their lives have been shaped by the landscape of the Arctic Ocean, fjords, and *tundra*, a Sami word, where generations have made their living from reindeer farming, fishing, hunting, and handicrafts. Located on the inland tundra of northern Norway, Kautokeino is the cultural capital of the Sami people and one of the most important reindeer districts.

Getting to Kautokeino

On August 9, 1976, with my new, bigger backpack, sleeping bag, and handful of maps, I set out on a scenic journey to the north, sightseeing along the way. Crossing the Hallingskarvet Mountain, I traveled by train from Drammen to Voss (near Bergen). Riding the bus from Voss to Gudvangen, I experienced one of northern Europe's steepest roads with thirteen hairpin bends at Stalheim. By ferry to Kaupanger, I crossed the Sognefjord, the longest, deepest fjord in the world. I rode the bus from Kaupanger to Sogndal, and then over the Jotunheimen Mountain to Otta. My favorite location was Sognefjellshytta, at the top of the highest mountain pass in northern Europe. Finally, I was back on the train from Otta to Trondheim and about one-third of the way from Drammen to Tromsø as the crow flies.

Clad in my blue-and-white-striped *busserull* (traditional work shirt) with the big *Norges Bygdeungdomslag* (Norwegian Young Farmers Organization) NBU patch and sporting waist-length, blond hair, I looked, as they say, *hele norsk* (whole Norwegian). Using my *Landslaget for Norske Ungdomsherberger* (Norwegian Youth Hostel) or NUH card, I stayed economically along the way. From Trondheim, I hitched four rides to Namsos.

Hitchhiking at this time in northern Norway was considered a common way to travel and almost a necessity for students. There were and still are no trains in the northern one-third of the country. In all, I hitchhiked over 1,500 miles on this trip.

Norway has one of the roughest and longest coastlines in the world. From Namsos, I traveled the short ride by boat to Rørvik and then boarded the *Hurtigruten* (coastal steamer) "M/S Polarlys." The 46-hour express ride along the coast crossed over the Arctic Circle just south of Bodø. I was now about two-thirds of my way to the far north. From Bodø, the Hurtigruten crossed over the rough open sea to the Lofoten Islands, renowned for their sheer, jagged mountain peaks and traditional cod fishing. Meandering through the chain of islands, the coastal steamer arrived in Tromsø on August 19, and I

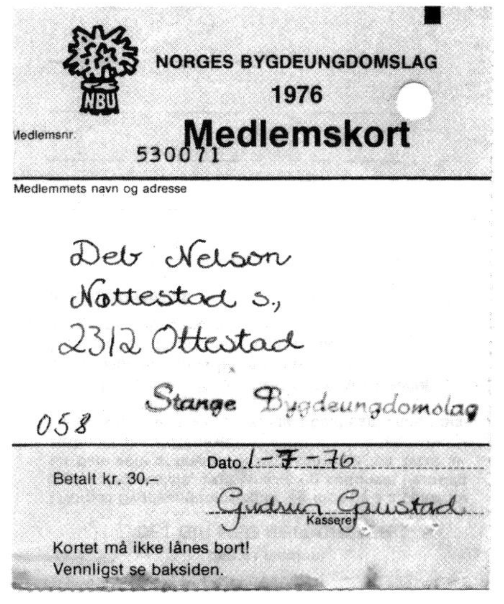

NORGES BYGDEUNGDOMSLAG
1976
Medlemskort
Medlemsnr. 530071

Medlemmets navn og adresse

Deb Nelson
Nøttestad s.,
2312 Ottestad

Stange Bygdeungdomslag
058

Dato 1-7-76
Betalt kr. 30,–
Gudrun Gaustad
Kasserer

Kortet må ikke lånes bort!
Vennligst se baksiden.

NBU

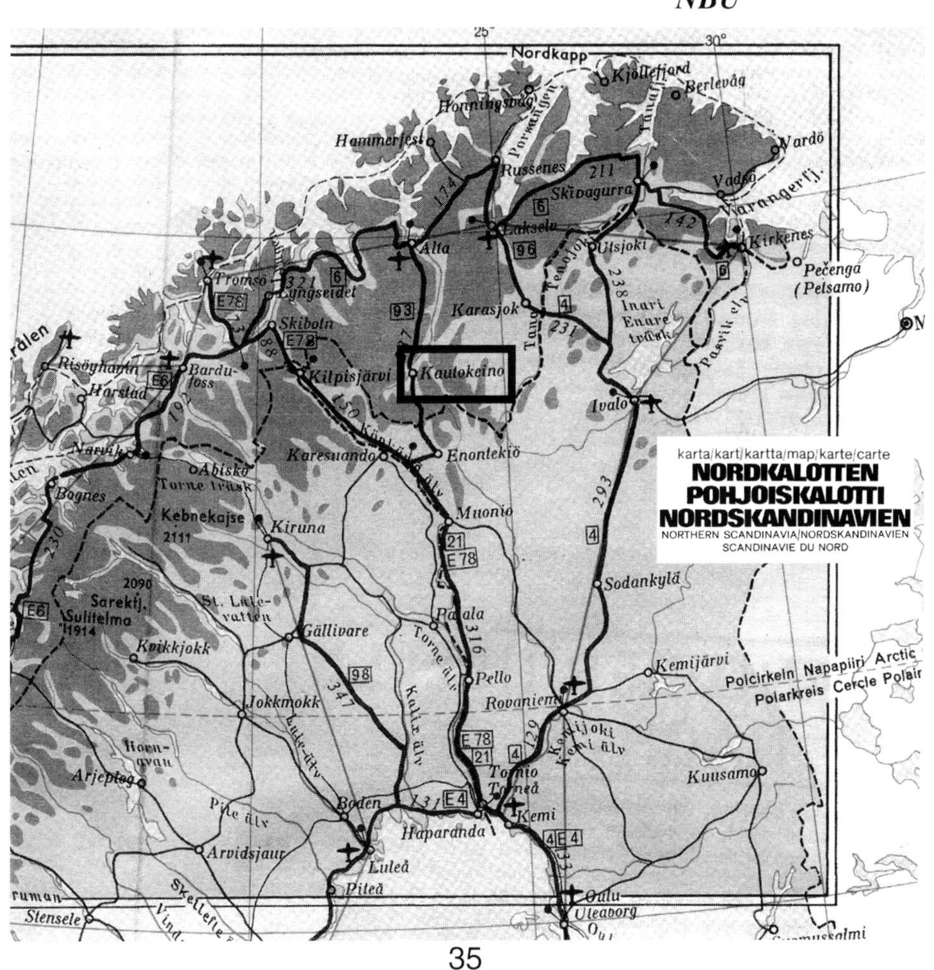

was welcomed with open arms by Wilhelm, his wife, Aud, and their sons.

My eleven-day trip from the strawberry and tomato farm in Drammen to Tromsø had only wet my appetite for adventure. The days were long in the *Land of the Midnight Sun* and I too soon ignored my need for sleep. Some 250 miles north of the Arctic Circle, the sun never sets in Tromsø from May 21 to July 23, but also never rises from November 25 to January 21.

Snowflakes

by Sami Poet Pedar Jalvi
from Utsjok in the Tana Valley

Tiny snowflakes now descending
Hover through the silent air,
Dainty, frail, on rocks and birch groves,
White on white the earth they cover.

Small, so small, the snowflakes are,
Yet together number millions,
Cover hollows, valleys, trees,
Mould fine ridges on the birch grove,
Pile tall drifts behind the rocks.

But with the heat of vernal sun
Each flake melts to purest liquid.
And from each drop at last is gathered
Spring and river, lake and ocean,
Strength on strength from tiny snowflakes
–Great are then the frail, the small.

My favorite Sami poem was found at the Tromsø public library.

I was delighted when on August 21 William and Aud arranged for me to join John Launois, National Geographic/ Black Star Publishing Company photojournalist, for a ride on the cable car they managed. From 12:30 A.M., as Launois photographed the rising sun, I learned of his 1971-1972 documentation of the Tasaday tribe, an indigenous Philippine rain forest tribe living in what he referred to as *Primeval Eden.*

Another adventure of mine involved accompanying a crew, whom I had not previously met, delivering supplies to *Fugløykalven fry*, the lighthouse on the north side of *Fugløya* (Bird Island), at 70°19'N latitude and 20°09'E longitude. Although I didn't get to see them, a large colony of puffins nest here in the summer.

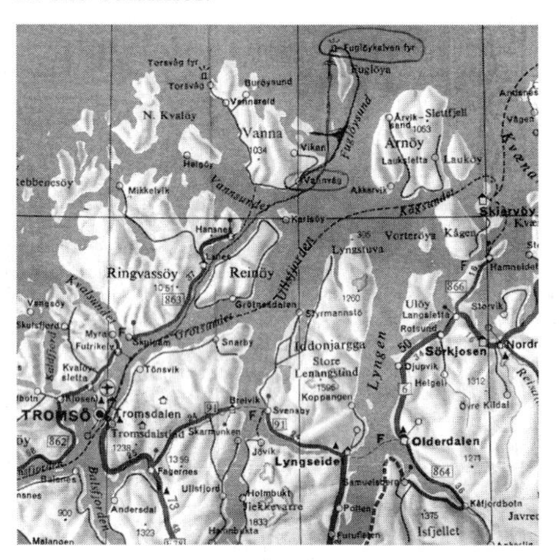

On August 27, I boarded the tugboat, "Blue Boy," which belonged to Aud's brother. We left just after midnight and were only two hours into the trip, crossing Fugløysund, when an unpredicted, violent storm hit. When we arrived at the lighthouse overlooking the Arctic Ocean at 4:30 A.M., the waves were spraying over the top of the tugboat, and the crew were unable to hook up the hoses to unload the oil and drinking water. I ended up hitchhiking back to Tromsø on the fishing boat "M/S Garnfisk," while the "Blue Boy" held out for better weather at Vannvåg, on the island Vanna. I had been seasick enough to last a lifetime.

Prior to hitchhiking 500 miles in three days from Tromsø to Kautokeino, I spent time at the local museum studying the numerous Sami exhibits. I also spent several days at the public library reading about Sapmi (Samiland or Lapland). Along the coastal route, I toured Hammerfest, which has the distinction of being the northernmost town in the world. *Nordcapp* (North Cape) was only a short distance away, but getting there meant crossing the sea again, which was not appealing.

During the last hour of my 23-day journey to Kautokeino, I hitched a ride with three Sami men who spoke their native language and Norwegian, but no English. They were dressed in their traditional colorful attire. Before driving me to the youth hostel, they taught me the local village saying: *We have nine months of winter and three months of poor skiing conditions.*

Indigenous People

The Sami people live in an area called Sapmi that stretches through four countries: Norway, Sweden, Finland,

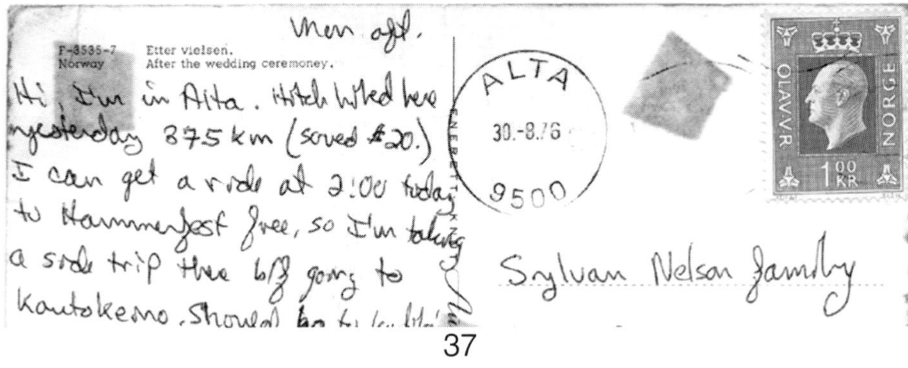

Mon aft.

F-3535-7 Norway — Etter vielsen. After the wedding ceremoney.

Hi, I'm in Alta. Hitch hiked here yesterday 375 km (saved $20.) I can get a ride at 2:00 today to Hammerfest free, so I'm taking a side trip there b/f going to Kautokeino. Should be [illegible]

Sylvan Nelson family

and Russia. The small, indigenous group is estimated at 100,000 with half of the population living in Norway and most of them living in Finnmark, the northernmost county of Norway. The Sami people are considered indigenous because their ancestors inhabited the area before it was settled or the present borders were drawn. They also have their own distinct social, economic, cultural, and political institutions.

Each Sami group I observed had a slightly different type of costume, with Kautokeino's Sami having the most colorful of any in Sapmi. Men, women, and children wore bright, blue tunics every day. The women's tunics were dress length, and the men's were shorter. They were decorated over the shoulder, chest, neck, cuffs, and hem with bright red, green, and yellow bands. Both the men and women wore ornate leather belts; however, the men slid theirs down around their hips making the upper part of the tunic a storage place for anything they were likely to need. The women also wore a bright silk or woolen scarf over their shoulders.

Knowing the shape, color, and pattern of the Samis' headgear allows you to identify their native district. Hats worn by Kautokeino's men and boys are about a foot tall and decorated with colored bands. The floppy blue fabric in the back of their hats has four points, representing the four winds. Leather boots with turned up toes are used in the summer; whereas reindeer skin moccasins filled with dry grass are worn the rest of the year. During the winter both sexes wear narrow reindeer skin trousers under their tunics as well as heavy reindeer skin coats.

The Sami winter in renowned for its cold, snow, Northern Lights, and the silence of the boundless Finnmark Mountain Plateau. Located on the same latitude as Siberia, Greenland, and

Alaska, the coldest temperature on record in Kautokeino was in 1886, when it was minus 60.5ºF. As recent as January 26, 1999, a freezing wind from Siberia was blamed for the almost inhuman temperatures of minus 58.5ºF in the village. In 1976 most of the people in Kautokeino lived in simple wooden structures and were semi-nomadic. The majority still followed the reindeer on the big migrations, but they return to live in the village in between times.

At the Youth Hostel in Kautokeino, I lived in the same wooden house as the Sami owner, Anna, and her son, Alfred. Anna offered me a job for a few hours each day helping her clip out letters and reindeer from felt, for the *Hilsen fra Kautokeino* (Hello from Kautokeino) souvenirs she sold. It was a great opportunity to drink black coffee with Anna and listen to her stories about their unique way of life. I learned that the Sami people even walk differently, shifting their bodies from side to side, making long distance travel more efficient. I also learned that it is impolite to ask a Sami how many reindeer he has, the equivalent of asking how much money he has in the bank.

The everyday use of the Sami language is a decisive point in determining one's right to be classified as a Sami. Unlike Norwegian, which is a Germanic language, the Sami language belongs to the Finno-Ugric branch of

the Uralic family, which is more closely related to Finnish and Hungarian. Samis have 100 words for snow, some 400 words for reindeer, and about 50 different names for the color of the reindeer coat.

In English, the word *Lapp* has been replaced with *Sami*. Lapp is considered a derogatory term, since it means patch of cloth for mending, suggesting that the Samis are wearing patched clothing.

Staying in Anna's Youth Hostel, next to the main house, were two French students and one German. The language barrier became almost comical at times with the Frenchman speaking to me in English and the German student speaking in German, so that I could translate into Norwegian for Anna. I'll never forget the day the German student arrived and asked if Germans were allowed at the Youth

Anna and Deb

Hostel. Anna later explained to me that the Nazis during World War II burned to the ground every single building in Kautokeino and nearly every home in the county of Finnmark. Hard feelings still existed amongst her people.

The Samis observe not four but eight seasons a year, with each being a separate phase of reindeer breeding. The different tasks carried out in the different seasons bring a rhythm to their lives, controlled primarily by the movements of the reindeer. To identify ownership of the reindeer, a unique set of notches is cut with a knife in each animal's ear.

Both the reindeer bulls and cows annually grow antlers during the summer. After rutting and competing to breed the cows in the autumn, the males begin to shed their antlers, which is completed by mid-December. Female reindeer retain their antlers until after calving in the spring to protect their newborn against predators. Santa's reindeer, every single one of them from Rudolph to Blitzen, most likely were females.

Easter in Kautokeino is a special event with people converging from various parts of Sapmi. Although the vast majority of the Samis belong to the Lutheran Church, they celebrate Easter as more than just a religious holiday. Reindeer races are held to celebrate their culture and way of life, as the reindeer herders prepare to follow their herds to the mountains near the sea. Lively celebrations are held with marriages, Sami music, and theatre performances, using beautiful sets made of snow and taking advantage of the Northern Lights as dramatic backdrop.

During the winter, about 70,000 reindeer return to the Kautokeino area, where they feed chiefly on a type of lichen called reindeer moss. About 15,000 reindeer are slaughtered annually in the village's modern slaughterhouse. The reindeer were still in the mountains when I was in Kautokeino.

On September 29, I returned to the strawberry and tomato farm in the south. My 52-day trip that started on a whim had provided me with adventure beyond my wildest expectations and with memories to last a lifetime.

The city of Tromsø is applying to host the Olympic winter games in 2014. If their offer is accepted, it would be the first ever games within the arctic region. The event would have a distinct Sami influence promoting Norway as a nation of culture and sports. What a tribute this would be to one of the oldest surviving cultures in the world, the beautiful indigenous Sami people of the arctic.

Nord for polarsirkelen

Et besøk i Kautokeino i 1976, hvor det bor 2500 samer og 70 000 reinsdyr

Jeg var en ung student åpen for eventyr, og fløy til Norge dagen etter at jeg hadde tatt avsluttende eksamen ved Universitetet i Minnesota. Da jeg 12. juli 1976 tok imot en invitasjon til å besøke en familie i Tromsø (Wilhelm og Aud Schreuder), hadde jeg ingen ide om at de levde blant den samiske urbefolkningen nord for polarsirkelen i Norge. Jeg hadde bare snakket litt norsk med mine nye bekjentskaper i løpet av en togreise fra Sandefjord til Drammen ved Oslo, i det sørlige Norge. Impulsivt sa jeg ja til invitasjonen, uten å vite, eller en gang å spørre, hvor Tromsø var.

På togstasjonen i Drammen ble jeg møtt av min beste venninne, Marit Waaler, som jeg hadde møtt tidligere den våren på trappa på Universitetet i Minnesota. Vel tilbake på deres jordbær- og tomatgård i Egge i Lier, fortalte jeg om samtalen på toget og om mine gryende planer om å dra til Tromsø, hvor nå det kunne være. Marit og søsteren, Bjørg, viste meg kartet, lo og sa: *"Vel, du trenger en større ryggsekk om du skal komme deg dit."* Det var bare ved hjelp av Marits og Bjørgs lynkurs i hvordan man reiser alene i Norge, og overlevelsesrådene deres far, Sigmund, gav meg, at jeg nådde Tromsø.

I luftlinje er det 175 norske mil fra sør til nord i Norge. Mens jeg reiste med bil, tog, buss, ferge og hurtigrute på min vei til Nordens Paris, Tromsø, så jeg noen av de mest utrolige landskap i verden. Jeg var i midnattsolens og nordlysets land. Dette var bare en forsmak på hva som ventet meg etter hvert som jeg våget med stadig lenger nord og inn i landet til Kautokeino, hvor det i vintermånedene befant seg 2500 samer og 70 000 reinsdyr.

Jeg dykket ned i en unik kultur basert på samenes nære forhold til naturen. Livene deres var formet av et landskap av arktisk hav, fjorder og tundra, som er et samisk ord, i et område hvor generasjoner hadde skapt seg et levebrød av reindrift, fiske, jakt og håndverk. Beliggende på innlandets tundra i det nordligste Norge, er Kautokeino kulturhovedstaden for det samiske folk, og et av de viktigste reindistriktene.

Veien til Kautokeino

Jeg la ut på turen 9. august 1976 med en ny og større ryggsekk, sovepose og en håndfull med kart, og det ble en naturskjønn reise mot nord mens jeg nøt

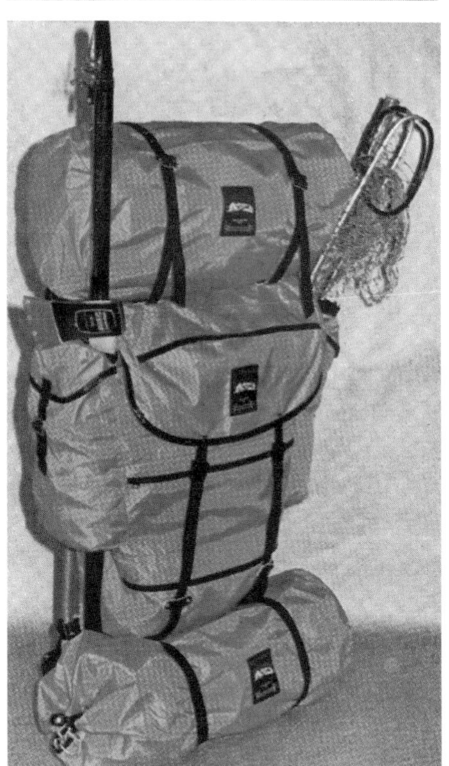

utsikten langs ruta. Jeg reiste med tog fra Drammen til Voss, over Hallingskarvet. Fra Voss til Gudvangen tok jeg bussen, og opplevde en av Nord-Europas bratteste veier med sine tretten hårnålsvinger ved Stalheim. Med ferge til Kaupanger, krysset jeg Sognefjorden, den lengste og dypeste fjorden i verden. Jeg kjørte buss fra Kaupanger til Sogndal, og videre over Jotunheimen til Otta. Mitt favorittsted var Sognefjellshytta, på toppen av den høyeste fjellovergangen i Nord-Europa. Til slutt var jeg tilbake på toget, fra Otta til Trondheim, og hadde tilbakelagt omtrent en tredel av veien mellom Drammen og Tromsø, regnet i luftlinje.

Kledd i blå- og kvitstripet busserull (en tradisjonell arbeidsskjorte) med et stort Norges Bondeungdomslag-merke på, og med sporty, midjelangt blondt hår, så jeg såkalt helnorsk ut. Jeg brukte NHU-kort fra Landslaget for Norske Ungdomsherberger, og reiste rimelig hele veien. Fra Trondheim haiket jeg i fire etapper til Namsos.

Å haike var på denne tiden betraktet som en vanlig måte å reise på i det nordlige Norge, og nærmest nødvendig for studenter. Der var og er fremdeles ingen jernbane i den nordligste tredelen av landet. Alt i alt haiket jeg mer enn 2400 kilometer på denne turen.

Norge har en av de tøffeste og lengste kystlinjene i verden. Fra Namsos reiste jeg den korte turen med båt til Rørvik, og gikk der ombord på Hurtigruten "M/S Polarlys". I løpet av den 46 timer lange turen langs kysten, passerte vi polarsirkelen litt sør for Bodø. Jeg var nå kommet om lag to tredeler av veien til det fjerne nord. Fra Bodø krysset hurtigruten over det åpne havstykket til Lofotøyene, kjent for sine bratte, taggete fjelltopper og tradisjonelle torskefiske. Etter å ha buktet seg gjennom kjeden av øyer, kom hurtigruten til Tromsø den 19. august, og jeg ble tatt imot med åpne armer av Wilhelm, hans kone Aud, og sønnene deres.

Min elleve dagers reise fra jordbær- og tomatgården ved Drammen til Tromsø hadde bare skjerpet appetitten på eventyr. Dagene var lange i Midnattsolens land, og jeg ignorerte fort behovet for søvn. Om lag 40 norske mil nord for polarsirkelen går sola aldri ned mellom 21. mai og 23. juli, men den står heller aldri opp mellom 25. november og 21. januar.

Jeg var henrykt da William og Aud den 21. august fikk ordnet det slik at jeg kunne ledsage John Launois, som var fotograf for National Geographic/Black star Publishing Company, på en tur med kabelbanen. Fra en halvtime over midnatt fotograferte Launois soloppgangen,

Treasured gifts given to Deb by Wilhelm and Aud Schreuder

Samebarn
by Odd Harrong 28/300

Kamp for tilvarelsen
by Odd Harrong 31/100

mens han fortalte om sin dokumentasjon fra 1971 til 1972 av Tasaday-stammen, en urbefolkningsstamme i den filippinske regnskogen, som levde i det han kalte *"Det opprinnelige Eden."*

Et annet eventyr var det å følge et mannskap jeg ikke hadde møtt før, og som leverte forsyninger til Fugløykalven fyr, fyrtårnet på nordsiden av Fugløya ved 70° 19' nordlig bredde og 20° 9' lengde. Jeg fikk ikke se dem, men det hekker en koloni med lundefugler her om sommeren.

Den 27. august gikk jeg om bord på slepebåten "Blue Boy", som tilhørte Auds bror. Vi gikk ut rett etter midnatt,

og hadde bare lagt bak oss to timer av turen over Fugløysundet, da det kom en sterk, uanmeldt storm. Da vi ankom fyret med sin utsikt over Nordishavet klokken 4.30 om morgen-en, plasket bølgene over toppen av slepebåten og mannskapet var ute av stand til å få i land slangene for å losse olje og drikkevann. Jeg endte opp med å haike tilbake til Tromsø med fiskebåten "M/S Garnfisk", mens "Blue Boy" ventet på bedre vær ved Vannvåg, på øya Vanna. Jeg hadde vært sjøsyk nok for resten av livet.

Forut for den 80 mil lange tredagersturen fra Tromsø til Kautokeino, tilbrakte jeg en del tid på det lokale museet, hvor jeg studerte de tallrike samiske utstillingene. Jeg tilbrakte også flere dager på det offentlige biblioteket, hvor jeg leste om Sapmi (Sameland eller Lappland). Langs landeveien besøkte jeg også Hammerfest, som er kjent for å være verdens nordligste by. Nordkapp var ikke langt unna, men å dra dit betydde at jeg måtte ut på sjøen igjen, og det fristet ikke.

I løpet av de siste timene av min 23-dagers reise til Kautokeino, haiket jeg med tre samiske menn som snakket både sitt eget språk og norsk, men ikke engelsk. De var kledd i sine tradisjonelle, fargerike drakter. Før de kjørte meg til ungdomsherberget, lærte de meg det lokale uttrykket: *"Vi har ni måneder med vinter og tre måneder med dårlig skiføre."*

"Vi har ni måneder med vinter og tre måneder med dårlig skiføre."

Urbefolkningen

Samene lever i et område kalt Sapmi som strekker seg over fire land: Norge, Sverige, Finland og Russland. Den lille urbefolkningsgruppen er anslått til om lag 100 000, og halvparten av befolkningen lever i Norge, de fleste i Finnmark, det nordligste fylket i Norge. Samene er betraktet som urbefolkning fordi deres forfedre bodde i området før det ble bebygd, eller før de nåværende grensene ble lagt. De har også sine egne spesielle sosiale, økonomiske, kulturelle og politiske institusjoner.

Hver samegruppe jeg så hadde forskjellige drakttyper, og Kautokeinos samer var de mest fargerike av alle. Menn, kvinner og barn bar skinnende blå tunikaer til hverdags. Kvinnenes drakt var kjolelange, mennenes var kortere. De var dekorert over skuldrene, brystet, i nakken og langs mansjetter og kanter med klare røde, grønne og gule bånd. Både menn og kvinner bar utsmykkede lærbelter, men mennene spente sitt rundt hoftene slik at den øvre delen av koften skapte en plass hvor de kunne bære med seg det de kunne ha bruk for. Kvinnene bar også skinnende silke- eller ullsjal over skuldrene.

Om du kjenner de samiske hodeplaggenes fasong, farge og mønster, kan du identifisere samenes hjemdistrikt. Hodeplagg båret av Kautokeinos menn og gutter er om lag 30 centimeter høye og dekorert med fargerike bånd. Den blå stoffpynten som henger bakpå luene har fire punkter, disse representerer fire vinder. Lærstøvler med oppovervendte tær blir brukt om sommeren, mens mokkasiner av reinskinn, fylt med tørket gress, blir brukt resten av året. I løpet av vinteren bruker begge kjønn trange reinskinnbukser under koften sammen med tunge reinskinnkåper.

Den samiske vinteren er kjent for sin kulde, sin snø, nordlyset og stillheten på den uendelige Finnmarksvidda. Med sin beliggenhet på samme breddegrad som Sibir, Grønland og Alaska, var kulderekorden fra Kautokeino i 1886 på minus 45°

Photo taken near Tromsø by Aud Schreuder

Celsius. Så sent som 26. januar 1999 kom det en isvind fra Sibir som fikk skylden for den umenneskelige temperaturen på minus 41° Celsius på stedet. I 1976 bodde de fleste menneskene i Kautokeino i enkle trebygninger og var seminomader. Majoriteten følger fortsatt reinsdyrene på deres lange streifinger, men de returnerer til samebyene innimellom.

Ved ungdomsherberget i Kautokeino bodde jeg i samme trebygning som den samiske eieren Anna, og hennes sønn Alfred. Anna tilbød meg jobb noen timer hver dag for å hjelpe henne med å klippe ut bokstaver og reinsdyr av filt til *Hilsen fra Kautokeino*-souvenirene som hun solgte. Det var en utmerket anledning til å drikke svart kaffe sammen med Anna mens jeg hørte på historier om samenes unike levemåte. Jeg fikk vite at samene til og med går annerledes enn andre, idet de rugger kroppen fra side til side, for å gjøre en lang ferd lettere. Jeg fikk også vite at det er uhøflig å spørre en same om hvor mange rein han har, det er det samme som å spørre etter hvor mange penger han har i banken.

Den daglige bruken av samisk språk er helt vesentlig for å bestemme retten til å bli klassifisert som same. I motsetning til norsk, som er et germansk språk, hører det samiske språket til den finsk-ugriske greina av den uralske språkfamilien, og er nært beslektet med

finsk og ungarsk. Samisk har 100 ord for snø, om lag 400 ord for reinsdyr, og omtrent 50 forskjellige navn på fargen på reinsdyrskinnet.

Ettersom ordet "lapp" er betraktet som en nedsettende term, som betegner et tøystykke man bruker for å reparere klær med, hvilket kan insinuere at samene bærer lappede klær, er ordet "lapp" i engelsk erstattet med "sami".

På ungdomsherberget i Kautokeino, ved siden av hovedhuset, bodde det to franske og en tysk student. Språkbarrieren ble nesten komisk til tider, da franskmannen snakket til meg på engelsk og den tyske studenten snakket tysk, slik at jeg kunne oversette til norsk for Anna. Jeg glemmer aldri den dagen den tyske studenten ankom og spurte på tysk om tyskere hadde adgang ved ungdomsherberget. Anna forklarte meg senere at Kautokeino, og nesten hvert eneste hjem i Finnmark fylke, ble brent ned til grunnen av nazistene under andre verdenskrig. Bitterheten sitter fortsatt i blant folket hennes.

Samene observerer ikke fire, men åtte årstider, der hver årstid utgjør en fase i oppdretten av reinsdyrene. De forskjellige oppgavene som er knyttet til hver sesong, gir en rytme til livene deres, først og fremst styrt av reinsdyrenes bevegelser. For å identifisere eierskapet til reinen, blir det med kniv skåret inn et spesielt sett med hakk i dyrets øre.

Både reinoksen og kua får i løpet av hver sommer et nytt sett med horn. Etter brunsten, der de rivaliserer om hunnene om høsten, begynner hannene å felle hornene, noe som er gjort midt i desember. Hundyrene beholder sine horn til etter kalvingen om våren for å beskytte sine nyfødte mot rovdyr. Julenissens reinsdyr, hvert eneste ett av dem, fra Rudolf til Blitzen, må øyensynlig være hundyr!

Påsken i Kautokeino er en spesiell begivenhet der menneskene samler seg fra forskjellige deler av Sameland. Selv om den store majoriteten av samer hører til den lutherske kirken, feirer de påske som mer enn en religiøs høytid. Reinsdyrløp blir avholdt for å feire kultur og levemåte, idet reindriftssamene forbereder seg til å følge flokken til fjellene nær havet. Da blir det avholdt livlige feiringer med bryllup, samisk musikk og teaterforestillinger med vakre settinger av snø, og med nordlyset som dramatisk bakteppe.

I løpet av vinteren vender omlag 70 000 reinsdyr tilbake til Kautokeino-området, hvor de hovedsakelig lever av en form for lav som kalles reinmose. Omlag 15 000 rein blir slaktet årlig i byens moderne slaktehus. Da jeg var i Kautokeino var reinen fortsatte oppe i fjellene.

Jeg kom tilbake til jordbær- og tomatgården i sør den 29. september. Min 52 dager lange reise som startet som et innfall, hadde utstyrt meg med eventyr langt ut over mine villeste forventninger og med minner nok for resten av livet.

Tromsø by søker om å få være vertsby for de olympiske vinterleker i 2014. Hvis deres tilbud blir akseptert, blir det de første leker som noensinne er arrangert i en arktisk region. Begivenheten burde gi en særegen samisk innflytelse som fremmer Norge som nasjon for kultur og sport. Hvilken anerkjennelse ville ikke det ha vært for en av de eldste overlevende kulturer i verden, den vakre, samiske urbefolkningen i nordområdene.

4

The Little Red Jacket

World War II gift leads to Norway visit 31 years later

In a 1977 interview with the Norwegian newspaper *Adresseavisen*, 73-year-old Petra Størseth from Stadsbygd, near Trondheim, Norway, recalled the post-war years and very day, October 27, 1948, when she received a heartily welcomed package from America.

"At one time it was so bad that I thought the young would have to go naked. We had of course ration cards, but that was no help so long as there wasn't so much as a yard of material to find! So then came a call from the Creamery Station that new 'American packages' had arrived in. I was so happy the tears rolled. When the package was opened, it contained clothes that fit all of the children and then I really cried. Still today 31 years later I don't think I can give thanks enough for this package."

"At one time it was so bad that I thought the young would have to go naked."

Amongst the clothing was a little red jacket with a piece of paper in the pocket containing the words: *"Charlotte Knudson, Canton, Minnesota."* My mother, at age fourteen, had included her name and address in the pocket of her jacket destined for Norway.

A clothing drive had taken place two years earlier, in 1946, at the Henrytown Lutheran Church in Fillmore County, Minnesota. At the time, radio and newspapers kept everyone informed of the war and conditions in Norway. Charlotte's mother, Esther Knudson, hearing about the church event, collected good used clothing for her ancestor's homeland.

Post-World War II letter

The very same day that Petra received the American package, she wrote the following thank-you letter to my mother and mailed it: *Frk Charlotte Knutson, Canton, Minnesota, US Amerika.*

> *October 27, 1948*
>
> *Dear friend,*
>
> *Actually, the package arrived two years ago. Some of the gifts were distributed at that time; others were put away until now, when I received a red jacket, which just fits my six-year-old daughter. She was so happy, so I wanted to write and thank you at once . . .*
>
> *It was wonderful to receive the clothes, since times have been very difficult here - we have survived on almost nothing. But one has to be thankful that we now have peace, and we're finally able to get food again. During the war we couldn't get coffee or sugar, and ate a lot of dark, coarse bread. But - we survived that too . . .*
>
> *My husband was trained as a house painter, and now there are beginning to be more and more work opportunities for him, but during the war there was not work available for him. Now there are quite a few from my home community that have moved to Minnesota . . .*
>
> *It's a bit unusual to be writing to someone I don't know, but I want to express my deepest thanks for the little red jacket . . . Those who sent the gifts more than two years ago must have wondered what happened. So I wanted to sit down at once and respond. It's wonderful to have a contact in America.*
>
> *Mrs. Petra L. Størseth*
>
> (Translated December 2002 by Harley Refsal, Decorah, Iowa)

At the sight of the envelope from Norway, my mother knew that her little red jacket had made the journey and was eager to read the letter. Unfortunately, Charlotte's family was unable to translate the Norwegian, as it was written in an older rural Trondheim dialect unfamiliar to the family. Disappointed, my mother tucked away the treasured Norwegian response. For the next twenty-eight years the unread letter remained in a wooden tea box given to Charlotte by her father, Henry Knudson.

Accidental meeting in 1976

This is where I come into the story. In the fall of 1976, I had been hitchhiking near the North Cape in the extreme north of Norway and stayed a couple of extra adventurous weeks in the Sami (formerly called Lapp) town of Kautokeino. Since I had fallen behind in my travel schedule, I caught the train near the Arctic Circle to speed my journey towards Oslo, hundreds of miles to the south.

Having taken the night train from

Stadsbygdfamilie fikk uventet amerikabesøk

31 år gammelt brev dukket fram

From the left: Esther Knudson, Carol Gerard (Esther's niece), Petra Størseth, and Charlotte (Knudson) Nelson in Stadsbygd near Trondheim, Norway in 1977.

Trondheim, I arrived about 5:00 A.M. in the town of Hamar, a couple hours north of Oslo, and waited for my bus ride out in the countryside along Lake Mjøsa. There I would visit with my host farm family, Veterinarian Mads and Anna Gaustad, before beginning my sheep artificial insemination project at the Norges Veterinærhøgskole in Oslo.

Also waiting at the train station at this early hour was a teenage boy named Stig Lorentzen, from Trondheim, Norway. Since Stig and I were the only pre-dawn travelers, we visited in a blending of Norwegian-English, and I showed him a handful of pictures from southeastern Minnesota. Stig dreamed of traveling to America, and when he discovered I was from a farm and had four younger brothers near his age, he wanted to visit my family.

Within hours I telephoned my parents, waking them up during the night to ask if Stig could stay with them. They were thrilled at the thought of having a Norwegian visitor. Stig arrived at my parents' farm in Fillmore County in November 1976, as he stated, *"to work as a cowboy."*

Shortly after Stig's arrival in

Amherst, mom was preparing for Christmas and happened upon her wooden tea box that contained her special keepsakes, including Petra's letter. Stig, being from Trondheim, recognized Petra's town name of Stadsbygd, located only a short distance across the fjord from where he lived. He verbally translated Petra's post-war letter and mom was overjoyed, after twenty-eight years, to finally learn its contents.

Utrolige tilfeldigheter førte til Amerika-besøk i Stadsbygd

Takkebrev dukket opp etter 30 år

Av ANN BRITT HANGERAAS

— En tid var det så ille at jeg trodde ungene måtte gå nakne. Vi hadde jo klesmerker, men hva hjalp vel det så lenge det ikke var så mye som en meter stoff å få tak i! Så da det kom oppringning fra meierisentralen om at det var kommet nye «Amerika-pakker», ja da ble jeg så glad at tårene trillet. Og da pakken ble åpnet og den viste seg å inneholde klær som passet til alle barna, ja da tutet jeg virkelig. Ennå i dag — 31 år etter — synes jeg ikke at jeg kan få takket nok for denne pakken.

om de vanskelige forholdene i etterkrigstidens Norge, sporenstreks samlet sammen pent brukt tøy og sendte det til det land hennes bestefar kom fra.

Tirsdag møttes de to for første gang. Og når man vet at Esther Knudsen så sent som julen -76 ikke visste om Petra Størseths eksistens, skjønner en at det bak dette

møtet skjuler seg mange tilfeldigheter. Ja, bent ut sagt utrolig virker det når de to kvinnene og noen av deres barn sitter rett overfor hverandre ved et kafebord i Trondheim. Sammen med dem sitter også Stig Lorentzen, 20-åring fra Trondheim. Og han er en av hovedrolleinnehaverne i det rørende eventyret fra virkeligheten som her skal fortelles.

For hadde ikke Stig, en grytidlig sommermorgen i 1976 befunnet seg på jernbanestasjonen i Hamar, ville ikke Petra fra Stadsbygd og Esther fra Minnesota møtt hverandre.

— Hvordan kan så det ha seg?

— Jo her, klokken fem om morgenen kom jeg i prat med en amerikansk jente, Debra, som var på Inter-Rail-ferie. Vi snakket lenge sammen og før vi skiltes rakk hun å invitere meg over til den farmen hennes foreldre drev i Minnesota. Litt tøft kanskje, men jeg hadde nettopp tatt artium og var lysten på å se meg om i verden. Så utpå høstparten dro jeg like godt over for å jobbe som cowboy i noen måneder. Og så, sier Stig, hendte det morsomme at familien under julesjauen kom over et brev fra Norge. Fordi ingen av dem kunne norsk, var brevet aldri blitt lest. Nå oversatte jeg det for dem og da viste det

Petra's American visitors

Immediately Charlotte wanted to try to contact Petra. As she dictated, Stig wrote a response in Norwegian to Petra's thank-you. *"I didn't know if I should believe my own eyes,"* said the 73-year-old Petra when she received the response that Christmas. She quickly replied and letters were sent back and forth regularly for the next few months. One of the letters from Petra included an invitation to visit her home, which Charlotte, Esther, and Stig graciously accepted.

Stig returned to Norway in 1977 and made arrangements for the upcoming American visit. Petra was so ecstatic about their impending arrival that she redid the whole house including painting, curtains, rugs, and tablecloths. She even considered removing a wall to make the rooms larger.

Upon arrival, the American visitors met Stig in Trondheim, crossed the fjord on the car ferry, and proceeded to Petra's farm. There they met Petra, her husband, and two daughters, one of whom had received the little red jacket.

Norwegian newspaper reporters were on hand in 1977 to publish the touching story of the visitors: *"Today, 31 years after the first contact was made, Petra Størseth got to meet the two, Esther Knudsen* [Knudson] *and her daughter, Charlotte* [Knudson] *Nelson, who in the hard post-war time sent a warm sunbeam in the form of much needed clothing to the family with so many children in the small Trøndelag town. All this, thanks to an accidental meeting between two young people at a train station far away from both Stadsbygd and Minnesota."*

I think about Petra and the unwavering gratitude she showed for the little red jacket. Who would have thought that this small act of kindness would result in an enduring friendship and a trip to Norway.

Den lille røde jakken

Etterkrigsgave førte til Norge etter 31 år

I et intervju med *Adresseavisen* i 1977 fortalte den 73 år gamle Petra Størseth fra Stadsbygd ved Trondheim om etterkrigsårene og om den spesielle dagen, 27. oktober 1948, da hun mottok en amerikapakke som varmet hjertet.

"En tid var det så ille at jeg trodde ungene måtte gå nakne. Vi hadde jo klesmerker, men hva hjalp vel det så lenge det ikke var så mye som en meter stoff å få tak i! Så da det kom oppringning fra meierisentralen om at det var kommet nye Amerikapakker, ja, da ble jeg så glad at tårene trillet. Og da pakken ble åpnet og den viste seg å inneholde klær som passet til alle barna, ja, da tutet jeg virkelig. Ennå i dag – 31 år etter – synes jeg ikke at jeg kan få takket nok for denne pakken."

Fra venstre: Stig Lorentzen, Charlotte (Knudson) Nelson, Esther Knudson og Petra Størseth i Stadsbygd ved Trondheim i 1977. De besøkende dukket opp først 31 år etter at Charlotte hadde etterlatt navnet sitt på en lapp i en liten rød jakke som var del av en klesforsendelse til Norge etter krigen. Overskriften i Adresseavisen lød: *"Utrolige tilfeldigheter førte til Amerikabesøk i Stadsbygd."*

From the left: Stig Lorentzen, Charlotte (Knudson) Nelson, Esther Knudson, and Petra Størseth in Stadsbygd near Trondheim, Norway in 1977. The visit occurred 31 years after Charlotte had included her name in the pocket of a little red jacket that was part of a post-war clothing donation to Norway. The Norwegian newspaper, headline reads: *"Remarkable coincidence leads to an American visit in Stadsbygd."*

Blant klærne var en liten rød jakke, og den hadde en papirlapp i lommen hvor det stod: *"Charlotte Knudson, Canton, Minnesota."* Min mor, som da var fjorten, hadde lagt navn og adresse i lommen før jakken ble sendt til Norge.

En klesinnsamling hadde funnet sted to år før, i 1946, ved Henrytown lutherske kirke i Fillmore County i Minnesota. På den tiden holdt radio og aviser alle informert om krigen og forholdene i Norge, og Charlottes mor, Esther Knudson, samlet inn pent brukte klær til forfedrenes hjemland da hun hørte om kirkens innsamling.

Etterkrigsbrevet

Samme dag som Petra mottok amerikapakken skrev hun følgende takkebrev til min mor, og gav det adressen: *Frk Charlotte Knutson, Canton, Minnesota, US Amerika.*

Charlottes familie i stand til å forstå hva som stod, da det var skrevet på et alderdommelig og muntlig preget språk som familien var ukjent med. Skuffet stakk min mor det verdsatte svaret vekk. I de neste tjueåtte årene lå det uleste brevet i en teboks av tre som Charlotte hadde fått av faren, Henry Knudson.

"ikke kaffe – ikke sukker, og vi spiste tørt, sort brød. Men vi levet over det også..."

Tilfeldig møte i 1976

Det var her jeg kom inn i historien. Høsten 1976 hadde jeg haiket til Nordkappområdet, helt oppe i det

Størseth den 27/10-48

Kjære veninde,

Ja, det har været utdeling av de gavepakker som er kommet fra Amerika, ja, det vil si de kom for 2 år siden, da delte de ut noget og så har de gjemt noget til nu, da fikk jeg en rød jakke og den blev passende til min pike som er 6 år. Hun blev så glad, jeg måtte sende takk med en gang...

Det var kjekt å få klær, for her må jeg si det er lite å få i, ja, nesten ingen ting, så jeg må si jeg har været opprådd mange ganger, men man må være glad for at det blir fred, og så at det blev litt mat å få i, her var det trasigt i krigsåra – ikke kaffe – ikke sukker, og vi spiste tørt, sort brød. Men vi levet over det også...

Min mand er utlært maler og nu begynner det å bli lit maling å få i, så da blir det lit arbeide nu, men under krigen var det ikke noget å gjøre...Ja, det kunde jo snart være mange fra min bygd i Minnesota...

Ja, jeg skriver nu vel lit vidløftig til at vi er ukjent... jeg må si så mange takk...De synes nu vel det er rart De som sendte for 2 år siden... men jeg satte meg ned og skrev samme dag...det er nu morsomt å ha forbindelse med nogen i Amerika...

Fru Petra L. Størseth

Da min mor så konvolutten fra Norge, skjønte hun at den lille røde jakken var kommet fram og var spent på å lese brevet. Uheldigvis var ikke

nordlige Norge, og oppholdt meg et par særdeles eventyrlige uker i samenes Kautokeino. Siden jeg lå etter reiseplanen, tok jeg toget fra et sted i nærheten av Polarsirkelen for å komme raskere til Oslo, mer enn hundre norske mil lenger sør.

Jeg hadde tatt nattoget fra Trondheim og kom ved femtiden om morgenen til Hamar, et par timer nord for Oslo, og ventet på bussen som skulle føre meg til Oslo gjennom jordbruksområdene langs Mjøsa. Der skulle jeg besøke min vertsfamile, veterinærene Mads og Anna Gaustad, før jeg begynte på min oppgave om kunstig inseminasjon av sauer ved Norges Veterinærhøgskole i Oslo.

På togstasjonen tidlig denne morgenen ventet også en tenåringsgutt fra Trondheim, Stig Lorentzen. Siden Stig og jeg var de eneste som reiste før daggry, kom vi i snakk på en blanding av norsk og engelsk, og jeg viste ham en håndfull bilder fra det sørøstlige Minnesota. Stig drømte om å reise til Amerika, og da han skjønte at jeg kom fra en gård, og hadde fire yngre brødre som ikke var så langt fra hans egen alder, hadde han lyst til å besøke familien min.

Innen noen timer hadde jeg ringt og vekket foreldrene mine om natta, for å spørre om Stig kunne bo hos dem. De var henrykt ved tanken på å få norsk besøk. Stig ankom mine foreldres gård i Fillmore County i november 1976, og erklærte at han skulle *"jobbe som cowboy."*

Kort tid etter Stigs ankomst til Amherst, stelte mor i stand til jul, og hun kom da over treboksen, som en gang var brukt til å oppbevare te i, men som nå rommet hennes spesielle minner, inklusive Petras brev. Stig, som var fra Trondheim, gjenkjente navnet på Petras hjemsted, Stadsbygd, som lå rett over fjorden der han bodde. Han oversatte Petras etterkrigsbrev, og mor var overlykkelig, for etter tjueåtte år ble hun endelig gjort kjent med innholdet.

Petras amerikabesøk

Charlotte ville øyeblikkelig prøve å kontakte Petra. Mens hun dikterte, skrev Stig et brev på norsk for å besvare Petras takk. *"Jeg visste ikke om jeg skulle tro mine egne øyne,"* sa den 73 år gamle Petra da hun mottok svaret den julen. Hun svarte raskt, og brevene gikk jevnlig fram og tilbake i de neste månedene. Ett av brevene rommet en invitasjon til å besøke hennes hjem, og Charlotte, Esther og Stig svarte takknemlig ja.

Stig dro tilbake til Norge i 1977, og han tok seg av forberedelsene før det ventede amerikabesøket. Petra var så opprømt over besøket at hun gjorde om på hele huset inkludert maling, gardiner, tepper og duker. Hun vurderte til og med å fjerne en vegg for å gjøre rommene større.

De amerikanske gjestene møtte Stig i Trondheim, krysset fjorden med bilferga og fortsatte til Petras gård. Der møtte de Petra, hennes ektemann og to døtre, den ene var den som hadde fått den lille røde jakken.

Norske avisreportere var til stede i 1977 for å trykke den rørende historien om besøket: *"I dag, 31 år etter at den første kontakt ble opprettet, fikk Petra Størseth oppleve å møte de to - Esther Knudsen* [Knudson] *og hennes datter Charlotte* [Knudson] *Nelson, som i den harde etterkrigstiden sendte en varm solstråle i form av hardt tiltrengte klær til den barnerike familien i trønderbygda. Og alt altså takket være et tilfeldig møte mellom to unge mennesker på en jernbanestasjon langt borte fra både Stadsbygd og Minnesota."*

Jeg tenker på Petra og den varige takknemligheten hun viste over den lille røde jakken. Hvem skulle ha trodd at en slik liten, vennlig handling ville ende i et varig vennskap og en reise til Norge.

Air mail

Miss Deb Nelson,
Bailey 216 A.U.
St. Paul
Mn. 55101
U.S.A.

Dear Deb. 24. 4. 76

Here we send you a picture of our farm so you find it. In the back-ground you will see the lake "Mjøsen".

Welcome to us

Anne og Mads Gaustad

Mads and Anna Gaustad family & Deb

Anna hand-knitted my sweater and hat after my return from Kautokeino

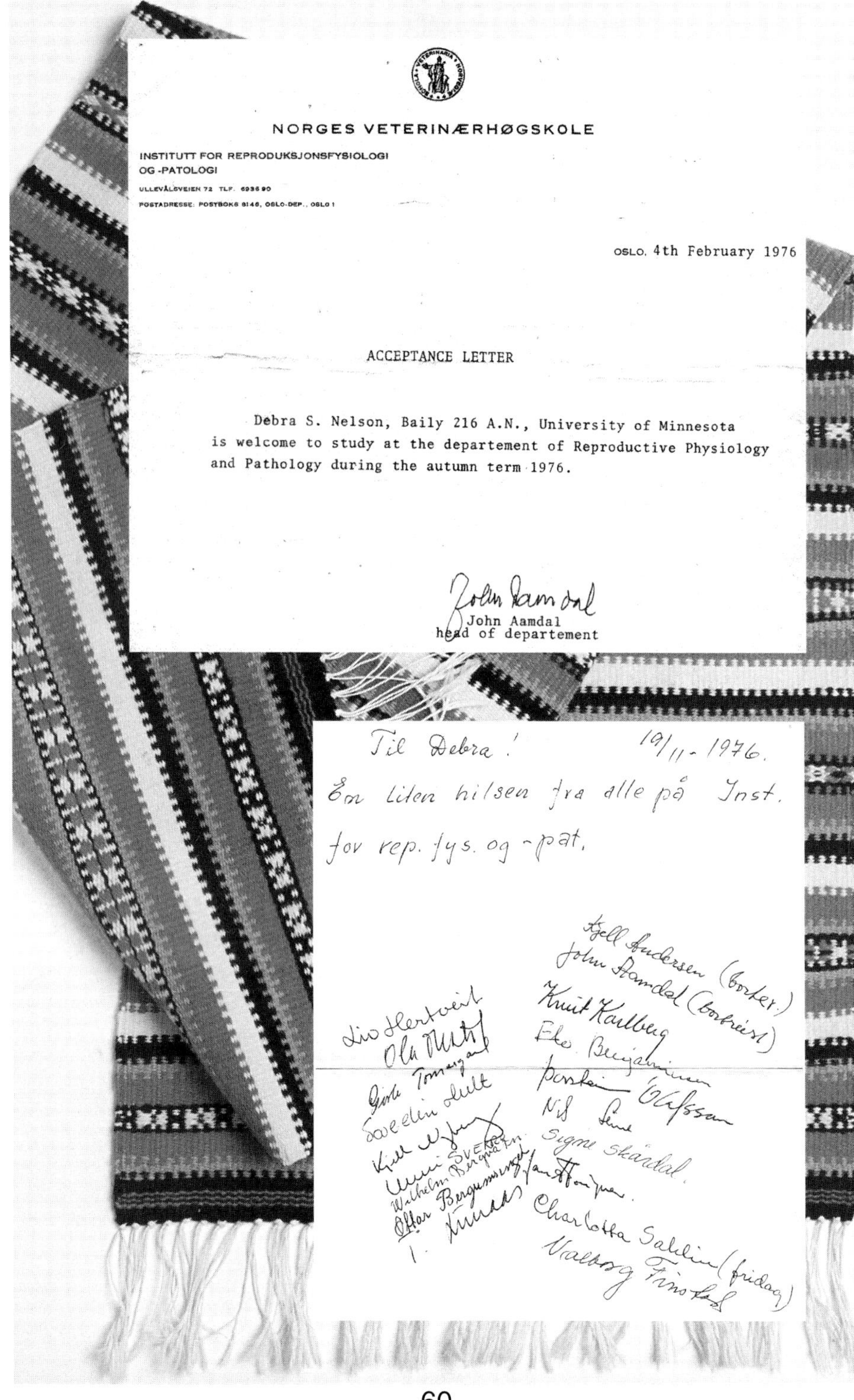

NORGES VETERINÆRHØGSKOLE

INSTITUTT FOR REPRODUKSJONSFYSIOLOGI
OG -PATOLOGI

ULLEVÅLSVEIEN 72 TLF. 693690

POSTADRESSE: POSTBOKS 8146, OSLO-DEP., OSLO 1

OSLO, 4th February 1976

ACCEPTANCE LETTER

Debra S. Nelson, Baily 216 A.N., University of Minnesota is welcome to study at the departement of Reproductive Physiology and Pathology during the autumn term 1976.

John Aamdal

John Aamdal
head of departement

Til Debra! 19/11 - 1976.

En liten hilsen fra alle på Inst. for rep. fys. og -pat.

Kjell Andersen

John Aamdal

Knut Karlberg

Signe Skårdal

Charlotta Sahlin (fridag)

5

Astri, my Astri, where art thou?

A primer for searching Fillmore County, MN genealogy records for pioneer ancestors

Imagine a class called Genealogy 101: Fillmore County Pioneers. You are given only the following information for your assignment: *Astri Herbrandsdatter, age 65, and her second husband Tosten Larson Nøbben immigrated to America in 1857, a year before Minnesota became a state, with their two daughters, Gunhild [#2], born August 13, 1832 and Ingeborg, born March 12, 1837. To complete the course you need to find out where Astri is buried.*

Genealogy 101: Fillmore County Pioneers *find out where Astri is buried*

Given an assignment like this, would you know how to research your pioneer ancestors and their families? During January and February of 2002, my mother, Char Nelson, and I were in such a genealogy course. We not only learned what resources are available in southeastern Minnesota's Fillmore County but found an incredible amount of information about our pioneer ancestors as well.

At age eight, I had rescued from the burn pile the decorated trunk that belonged to my great-great-great-grandmother, Astri Herbrandsdatter Børtnes Syversrud. This single event set in motion my lifelong interest in genealogy. Shortly after my *Astri Herbrandsdatter 1812* trunk story appeared in the *Fillmore County Journal*, a reader, Delphin M. Johnson, Astri's first cousin four times removed from Superior, Wisconsin, contacted me. Del informed me that Astri and her family had immigrated to America. I was ecstatic. My interest had taken me from the trunk to the family tree.

For the past 26 years, since 1976, I had been searching for Astri's death records only in Norway. Now, within a few days of my trunk story being published, I learned that my great-great-great-grandmother had actually immigrated to America. But the important question of where the owner of my trunk was buried remained unanswered.

Mom and I headed straight to the Fillmore County History Center and Genealogy Library in Fountain, which contains thousands of books, photographs, microfilmed newspapers, as well as county records, State and Federal Census reports, and other government sources. We specifically wanted to research the Center's death records, cemetery transcriptions, and obituaries to see if Astri came to Fillmore County.

No church records at genealogy library

We suspected Astri settled in Fillmore County since her older daughter by her first marriage, Gunhild (#1) Guttormsdatter, had immigrated nine years earlier. Gunhild (#1) and her husband, Knud Knudson, were buried in the Elstad Lutheran Church Cemetery near Highland. Thus, we requested to see all the Amherst Township Church records prior to 1900. To my disbelief we were told: *at this point in time the Fillmore County Genealogy Library does not have any microfilmed church records for Fillmore County.*

Having no pioneer church records at the Genealogy Library became my greatest frustration in trying to find Astri. I was discouraged. How was I to find Astri and her family if there were no available church records at the Genealogy Library for birth, baptism, confirmation, marriage, but most of all death and burial records? The thought of having to contact each individual church in the county was quite staggering.

Missing church records

A brief sketch from the *Elstad Lutheran Church Menighet Historie 1854-1979*, described the missing church records and my great-great-grandparents as follows: *To write a complete history of the Elstad Lutheran Church is an impossible task due to loss of pioneer church records over the years; and due to the fact that some ministerial records were destroyed by a parsonage fire in Washington Prairie in 1870 . . . Knud Knudson and family established their home on the land where Amherst Village was to be located. The Knudson family opened their home to many of the pioneer families who arrived in the next few years.* How was I ever going to find Astri when there were no duplicate copies of these records?

Mom and I located one tombstone in the Elstad Cemetery that had four Knudson children listed on it; two Birgit Knudsons on the front side and two Guttorm Knudsons on the backside. Beside these four children was buried a Kjersti Knudson. We found the existing Elstad Church death and burial records did not include the parents' names of any of the five Knudson children, yet we suspected they belonged to Knud and Gunhild.

By researching the *Riksarkivaren National Archives of Norway Digitalarkivet* website http://digitalarkivet.uib.no/index-eng.htm, I was able to find that my great-great-grandparents, Knud and Gunhild, were the parents of all five Knudson children listed on the two tombstones. Included on the website are 6,480 baptisms during the years 1854-1883 and 1,888 conformations during the years 1860-1885 that were transcribed by Lars E. Øyane from Norway. The database includes the following Fillmore County churches: Arendahl, Elstad, Greenfield, Highland, North Prairie, N.P. Hauge, Rushford, Rushford 2, and Union Prairie. Within the Elstad parish are records for Highland Prairie, Newburg (Garness), and Whalan.

To locate the Fillmore County church records in the Norwegian database, I started at the above *Digitalarkivet* home page and used the following sequence: *categories, church registers, baptized, abroad, and MN Fillmore Co baptisms 1854-1883*. Under the section entitled *the following sources are available*, I then selected *baptisms or confirmations* (available for a limited number of churches).

It became clear to me at this point that it would be very beneficial for the Genealogy Library to have access to pioneer records from all of the Fillmore County churches in order to help people research their families. Inquiring, I learned that in order for the Library to have such records, permission had to be granted from each individual church congregation.

Sources sorted on:

Source category

Censuses
Tax lists
Military rolls
Church registers
- baptised
- - Akershus
- - Oslo
- - Hedmark
- - Oppland
- - Buskerud
- - Vestfold
- - Telemark
- - Vest-Agder
- - Rogaland
- - Hordaland
- - Bergen
- - Sogn og Fjordane
- - Møre og Romsdal
- - Sør-Trøndelag
- - Nord-Trøndelag
- - Nordland
- - Troms
- - Finnmark
- - Abroad
- confirmed
- married
- buried
- communicants
- marriage licenses
- out migrants
- in migrants

"A very interesting group of Fillmore County Pioneers"
October 19, 1916 photo from Levang's Weekly in Lanesboro, MN

Front row from left: Christine Stenshoel, 81 years; Gunhild Evans, 84 years (Astri's daughter); Ingeborg Western, 86 years; Maren Elstad, 75 years; M.O. Elden, 72 years;
Back row from left: Andrew O. Wang, 81 years; M.O. Elden, 78 years; Mons Anderson, 70 years; Erik Hanson, 73 years; A.P. Storhofff, 76 years

Saturday, September 23, 1916, Mr. Mons Anderson celebrated his 70th birthday at his farm home just south of Lanesboro. Across the road is the farm home of his stepson, Mr. Peter Abrahamson. This gentleman had arranged a surprise for Mr. Anderson by inviting the above group of youngsters to come and help celebrate the day. And a most jolly time they had, swapping stories of the good old days.

It does not happen every day that such a group of Fillmore County pioneers can be photographed, and it was a happy idea of Mr. Abrahamson to send for Mr. Bue, the Lanesboro artist. The combined age of these pioneers is 776 years.

Photo courtesy of Fillmore County History Center and Genealogy Library

Norwegian traditional naming system

To research Norwegian genealogy, one needs to have an understanding of the Norwegian traditional naming system. As if part of the *Ten Commandments*, these traditions were considered almost unbreakable.

The child's first name came from:

• 1st son named after his father's father
• 2nd son named after his mother's father
• 1st daughter named after her father's mother
• 2nd daughter named after her mother's mother
• If a spouse died the next child of the same sex was named after the deceased
• If a child died the next child of the same sex was named after the deceased.

This explained why Knud and Gunhild Knudson had two daughters named Birgit and two sons named Guttorm.

The child's second name came from the father. *Datter* translates to daughter. Daughters of Guttorm or Tosten, were named Guttormsdatter or Tostensdatter, respectively. Understanding this traditional naming system explained why Astri had two daughters named Gunhild. The second Gunhild was named after her second husband's mother, Gunhild.

The child's third name came from the address or farm that the family currently lived on. Astri was born in 1792 and in the 1801 Norwegian census her family was documented as living on the Børtnes farm. Astri descended from Gaute Olson Børtnes, born in the 1500's and known as one of the wealthiest landowners in Hallingdal during his time. Thus, Astri's Børtnes and Syversrud names came from the farms she had lived on near *Nes i Hallingdal* (Nes in the valley of Hallingdal).

Astri was first married to Corporal Guttorm Jensen Gulbrandsrud. Their son, Jens Guttormsen, and my great-great-grandmother, Gunhild Guttormsdatter Knudson, both immigrated to America. After Guttorm's death, Astri married Tosten Larson Ursdalen. My previous 26-year search for Astri had ended at this point, as I was unable to find further documents about her life, until my trunk story was published.

References from *Emigranter fra Nes og Flå i Hallingdal* by Sigmund Sevre and *Boka om Gol* by Terje Østro provided me with the missing information. Astri and Tosten had moved to Nøbben, changing their last name, which explained why I did not know that Astri came to America.

Cemetery transcriptions

Genealogy Library employees, volunteers, or Works Project Administration (WPA) have over the years walked more than 150 burial sites in Fillmore County which include church, city, private, abandoned, and Indian Mounds. Visual transcriptions were made of what is written on the existing tombstones. These records unfortunately do not include stones that are illegible or missing, which can be found only in church or sexton records.

Our first big discovery came when the names and birth dates of Gunhild and Ingeborg, the two daughters who immigrated with their mother Astri, matched perfectly to those in the Highland cemetery transcriptions. We found that Gunhild married Nels Evans and Ingeborg married Hans Gunvalson. We now knew that Astri had two daughters buried in Highland and one daughter buried in Elstad, located only a couple miles away. Sadly, there was no cemetery transcription for the half-sisters' mother, Astri.

We photocopied the cemetery transcriptions from Highland and Elstad, so mom and I could study them into the night. I recall late one January evening when mom and I read in the records: *stone is lying flat and is illegible*. The tombstone was located right next to Astri's daughter, Ingeborg. Did this tombstone belong to Astri?

Although the snow had melted and we could see the bare ground, because of a recent January thaw, it was still bitterly cold outside. Regardless of the howling wind, Mom and I, of course, could not wait until daylight to try our hand at reading the stone. So out came the flashlights and off to the Highland Cemetery we went. Chilled to the bone, we too conceded the stone was illegible, so the search for Astri continued.

Only days later, we were wild with excitement, when we thought we had found Astri in the cemetery transcriptions of an abandoned burial site. There are private cemeteries throughout Fillmore County, including one located on what was known as the Poor Farm near Henrytown. We immediately called my 93-year-old grandmother, Esther Knudson, but she assured us that the fenced in area of the very far corner of our Knudson ancestral farm had only been a potato patch.

By obtaining the land description of the one-forth acre burial site, we determined the private cemetery was actually located across the fence from the Knudson property. Of the nine known graves, three belonged to wives of Mr. Smith. A Quit Claim showed that Mr. Smith had moved to Missouri and had sold the one-fourth acre to Henry Ness in 1867. The Eiken family now owns the land.

Cemetery plots

To continue our research on the illegible tombstone thought to belong to Astri, we located the cemetery plot records. However, we came to another roadblock when the old pioneer section of the Highland Cemetery was not plotted. These non-plotted stones even included the Evans and Gunvalson tombstones that we had just photographed days before in the church cemetery.

Mom and I provided the Highland Church with a copy of the cemetery transcriptions from the Genealogy Library. Hopefully, the transcriptions will help fill in their records and also help identify the numerous pioneer stones that are no longer standing. Apparently, Volume I of the Highland Lutheran Church records was accidentally misplaced about 17 years ago.

Mom, seeing my disappointment in not finding Astri, called the Minnesota

Historical Society. She visited the Fillmore County Courthouse to further research cemetery plot layouts and land ownership, as well as contacted the Vesterheim Genealogical Society in Madison, Wisconsin. However, there were no Volume I records of the Highland Lutheran Church to be found.

None of my earlier research had left me quite as starchless as not being able to identify the *stone is lying flat and is illegible* located next to Astri's daughter. I again contacted the Genealogy Library only to learn that missing cemetery plot records are very common. According to the Genealogy Library, a dog ate one set of cemetery records, while others have been burned in fires or lost. Even worse, whole sections of some cemeteries cannot be used because of the unknown location of caskets.

Census reports and indexes

I found the census reports to be a helpful resource, since the names of the whole family household are listed along with their ages. Census Reports cover every five years from 1860 to 1920, except 1890 and 1915. State of Minnesota Census Indexes for the years 1860 and 1870 as well as the Minnesota Veterans 1890 books are also available at the Genealogy Library. The Genealogy Library shared in our triumph each time we found Astri and Tosten in the census. We found they were living in their daughters' Amherst Township households during the years 1865, 1870, and 1875.

It became very apparent that during the pioneers' Americanization process, the traditional Norwegian naming system was left behind as they took on new American names. A search of the census revealed an almost total loss of identity for the immigrants in the U.S. records. For example, Astri Herbrandsdatter Børtnes became Mrs. Tosten Larson. In my family alone, last names were changed to Knudson, Larson, Bendickson, Thompson, and Nelson, leaving no clues as to what farm they immigrated from in Norway.

Histories and vital statistics

History of Fillmore County for 1858, 1882, 1912, and 1984, church anniversary books, and town histories can be researched at the Genealogy Library. Vital statistics including marriage, birth, and death records are also available at the Genealogy Library. The death records are indexed by the last name and contain valuable information including name of deceased, date of death, sex, color, marital status, age, place of birth, name of father, place of birth of father, name of mother, place of birth of mother, cause of death, and occupation. The Amherst Township documents revealed:

- *Tosten Larson died January 16, 1877 of tuberculosis*
- *Astri (Herbrandsdatter) Larson died May 13, 1878 of rheumatism*

We not only learned the dates and causes of their deaths, but we now knew Tosten and Astri died in Amherst Township.

Obituaries

Incredible stories can be found in the large collection of obituaries in the Fillmore County History Center and Genealogy Library including this one from Astri's daughter: *As a young girl of 25 years, Gunhild Tostensdatter came with her parents, Tosten Larson and Astri Herbrandsdatter, to Fillmore County in 1857. The family, including her sister Ingeborg Tostensdatter, made the last lap of the trip on foot walking all the way from McGregor, Iowa to Amherst Township, where they located on a farm.*

An obituary of Astri's granddaughter, Anna (Evans) Gilbertson, tells an additional story: *On April 26, 1878, she was united in marriage to Thor Gilbertson, also of Fillmore County. Shortly after their marriage they came to Norman County, making the journey by ox team and also drove cattle, the entire trip occupying about a month.*

Mrs. Gilbertson walked a great deal of the way helping drive the cattle.

An ox cart could carry about 800 to 1000 pounds for 20 miles in a 10-hour day. However, each ox cart had its own peculiar wobble and screech. Rarely are ox carts mentioned in early letters and diaries without mention of their horrible sound . . . *it can be heard six miles away . . . it is like no other sound you ever heard in your life and makes your blood run cold.*

The following is taken from the obituary of Astri's son-in-law Hans Gunvalson: *Immediately after the famous First Minnesota regiment had been shot all to pieces in the battle of Gettysburg, Mr. Gunvalson enlisted in Company A of that regiment. He began his military service on February 29, 1864 and was honorably mustered out on July 14, 1865. But in the sixteen months he saw active service he participated in some of the bloodiest battles of the Civil War, for instance the battle of Petersburg. He was with General Grant at the surrender of General Robert Lee . . . He treasured a memento from that occasion, a silver fork from General Lee's private dinner table on the day of the surrender.*

Plat books, maps and newspapers

Plat books are an excellent source to obtain ownership data gathered from the Official Public Records at the Courthouse. Illustrative maps in the plat book include the landowner's name and acreage size, township section numbers, local and state roads, and incorporated towns. Plat books for 1878, 1896, and 1915 as well as maps

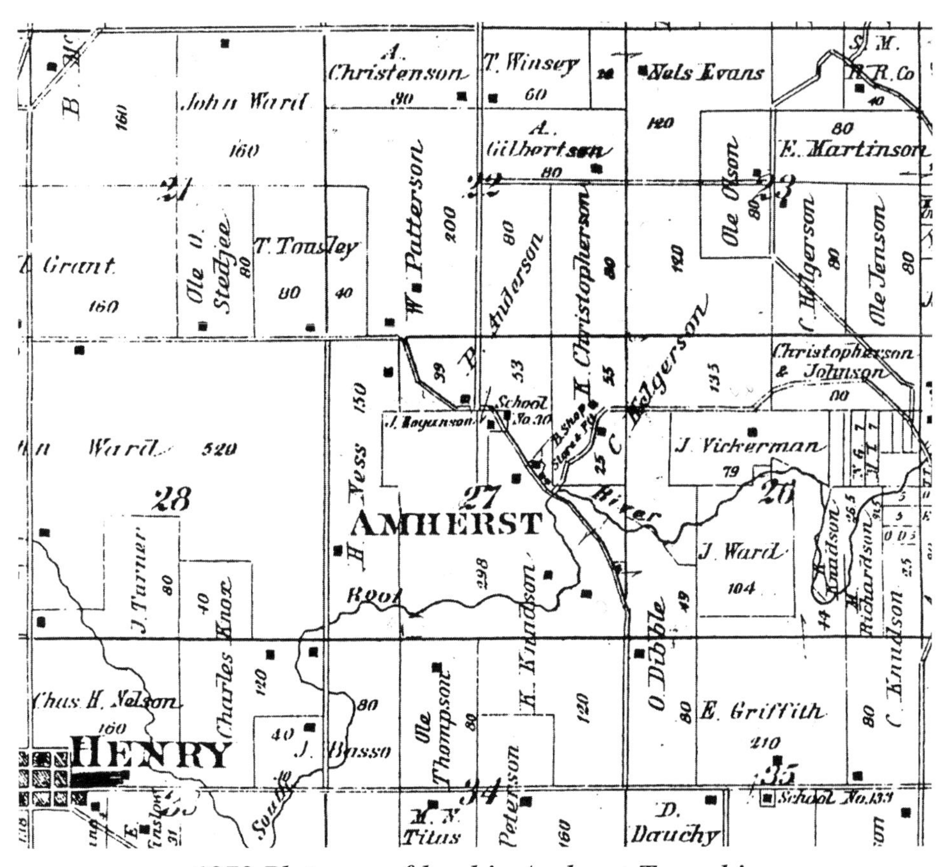

1878 Plat map of land in Amherst Township

for 1904 and 1911 were helpful, showing where the Knudson, Evans, and Gunvalson families lived and owned land.

The Genealogy Library also has various years of old newspapers on microfilm from Chatfield, Harmony, Lanesboro, Mabel, Peterson, Preston, Rushford, Spring Valley, and Wykoff.

Military data, surname and photo files

Civil War, Spanish American War, World War I, and World War II data of Fillmore County veterans can be found at the Genealogy Library. The surname file is an index that directs you to research completed by others looking for the same family members. The photo file provides valuable pictures. We found one of Gunhild Evans at age 84 entitled: *A very interesting group of Fillmore County Pioneers.*

From these types of records we were able to construct the following story of Astri's son-in-law: Nels Evans joined Company F, 5th Regiment and fought in the Battle of Nashville. He became extremely ill with chronic dysentery, contracted in Mississippi. By the time the regiment reached Demopolis, Alabama (west of Montgomery), Nels was a mere skeleton and released from the army in September 1865. A casualty of the Civil War, Nels was never well again and died seven years later in 1872, at age 47. Research shows that more Civil War solders died of diseases, especially dysentery, than in battle.

Gunhild Evans was left a widow at age 40 with seven children. Undaunted, this pioneer woman set to work to support the family and to pay off the debt on the farm, and she succeeded. In 1902 she quit the farm and moved to Lanesboro, where she was a resident for 21 years. Gunhild was nearly 91 when she died.

Land patents

Fillmore County land patents, which document the original transfer of land ownership from the federal government to individuals, are located in the Fillmore County Courthouse Recorder's office in Preston, Minnesota. Fillmore County consists of 24 townships, with Amherst Township being divided into 36 sections. Mom and I needed a lesson in the Bureau of Land Management/General Land Office Records identification system in order to understand that Township (T)-102-N and Range (R)-9-W was another way of describing Amherst Township section 27, where Amherst Village is located.

My great-great grandparents, Knud and Gunhild Knudson, settled 1/4 of a section (160 acres) on the south fork of the Root River located across from the now Amherst Store. Signed by President Abraham Lincoln, the land patent describes the location of our family's ancestral farm, which is now over 150-years-old.

In 1857, Nels Evans purchased Bounty Land that had earlier been given to an officer for engagement in the military service of the US during the Frontier Disturbances. Likewise in 1860, Hans Gunvalson's patent was Bounty Land originally given to an officer for military service in the War of 1812.

Astri's song

There is an old Norwegian folksong called "Astri, my Astri" about happy memories. As I look back on the early months of 2002, my fondest memories were the many hours I spent with my mother doing research on Astri. So many hours, in fact, that at the sound of our voices, the folks at the Genealogy Library knew that we had returned.

Genealogy 101, which took us from the trunk to the family tree, also demonstrated some of the trials and tribulations of genealogy research. Although, we didn't find out exactly where Astri is buried, we feel we have narrowed it down to the Elstad and Highland Cemeteries, since she has daughters buried in both places.

THE UNITED STATES OF AMERICA,

To all to whom these presents shall come, greeting:

Pre-emption
CERTIFICATE
No. 133.

Whereas, Knud Knudson, of Fillmore County, Minnesota has deposited in the GENERAL LAND OFFICE of the UNITED STATES, a CERTIFICATE of the **Register of the Land Office** at Brownsville whereby it appears that FULL PAYMENT has been made by the said Knud Knudson according to the provisions of the act of Congress of the 24th of April, 1820, entitled "An act making further provision for the sale of the public lands," for the West half of the South East Quarter, and the East half of the South West Quarter of Section Twenty-seven in Township One hundred and two, of Range Nine West, in the District of Lands formerly subject to sale at Brownsville, now Winnebago City, Minnesota, containing One hundred and sixty Acres.

according to the OFFICIAL PLAT of the Survey of the said lands, returned to the GENERAL LAND OFFICE by the **Surveyor General**, which said tracts have been purchased by the said Knud Knudson

Now know ye, That the ***UNITED STATES OF AMERICA***, in consideration of the premises, and in conformity with the several Acts of Congress in such case made and provided, HAVE GIVEN AND GRANTED, and by these presents DO GIVE AND GRANT, unto the said Knud Knudson and to his heirs, the said Tract above described; **TO HAVE AND TO HOLD** the same, together with all the rights, privileges, immunities, and appurtenances, of whatsoever nature, thereunto belonging, unto the said Knud Knudson and to his heirs and assigns forever.

In testimony whereof, I, Abraham Lincoln. PRESIDENT OF THE UNITED STATES OF AMERICA, have caused these Letters to be made Patent, and the Seal of the GENERAL LAND OFFICE to be hereunto affixed.

Given under my hand, at the **CITY OF WASHINGTON**, the first day of March in the YEAR OF OUR LORD one thousand eight hundred and sixty-two, and of the **Independence of the United States** the Eighty-sixth.

BY THE PRESIDENT: Abraham Lincoln

Astri, mi Astri, hvor er du?

Innføring for nybegynnere om hvordan man søker etter genealogiske kilder om pionerene i Fillmore County, MN

Forestill deg et kurs som får navnet Genealogi 101: Fillmore Countys første innbyggere. Du får bare tildelt en oppgave med følgende informasjon: *Astri Herbrandsdatter, alder 65, og hennes andre ektemann, Tosten Larson Nøbben, immigrerte til Amerika i 1857, et år før Minnesota ble en stat, med sine to døtre, Gunhild [#2], født 13. august 1832, og Ingeborg, født 12. mars 1837. For å fullføre kurset må du finne ut hvor Astri er gravlagt.*

Ville du med utgangspunkt i denne oppgaven vite hvordan du skulle søke etter ættens første nybyggerne og deres familier? I løpet av januar og februar 2002 tok min mor, Char Nelson, og jeg et slikt kurs. Vi fikk ikke bare vite hvilke kilder som var tilgjengelige i det sørøstlige Minnesotas Fillmore County, men fant en utrolig mengde med informasjon om pionerfamiliene i tillegg.

Da jeg var åtte, hadde jeg reddet en rosemalt kiste som hadde tilhørt min tipp-tipp-oldemor, Astri Herbrandsdatter Børtnes Syversrud, fra bålet. Denne ene begivenheten satte i gang en livslang interesse for slektsforskning. Kort tid etter at jeg hadde trykket historien om *Astri Herbrandsdatter 1812*-kisten i *Fillmore County Journal*, kontaktet en leser meg. Det var Delphin M. Johnson fra Superior, Wisconsin, som var Astris fetters tipp-oldebarn. Del kunne fortelle meg at Astri og familien hadde immigrert til Amerika. Jeg var ekstatisk. Min interesse hadde ført meg fra kisten til familietreet.

De forutgående 26 årene, siden 1976, hadde jeg søkt etter Astris dødsdata bare i Norge. Nå, bare få dager etter at historien var blitt publisert, skjønte jeg at min tipp-tipp-oldemor faktisk hadde immigrert til Amerika. Men det viktige spørsmålet, hvor eieren av kisten var gravlagt, forble ubesvart.

Mor og jeg satte kursen rett til Fillmore County History Center and Genealogy Library i Fountain, som inneholder tusener av bøker, fotografier og mikrofilmer av aviser, i tillegg til fylkesnedtegnelser, statlige og føderale manntall, og andre statlige kilder. Vi ønsket spesifikt å undersøke senterets arkiver over døde, gravinnskrifter og nekrologer for å se om Astri kom fra Fillmore County.

Genealogi 101: Fillmore Countys første innbyggere *finne ut hvor Astri er gravlagt*

Ingen kirkebøker ved slektsforskningsbiblioteket

Vi mistenkte at Astri hadde bosatt seg i Fillmore County, siden hennes eldste datter fra første ekteskap, Gunhild (#1) Guttormsdatter, hadde immigrert ni år tidligere. Gunhild (#1) og mannen, Knud Knudson, ble gravlagt på kirkegården ved Elstad lutherske kirke i nærheten av Highland. Derfor bad vi om å få se alle Amherst Townships kirkebøker forut for 1900. Overrasket måtte jeg konstatere: *på denne tiden hadde ikke Fillmore Countys slektsforsknings-bibliotek noen kirkebøker fra Fillmore County på mikrofilm.*

At det ikke fantes noen kirkebøker ved Genealogy Library fra pionertiden, ble min største frustrasjon i forsøket på å finne Astri. Jeg mistet motet. Hvordan skulle jeg kunne finne Astri og familien hennes, om ingen kirkebøker som kunne opplyse om fødsel, dåp, konfirmasjon, ekteskap, og mest av alt død og begravelse, var tilgjengelige ved slektsforskningsbiblioteket? Tanken på å måtte kontakte hver enkelt kirke i fylket var nokså rystende.

Tapte kirkebøker

En kort tekst fra *Elstad Lutheran Church Menighet Historie 1854-1979*, beskrev de manglende kirkebøkene, og mine tipp-oldeforeldre, på følgende måte: *Å skrive Elstad lutherske kirkes fullstendige historie er en umulig oppgave på grunn av mange års mangel på kirkebøker fra nybyggertiden, og det faktum at noen kirkearkiv ble ødelagt av en prestegårdsbrann i Washington Prairie i 1870...Knud Knudson og familie etablerte sitt hjem på det land hvor Amherst Village skulle komme til å ligge. Familien Knudson åpnet sitt hjem for mange av de nybyggerfamilier som ankom de påfølgende årene.* Hvordan skulle jeg noen gang kunne finne Astri når det ikke fantes duplikater av disse fortegnelsene?

Mor og jeg fant en gravstein på kirkegården i Elstad som listet opp fire Knudson-barn, to Birgit Knudson på framsiden, og to Guttorm Knudson på baksiden. Ved siden av disse fire var det gravlagt en Kjersti Knudson. Vi fant at de eksisterende nedtegnelsene over døde og gravlagte ikke inkluderte foreldrenes navn på noen av de fem Knudson-barna, selv om vi hadde en mistanke om at de tilhørte Knud og Gunhild.

Ved å undersøke websiden til *Riksarkivarens nasjonale arkiver i Norge, Digitalarkivet*, http://digitalarkivet.uib.no/index-eng.htm, greide jeg å finne at mine tipp-oldeforeldre, Knud og Gunhild, var foreldrene til alle de fem Knudson-barna som var nevnt på de to gravsteinene. Denne websiden omfatter også 6480 døpte i løpet av årene 1854-1883, og 1888 konfirmerte i løpet av årene 1860-1885, transkribert

2 Birgit Knudson på framsiden

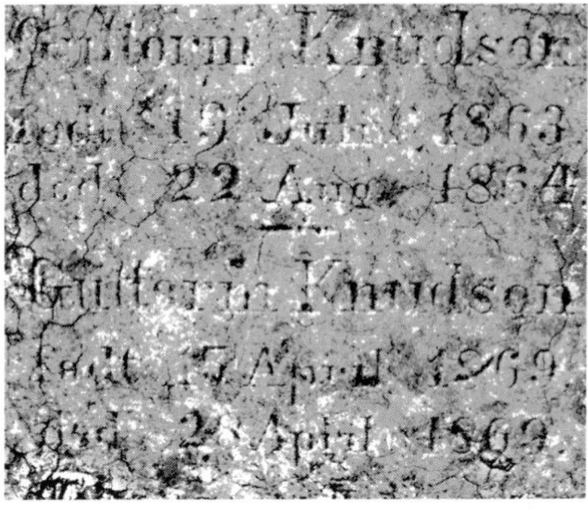

2 Guttorm Knudson på baksiden

Kjersti Knudson

av nordmannen Lars E. Øyane. Databasen rommer opplysninger fra de følgende kirkene i Fillmore County: Arendahl, Elstad, Greenfield, Highland, North Prairie, N.P. Hauge, Rushford, Rushford 2 og Union Prairie. Innenfor Elstad prestegjeld finnes fortegnelser fra Highland Prairie, Newburg (Garness) og Whalan.

For å finne kirkebøkene fra Fillmore County i den norske databasen, startet jeg øverst på *Digitalarkivets* hjemmeside, og brukte følgende sekvens: *categories, church registers, baptized, abroad og MN Fillmore Co baptisms 1854-1883.* Under kategorien *the following sources are available,* valgte jeg så *baptisms eller confirmations* (tilgjengelig for et begrenset antall kirker).

Det stod nå klart for meg at det ville ha vært svært fordelaktig for Genealogibiblioteket å ha tilgang til pionerfortegnelsene fra alle kirkene i Fillmore County, for å hjelpe folk med å søke etter sine familier. Mens jeg holdt på med granskingen, fant jeg ut at i stedet for at biblioteket hadde slike bøker, så måtte hver enkelt kirkes menighet gi sin tillatelse.

Det tradisjonelle norske navnesystemet

For å søke etter norsk slekt, trenger man å forstå det tradisjonelle navnesystemet. Som om de var del av de *ti bud,* var disse tradisjonene betraktet som nærmest ufravikelige.

Barnets første navn kom fra:

- Første sønn fikk navn etter farens far
- Andre sønn fikk navn etter morens far
- Første datter fikk navn etter farens mor
- Andre datter fikk navn etter morens mor
- Hvis en ektefelle døde, ble avdødes navn gitt videre til det første barnet av samme kjønn
- Hvis et barn døde, fikk det neste barnet av samme kjønn navn etter avdøde. Dette forklarte hvorfor Knud og Gunhild Knudson hadde to døtre som het Birgit, og to sønner ved navn Guttorm.

Barnets andre navn kom fra faren. Datter ble brukt som suffiks. Døtre av Guttorm eller Tosten fikk henholdsvis navnene Guttormsdatter eller Tostensdatter. Da vi forstod det tradisjonelle navnesystemet, skjønte vi også hvorfor Astri hadde to døtre som het Gunhild. Den andre Gunhild hadde navn etter hennes andre ektemanns mor, Gunhild.

Barnets tredje navn kom fra det stedet eller gården familien bodde på i øyeblikket. Astri ble født i 1792, og i 1801 dokumenterer en norsk folketelling at familien bodde på gården Børtnes. Astri nedstammet fra Gaute Olson Børtnes, født på 1500-tallet og kjent som en av de rikeste landeierne i Hallingdal på den tiden. På denne måten kom Astris navn, Børtnes og Syversrud, fra gårdene hun hadde bodd på i nærheten av Nes i Hallingdalen.

Astri ble først gift med korporal Guttorm Jensen Gulbrandsrud. Deres sønn, Jens Guttormsen, og min tippoldemor, Gunhild Guttormsdatter Knudson, immigrerte begge til Amerika. Etter Guttorms død, giftet Astri seg med Tosten Larson Ursdalen. Mitt tidligere 26-årige søk etter Astri hadde sluttet her, ettersom jeg var ute av stand til finne videre dokumentasjon om livet hennes før historien om kisten ble trykket.

Referanser fra *Emigranter fra Nes og Flå i Hallingdal* av Sigmund Sevre, og *Boka om Gol* av Terje Østro, gav meg den informasjonen jeg manglet. Astri og Tosten hadde flyttet til Nøbben, og hadde dermed endret etternavn, noe som forklarte hvorfor jeg ikke kunne vite at Astri kom til Amerika.

Gravtranskripsjoner

Ansatte og frivillige ved Genealogy Library, eller Works Project Administration (WPA), har over år gått over

Torsten Larsen Nubben 57-57, 69, *Torsten Larsen Ulsdalen, 32, g 14.11.1831 enke*
k Astrid Herbrandsd Børtnæs Syversrud 58-57, 64 *(Herbrand Børtnæs-Ragne), f juni 1792*
d Gunhild Torstensd Nubben 59-57, 25, 17.8.32, *f 13.8.1832*
d Ingeborg Torstensd Nubben 60-57, 20, f 16.4.1837

4. Torstein Larson f 1795 d i Am. g 1831 m enkja Astri Herbrandsdtr. Syversrud; budde på Nøbben, til Am. 1857 med 2 born, farma i Minn.

mer enn 150 kirkegårder i Fillmore County, noe som omfatter kirke, by, private og forlatte [gravplasser] og indianske gravhauger. De har transkribert det som står skrevet på de eksisterende gravsteinene. Disse nedtegnelsene innbefatter dessverre ikke steiner som er uleselige eller savnet, og som bare kan finnes i kirkenes eller kirketjenernes protokoller.

Vår første store oppdagelse kom da både navn og fødselsdataene til Gunhild og Ingeborg, de to døtrene som immigrerte sammen med moren Astri, passet perfekt til det vi fant i transkripsjonene fra kirkegården i Highland. Vi fant at Gunhild giftet seg med Nels Evans, mens Ingeborg giftet seg med Hans Gunvaldson. Vi vet at Astri hadde to døtre som var gravlagt i Highland, og en datter som var gravlagt i Elstad, bare noen kilometer unna. Dessverre fantes det ingen transkripsjon av noen gravskrift for halvsøsteren mor, Astri.

Vi fotokopierte gravtranskripsjonene fra Highland og Elstad, slik at mor og jeg kunne studere dem utover kveldene. Jeg husker en sen januarkveld mor og jeg leste i fortegnelsene: *steinen ligger flatt og er uleselig*. Gravsteinen var plassert rett ved siden av Astris datter, Ingeborg. Tilhørte denne gravsteinen Astri?

Selv om snøen var smeltet, og vi på grunn av et mildvær vi nylig hadde hatt i januar, kunne se barmark, var det likevel bitende kaldt ute. Uten hensyn til den ulende vinden, kunne selvsagt ikke mor og jeg vente til dagslyset kom før vi prøvde å kjenne etter hva som stod på steinen. Fram kom lommelyktene, og vi i vei til Highland kirkegård. Mens kulden trengte inn i margen, måtte vi innrømme at steinen var uleselig, så jakten på Astri fortsatte.

Bare dager etter var vi vilt begeistret, for da trodde vi at vi hadde funnet Astri i transkripsjonene av gravskifter fra en forlatt gravplass. Det finnes private kirkegårder i Fillmore County, inkludert en som befant seg på det som var kjent som Fattiggården i nærheten av Henrytown. Vi ringte øyeblikkelig min 93 år gamle bestemor, Esther Knudson, men hun forsikret oss om at det inngjerdede området i ytterkanten av Knudssons slektsgård ikke hadde vært annet enn en åkerlapp med poteter.

Ved å få tak i målebrevet over denne gravplassen på om lag et mål, bestemte vi den private kirkegården til å ligge tvers over gjerdet fra Knudsons eiendom. Av de ni kjente gravene tilhørte tre av dem konene til Mr. Smith. En flyttemelding viste at Mr. Smith hadde flyttet til Missouri, og hadde solgt denne jordlappen på drøyt et mål til Henry Ness i 1867. Familien Eiken eier nå jorda.

Kirkegårdsparseller

For å fortsette arbeidet med den uleselige gravsteinen vi trodde tilhørte Astri, fikk vi tak i kirkegårdens jordoppmålingsdokumenter. Uansett kom vi til en ny veisperring da den gamle nybyggerseksjonen på kirkegården i Highland ikke var inntegnet. Disse steinene som ikke var tegnet inn, omfattet til og med Evans og Gunvalsons gravsteiner, som vi hadde fotografert bare dager før på kirkegården.

Mor og jeg utstyrte Highland kirke med en kopi av kirkegårdstranskripsjonene fra Genealogy Library. Forhåpentligvis vil transkripsjonene hjelpe til med å utfylle fortegnelsene og med å identifisere de tallrike pionersteinene som ikke lenger står. Øyensynlig ble bind I av kirkeboken fra Highland lutherske kirke tilfeldigvis feilplassert for omkring 17 år siden.

Mor så min skuffelse over ikke å finne Astri, og ringte historieselskapet i Minnesota. Hun besøkte Tinghuset i Fillmore County for å undersøke mer om kirkegårdsparseller og jordeierskap, og hun kontaktet Vesterheim slektsforskningsselskap i Madison, Wisconsin. Uansett var der ikke noe første bind av kirkebøkene fra den lutherske kirken i Highland å finne.

Ingen av mine tidligere søk har gjort meg så motløs som det å ikke være i stand til å identifisere *steinen som lå flatt og var uleselig*, og som befant seg ved siden av Astris datter. Jeg kontaktet igjen Genealogy Library bare for å finne at det at det mangler bøker over kirkegårdsparseller, er svært så alminnelig. I følge Genealogy Library spiste en hund et sett med kirkegårdsbøker, mens andre var blitt borte i branner eller var forsvunnet. Verre er det at hele seksjoner på noen kirkegårder ikke kan brukes, fordi man ikke vet hvor kistene er plassert.

Folketellinger og registre

Jeg fant at folketellinger kunne være en viktig kilde, siden navnene på hele familiehusholdninger var oppført der sammen med personenes alder. Folketellingene dekker hvert femte år fra 1860 til 1920, unntatt 1890 og 1915. Staten Minnesotas manntall for årene 1860 og 1870, liksom Minnesota-veteranenes 1890-jubileumsbok, er også tilgjengelig ved Genealogy Library. Biblioteket delte vår triumf hver gang vi fant Astri og Tosten i manntallet. Vi fant at de var del av datterens husholdning i Amherst Township gjennom årene 1865, 1870, og 1875.

Det ble svært tydelig at det norske navnesystemet ble forlatt etterhvert som man gjennom pionertidens amerikaniseringsprosess tok nye, amerikanske navn. Et søk i folketellingene avslørte et nesten totalt tap av identitet blant immigrantene i de amerikanske nedtegnelsene. For eksempel ble Astri Herbrandsdatter Børtnes til Fru Tosten Larson. Bare i min familie ble etternavnene forandret til Knudson, Larson, Bendickson, Thompson og Nelson, noe som ikke etterlot noen som helst spor etter hvilke gårder de hadde immigrert fra i Norge.

Historiebøker og viktig statistikk

Fillmore Countys historie for 1858, 1882, 1912 og 1984 samt kirkens jubileumsbøker og byhistoriebøker, er alle å finne ved Genealogy Library. Viktig statistikk, inkludert nedtegnelser over ekteskap, fødsel og død, er også tilgjengelig ved Genealogy Library. Nedtegnelsene over døde har stikkordsregister som benytter etternavn og inneholder verdifull informasjon, inkludert navn på døde, dødsdato,

Henry Knudson and Oscar Knudson

kjønn, farge, sivil status, alder, fødested, fars navn, fars fødested, mors navn, mors fødested, dødsårsak og yrke. Dokumentene fra Amherst Township avslørte:

• *Tosten Larson døde 16. januar 1877 av tuberkulose*

• *Astri (Herbrandsdatter) Larson døde 13. mai 1878 av revmatisme*

Vi fikk ikke bare vite datoer og dødsårsak, men vi visste nå at Tosten og Astri døde i Amherst Township.

Gravskrifter

En kan finne utrolige historier i de store samlingene av gravskrifter ved Fillmore Countys historiesenter og slektsbibliotek, inkludert denne om Astris datter: *Som ung pike på 25 år kom Gunhild Tostensdatter sammen med foreldrene, Tosten Larson og Astri Herbrandsdatter, til Fillmore County i 1857. Familien, også søsteren Ingeborg Tostensdatter, gjorde den siste delen av reisen til fots, og hun gikk hele veien fra McGregor, Iowa til Amherst Township, hvor de slo seg ned på en gård.*

En gravskrift over Astris barnebarn, Anna (Evans) Gilbertson, gir en historie til: *Hun ble forent i ekteskap med Thor Gilbertson 26. april 1878, også han fra Fillmore County. Kort tid etter giftemålet kom de til Norman County, de reiste med oksespann og drev også kveg på hele turen, som tok omtrent en måned. Fru Gilbertson gikk til fots en stor del av veien og hjalp til med å drive kveget.*

En oksekjerre kunne bære mellom 350 og 450 kilo drøye 30 kilometer i løpet av en 10-timers dag. Imidlertid hadde hver oksekjerre sin egen spesielle rugging og remjing. Nesten ingen oksekjerrer er nevnt i tidlige brev og dagbøker uten at den fryktelige lyden også er nevnt...*den kan høres nesten en mil unna...den likner ikke noen annen lyd du har hørt i ditt liv og får blodet til å fryse i årene.*

Det følgende er tatt fra gravskriften over Astris svigersønn, Hans Gunvaldson: *Rett etter at det berømte Minnesota-regimentet hadde blitt skutt*

Knudson farm

sønder og sammen i slaget ved Gettysburg, ble Herr Gunvaldson innskrevet i kompani A i samme regiment. Han begynte sin militærtjeneste den 29. februar 1864 og ble utskrevet med ære 14. juli 1865. Men i den sekstende måned av aktiv tjeneste deltok han i noen av de blodigste slag under borgerkrigen, eksempelvis slaget om Petersburg. Han var sammen med general Grant da general Robert Lee overgav seg...Han oppbevarte et minne fra den anledningen, en sølvgaffel fra general Lees private middagsbord fra den dagen han kapitulerte.

Matrikler, kart og aviser

Matrikler er utmerkede kilder når det gjelder å finne eiendomsdata i de offentlige arkivene på tinghuset. Illustrerende kart i matriklene inkluderer jordeiernes navn og områdenes størrelse, kommunale seksjonsnummer, lokale og statlige veier, og innlemmede byer. Matrikler fra årene 1878, 1896 og 1915 sammen med kart fra 1904 og 1911 var til hjelp, idet de viste hvor familiene Knudson, Evans og Gunvaldson bodde og eide jord.

Genealogy Library har mikrofilmer av forskjellige årganger av gamle aviser fra Chatfield, Harmony, Lanesboro, Mabel, Peterson, Preston, Rushford, Spring Valley og Wykoff.

Militære data, etternavn og fotofiler

Data om Fillmore County-veteraner fra borgerkrigen, den spanskamerikanske krigen og første og andre verdenskrig er å finne ved Genealogy Library. Etternavnsfilen er en indeks som leder deg til fullførte søk gjort av andre som har sett etter de samme familiemedlemmene.

Fotofilen sørger for verdifulle bilder. Vi fant et av Gunhild Evans som 84-åring under tittelen: *Et svært interessant gruppe med nybyggere fra Fillmore County.*

Fra disse typene med arkiver var vi i stand til å konstruere følgende historie om Astris svigersønn: Nels Evans gikk inn i Kompani F i 5. regiment, og deltok i slaget ved Nashville. Han ble svært syk av kronisk dysenteri, som han pådro seg i Mississippi. Da regimentet nådde Demopolis i Alabama (vest for Montgomery) var Nels mest et skjelett og ble utskrevet fra armeen i september 1865. Borgerkrigen ble en ulykke, for Nels ble aldri bra igjen, og han døde sju år senere i 1872, 47 år gammel. Forskning viser at flere soldater fra borgerkrigen døde av sykdom enn i kamp, særlig døde de av dysenteri.

Gunhild Evans ble etterlatt som enke med sju barn da hun var 40 år gammel. Med sterkt mot satte denne nybyggerkvinnen i gang med å arbeide for å forsørge familien og betale ned gjelden på gården, og hun greide det. I 1902 forlot hun gården og flyttet til Lanesboro, hvor hun bodde i 21 år. Gunhild var nesten 91 da hun døde.

Skjøter

Skjøter fra Fillmore County, som dokumenterer overdragelsen av jordeiendommer fra den føderale regjeringen til individer, er å finne i arkivene i Fillmore Countys tinghus i Preston, Minnesota. Fillmore County består av 24 "township", og Amherst Township er delt inn i 36 seksjoner. Mor og jeg trengte en leksjon i identifikasjonssystemet til arkivene i Bureau of Land Management/General Land Office for å kunne forstå at Township (T)-102-N og Range (R)-9-W var en annen måte å beskrive Amherst Townships seksjon 27 på, hvor landsbyen Amherst lå.

Mine tipp-oldeforeldre, Knud og Gunhild Knudson, overtok en fjerdedels seksjon (160 acres, drøyt 160 mål) på den sørlige avgreiningen av Root River, beliggende rett imot der Amherst Store nå ligger. Skjøtet er signert av presiden Abraham Lincoln, og beskriver plasseringen av familiens slektsgård, som nå er over 150 år gammel.

Nels Evans kjøpte i 1857 Bounty Land, som tidligere var blitt gitt til en offiser for innsatsen under militærtjenesten for De forente stater under grenseurolighetene. Likeså ble Bounty Land i følge Gunvaldsons skjøte fra 1860, opprinnelig gitt til en annen offiser for tjenesten i krigen i 1812

Astris sang

Det finnes en gammel norsk folkesang om gode minner som heter "Astri, mi Astri." Når jeg ser tilbake på de første månedene av 2002, er de mange timene jeg tilbrakte sammen med mor mens vi forsket på Astri, mine kjæreste minner. Så mange timer faktisk at de ansatte på Genealogy Library visste at vi var der igjen når de hørte lyden av stemmene våre.

Genealogy 101, som tok meg *fra kisten til familietreet*, demonstrerer noe av det "syt og strev" slektsforskning bringer med seg. Selv om vi ikke fant ut akkurat hvor Astri ble gravlagt, så følte vi at vi hadde avgrenset det til kirkegårdene i Elstad og Highland, ettersom hun hadde døtre som var gravlagt begge steder.

Genealogy Resources

- Ancestry.com - http://www.ancestry.com

- Bygdebøker (local history books) and Gards og Ættesoge (farms and family sagas) to research rural communities in Norway

- Cyndi's List Norwegian Genealogy Sites http://www.cyndislist.com/norway.htm

- Decorah Genealogy Association (basement of Decorah Public Library), 202 Winnebago, Decorah, IA 52101, phone 563-382-8559

- Digitalarkivet - http://digitalarkivet.uib.no/index-eng.htm

- Fillmore County History Center, 202 Co. Rd. 8, Fountain, MN 55935, phone 507-268-4449, http://www.rootsweb.com/~mnfillmo/sources.htm

- Galleri NOR photo database - http://www.nb.no/gallerinor/e_sok.php

- Houston County Historical Society , 104 History Lane, Caledonia, MN 55921, phone 507-725-3884, http://www.lacrosselibrary.org/guide/houston_hs.html

- Norwegian-American Historical Association, 1510 St. Olaf Avenue, Northfield, MN 55057-1097, phone 507-646-3221, http://www.naha.stolaf.edu

- "Norwegians in the Civil War," searchable database of over 6,500 Norwegians, written by Jerry Rosholt, http://www.vesterheim.org/CivilWar/db

- Oluf Rygh's Norske Gaardsnavne (Norwegian Farm Names), Volumes 1-17, http://www.dokpro.uio.no/rygh_ng/rygh_form.html

- Telelaget of America - http://www.telelaget.com

- Vesterheim Genealogical Center and Naeseth Library, 415 West Main St., Madison, WI 53703, http://www.vesterheim.org/genealogy.html

- Vesterheim Norwegian-American Museum, 523 West Water St., Decorah, IA 52101, phone 563-382-9681, http://www.vesterheim.org

- WorldConnect Project - http://worldconnect.rootsweb.com

Land Patents

Land patents document the transfer of land ownership from the Federal Government to individuals. The following land patents glossary is taken from the Bureau of Land Management (BLM) General Land Office (GLO) Records database: http://www.glorecords.blm.gov/PatentSearch

Land Description - A sub-part of a legal land description on a land patent. Land descriptions uniquely identify the parcel or parcels of land for which title is given by the land patent. Land descriptions are based on the rectangular survey system.

Legal Land Description - Each land patent contains a legal land description that describes in legal (survey) terms the land to which title is given. A legal land description in turn consists of one land description for each parcel of land for which title is given by the land patent.

Range - A row or tier of townships lying east or west of the principal meridian and numbered successively to the east and to the west from the principal meridian.

Range Direction - The Range Direction indicates which side of the principal meridian the township is on. In the example "Township 5 North, Range 12 West," West indicates the direction of the township from the (vertical) meridian. Range directions can be either east or west.

Range Number - A Range Number identifies a township's East or West relation to its principal meridian. In the example "Township 5 North, Range 12 West," the number 12 represents the Range Number used to identify the township that is 12 tiers to the left of the principal meridian.

Section - A section is a regular tract of land, 1-mile square, containing 640 acres, within a township. It is approximately 1/36 of a township.

Section Number - Identifies a section within a township. Sections are usually numbered 1 to 36 but can be higher in some states. Alphabetic characters may be included in the section number. In some instances there are surveys with duplicate section numbers that are identified by a numeric-alpha (e.g., 12 or 12U).

Township - A township is a major subdivision of the public lands under the rectangular system of surveys. It is a tract of land contained within the boundaries of the north-south range lines. Most townships are 4-sided, measuring approximately 6 miles on each side and containing approximately 36 square miles, or 23,040 acres.

Township Direction - The Township Direction indicates which side (north or south) of the baseline the township is on. In the example, Township 5 North, Range 12 West," North indicates the Township Direction from the (horizontal) baseline.

Township Number - A township number is identified by its relation to a base line and a principal meridian. For example, "Township 5 North, Range 12 West" identifies a particular township that is 5 tiers up from the base line. In this example, the number 5 represents the Township Number. Some townships may be fractional.

6

A Tour of Norway's Medieval Stavkirker

Finding ancestral links to Stave Churches

Truly unique to Norway, the *stavkirke* (Stave Church) is a 900-year-old wooden temple filled with the history of the Viking Era and Christianity. Approximately 1,000 of these churches, built between the 1100s and 1300s, were once scattered throughout Norway's routes of trade. Today, only 29 stavkirker remain in Norway to deliver their *messages in wood.*

Christianity was introduced into Norway over a lengthy period of about two hundred years. Through trading connections and Viking raids, Norwegians came in contact with Christian Europe, which contributed to a weakening of the traditional belief in the Nordic gods. Three missionary Viking kings gave the church their final victory: Håkon I the Good, Olaf I Tryggvason, and Olaf II Haraldsson (Saint Olaf).

Norwegians used their extensive woodworking and shipbuilding skill to craft the pointed gables, narrow archways, and the same dragonheads that decorated the bows of the Viking longboats. The dark tarred timber structures spoke of a pagan past on the exterior, but provided a quiet place of Christian worship on the inside.

Stavkirkene marked a transition of the Norsk people from pagan beliefs to those of Christianity and helped drive the Norse gods from the Norwegian valleys, mountain, and fjords. After

touring numerous stavkirker during the summers of 2001 and 2003, my family not only learned of our own ancestral pagan temple sites, but also found benches in the Uvdal stavkirke i Numedal labeled with our Imingen family name.

We found ancestral links to a Hallingdal stavkirke, when we located a 300-year-old memorial painting of my 8th great-grandfather Bjørn Frøysok and his family. The 1699 epitaph is the first portrait and the only known church painting of a Norwegian farm family. The painting hung in the Gol stavkirke and is now displayed at the *Norsk Folkemuseum* (Norwegian Folk Museum) in Bygdøy, Oslo.

Norse mythology

In the pagan religion, the gods and goddesses each had power over their own domain. Odin, old and wise, was the chieftain and ruled over all the gods. Odin's son Thor, the second mightiest god, was the strong and quick-tempered god of the warriors and was always ready to do battle with the giants and trolls. Many types of supernatural beings were believed to live in the forests and mountains. Thor's chariot rolling across the sky made the sound of thunder.

The pagan gods are best known from descriptions written down in early Christian times. Some of the Norwegian farms such as Torshov, Frøyshov, and Onsaker kept their original pagan god names. Present day Norwegian sites with the last syllable *hov* indicate that there once was a heathen temple at the site.

Prior to 1000 AD and Christianity, the god Frey was worshiped at Frøysok (Frosager) i Gol, Hallingdal, my ancestral farm. Frey was responsible for the fertility of the soil and livestock and for peace and prosperity. An image of Frey was worshiped close to the crop fields. After splashing the image with blood, it was washed in the pond behind the farm living quarters or in the river.

A sacrificial temple was also believed to be located in pre-Christian times at another of my ancestral farms, the Ve farm. A translation of the Old Norse word Ve means "sacred place." The Flå stavkirke in Hallingdal once stood on the Ve farm, but it was torn down due to its deterioration. The term *farmer in the mound* was a commonly held pagan belief that the spirit of the original owner of an estate continued to offer protection from the grave.

Stavkirke Construction

The stavkirke construction technique of building with wood was a legacy of the Vikings. Like the Viking ships, the wooden structure was a display of amazing technical skills. The intricate system and precise structural details gave the stavkirke durability to resist centuries of wear and tear.

The term *stav* originates from the high wooden supporting pillars, which are a characteristic part of the skeleton structure of the stavkirker. In the 12th century, it became customary to place horizontal beams (sills) on a wall of flat stone footings to raise the stavkirke above ground level. This sill technology became a way of preventing the staves from rotting.

The stavkirke structure was completely flexible; each joint could expand or contract depending upon the damp or dry weather. This was made possible by the way the columns, planks and supports were dovetailed, pegged and wedged, never nailed or glued. Construction was accomplished with

Deb Nelson Gourley with her mother, Char Nelson, at Hopperstad stavkirke Vik i Sogn during 2001

Hopperstad stavkirke

axes, since the use of saws and planes was almost unknown. Knives were used to carve simple crosses and arrogant dragonheads. Tarred wooden shingles were used for the roof. The entire wooden structure was painted with a mixture of natural tar, turpentine, and linseed oil.

Norwegian pine trees, which grow to 115 feet, were used to build the stavkirker. The tree curing process took a couple decades to complete, since the process began while the trees were still alive. In order to make the pine tree more rot resistant, they were first debranched and topped, then left to bleed the resin into the branch ends, and finally to dry.

Among the most distinctive works of art to be found in Norway are the stavkirke doorframes. Virtually all of the doorframes are richly decorated from top to bottom with carvings from the pagan animal world of the Viking era.

Axes and swords were deposited near the doorway before entering the stavkirke. Other than the flickering candlelight by the altar, which was beautified with vessels of silver and gold, the long service was held in almost total darkness. The room was filled with intense odors of tar, wood, wool, fur, candles, and incense.

Only the elderly or feeble had benches along the wall, while the others stood on dirt floors in the cold, dark room. The non-baptized followed the church service from the galleries. Lepers viewed the service from the outside through a hole in the wall.

Bjørn Tolleivson Frøysok
Epitaph 1699

My 8th great-grandfather, Bjørn Tolleivson Frøysok (1634-1709), was a descendant from Frøysok (Frosager) i

Description of the 1699 Bjørn Tolleivson Frøysok Epitaph displayed in the Norsk Folkemuseum in Bygdøy, Oslo.

Bjørn Froysok together with his family. Memorial picture, 1699. The clothing shown in the picture is a combination of medieval tradition and Renaissance fashion.

• • • • • • • •

Bjørn Frøysok med huslyd. De eldste og einaste bilete av ein odelsbonde, mala I 1699. Kleda vist pa biletet sameiner mellomaldertradisjon og renessanse-mote.

Bjørn og sønene har koll-luve og steglatrøye av mellomalderutspring. Ermebryningen er eit renessanse-trekk. Skorne med raudmåla høge hæler er likeins nymotens.

Kone-ketta og jentehovudbunaden er truleg mellomalderplagg. Trøya og forkleet er renessance-påverka.

Fellebukse og –stakk kan vera moderne eller ei vidareføring av ein forhistorisk tradisjon.

Gol, Hallingdal, the site of the once pagan temple and sacred cultivated farm fields. His parents were *Bonde* Tolleiv Arneson Frøysok, whose name is painted on the wall in the front of the Gol stavkirke, and Jørand Johannesdatter Hove. Bonde was a term used for owners of large rural properties.

Bjørn and his first wife, Ingebjørg Halvorsdatter Hersgard Børtnes, had ten children. I am a descendant of their son, Per Bjørnson Frøysok, on my Knudson side of the family. Ingebjørg died about 1680. Bjørn then married Guri Eivindsdatter Tolleivsgard and eight more children were born. In 1699, Bjørn had a memorial painting made depicting both of his families and donated it to the Gol stavkirke.

Dominating the 52" by 78" painting, which was probably chalk paint on

Borgund stavkirke located at the head of the Sognefjord near Lærdal

canvas, is Bjørn holding a battle hammer in his hand. To the left the artist painted Bjørn's deceased first wife and their ten children. On the right are his then living wife and their eight children. Above Bjørn is the year *1699* and the Gothic inscription: *Have thanks O God our creator for nourishment from land and water. Thank you the Holy Spirit for our minds and thank God for our hearts and our happiness and bread shall be delivered us until our death and give us luck and health and life and gain eternity in Jesus name. Amen.*

Bjørn Frøysok's costume is a variation of the Renaissance style of the 1500s. Bjørn and his sons are wearing a type of cap and shirt, which dates back to the Middle Ages. The men's short, wide pantaloons and red high-heeled shoes, as well as the women's skirts, narrow aprons, and blouses, are signs of Renaissance fashions. Outside influences were late in arriving to the mountain districts.

Bjørn and his family were many times in court over quarrels of property and inheritance. According to the laws of the time, ancestral land had to be offered for sale to the descendants of the original owner.

This reference found in *Norway's Stave Churches - Architecture, History and Legends* by Eva Valebrokk and Thomas Thiis-Evensen describes my Frøysok ancestor: *We know that many of those who were a part of financing the artwork in the church were certainly not the most unobtrusive in manner and mood. On the contrary, many of them were fined and censured for fighting and bloodshed and many kinds of lawbreaking.*

29 stavkirker in Norway

No trip to Norway would be complete without a tour of the stavkirker, where wooden crosses and fierce dragonheads sprouting from the roofs still survive side by side. About 1600, monarchs began to dip into church funds to pay for wars and, consequently, churches often fell into decay. About half of the country's churches were sold to private persons to raise needed funds.

These remaining 29 stavkirker are among the oldest wooden buildings in the world and each tells its own unique story:

1. Borgund - Located at the head of the Sognefjord near Lærdal, this ancient structure built in 1150 is the best preserved of all stavkirker and serves as a model for many church restorations. In 1782, a mentally disturbed woman set fire to the stavkirke. A passerby called for help and the wooden structure was saved.

2. Urnes - Known as the Queen of the stavkirker, this Luster i Sogn structure with ornaments dating from about 1060 rises high above the sea. It was constructed around 1131 on the site of a pagan temple. The Urnes stavkirke is home to the Danish saga about Habor and Signe's tragic love. Legend tells of the gallows where Habor was hanged and the cage where the grieving Signe took her life.

3. Kaupanger - The Sogndal i Sogn stavkirke, built in 1180, is the largest stavkirke in the Sogn area and still serves as the local parish church. The Old Norse word *kaupangr* meant trading post or marketplace.

4. Hopperstad - Located at Vik i Sogn, the Hopperstad stavkirke is used only on Midsummer's Eve. The stavkirke recently constructed in Moorhead, MN is a replica of the Hopperstad.

5. Undredal - The Undredal i Sogn stavkirker is not only one of Norway's oldest stavkirker, but also one of the smallest, seating about 40 people. Built as early as 1147 in the Aurlandsfjord, the ancient structure has been in use ever since.

6. Røldal - The crucifix located in Hordaland's Røldal i Odda stavkirke was believed to have a healing aspect. On Midsummer's Eve the paralyzed, lame, blind, and sick were helped to the altar.

7. Heddal - Called a *gothic cathedral in wood*, the Heddal stavkirke near Notodden, Telemark is Norway's largest stavkirke. The church records show it was consecrated in 1147 and mentioned in the sagas in 1315. Because of its five levels of roof-upon-roof and tower-upon-tower, it is also known as the *Wedding Cake Temple*.

8. Eidsborg - The Eidsborg stavkirke in Lårdal is distinctive due to roof, posts, and walls being entirely clad with wooden shingles. This structure near Dalen i Telemark was one of the last built before the Black Death (Bubonic Plague) in 1349.

9. Rollag - It is thought that in early days of Christianity, the congregation gathered at a large stone cross. Later this cross was found in a burial chamber beneath the Rollag i Numedal stavkirke and placed outside the church. The cross is perhaps older than the stavkirke.

10. Flesberg - Still the parish church, the Flesberg i Numedal stavkirke has undergone extensive restorations. One of the few remaining remnants of this wooden structure is a medieval dragon entrance.

11. Nore - The Nore i Numedal stavkirke is noted for having its walls covered with Biblical sites presented in riddle form. Mass was said in Latin and Biblical paintings were used for education.

12. Uvdal – Built in the late 1100s, the Uvdal i Numedal stavkirke has three wooden benches with my family's ancestral name, Imingen, painted on them, signifying where they sat during church service. My great-great-grandfather who emigrated from Numedal used four last names during his lifetime: Imingen, Kjosa, Tovsson, and finally Thompson. During excavation beneath the flooring, knotted cords and pouches holding objects were found that were thought to have magical powers.

13. Hedalen - Legend tells this Valdres stavkirke was deserted for nearly 200 years after the Black Death, only to be discovered by a hunter. A bear hibernating at the foot of the altar was found and killed by the hunter. The bear's pelt is still kept in the church.

14. Lomen - The Lomen stavkirke was in continuous use during the Middle Ages. The Black Death did not seen to depopulate this isolated Vestre Slidre community in Valdres.

15. Høre - Consecrated in 1180, the Høre stavkirke was located close to yet another of my ancestral farms, the Kvie farm in Vang, Valdres. Future Queen Gyda was raised at Kvie. Gyda married King Harald Hårfagre, the first king of all of Norway. Coins dating back to 1040 indicate the Høre stavkirke and the Kvie farms were important religious and trading centers.

16. Øye – Woodcarvings date the Øye i Valdres stavkirke to 1125. Because of its location in a flood area, stones were placed on any casket lowered into the ground during the flooding season. Damaged by a flood in 1746, the structure was dismantled and a new church was built. During repair in 1935, the timbers of the old stavkirke were found stored beneath the floor and the ancient structure was restored.

17. Hegge - The Hegge stavkirke is the only remaining medieval stavkirke in Østre Slidre i Valdres. Unique are eight one-eyed masks representing the Norse god, Odin.

18. Reinli - Legend tells that the Reinli stavkirke was first located at the base of the valley in Sør-Aurdal i Valdres; however, the huldre (underground creatures with a long, cowlike tail) were annoyed and transported the structure to its present location far up on the hillside.

19. Torpo - Located next to my Nubgarden ancestral farm, the Torpo stavkirke built in 1160 is the oldest building in Hallingdal. Its rare ceiling paintings are rated among the finest of European church art. Almost 800 years ago an unknown artist portrayed in

Heddal stavkirke in Telemark roof-upon-roof, tower-upon-tower

graphic scenes, the life of Jesus and the martyrdom of St. Margaret, who had professed to be a Christian and refused to marry a pagan.

20. Gol - The 1699 painting of the Bjørn Frøysok family hung in the original Gol stavkirke. The stavkirke was dismantled and moved in 1885 to the Norsk Folkemuseum in Bygdøy, Oslo, where the painting also hangs. In 1994 a new stavkirke was consecrated at Gol i Hallingdal replacing the old church.

21. Høyjord - Norway's southernmost stavkirke, located in Andebu near Tønsberg, had consecrated crosses carved into the walls to keep the evil spirits away.

22. Rødven - Considered a masterpiece, a life-size crucifix is located in the front of the Rødven stavkirke. The Rauma i Romsdal church was sold at public action by the monarchs to raise funds.

23. Kvernes - Exposed to the open sea at Averøy i Romsdal, the Kvernes stavkirke has withstood all storms and remains a place of worship in Nordmøre. Although having undergone numerous reconstructions, the main part from the original stavkirke was saved.

24. Grip - Located on an island 14 kilometers off the coast of Norway near Kristiansund, the Grip stavkirke has withstood storms and tidal waves. This included the nighttime storm in 1796 that washed nearly 100 buildings into the sea.

25. Holtålen - During the *Catholic Era*, a quick solution to no warm water for a baptism in Gauldal resulted in the priest asking the parishioners to spit into the baptismal dish. Word reached Rome angering the Pope enough to call the people of Holtålinger barbarians and demand that the incident not be repeated. From 1881 to 1884, the Holtålen stavkirke was dismantled and reconstructed at the Trøndelag Folk Museum in Trondheim.

26. Garmo - According to a legend, Torgeir the Old from the Garmo farm in Lom negotiated with St. Olaf. Torgeir accepted the Christian faith and built a church on his farm in exchange for Lake Tessevann, a lake rich with fish. The Oppland stavkirke was moved to the Maihaugen museum in Lillehammer in 1921.

27. Vågå – The second oldest in Norway, Vågå's *Vatican Church* was built about 1100 to 1130. My parents attended the wedding of their exchange student, Thor Ekre, in the Vågå i Gulbrandsdal stavkirke.

28. Ringebu - The Ringebu i Gudbrandsdal stavkirke, with its distinctive now red towering steeple, still functions as the local parish church. The main section from the original stavkirke is especially known for its beautiful altarpiece and pulpit.

29. Lom – The Lom i Gulbrandsdal stavkirke was built about 1200 and is still used for services. While hiding in the mountain to avoid the death penalty, two young boys from Lom each carved a wooden angel for the altar. Upon returning with the angels they were pardoned for deserting the war.

There are no other wooden structures anywhere in the world like stavkirkene fusion of Viking and Christian cultures. Finding ancestral links, including pagan temple sites, a 300-year-old Frøysok painting, and wooden Imingen benches has only heightened my interest in the legends, history, and medieval architecture of the imposing *messages in wood*.

Reise mellom norske stavkirker

Stavkirkene forteller familiehistorie

De ni hundre år gamle stavkirkene er fylt med historie fra vikingtid og kristendom, og som helligdommer bygd i tre er de et unikt norsk fenomen. Omtrent 1000 slike kirker ble reist mellom 1100 og 1300, da de ble strødd ut langs Norges handelsveier. I dag står det bare 29 stavkirker igjen i Norge og bringer trearbeidernes budskap videre.

Kristendommen ble introdusert i Norge over en lengre periode på to hundre år. Gjennom handelsforbindelser og vikingtokter kom nordmennene i kontakt med det kristne Europa, noe som bidro til å svekke den tradisjonelle troen på de nordiske gudene. Tre misjonerende vikingkonger gav kirken dens endelige seier: Håkon I Den gode, Olav I Tryggvason, og Olaf II Haraldsson (Hellige Olaf).

Nordmenn brukte sine omfattende trearbeids- og skipsbyggingsferdigheter for å bygge de spisse gavlene, de trange buegangene, og de samme dragehodene som prydet baugen på vikingenes langskip. Det mørke, tjærebredde tømmeret på utsiden forteller om en hedensk fortid, mens det var sørget for et stille rom for kristen tilbedelse på innsiden.

Stavkirkene markerte for folket i Norge overgangen fra hedensk til kristen tro, og bidro til å fordrive norrøne guder fra norske daler, fjell og fjorder. Da min familie besøkte utallige stavkirker somrene 2001 og 2003, fikk vi ikke bare høre om våre forfedres hedenske helligsteder, men vi fant også benker i Uvdal stavkirke i Numedal som var merket med vårt eget familienavn, Imingen.

Char Nelson - Uvdal stavkirke i Numedal

Vi fant forbindelser til familien i Hallingdal stavkirke, hvor vi lokaliserte en tre hundre år gammel minnetavle over min oldefar i åttende ledd, Bjørn Frøysok, og hans familie. Epitafet fra 1699 er det første portrett og det eneste kjente kirkemaleri som framstiller en norsk bondefamilie. Maleriet hang i Gol stavkirke, og det er nå utstilt på Norsk Folkemuseum på Bygdøy i Oslo.

Norrøn mytologi

I den hedenske religionen hadde hver gud og gudinne makt over sitt eget område. Odin, gammel og vis, var overhodet, og regjerte over alle gudene. Odins sønn, Tor, den nest mektigste guden, var den sterke og temperamentsfulle guden for krigerne, og han var alltid rede til å sloss mot jotner og troll. Mange slags overnaturlige skapninger levde i følge folketroen i skoger og fjell. Tors vogn laget lyden av torden når den rullet over himmelen.

De hedenske gudene er best kjent fra skriftlige beretninger fra tidlig kristen tid. Noen av de norske gårdene, så som Torshov, Frøyshov og Onsaker, beholdt sine opprinnelig hedenske gudenavn. I dag indikerer den siste stavelsen *hov* at det har vært en hedensk helligdom på stedet.

Forut for år 1000 og kristendommen ble Frøy dyrket på mine forfedres gård, Frøysok, (Frosager) i Gol i Hallingdal. Frøy hadde makt over jordas og gårdsdyrenes fruktbarhet, og brakte fred og trivsel. Et bilde av Frøy ble helligholdt i nærheten av åkrene. Etter å ha skvettet blod på bildet, ble det vasket i dammen bak gårdens oppholdsrom, eller i elva.

Man mener også at det i førkristen tid skal ha vært en helligdom på en annen av mine forfedres gårder, gården Ve. Oversetter man det norrøne ordet Ve, betyr det *"hellig sted"*. Flå stavkirke i Hallingdal stod en gang på gården Ve, men ble revet på grunn av skader. Uttrykket *haugkall* var uttrykk for en vanlig hedensk forestilling om at den opprinnelige eieren av gården fortsatt ga sin beskyttelse fra graven.

Norges 29 stavkirker

1. Borgund
2. Urnes
3. Kaupanger
4. Hopperstad
5. Undredal
6. Røldal
7. Heddal
8. Eidsborg
9. Rollag
10. Flesberg
11. Nore
12. Uvdal
13. Hedalen
14. Lomen
15. Høre
16. Øye
17. Hegge
18. Reinli
19. Torpo
20. Gol
21. Høyjord
22. Rødven
23. Kvernes
24. Grip
25. Holtålen
26. Garmo
27. Vågå
28. Ringebu
29. Lom

Stavkirkekonstruksjonen

Stavkirkenes trebygningsteknikk var en arv fra vikingene. Som i vikingskipene ble trekonstruksjonen en framvisning av forbløffende tekniske ferdigheter. Det innviklede systemet og de presise strukturelle detaljene gav stavkirkene styrke til å motstå århundrer med tyngde og slitasje.

Termen *stav* har sitt navn etter de høye bærepilarene av tre som utgjør en karakteristisk del av stavkirkenes bærekonstruksjon. På 1200-tallet ble det vanlig med horisontale bunnstokker (syllstokker) på en grunnmur av flate steiner for å heve stavkirken over bakkenivået. Bruken av slike syllstokker hindret stavene fra å råtne.

Stavkirkestrukturen var fullstendig bevegelig; hver tømmerstokk kunne utvide seg eller trekke seg sammen alt etter hvor vått eller tørt været var. Dette ble muliggjort gjennom måten stokker, planker og støttepilarer ble sinket, plugget og kilt sammen, aldri spikret eller limt. Konstruksjonen ble fullført ved at man hogg den til med øks, ettersom sag og høvel var nesten ukjent. Kniver ble brukt for å skjære inn enkle kors og arrogante dragehoder. Tjærebredd treshingel ble brukt for å dekke taket. Hele trestrukturen ble malt med en

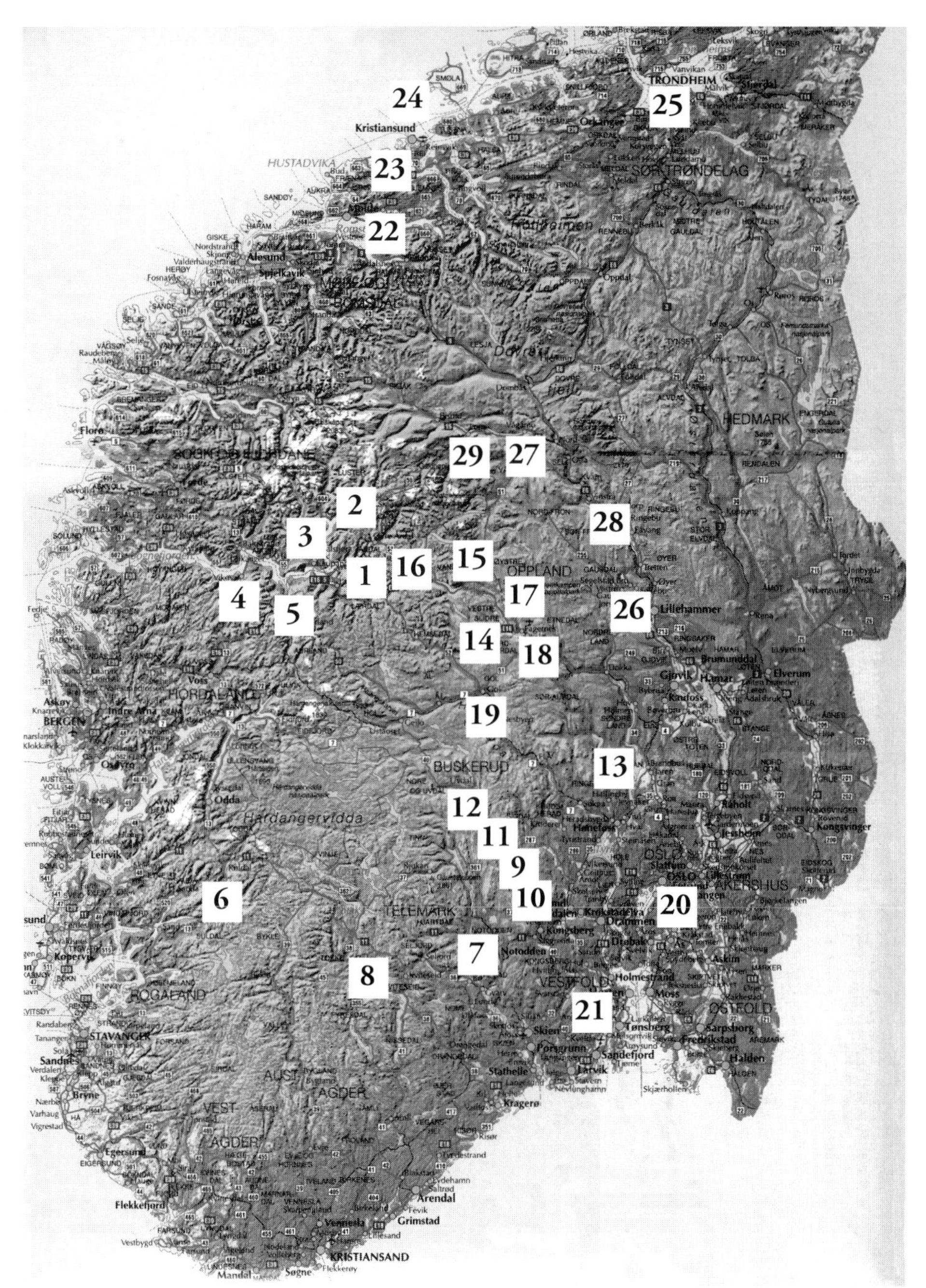

blanding av naturlig tjære, terpentin og linolje.

Norske furutrær, som kan bli om lag 35 meter høye, ble brukt for å bygge stavkirkene. Prosessen med å klargjøre treet tok et par tiår å fullføre, siden prosessen begynte mens treet fortsatt var i live. For å gjøre furutreet mer motstandsdyktig mot råte, ble det først greinet og toppet, så forlatt for å blø ut harpiks der greinene var fjernet før det kunne tørke.

Blant de mest utpregede kunstverkene vi finner i Norge er dørrammene i stavkirkene. Praktisk talt alle dørrammer er rikt dekorert fra topp til bunn med treskjæringsarbeider som henter sine motiver fra vikingtidens hedenske dyreverden.

Man satte fra seg økser og sverd ved døra før man gikk inn i en stavkirke. Bare opplyst av de flakkende flammene fra talglysene på alteret, som var vakkert dekorert med kar av sølv og gull, ble den lange gudstjenesten holdt i nær sagt totalt mørke. Rommet var fylt med intense dufter av tjære, tre, ull, skinn, talglys og røkelse.

Bare de eldste og svakeste hadde benker langs veggen, mens de andre stod på jordgulvet i det kalde, mørke rommet. De som ikke var døpt, fulgte gudstjenesten fra utsiden gjennom et hull i veggen.

Bjørn Tolleivson Frøysok-epitafet fra 1699

Min oldefar i åttende ledd, Bjørn Tolleivson Frøysok (1634-1709), var en etterkommer fra Frøysok (Frosager) i Gol i Hallingdal, hvor det en gang lå et hedensk kultsted og helligholdte åkermarker. Hans foreldre var bonde Tolleiv Arneson Frøysok, hvis navn er malt på frontveggen på Gol stavkirke, og Jørand Johannesdatter Hove. *Bonde* var en benevnelse som ble brukt på eierne av større landeiendommer.

Bjørn og hans første kone, Ingebjørg Halvorsdatter Hersgard Børtnes, hadde ti barn. Jeg er på Knudson-siden i familien etterkommer etter en av deres sønner, Per Bjørnson Frøysok. Ingebjørg døde ca 1680. Bjørn giftet seg så med Guri Eivindsdatter Tolleivsgard, og det ble født åtte nye barn. I 1699 fikk Bjørn malt en minnetavle som avbilder begge familier, og donerte den til Gol stavkirke.

I sentrum av det 132 x 199 cm store bildet, som trolig er malt med limkalk på lerret, står Bjørn og holder en stridshammer i hånden. Til venstre har kunstneren malt Bjørns avdøde første kone og deres ti barn. Til høyre står hans dalevende kone og deres åtte barn. Over Bjørn er malt året *1699* og den gotiske inskripsjonen (horisontalt i bildet):

HavTak O Gud vaar Skaber Mand
for Næring udaf Land og Vand
hav Tak du rette Livsens brød
Tak hellig Aand oplius vort Sind
og Gud til vore hierter bind
Gud tænk opaa os arme smaa
som i din Forsyns øye staa
du veedst Hvordan vor Lykk og brød
skal skieres For oss til vor Død
Giv Lykke Helbred liv og gafn
og salighed i Jesu Nafn - Amen

Bjørn Frøysoks påkledning er en variant av renessansestilen på 1500-tallet. Bjørn og sønnene hans bærer en lue- og jakketype som daterer seg tilbake til middelalderen. Mennenes korte, vide bukser og røde, høyhælte sko, liksom kvinnenes skjørt, trange forklær og bluser, vitner om renessansemotene. Påvirkning utenfra kom sent til fjelldistriktene.

Bjørn og familien hans var mange ganger i retten på grunn av uenighet om eiendom og arv. I henhold til lovene på den tiden måtte slektens eiendommer tilbys for salg til etterkommerne etter den opprinnelige eieren.

Denne referansen fra *Levende fortid – De utrolige stavkirkene* av Eva Valebrokk og Thomas Thiis-Evensen, beskriver min ane fra Frøysok: *"Me veit om fleire av desse som var med og bekostet kunstverket i kyrkja at dei slett ikkje var av dei mest stillfarende i lag og lyd. Tvertimot fekk fleire av dei bøter og påtale for slagsmål og "bloduir", og mange slags lovbrot."*

Norges 29 stavkirker

Ingen Norgestur vil være fullstendig uten en rundtur til stavkirkene, hvor trekors og heftige dragehoder som spirer ut fra takene, fortsatt overlever side ved side. Rundt 1600 begynte monarkene å forsyne seg av kirkekassene for å betale for kriger, og kirkene endte derfor ofte i forfall. Omtrent halvparten av landets kirker ble solgt til private for å reise tilstrekkelig med midler.

De gjenværende 29 stavkirkene er blant de eldste trebygningene i verden, og hver og en forteller sin egen enestående historie:

1. Borgund – Ligger innerst i Sognefjorden nær Lærdal. Den gamle bygningen som ble reist i 1150, er den best bevarte av alle stavkirker, og tjener som modell for mange kirkerestaureringer. I 1782 satte en mentalt forstyrret kvinne fyr på stavkirken. En forbipasserende tilkalte hjelp, og trebygningen ble reddet.

2. Urnes – Kjent som dronningen blant stavkirker, reiser denne bygningen med sin ornamentikk fra 1060 seg høyt over havet i Luster i Sogn. Den ble bygd rundt 1131 på samme sted som et hedensk hov. Urnes stavkirke er stedet hvor den danske sagaen om Hagbard og Signes tragiske kjærlighet utspiller seg. Legenden forteller om galgen hvor Hagbard ble hengt og om "jomfruburet" hvor den sørgende Signe tok sitt liv.

3. Kaupanger – Stavkirken i Sogndal i Sogn ble bygd i 1180, den er den største stavkirken i Sogn og tjener fortsatt som lokal soknekirke. Det gamle navnet *kaupanger* betyr *kjøpstad* eller *markedsplass*.

4. Hopperstad – Ligger i Vik i Sogn. Hopperstad stavkirke blir bare brukt på sankthanskvelden. Stavkirken som nylig ble bygd i Moorhead i Minnesota, er en kopi av Hopperstadkirken.

5. Undredal – Undredal stavkirke i Sogn er ikke bare en av Norges eldste stavkirker, men også en av de minste, med plass for omtrent 40 personer. Den gamle bygningen i Aurlandsfjorden har vært i bruk siden den ble bygd så tidlig som i 1147.

6. Røldal – Krusifikset i Røldal stavkirke i Odda i Hordaland skal ha hatt en legende virkning. På sankthanskvelden ble lamme, halte, blinde og syke hjulpet fram til alteret.

7. Heddal – Heddal stavkirke nær Notodden i Telemark er Norges største stavkirke og blir kalt en gotisk trekatedral. Kirkebøkene viser at den ble vigslet i 1147, og den nevnes i sagaer i 1315. På grunn av sine fire etasjer med tak over tak og tårn over tårn, er den også kjent som *bryllupskakekirken*.

8. Eidsborg – Eidsborg stavkirke i Lårdal er spesiell på grunn av at tak, stolper og vegger er helt dekket med treshingel. Denne bygningen nær Dalen i Telemark var en av de siste som ble bygd før svartedauden (byllepesten) i 1349.

9. Rollag – Man mener at menigheten i kristendommens første dager samlet seg ved et stort steinkors.

Senere ble dette korset funnet i et gravkammer under Rollag stavkirke i Numedal og plassert utenfor kirken. Korset er kanskje eldre enn stavkirken.

*10. **Flesberg*** – Flesberg i Numedal er fortsatt soknekirke, og har gått gjennom omfattende restaureringer. En av de få levningene av den opprinnelige trebygningen er den middelalderpregede drageinngangen.

*11. **Nore*** – Nore i Numedal er kjent for å ha veggene dekket med bibelsitater presentert i gåteform. Messen ble framsagt på latin og malerier med tema fra Bibelen ble brukt til opplæring.

*12. **Uvdal*** – Uvdal stavkirke er bygd sent på 1100-tallet og har mitt familienavn, Imingen, malt på tre trebenker, hvilket forteller hvor de satt under gudstjenesten. Min tipp-oldefar som emigrerte fra Numedal, brukte fire etternavn mens han levde: Imingen, Kjosa, Tovsson og til sist Thompson. Under utgravinger under gulvet fant man knyttede bånd og poser som rommet gjenstander som skal ha vært tillagt magiske krefter.

*13. **Hedalen*** - Legenden forteller at Valdres stavkirke ble forlatt i nærmere 200 år etter svartedauden, og at den ble gjenfunnet av en jeger. En bjørn som var gått i dvale ved foten av alteret ble funnet og drept av jegeren. Bjørneskinnet er fortsatt oppbevart i kirken.

*14. **Lomen*** – Lomen stavkirke var i kontinuerlig bruk gjennom middelalderen. Svartedauden synes ikke å ha avfolket det isolerte samfunnet Vestre Slidre i Valdres.

*15. **Høre*** – Høre stavkirke ble innvidd i 1180, og er lokalisert i nærheten av en av mine forfedres gårder, Kviegården i Vang i Valdres. Den kommende dronning Gyda vokste opp i Kvie. Gyda giftet seg med kong Harald Hårfagre, den første kongen over et samlet Norge. Mynter som dateres til 1040 indikerer at Høre stavkirke og gården Kvie var viktige religiøse og handelsmessige sentra.

*16. **Øye*** – Treskjæringene daterer Øye stavkirke i Valdres til 1125. På grunn av plasseringen i et flomområde, la man steiner på enhver likkiste som ble senket ned i grunnen i flomtiden. Da bygningen ble ødelagt av en flom i 1746, ble den demontert, og en ny kirke ble bygd. Under reparasjoner i 1935 ble tømmeret til den gamle stavkirken funnet lagret under gulvet, og den gamle bygningen ble gjenreist.

*17. **Hegge*** – Hegge stavkirke er den eneste gjenværende stavkirken i Østre Slidre i Valdres. Enestående er åtte enøyde masker som forestiller den norrøne guden Odin.

*18. **Reinli*** – Historien forteller at Reinli stavkirke først var plassert i dalbunnen i Sør-Aurdal i Valdres, men at huldrene (underjordiske skapninger

Gol stavkirke, Bygdøy, Oslo

Vågå stavkirke
photos by Thor Ekre

med lang kuhale) ble forstyrret og derfor flyttet bygningen til sin nåværende lokalitet langt oppe i åsen.

19. Torpå – Er nabo til min slektsgård, Nubgarden. Bygd i 1160, er dette den eldste bygningen i Hallingdal. Dens sjeldne takmalerier gjelder som noen av de fineste i europeisk kunst. For nesten 800 år siden framstilte en ukjent kunstner i bilder scener fra Jesu liv og den Hellige Margarets martyrium, hun hadde erklært seg som kristen og nektet å gifte seg med en hedensk mann.

20. Gol – Maleriet fra 1699 av Bjørn Frøysok-familien hang i den originale Gol stavkirke. Stavkirken ble tatt fra hverandre, og ble i 1885 flyttet til Norsk Folkemuseum på Bygdøy i Oslo, hvor også maleriet henger. I 1994 ble en ny stavkirke vigslet i Gol i Hallingdal på den gamle kirkens sted.

21. Høyjord – Norges sørligste stavkirke, lokalisert i Andebu nær Tønsberg, hadde vigslede kors skåret inn i veggene for å holde de onde åndene unna.

22. Rødven – Betraktet som et mesterverk er et mannshøyt krusifiks i fronten av Rødven stavkirke. Kirken i Rauma i Romsdal ble solgt på en offentlig auksjon av monarkene for å reise penger.

23. Kvernes – Utsatt for åpen sjø ved Averøy i Romsdal, har Kvernes stavkirke stått mot alle stormer, og er forblitt et sted for gudsdyrking på Nordmøre. Etter å ha gjennomgått utallige ombygginger, ble hoveddelen av den originale stavkirken reddet.

24. Grip – Plassert på en øy 14 kilometer fra fastlandet i nærheten av Kristiansund, har Grip stavkirke overlevd stormer og tidevannsbølger. Det innbefatter stormen i 1796 som vasket nesten 100 bygninger på havet.

25. Holtålen – I katolsk tid ble en rask løsning på at det manglet varmt vann til en dåp i Gausdal at presten bad sine sognebarn om å spytte i døpefonten. Dette nådde Roma og ergret paven tilstrekkelig til at han kalte holtålingene for barbarer og bad om at opptrinnet ikke måtte gjentas. Fra 1881 til 1884 ble Holtålen stavkirke tatt fra hverandre og rekonstruert ved Trøndelag Folkemuseum i Trondheim.

26. Garmo – I følge historiene forhandlet Torgeir fra den gamle Garmogården i Lom med Hellige Olaf. Torgeir tok den kristne troen og bygde en kirke på gården sin i bytte mot Tessevann, en fiskerik innsjø. Oppland stavkirke ble flyttet til Maihaugen museum på Lillehammer i 1921.

27. Vågå - Den nest eldste stavkirken i Norge, Vågås "vatikankirke", ble bygd mellom 1100 og 1130. Mine foreldre overvar bryllupet til sin utvekslingsstudent, Thor Ekre, i Vågå stavkirke i Gudbrandsdalen.

28. Ringebu – Ringebu stavkirke i Gudbrandsdalen med sitt karakteristiske, nå røde, bratte tårn, fungerer fortsatt som lokal soknekirke. Hoveddelen fra den originale stavkirken er spesielt kjent for sin vakre altertavle og døpefonte.

29. Lom – Lom stavkirke i Gudbrandsdalen ble reist omkring 1200 og er fortsatt i bruk til gudstjenester. Mens de gjemte seg i fjellene for å unngå en dødsstraff, skar to unge gutter fra Lom ut en treengel til alteret. Da de kom tilbake med engelen, ble de tatt i nåde etter å ha desertert fra krigen.

Det finnes ingen andre trebygninger i verden som på samme måte som stavkirkene smelter sammen vikingtid og kristen kultur. Å finne familiebånd, inkludert hedenske helligsteder, et tre hundre år gammel Frøysokmaleri og Imingen-familiens trebenker, har bare forsterket min interesse for de overveldende budskap treskjærerne etterlot seg gjennom legender, historie og middelalderarkitektur.

7

Garness Church roots go back to Garnås farm in Hallingdal

Starting a Norwegian Lutheran Church in America

The familiar sounds I grew up with, the unloading of the horses, the snorting and pawing, and the cinching of the saddles were all heard that cold blustery day, January 14, 1996. However, someone very important to me was missing from this gathering of horses and riders. It was my father, Sylvan Nelson, who always went from rider to rider with a big smile, shaking hands, and making everyone feel welcome.

Star, my father's horse, was led riderless by my nephew, Nathan O'Connor. Joining them on horseback for the tribute ride were six members of the Minnesota Cutting Horse Association, each solemnly taking their pallbearer positions behind the wagon carrying my father's casket. Family and friends followed the wagon tracks two miles up the hill from the village of Newburg to the Garness Church in rural Mabel, Minnesota.

Sylvan, my father, died at age 67. He was a well-known farmer in the Mabel-Canton area, a former president of the Mabel Lions Club, member of the Cattlemen's Association, and an avid rider since childhood. Prior to his illness, he checked the cattle on horseback every day all year round, regardless of the weather. An annual two-day memorial cutting horse show, an event my father loved, has been hosted by my mother, Char, and attended by riders from several states.

Star, my father's horse, was led riderless by my nephew, Nathan O'Connor

Garness Trinity Lutheran Church, Mabel, Minnesota

Garness Church

In early 1868, the *Norwegian Evangelical Lutheran Trinity Church of Newburg* was organized in southeast Minnesota. It was built on land owned and donated by my father's great-great-grandparents, Bjørn Olson Sata and Sidsel Nilsdatter Nubgarden, who used the surname *Garnås* in America. The church, whose name was later changed to Garness Trinity Lutheran Church, was completed in 1869 at a cost of about $1,023.

The church sits high on top of a rural hill catching all inclement weather. On July 25, 1901, the original church was struck by lightning and burned. A new brick church was completed the following year at a cost of over $5,000. The altar, altar rail, and pulpit were made in 1902 by L.A. Lund of Mabel at a cost of $130. Norway pines planted around the cemetery still stand there today.

Before the church was built, the early Norwegian pastors traveled by foot or by horse to serve the settlement. A cornerstone of the Garness Church reads: *Pastor Ulrik Vilhelm Koren, from Washington Prairie Church near Decorah, was the first Pastor serving from 1854-1856. In 1857, services were held in the home of Bjørn and Sidsel Garnås.*

The first pioneers brought with them a strong heritage of the Lutheran Church in Norway. The Bible, hymnal, and catechism used in their homes were sources of comfort and inspiration as the early settlers endured the hardships and struggles of pioneer life.

The early Sunday worship services were in Norwegian and lasted for more than an hour. Separate seating was a custom for many years, with the women and smaller children on one side of the church and the boys with their fathers on the other.

Herbjørn N. Gausta painted the Garness Church altar. In 1867 at age 13, he emigrated with his family from *Vestfjorddalen i Telemark*, Norway to a farm in nearby Harmony, Minnesota. He studied and taught art at Luther College in Decorah, Iowa, and had studied in Europe as well. He is perhaps the best known of the Norwegian-American artists, painting approximately 400 altarpieces for Norwegian-American churches.

In 1958, the congregation voted to share a parsonage and a pastor with Scheie Lutheran Church, located to the north. Today the parsonage for the two sister churches is in Mabel.

Garnås farm in Norway

Bjørn and Sidsel descended from a long line of Norwegian farmers in *Ål i Hallingdal*. Their ancestors were well documented as *bønder* (highly respected farmers or landowners) throughout the 1600s and 1700s in the *Aal Bygde Soge*. In 1833, Bjørn and Sidsel moved with their two sons, Ole and Niels, from *Ål* to the *Garnås* farm in *Nes*, located high above the *Hallingdal* valley. During the time they lived on and owned a small part of the *Garnås* farm, five more children were born: Hans Jørgen, Mari, Engebret (great-grandfather to Sylvan), Guri, and Kari.

Garnås and *Garnaas* are two ways of spelling the Norwegian farm name. The three additional vowels (*æ, ø,* and *å*), which follow the "z" in the Norwegian alphabet, are written in English as *ae, oe,* and *aa*, respectively. Hence the two spellings.

Garnås in America

On June 13, 1853, Bjørn and Sidsel, along with their seven children, left *Nes i Hallingdal* for America. They immigrated to Rock Prairie, Wisconsin, and in 1854 settled in Newburg Township in Fillmore County, Minnesota. Garnås, the name of the farm they had lived on for the previous 20 years in Norway, became their last name in America.

The *Garnås* children used their father's name *Bjørnson* (Bjørn's son) or *Bjørnsdatter* (Bjørn's daughter). The

Ole B. Gornaas	1	10	00
Bjørn O. Gornaas	"	30	00
Iver G Ellestad	"	80	00
Niels B. Gornaas	1	00	00
Nils O Nyhus	"	15	00
~~Endrik B. Gornaas~~	"	45	00
Johannes A Ellestad	"	25	00
Ole O. Nyhus	"	10	00
Gulbrand G. Ellestad	"	80	00
Lars T Haugen	"	15	00
Merkel T. Lunde	"	65	00
Hans B. Gornaas	"	55	00
Thrond Olsen	"	15	00
Lars O Stensgaard	"	2	00
Ole Aslesen	"	4	00
Benjamin Johnsen	"	2	00
Bottel Olsen	"	15	00
Tollef Endresen	"	6	25
Iver Vadla	"	2	00
Peder Eikstad	"	10	00
Bjørn Spande	"	5	00
	6	91	25

18

List of contributors to the first church building fund in 1868

Name		Amount
Iver Thomsen	"	.5 00
Hans Kvalder	"	.2 00
O. Rövang	"	70 00
Ole Halvorsen	"	.5 00
Lars Johnsen	"	.5 00
Ole Larsen	"	.5 00
H. Iversen	"	18 00
Ole S. Berge	"	12 00
John Eriksen	"	.5 00
G. Gabrielsen	"	.5 00
Gulbrand Olsen	"	.6 00
Ole Horten	"	.2 00
Ole Smed	"	.4 00
O. Oarelsen	"	.5 00
Ole Bagli	"	15 00
Morten O. Kjelsberg	"	15 00
Anders P. Forde	"	10 00
Jan P. Forde	"	10 00
Hans Pedersen	"	.5 00
John Andersen	"	.1 00
Ole Andersen Dalles	"	.5 00
Lars Gabrielsen	"	.1 50
		211.50

19

Handwriting of Iver Ellestad, father of Sophie Ellestad

direct translation of the Norwegian word *bjørn* is *bear*. Some of the many Garnås offspring took the last name *Bearson*.

Homestead in North Dakota

Signed by President Abraham Lincoln on May 20, 1862, The Homestead Act of 1862 has been called one of the most important pieces of Legislation in the history of the United States. In all, about 270 million acres or 10% of the United States was claimed and settled under this act. The act granted 160 acres of surveyed public land to citizens who were the head of a family, or at least twenty-one years of age, who would occupy and improve the homestead for five consecutive years.

Great-grandparents to Sylvan, Engebret (*Garnås*) Bearson and Gunhild Syversdatter Krosshaug, after nearly forty years of married life, sold their farm near Mabel, Minnesota. They moved first to Dodge Center, Minnesota, in 1896 and then to Kermott, North Dakota, in 1901, where they filed a homestead claim. It was thought that they moved in their advanced age to ease the pain of losing six children in fifteen years.

Engebret and Gunhild's oldest daughter, Sidsel Bearson and her husband Syvert Bårdsgård, also homesteaded on the North Dakota prairie somewhere between 1901 and 1903. Syvert had emigrated from Selbu, Norway. Their daughter, Stella M. (Baarsgard) Nelson, was born in Bowbells, North Dakota in 1905. When she was three years old, the family returned to Mabel.

Nelson family matriarch

Grandma Stella was the matriarch of our Nelson family. She shared her strong faith in God with her fifteen grandchildren and thirty-three great-grandchildren. She taught Sunday School at Garness and often gave her grandchildren as well as other children in the neighborhood rides to the church. The hundreds of homemade quilts made by her and her daughter, Glorianne Knox, for Lutheran World Relief were a true labor of love.

Grandma Stella lived at Green Lea Manor Nursing Home in Mabel the final four years of her life, still enjoying quilt making. On my last visit to see her, she smiled, gently held my hands, and softly spoke the *Lord's Prayer* in Norwegian. Little did I know that this would be our last time together.

She passed away November 26, 2001, at the age of 96. Grandma Stella made her final journey to the Garness Church on December 1, 2001 where she was laid to rest near her son, Sylvan Nelson.

Reflecting on my ancestors' long journey from Norway to Fillmore County, I realize the sacrifices they made and the hardships they endured were not in vain. Their spirit lives on in the community and in the Garness Church, the beautiful house of worship they helped provide for the generations to come.

• Further information about the Garnås descendants in America can be found in *The Ancestors and Descendants of Bjørn Olson Sata Garnaas 1798-1868 and Sidsel Nilsdatter Nubgaard 1803-1883*, by Oscar Garness, at the Fillmore County Historical Society in Fountain, Minnesota.

Garness kirke har røtter på gården Garnås i Hallingdal

Etableringen av en norsk-luthersk kirke i Amerika

Lydene som hørtes når man lesset av hestene, prustingen og stampingen mens sadlene ble løsnet, var kjente lyder jeg vokste opp med, og de var alle der denne kalde og forblåste dagen, 14. januar 1996. Likevel manglet for meg noe helt vesentlig da hester og ryttere var samlet. Det var min far, Sylvan Nelson, som alltid gikk fra rytter til rytter med et stort smil, tok dem i hånden og fikk alle til å kjenne seg velkomne.

Min fars hest, Star, var uten rytter og ble leid av min nevø, Nathan O' Connor. Sammen med dem på denne siste ferden, fulgte seks medlemmer fra Minnesota Cutting Horse Association, og hver og en tok høytidelig bærerens plass bak vogna med fars kiste. Familie og venner fulgte vogna de vel tre kilometerne oppover åsen fra landsbyen Newburg til Garness kirke i det landlige Mabel i Minnesota.

Min far, Sylvan, døde da han var 67 år gammel. Han var en velkjent farmer i Mabel-Canton-området, tidligere president i Mabel Lions Club, medlem i Kvegeiernes forening og en ivrig rytter siden barndommen. Forut for sykdommen sjekket han kveget hver dag året

Altar painting by Herbjørn N. Gausta

rundt fra hesteryggen, uansett vær. Et årlig "cutting horse-show", et minneløp som gikk over to dager hvor det deltok ryttere fra flere stater, var en begivenhet min far elsket. Det ble ført videre av min mor, Char.

Garness kirke

Tidlig i 1868 ble Den norske evangelisk-lutherske trefoldighetskirken i Newburg etablert i det sørøstlige Minnesota. Den ble bygd på land som var eid og donert av min fars tipp-oldeforeldre, Bjørn Olsen Sata og Sidsel Nilsdatter Nubgarden, som brukte etternavnet Garnås i Amerika. Kirken endret senere navn til Garness lutherske trefoldighetskirke, og ble fullført i 1869 til en kostnad på 1023 dollar.

Kirken står høyt oppe på en landlig ås, og er utsatt for all slags vær. 25. juli 1901 ble den opprinnelige kirken truffet av lynet og brant ned. En ny mursteinskirke ble fullført året etter til en kostnad på vel 5000 dollar. Alteret, rekkverket og prekestolen ble laget i 1902 av L. A. Lund fra Mabel, og kostet 130 dollar. Norsk furu ble plantet rundt kirkegården og står fortsatt der i dag.

Før kirken ble bygget, reiste de norske prestene omkring til fots eller til hest for å avholde gudstjenester i nybyggersamfunnet. En av Garness kirkes hjørnesteiner har innskriften: Pastor Ulrik Vilhelm Koren, fra Washington Præriekirke ved Decorah, var den første pastor som tjente her fra 1854 til 1856. I 1857 ble gudstjenestene avholdt hjemme hos Bjørn og Sidsel Garnås.

De første pionerene brakte med seg en sterk arv fra den lutherske kirken i Norge. Bibelen, salmeboka og katekismen ble brukt hjemme som kilde til trøst og inspirasjon av de første nybyggerne, og hjalp dem til å holde ut pionerlivets motgang og strev.

Den tidlige søndagsgudstjenesten foregikk på norsk og varte i over en time. I mange år var skikken at kirken var delt, slik at kvinner og små barn satt på den ene siden, mens guttene satt sammen med fedrene på den andre siden.

Herbjørn N. Gausta malte altertavlen i Garnesskirken. I 1867 emigrerte han som trettenåring sammen med familien fra Vestfjorddalen i Telemark til en gård i nærheten av Harmony i Minnesota. Han studerte og underviste kunst ved Luther College i Decorah, Iowa, og hadde også studert i Europa. Han er kanskje den mest kjente av de norsk-amerikanske kunstnerne, da han malte om lag 400 altermalerier i norsk-amerikanske kirker.

I 1958 stemte menigheten for å dele prestegård og pastor med Scheie lutherske kirke, som lå i nord. I dag ligger prestegården for de to søsterkirkene i Mabel.

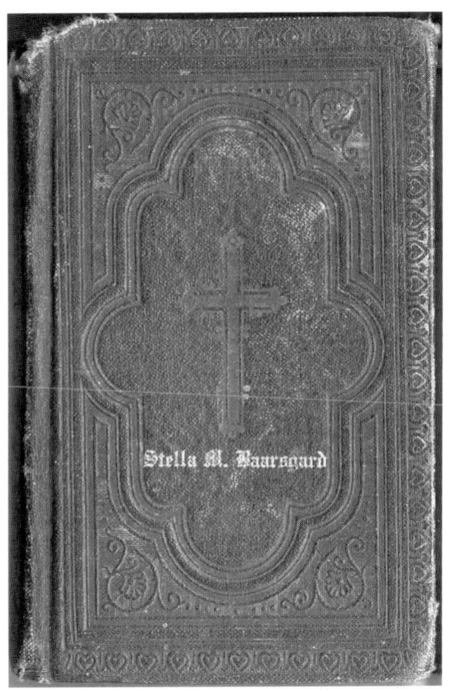

Gården Garnås i Norge

Bjørn og Sidsel nedstammet fra en lang rekke norske bønder fra Ål i Hallingdal. Deres forfedre er i *Aal Bygde Soge* vel dokumentert som bønder (høyt respekterte gårdbrukere og landeiere) gjennom 1600- og 1700-tallet. I 1833 flyttet Bjørn og Sidsel med sine to sønner, Ole og Niels, fra Ål til gården Garnås, som lå i Nes, høyt over Hallingdalen. I løpet av den tiden de eide og drev en liten del av gården Garnås, ble det født fem nye barn: Hans Jørgen, Mari, Engebret (Sylvans oldefar), Guri og Kari.

Det norske gårdsnavnet blir skrevet både som Garnås og som Garnaas. De tre ekstra vokalene æ, ø og å, som følger etter z i det norske alfabetet, skrives på engelsk som henholdsvis ae, oe og aa. Derfor de forskjellige stavemåtene.

Garnås i Amerika

13. juni 1853 forlot Bjørn og Sidsel Nes i Hallingdal sammen med de sju barna, og dro til Amerika. De immigrerte til Rock Prairie, Wisconsin, og i 1854 slo de seg ned i herredet Newburg i Fillmore County, Minnesota. Garnås, som var navn på gården de hadde bodd på i de forutgående 20 årene i Norge, ble deres etternavn i Amerika.

Garnåsbarna brukte familiens navn Bjørnson eller Bjørnsdatter. Fordi det norske ordet *bjørn* på engelsk har betydningen bear, tok mange etterkommere fra Garnås etternavnet *Bearson.*

Nybruk i Nord-Dakota

President Abraham Lincoln signerte 20. mai 1862 "Homestead Act", og den er blitt kalt en av de viktigste lovene i De forente staters historie. I alt ble om lag 1092 millioner dekar, eller 10 prosent av De forente stater, overdratt og bebygd på grunn av denne loven. Loven bevilget 647 dekar med oppmålt offentlig land til borgere som hadde familie å forsørge, eller som var minst 21 år gamle, hvis de tok over og forbedret jorda i fem etterfølgende år.

Oldeforeldrene til Sylvan, Engebret (Garnås) Bearson og Gunhild Syversdatter Krosshaug, solgte etter nærmere førti års ekteskap gården ved Mabel i Minnesota. De flyttet først til Dodge Center i Minnesota i 1896, og så til Kermott i Nord Dakota i 1901, hvor de etablerte et *homestead.* Det ble forstått slik at de flyttet i relativt høy alder for å lette smerten etter å ha mistet seks barn på femten år.

Engebret og Gunhilds eldste datter, Sidsel Bearson, og ektemannen, Syvert Bårdsgård, slo seg også ned på prærien et sted i Nord Dakota mellom 1901 og 1903. Syvert hadde emigrert fra Selbu i Norge. Deres datter Stella M. (Baardsgard) Nelson, ble født i Bowbells, Nord Dakota i 1905. Da hun var tre år, dro familien tilbake til Mabel.

Nelsonfamiliens martriark

Bestemor Stella var Nelsonfamiliens kvinnelige overhode. Hun delte sin sterke tro på Gud med sine femten barnebarn og trettitre oldebarn. Hun holdt søndagsskole i Garness, og gav ofte både egne barnebarn og andre barn i nabolaget skyss til kirken. De flere hundre lappeteppene som hun og datteren, Glorianne Knox, laget for Lutheran World Relief, var laget med kjærlig hånd.

Bestemor Stella bodde på sykehjemmet Green Lea Manor i Mabel de siste fire årene av sitt liv, og hun gledet seg fortsatt over å lage lappetepper. Siste gangen jeg besøkte henne, smilte hun vennlig og tok hendene mine, mens hun med mild stemme sa fram *Fadervår* på norsk. Lite visste jeg da at det skulle bli vårt siste møte.

Hun gikk bort 26. november 2001, 96 år gammel. Bestemor Stella gjorde sin siste reise til Garness kirke 1. desember 2001, hvor hun ble lagt til hvile ved siden av sin sønn, Sylvan Nelson.

Når jeg tenker over mine forfedres lange reise fra Norge til Fillmore County, forstår jeg hvilke offer de gjorde, og at motgangen de holdt ut ikke var forgjeves. Deres ånd lever fortsatt i samfunnet og i Garness kirke, det vakre gudshuset de hjalp til med å få laget for de kommende generasjonene.

• Videre informasjon om etterkommerne fra Garnås i Amerika er å finne ved Fillmore County Historical Society i Fountain, Minnesota, i *The Ancestors and Descendants of Bjørn Olson Sata Garnaas 1798-1868 og Sidsel Nilsdatter Nubgarden 1803-1883*, av Oscar Garness.

1853. Udflyttede, ifra Boru

No.	Datum	Navne	Alder	Tilhvad Sted
22.	2/5	Gjertrud Amundsd.	36.	Amerika
		[illegible] og Børn		
		Gjertrud . . .	22/10 36	
		Ingeborg . . .	18/4 40.	
		Herbrand . . .	27/1 43.	
		Olia . . .	16/3 48.	
27.		Herb. Olsen [illegible]	60.	
		Hustru Gjertrud [illegible]	47.	
29.	30/4.	Birgit Ols d. Gaardtejen?	24/8 29.	Gol.
30.	7/5.	Lavor? Halvorsen Kingle?	52.	Amerika..
		Hustru Margit Lavorsd.	37.	
		Børn Knud	17/8 42.	
		Ingeborg	3/9 46.	
		Margrethe .	12/6 50.	
35.	12/5	Johannes Olsen Bygg	29.	Voss.
		Hustru Berit Halvorsdatter	23½	
37.	30/5	Kari Thorkelsd. [illegible]	16/12 26	Modum.
38.	8/6	Ole Arnesen Bringebretten og Moder	16/2 30	Amerika.
39.		Gulhaug? Nilsdatter	50.	
40.	13/6	Bjørn Olsen Garnaas	54.	Aal
		Hustru Sidsel Nils datter	50.	
		Børn Ola . .	4/9 26	
		Nils . .	2/10 28.	
		Hans .	26/10 34.	
		Mari . .	1/4 37.	
		Engebret . .	16/12 39	
		Guri . .	20/3 42.	
		Kari . .	29/5 48.	

Bjørn Olson Sata Garnås

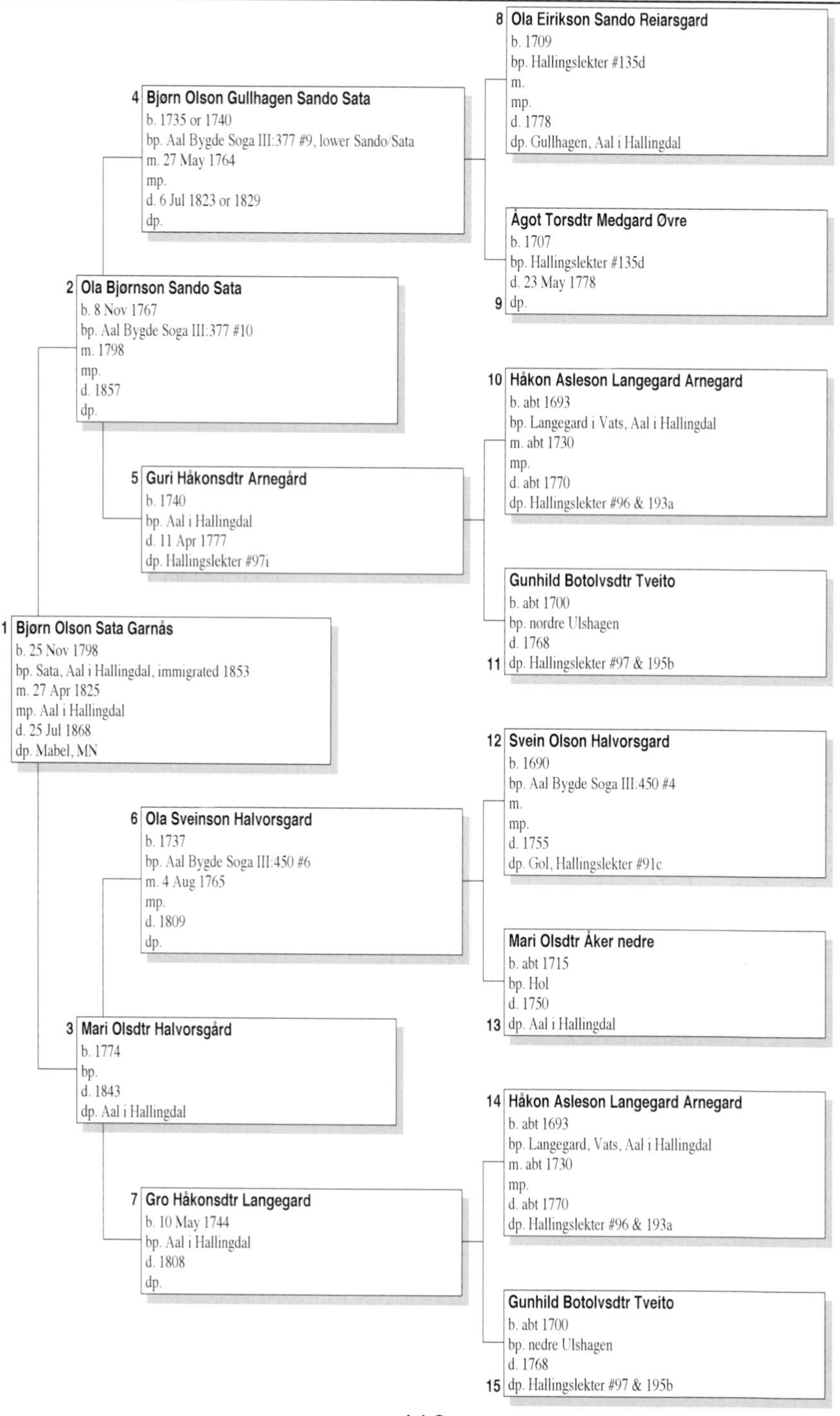

Sidsel Nilsdtr Nubgarden Garnås

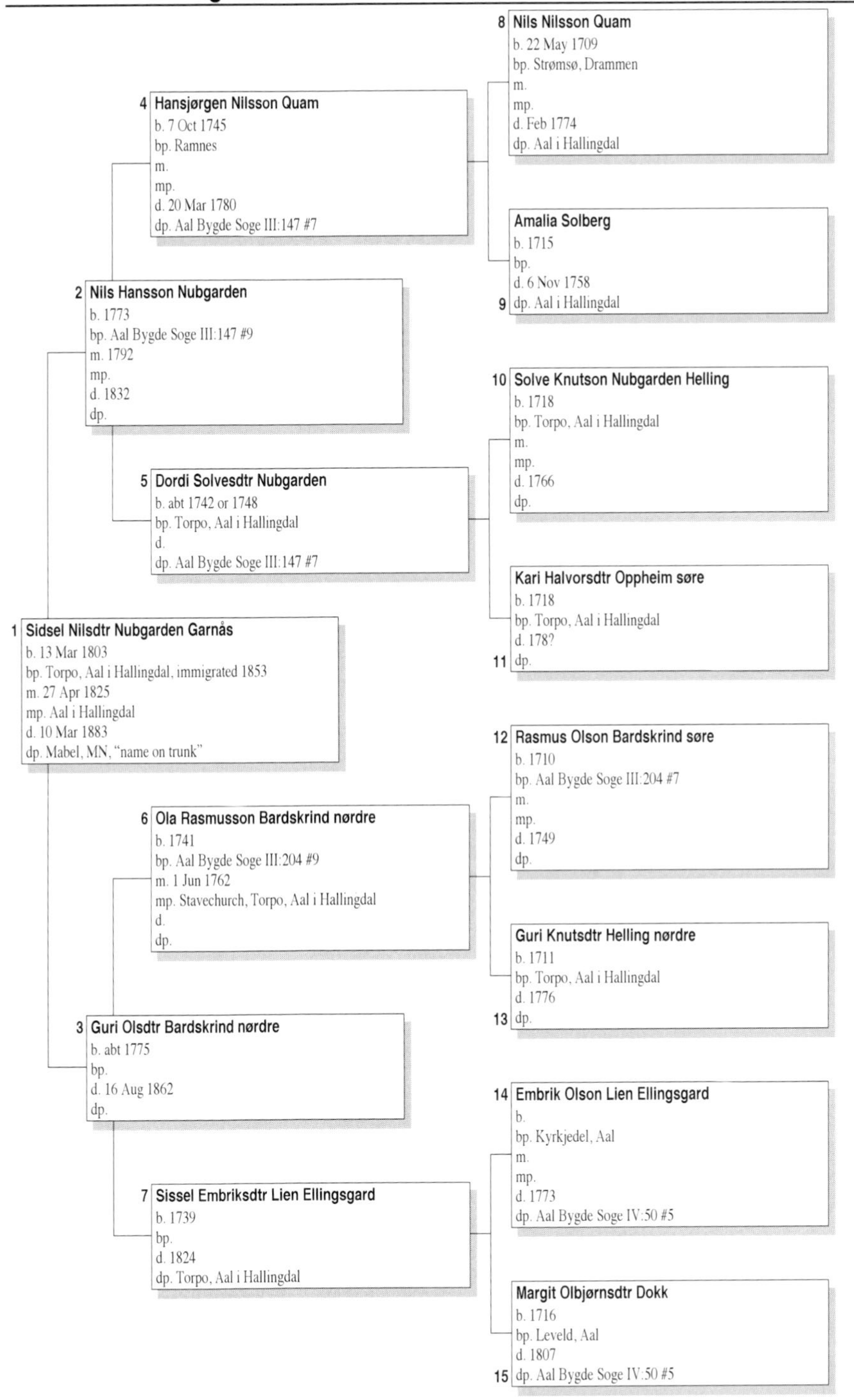

Photo courtesy of Vesterheim Norwegian-American Museum, Decorah, Iowa

Information Request Solved! was reprinted from Vesterheim Genealogical Center and Naeseth Library, Norwegian Tracks, Volume 29, Number 2, July 2004

Information Request Solved!

In the last issue of *Norwegian Tracks* we featured a 1997 Vesterheim acquisition [1997.91.1], a brightly painted cupboard, made in the United States, dated 1853. The names Sjur Hermansen Krosshaug and Helge Olsdatter Høyseth are painted across the top. Their great-great-great granddaughter, Deb Nelson Gourley of Waukon, Iowa, contacted us and supplied the following information taken from her files and from Oscar Garness', *The ancestors and descendants of Bjørn Olson Sato Garnaas, 1798-1868, and Sidsel Nilsdatter Nubgaard, 1803-1883.*

Sjur and Helge immigrated in 1849 and settled briefly at the Luther Valley settlement, Rock Co., Wisconsin, moving in 1850 to the Paint Creek settlement, Allamakee Co., Iowa. By 1853 they were living at Wilmington, Houston Co., Minnesota, later moving to Mabel, Minnesota. Sjur died on March 24, 1890, and his wife, Helga, on November 24, 1888. Both are buried in the Garness Cemetery, Mabel, Minnesota. Their daughter, Gunhild Syversdatter Krosshaug, who died in Kermit, North Dakota, ca. 1910, was married in Spring Grove, Minnesota, on April 6, 1861, to Engebret Bjørnsen Garnaas (Embric B.Garnaas Bearson), born in Nes, Buskerud, December 16, 1839, and died in Mabel, Minnesota, March 6, 1915. Their eight children used the Bearson and Garness names and have many descendants living today in Minnesota and North Dakota.

A special thanks to Deb Nelson Gourley for sharing this information with Vesterheim.

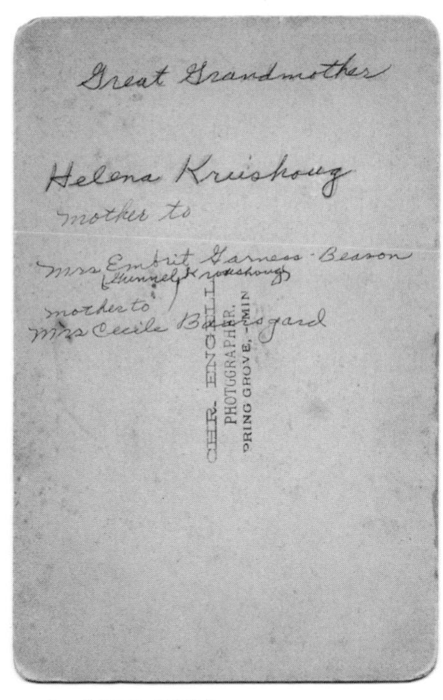

Helge Olsdatter Høyseth, 1812-1889,
the author's great-great-great-grandmother,
picture given to Deb by her grandma Stella M. (Baarsgard) Nelson

The Garness family reunion is held the last Sunday in June at the Sons of Norway building, Lanesboro, Minnesota.

A special thank you to Mervin and Evelyn Vatland for supplying the pictures and history of the original Garness Church organ.

"This organ was built in the 1860s. The church was struck by lightning and burned in 1901, but they were able to save the organ. Sometime in the 1940s it was moved from the Garness Church to the Thompson farm which was located about a mile West of the church. In the early 60s many old organs were being powered with an electric motor/vacuum system. It was at that time I wondered if the organ was still in the Thompson house. Knowing the farm had been sold I talked to the new owner, Lloyd Overland and found out that the organ was sold at the farm sale, but it was never picked up and was still in the house where we put it many years before. Lloyd said he wanted the house for grain and needed the organ moved. We offered to take it and it now is at the residence of Mervin and Evelyn Vatland near Wautoma, WI."

8

Garnås wheel still spinning after 200 years

Exploring the Hallingdal history behind my spinning wheel

Inheriting a 200-year-old *Garnås* family spinning wheel from my grandmother, Stella (Baarsgard) Nelson, was a dream come true. Being an avid handspinner, I could visualize the assembled spinning wheel from the cardboard box full of blue colored wooden parts.

My three-legged Saxon spinning wheel is a double-drive type that can be easily disassembled, transported, and reassembled. In reassembling the wheel I noticed the initials *OSSB* pressed into each individual piece of wood. On a visit to Norway in the summer of 2001, I learned from a staff researcher at the *Nes i Hallingdal Folkemuseum* that the initials belonged to Ola Syverson Breie, a carpenter in *Ål i Hallingdal* who built wheels. According to the *Aal Bygde Soge*, a district history book, the spinning wheel was constructed in the late 1700s or early 1800s.

A large rosemåled trunk, with the words *Sidsel Niels Datter Fød* [born] *1803 Malet* [painted] *1823*, was most likely used to transport my spinning wheel, when my great-great-great-grandparents, Bjørn Olson Sata and Sidsel Nilsdatter Nubgarden, moved in 1833 from their farm in *Ål* to the *Garnås* farm near *Nes i Hallingdal*, where they lived for twenty years. Once again their trunk carried my spinning wheel when they immigrated with their seven children to America in 1853, using *Garnås* for their last name. My father's sister, Glorianne (Gerard) Knox, now owns the distinctive *Hallingdal* trunk.

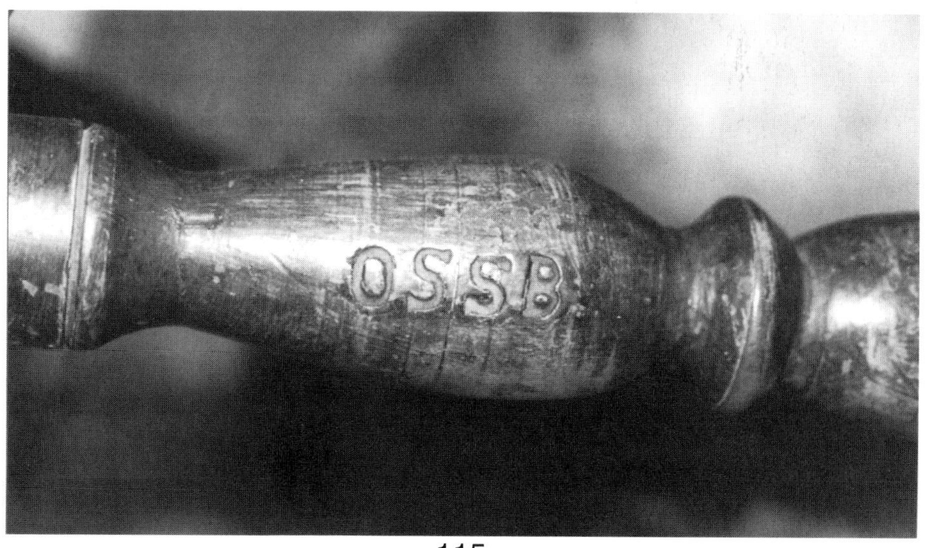

The spinning wheel belonged to the author's great-great-great-grandparents, Bjørn Olson Sata and Sidsel Nielsdatter Nubgarden from Ål i Hallingdal. They lived on the Garnås farm near Nes i Hallingdal for 20 years until they immigrated to America in 1853 and changed their last name to Garness. Pictured spinning in both pictures is the author's great-grand-mother, Sissel Baarsgard.

Sheep to shawl

Until about 1300, yarn was spun on a hand-held spindle. The spinning wheel made its European appearance during the 14th century. The Saxon wheel was introduced about 150 years later and became an important part of everyday living in Norway.

The Saxon spinning wheel was built for productivity by enlarging the driving wheel. A normal day's work can yield about 8,000 yards of single ply yarn. The blue paint on the treadle (foot pedal) of my spinning wheel is extremely worn, indicative of years of spinning by my ancestors. One of these spinners was my great-grandmother, Sidsel (Bearson) Baarsgard. I am fortunate to have a picture of her plying yarn.

I have taken part in several *sheep to shawl* spinning team exhibitions that included shearing, carding, spinning, plying, and weaving the yarn into a shawl. The wool is first sheared from the sheep and then sorted to remove the undesirable fleece. Wool is usually washed, air-dried, and then carded to separate, fluff, and align the fibers. The carded wool is spun into a single yarn. Plying is a process of re-spinning two or more yarns together, which can then be used for knitting, crocheting, or weaving.

Garnås farm saga

According to ancient sagas, *Hallingdal* became a kingdom about the year 800. The first king was *King Hadding*, who lived at *Ål* in the northern part of *Hallingdal*. His son, *Hadding*, married a daughter of the Chieftain of *Garnås* and succeeded him as king. The younger *King Hadding* lived on the *Garnås* farm near *Nes*, giving him an incredible view of the southern part of the *Hallingdal* valley. The name *Hallingdal* thus came from *King Hadding*, the name changing over time from *Hadding* to *Haddingjadal* to *Hallingdal*.

The discovery of iron in *Hallingdal* brought explorers to settle and farm the valley. With the production of quality iron, these *Hallings* could make farm tools and begin trade with other areas. In exchange for salt and fish, the Hallings also supplied iron to the Vikings, who hammered it into their tools and weapons.

In 1349, about one-half of the *Hallingdal* population died from the Black Death (Bubonic Plague) that had spread from Asia to Europe. In 1359-

1360, there was a smallpox epidemic that was followed by two more deadly epidemics. During this time in history, spinning and everyday life, as the Norwegians knew it, came to an abrupt standstill. Crops withered in the fields, farm animals wandered unattended, and panic prevailed.

Iron and coal were extracted on the *Garnås* farm leaving deep pits in the ground. Utilizing their resources, the Hallings then used these empty pits to trap wolves, reindeer, and moose. The pits were in use up to the 1400-1500s on the Garnås farm.

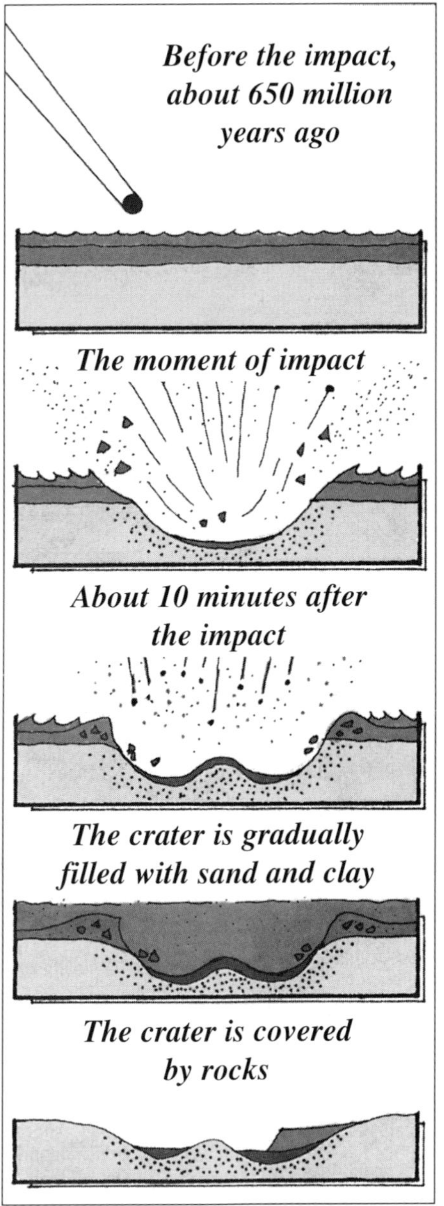

Gardnos meteorite crater Source: Nes kommune i Hallingdal

Garnås meteorite saga

About 650 million years ago, dramatic events took place on what was to become the *Garnås* farm. A meteorite, with the diameter of about 800 feet and a speed of about 600 miles an hour hit the area. The explosion was enormous with an equivalent power equal to several thousand bombs.

A meteorite crater was formed with a diameter of about three miles. The meteorite itself was vaporized and the rocks below the floor of the crater shattered. A type of rock called breccia was formed as fragments pressed and welded together. Most of this new solid rock was full of angular fragments.

Over the next millions of years, the rivers and glaciers changed the topography exposing the breccia far below the base of the original crater. However, it wasn't until 1941 that a geologist noticed the unusual breccia rock and named it *Gardnos breccia* after the *Garnås* farm it was located on.

In 1961, major problems arose when a hydroelectric tunnel was being blasted at *Garnås*. When drilling through the *Garnås breccia*, the boreheads wore down very rapidly and explosives did not produce the expected results.

Final conclusive proof that a meteorite had landed on what would eventually be the *Garnås* farm came in September 1990. The existence of special shock structures in the quartz grains was confirmed under the microscope: *Norway had gotten its first and, to date, only meteorite crater on land.* Source: *Gardnos Meteorittkrater, Hallingdal Geologipark, Nesbyen, Norway.*

200 years of ancestral spinning

My ancestral wheel has been passed down many generations, from Bjørn and Sidsel to their son Engebret (*Garnås*) Bearson, to his daughter Sidsel (Bearson) Baarsgard, to her daughter Stella (Baarsgard) Nelson, and finally to Stella's granddaughter, me.

Amidst the backdrop of fascinating Hallingdal history, the *Garnås* wheel has been spinning for more than 200 years. Still, no generations have spun straw into gold. Perhaps that strange little medieval man, Rumplestiltskin, will yet appear to help this *Garnås* granddaughter with her spinning.

Garnåsrokken spinner fortsatt etter 200 år

Familierokken forteller Hallingdalhistorie

Da jeg arvet den 200 år gamle familierokken etter min bestemor, Stella (Baarsgaard) Nelson, ble en drøm til virkelighet. Ettersom jeg var en ivrig håndspinner, kunne jeg over en pappeske full av blåmalte trebiter se for meg den fullstendige rokken.

Min treleggede saksiske rokk er en dobbeltdrevet type som lett kan demonteres, transporteres og settes sammen igjen. Da jeg monterte hjulet la jeg merke til initialene *OSSB*, som var presset inn i hver enkelt trebit. På et besøk i Norge i 2001 fikk jeg av en stabsforsker ved Folkemuseet i Nes i Hallingdal vite at initialene hørte til Ola Syverson Breie, en snekker fra Ål i Hallingdal som bygde hjul. I følge *Aal Bygde soge*, en lokalhistoriebok, ble rokken konstruert sent på 1700-tallet eller tidlig på 1800-tallet.

En stor rosemalt kiste med innskriften Sidsel Niels Datter [Fød] 1803 Malet 1823, ble sannsynligvis brukt for å transportere rokken min da mine tipp-tipp-oldeforeldre, Bjørn Olson Sata og Sidsel Nilsdatter Nubgarden, i 1833 flyttet fra gården i Ål til Garnåsgården ved Nes i Hallingdal, der de bodde i tjue år. Nok en gang bar kisten deres rokken da de i 1853 emigrerte til Amerika med sine sju barn, og tok Garnås som etternavn. Min fars søster, Glorianne (Gerard) Knox, eier nå den karakteristiske kisten fra Hallingdal.

Fra sau til sjal

Til om lag 1300 ble garnet spunnet på håndteiner. Rokken dukket opp i Europa i løpet av det 14. århundre. Det saksiske hjulet ble introdusert om lag 150 år senere og ble en viktig del av dagliglivet i Norge.

Den saksiske rokken ble bygd for å øke produktiviteten, hvilket ble oppnådd ved å gjøre drivhjulet større. En normal dags arbeid kan gi mer enn 7300 meter med enkeltspunnet garn. Den blå malingen på trøa på min rokk er svært slitt, noe som forteller om mine forgjengeres år ved rokken. En av disse spinnerne var min oldemor, Sidsel (Bearson) Baardsgaard. Jeg er så heldig å ha et bilde av henne når hun arbeider med garn.

Jeg har deltatt på flere spinneteamutstillinger som følger ulla fra sau til sjal, og som innbefatter klipping, karing, spinning, tvinning og bruk av garnet for å veve sjal. Ulla blir først klippet av sauen og så sortert for å fjerne uegnet materiale. Ulla blir vanligvis vasket, lufttørket og så karet til luftige, separate dotter hvor fibrene ligger i samme retning. Den karede ulla spinnes så til en enkel tråd. Tvinningen er en prosess der man spinner to eller flere tråder sammen, slik at garnet kan bli brukt til strikking, hekling eller veving.

Garnåsgårdens saga

I følge gamle sagaer ble Hallingdal et kongerike rundt 800. Den første kongen var kong Hadding, som levde i Ål i den nordlige delen av Hallingdalen. Hans sønn, Hadding, giftet seg med en datter av høvdingen på Garnås, og etterfulgte ham som konge. Den yngre kong Hadding levde på gården Garnås ved Nes, hvor han hadde en utrolig utsikt ut over den sørlige delen av Hallingdalen. Navnet Hallingdal kom dermed fra kong Hadding, da navnet over tid endret seg av Hadding til Haddingjadal og videre til Hallingdal.

Oppdagelsen av jern i Hallingdalen førte til at oppdagere bosatte seg og drev jordbruk i dalen. Ettersom de kunne produsere jern av god kvalitet, kunne disse hallingene også lage jordbruksredskaper av jern, og de etablerte handel med andre områder. I bytte mot salt og fisk, forsynte hallingene også vikingene med jern, og de hamret det om til verktøy og våpen.

I 1349 døde om lag halvparten av Hallingdalens befolkning av svartedauden (byllepesten) som hadde spredt seg fra Asia til Europa. I 1359-1360 kom det også en koppe-epidemi, som ble fulgt av to mer dødbringende epidemier. I løpet av denne tiden av historien ble spinningen og hverdagslivet slik nordmennene kjente det, brått satt tilbake. Avlingene visnet på markene, gårdsdyrene vandret omkring uten tilsyn og panikken spredte seg.

Jern og kull ble hentet ut på gården Garnås, og utvinningen etterlot seg dype groper i grunnen. For å utnytte ressursene brukte hallingene de tomme gropene for å fange ulv, reinsdyr og elg. Gropene var i bruk opp til 1400-1500-tallet på Garnåsgården.

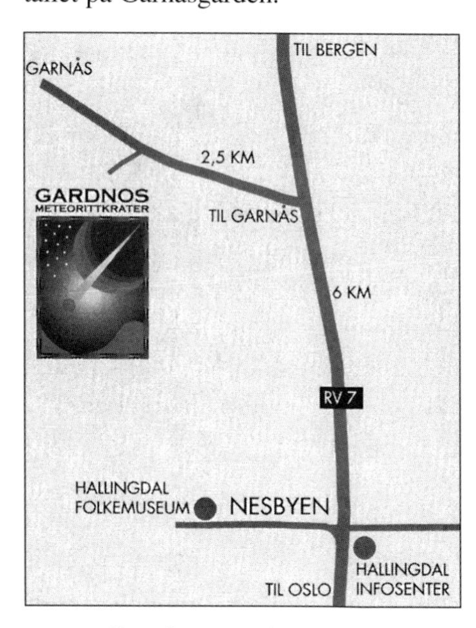

Garnåsmeteorittens saga

For rundt 650 millioner år siden skjedde det en dramatisk begivenhet der gården Garnås skulle komme til å ligge.

Steinar and Anna

Char Nelson and Kåre

A special thank you from both Deb and Char to the following for their genealogy assistance over the years:

- *Gene Estensen*
- *Blaine Hedberg*
- *Sigmund Sevre*
- *Kåre Sønsterud*
- *Steinar Vissebråten*
- *Terje Østro*

Sigmund and Deb

En meteoritt med en diameter på 244 meter og en fart på om lag 965 kilometer i timen, traff området. Eksplosjonen var enorm, og hadde samme kraft som flere tusen bomber.

Det ble skapt et meteorittkrater med en diameter på drøyt 4.8 kilometer. Meteoritten selv gikk i oppløsning og berget under kratergulvet ble knust. En type stein, kalt breccia, ble skapt av at fragmenter ble presset og sveiset sammen. Det meste av dette nye, solide berget var fullt av vinkelformede fragmenter.

I løpet av de neste millioner av år, forandret elver og isbreer topografien og blottla brecciaen langt under der den originale bunnen i krateret hadde ligget. Likevel var det ikke før i 1941 at en geolog oppdaget den uvanlige brecciasteinen og ga den navnet *Gardnos breccia*, etter gården Garnås hvor den befant seg.

I 1961 oppstod det store problemer da det skulle sprenges ut en hydroelektrisk tunnel ved Garnås. Da de boret seg gjennom Garnåsbrecciaen ble borehodene fort slitt ned, og eksplosiver ga ikke de forventede resultater.

Det endelige bevis på at en meteoritt hadde landet på det som skulle bli gården Garnås, kom i september 1990. Tilstedeværelsen av spesielle sjokkstrukturer i kvartskornene ble slått fast under mikroskopet: *Norge hadde fått sitt første og så langt eneste meteorittkrater på land.* Kilde: *Gardnos Meteorittkrater, Hallingdal Geologipark, Nesbyen, Norge.*

200 års spinnehistorie

Mitt slektshjul er blitt overlevert gjennom mange generasjoner, fra Bjørn og Sidsel til deres sønn, Engebret (Garnås) Bearson, til hans datter, Sidsel (Bearson) Baardsgard, til hennes datter, Stella (Baardsgard) Nelson, og til sist til meg, som er Stellas barnebarn.

Med Hallingdalens fascinerende historie som bakteppe, har Garnåsrokken spunnet i mer enn 200 år. Ennå har ingen generasjon spunnet halm til gull. Kanskje vil den merkelige lille middelaldermannen, Rumleskaft, snart dukke opp for å hjelpe denne etterkommeren fra Garnås med å spinne.

9

Hallingdal Rosemaling

Rosemaling on my great-great-great-grandmother's trunk by Nils Bæra, son of Herbrand Sata

During April 2004 I had the pleasure of meeting my distant relative, Nils Ellingsgard, from Norway for the first time. Nils was one of the keynote speakers at the first international rosemaling symposium, *The Art of Rosemaling: Tradition Meets the Creative Mind*, hosted by the Vesterheim Norwegian-American Museum, Decorah, Iowa.

I am very grateful to Nils for his

First International Rosemaling Symposium, *The Art of Rosemaling: Tradition Meets the Creative Mind*, during April 2004. Left to right: Harley Refsal, Sigmund Aarseth, Deb Nelson Gourley, Nils Ellingsgard, and Alex Huntrods. ***(Photo by Charlie Langton, courtesy of Vesterheim Norwegian-American Museum, Decorah, Iowa)***

identification of the trunk that my great-great-great-grandparents, Bjørn Olson Sata and Sidsel Nilsdatter Nubgarden, brought to America in 1853 (see Garness Church and Garnås spinning wheel stories). The outside of the trunk was decorated by Nils Herbrandson Bæra; however, the rosemaling on the inside of the lid is unknown.

I give special thanks to Nils Ellingsgard for allowing me to reprint his text on the Sata-Bæra school. To my aunt, Glorianne (Gerard) Knox, who owns this enormous five-feet-long by three-feet-wide by three-feet-deep trunk, a heartfelt thanks for letting me have the trunk photographed by Eaton Cote, Photographic Arts, Waukon, Iowa.

Herbrand Sata and his sons, Nils and Embrik Bæra, created a tradition generally referred to as the Sata-Bæra school, the very core of the Hallingdal style. The following information about them is taken from *Norsk Rosemåling: Dekorativ måling i folkekunsten* (Det Norske Samlaget, Oslo, 1999, p. 134-139) by Nils Ellingsgard.

(Translated by James Skurdall)

Glorianne (Gerard) Knox

The Sata-Bæra School

Herbrand Sata (1753-1830) from Sando in Ål is one of the most distinguished names in Norwegian folk art. As an independent artist and the creator of a regional style, he held a special position at the height of the classical period. His earliest known work dates from the end of the 1770s, so he was close to thirty years old before he emerged as a mature painter. His technical proficiency and his intimate knowledge of rococo style suggest that he had come in direct contact with urban artists. He had completely absorbed the new style and he stood on equal footing with skilled urban artists in his mastery of rocaille ornamentation, yet he could hardly have had any systematic training. A sense of naive hesitancy in his figures and images would seem to confirm this, even though he achieved more in this area than most of the other Hallingdal painters. An examination of old church walls reveals that he did decorative painting in the stave churches in both Ål and Nes.

To Charlotte Nelson
with best wishes.
Decorah, 1978.

Nils Ellingsgard.

Kista er måla av
Nils H. Boera (1785-
1873), Ål.
Innvendig: ukjent
målar.

ROSEMÅLING
I HALLINGDAL

To my cousin Deb Nelson Gourley
from Nils Ellingsgard

Decorah, April 2004

The 1790s were a particularly active and important period for Herbrand Sata as a painter. That decade was a golden age of rococo in Hallingdal and other rural areas. The style had fully established itself in the eastern part of Norway, and rural communities continued to enjoy an economic boom. One is struck by the large number of decorative paintings dating from the 1790s, whether as room interiors, or on trunks, cupboards, and bowls. In Hallingdal it was above all Herbrand Sata who set the standard. He cultivated his rococo style on trunks more than room interiors, and the trunks most easily allow us to study his development in the years that followed.

Immediately prior to the turn of the century we see that Sata was trying to find a more independent means of artistic expression. He may have begun to tire of the playfulness of rococo, but for whatever reason, he distanced himself more and more from the urban style from that time forward. This emancipation took place around the same time in Hallingdal and Telemark, but the two styles developed quite distinctly from one another in their respective districts. The Telemark painters continued to base their work on the asymmetrical rococo style, while Herbrand Sata returned to the flowers and vine tendrils of the baroque. He discarded rococo elements for the most part and painted his ornaments in a more symmetrical manner. (There are hints of the new Louix XVI style as well.) The flowers on the front of the trunk are arranged around a vertical axis with a primary motif in the center. But this central motif was seldom the same on each half of the trunk. The floral motif on the trunk lid was most often cross-symmetrical with a dominant flower or rosette in the middle.

Around the time that these changes in composition were taking place, there were also new developments in the stylization of surfaces, lines, and brush strokes. This represented yet another step away from urban rococo in the direction of the fully developed Hallingdal style. The flowers were unfolded in such a manner that they could be viewed either from the side or straight on. Tulips and roses were no longer depicted naturally with the effect of light and shadow, but rather produced in a play of C- and S-curves and simple brush strokes. Black foliage and leaves protruded from behind the petals. This legacy from the baroque was a distinctive element of the emerging Hallingdal style.

After the turn of the century, Herbrand Sata had settled into a style

that was well-established in its main features. But it never became rigid. He continued to experiment with new ideas in motifs, colors, and techniques. He might produce one painting in bold and vigorous strokes, then take great pains with the next, embroidering the pattern with droplets, dots, and small flowers. Characteristic for Herbrand Sata is a technique he began using around 1805 believed to be particular to him—a kind of "floral pointillism," in which each petal is created from an abundance of small white flecks closely packed in a shiny base color.

It was Herbrand Sata who shaped the Hallingdal style, and his sons, Nils

and Embrik Bæra, who perpetuated and continued to develop it. *Nils H. Bæra* (1785-1873) had been a rural schoolteacher as a young man, and he was called "School-Nils" for the rest of his life. He is remembered as a unique and colorful character, a man of eccentric qualities and a genuine artist temperament. No doubt he began learning from his father at an early age, and around 1820 he emerged as a painter in his own right. At that time he was still under the influence of his father's style, without the tidy lines and greater attention to detail that he later developed. Toward the end of the 1820s, he cultivated his own distinctive rococo style. Using blue as the primary color, he framed his wall and ceiling pictures in large laciniated cartouches (for example, Myking, 1827, and Sand, 1828, Norwegian Folk Museum). He did this twenty to thirty years after his father, Herbrand Sata, had abandoned the style forever, and forty to fifty years after it had gone out of fashion in Norwegian towns. Rococo elements became visible again in Nils Bæra's later work as well, but in a radically altered, almost schematic form, arranged symmetrically around the vertical central axis.

Some elements of Louix XVI and Empire styles are found in his painting beginning around 1835, usually as palmette borders used to frame wall depictions of biblical figures (for example, Bakkestova, 1855, Ål Bygdemuseum).

But this neoclassicism did not lead to innovations in Hallingdal rose painting. The style was fully developed by around 1830, and it did not incorporate many new elements after that.

What especially distinguishes the style of Nils Bæra from that of his father, Herbrand Sata, is the highly developed calligraphic play of lines in outlines and ornamentation. Nils was a matchless calligrapher and brush virtuoso. The fine, supple writing brush was an extremely important tool for his decorative art. He was the technical master par excellence and he set the standard for other painters in Upper Hallingdal. Today, when we examine the hundreds of registered works of "School-Nils," we must acknowledge that he looms large in the world of rose painting, both as technician and colorist. Equally impressive is the fact that he seems never to have painted two things alike, something certainly difficult to avoid in the course of a long career. This is true for his cupboards and trunks, and even more so for the countless ale bowls he decorated. His imagination was seemingly inexhaustible, yet he confined himself to the limits of the Hallingdal style, and in particular to its strict symmetric and concentric principles of composition. He must have poured his soul into every little piece.

In the decoration of interiors he often used figures, usually taken from biblical scenes that he found in books and graphic prints. These figures are drawn with a sure hand, yet they show strong traces of the *naivism* found in folk art. There is a marked distance between his pictures and the brilliant mastery he displays in ornamentation.

Embrik Bæra (1788-1876) was three years younger and somewhat overshadowed by his older brother. Although he was not of the same caliber purely in terms of technique, he was nonetheless in the variation of his motifs and the richness of his imagination equally successful. Embrik's work

Sidsel Niels Datter
Fød (born) 1803
Malet (painted) 1823

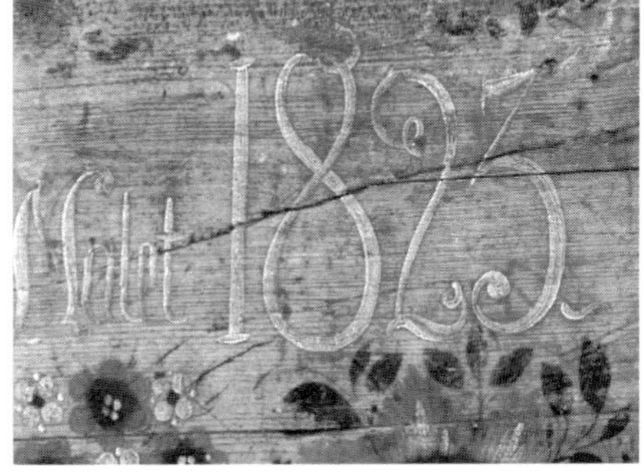

bears witness to a more solid and brooding disposition. He was a quiet-mannered, hardworking, earnest-minded, and deeply religious man. For his pictures he had a large repertoire of biblical motifs at his disposal—free renderings of his prototypes without concern for anatomy and proportion. These naive figures are often a powerful expression of simple religious pathos.

The years from around 1825 to 1850 were his most interesting and experimental period. In his later years he seemed to lose something of his sense of color. One distinctive feature was his almost exaggerated interest in yellow. He would sometimes work with two or three shades of yellow in the same composition, a predilection shared by some of the younger painters who tried to imitate him. To some extent Embrik Bæra's painting shows traces of the decline that characterized the late 1800s.

The Norwegian-American Museum
502 West Water Street
DECORAH, IOWA 52101
Tel. (319) 382-9681

August 20, 1991

Debbie Nelson Huntrods
R.R. 1, Box 143
Canton, Minnesota 55922

Dear Debbie,

Lila felt bad that the sails occupied her so much yesterday that she did not have time to talk. I am glad you left the information. It looks to me as if you might be in line with the painter Herbjørn Sata. I am sending your letter and the additional information to Nils Ellingsgard for analysis. He knows the genealogy of the painters well, primarily of Sata because he also descends from that line on his mother's side. I will try to get up and see the trunk owned by Mrs. Richard Knox. I think I could tell if it is by either Herbjørn or one of his two painter sons. I think they were all active in 1823. In fact, one of them was Niels, who later took the name Baera. I am meeting with Nils in Oslo about three weeks from now. By then he should have had time to go over this and comment.

I believe we already have some material from your family in the Museum. This includes a trunk from the 1600s in stave construction, a rare technique for an object of its size. It came from the Garness family in Mabel but was said to have Sata connections. A fine box bench on the second floor of the Museum is also from the Garness farm north of Mabel. I bought it for the Museum at an auction in the area years ago. You maybe have more information that should be here. Mine is sketchy.

Thank you for supplying this information and for keeping in touch with Vesterheim. It could be that Nils Ellingsgard would want a photograph of your aunt's trunk for the book he is writing on early Norwegian rosemaling in America. If time allows, I will try to get a simple photograph of it so he can try to determine who the painter was.

Sincerely,

Marion Nelson
Director

MJN:ln

Hallingdal Rosemaling

Min tipp-tipp oldemors rosemalte kiste, malt av Nils Bæra, sønn av Herbrand Sata

Av Nils Ellingsgard
Norsk Rosemåling: Dekorativ måling i folkekunst-en (Det Norske Samlaget, Oslo, 1999, p. 134-139)

Sata-Bæra-skolen

Herbrand Sata (1753-1830) frå Sando i Ål er eit av dei store namna i norsk folkekunst. Som sjølvstendig kunstnar og lokal stilskapar står han i ei særstilling midt i den klassiske blømingsperioden. Dei tidlegaste kjende arbeida hans skriv seg frå slutten av 1770-åra. Han var altså nærare tretti år før han stod fram som fullært målar. Den tekniske kunnskapen og kjennskapen til rokokkostilen han legg for dagen kan tyde på at han var i direkte kontakt med bykunsten. Han forstod den nye stilen fullt ut og meistra rocaille-ornamentikken på høgd med faglærte bymålarar. Men noka regulær læretid hadde han neppe hatt. Figurar og bilde verkar for naivt usikre til det, sjølv om han også på dette feltet nådde lenger enn hallingmålarar flest. Gransking av gamle veggtiler viser at han har utført dekor i stavkyrkjene både i Ål og Nes.

1790-åra var ein særleg aktiv og viktig periode for Herbrand Sata som målar. Dette tiåret var ei blømingstid i bygderokokkoen både i Hallingdal og andre stader. På Austlandet hadde stilen slege gjennom for godt og bygdene naut godt av eit vedvarande økonomisk oppsving. Påfallande mange målararbeid er daterte i 1790-åra, frå heile stoveinteriør til kister, skåp og bollar. I Hallingdal er det først og fremst Herbrand Sata som slår an tonen. Det er på kistene, meir enn i interiøret, han dyrkar rokokkoen mest ekte, og det er på kistene vi lettast kan følgje utviklinga hans i åra framover.

Like før hundreårsskiftet merkar vi hjå Sata ein trong til ei meir sjølvstendig uttrykksform. Kanskje tok han til å trøytna av rokokkoleiken, og frå no av er målinga hans i ferd med å frigjere seg frå bystilen. Denne frigjeringa skjer omtrent samstundes i Hallingdal og Telemark, men stilutviklinga tek ulike vegar i dei to distrikta. Telemarksmålarane byggjer framleis på den asymmetriske rokokkoen som grunnform, medan Herbrand Sata søkjer attende til barokkens blome- og rankeflora. Han skuvar rokokkoformene meir eller mindre til sides og byggjer ornamentet opp etter symmetriske grunnprinsipp. (Det er også mogleg at den "nye" louis-seize stilen har gjeve visse impulsar.) På framsida er kisterosene komponerte kring ein vertikal akse med eit sentralt motiv i midten. Men midtmotivet er sjeldan likt på kvar kistehalvpart. Loket får oftast kross-symmetrisk motiv med ein dominerande blome eller rosett i sentrum.

Omtrent samstundes med omlegginga i komposisjonen, går det føre seg ei stilisering i flater, liner og strøk. Dette er endå eit steg bort frå byrokokkoen mot den seinare fullt utvikla hallingstilen. Blomane blir bretta ut i flater slik at vi ser dei anten frå sida eller midt imot. Tulipanar og torneroser blir ikkje lenger naturalistisk skildra med lys- og skuggeverknad, men forma i C- og S-liner og enkle penselstrøk. Svarte blekkjer og lauv stikk fram mellom kronblada. Denne arven frå blomebarokken vart eit særmerk element i den framtidige hallingstilen.

Etter hundreårskiftet ser vi at Herbrand Sata har funne fram til ein stil som i hovuddraga er nokolunde fastlagd. Men han stivnar aldri til. Støtt eksperimenterer han vidare med nye påfunn i motiv, farge og teknikk. Stundom er målinga enkelt utført i djerve, saftige strøk. Andre gonger legg han stor flid i arbeidet og broderer mønsteret ut med droplar, prikkar og småblomar. Karakteristisk for Herbrand Sata, og han åleine, er ein teknikk han tek i bruk frå om lag 1805: eit slag "blomepointillisme" der kvart kronblad er forma av ei mengd små, kvite fargeklattar, lagde tett i tett i våt underfarge.

Det var Herbrand Sata som markerte hovudlinene i hallingstilen. Sønene hans, Nils og Embrik Bæra, førte linene

vidare og bygde stilen ut. *Nils H. Bæra* (1785-1873) var omgangsskulelærar i ungdomen og gjekk sidan under namnet “Skule-Nils.” I bygdesoga har han vorte ståande som ein original og fargerik figur, ein ekte kunstnarnatur med eksentriske drag. Truleg kom han tidleg i lære hjå far sin, men det er først frå om lag 1820 vi kjenner han som sjølvstendig målar. Då er han enno sterkt prega av farens stil, utan den sirlege lineteikninga og større detaljrikdomen han seinare la seg til. I slutten av 1820-åra dyrka han rokokkostilen i si eiga personlege form. Med blått som hovudfarge ramma han inn vegg- og takbilde i store, flikute kartusjar (t.d. Myking 1827 og Sand 1828, Norsk Folkemuseum). Dette skjer 20-30 år etter at far hans, Herbrand Sata, hadde lagt stilen til sides for godt, og 40-50 år etter at stilen var gått av moten i norske byar. Også i Nils Bæras seinare arbeid kjem rokokkoelement til syne, men då i ei radikalt omdikta og nærast skjematisk form, ordna symmetrisk kring den vertikale midtaksen.

Frå om lag 1835 får rosemålinga hans nokre innslag av louis-seize og empire, helst som palmettborder kring veggbilde med bibelske figurar (t.d. Bakkestova 1855, Ål bygdemuseum). Nokon nyskapande verknad fekk likevel ikkje nyklassisismen i hallingdalsk rosemåling. Lokalstilen var fullt utvikla kring 1830 og tok seinare imot få impulsar utanfrå.

Det som særleg skil Nils Bæra frå Herbrand Sata i stilen er det høgt utvikla kalligrafiske linespelet i konturar og utsiring. Nils var ein makelaus skriftkunstnar og penselvirtuos. Den fine, spenstige skrivepenselen var ein overmåte viktig reiskap i heile hans dekorative kunst. Han var den tekniske meisteren framom alle, og det store førebildet for andre målarar i øvre Hallingdal. Om vi i dag saumfer dei hundrevis av registrerte arbeid som finst att etter Skule-Nils, må vi erkjenne at han ruver i rosekunsten, både som teknikar og kolorist. Like imponerande er det å konstatere at han så godt som aldri målar to ting like, noko som må

vera vanskeleg å unngå gjennom eit langt målarliv. Dette gjeld for skåp og kister, og endå meir for det utal av ølbollar han er meister for. Fantasien synest utømmeleg, men han held seg alltid innanfor stilramma og det strengt symmetriske og konsentriske komposisjonsprinsippet i hallingstilen. Han må ha lagt si sjel i kvar minste ting.

I romprydnaden nyttar han ofte figurar, helst bibelske scener etter førebilde i bøker og grafiske trykk. Figurane er nokolunde sikkert teikna, men likevel prega av folkekunstens naivisme. Det er stor avstand mellom bilda og den suverene meisterskapen han viser i ornamentikken.

Embrik Bæra (1788-1876) var tre år yngre og kom litt i skuggen av storebror Nils. Han var heller ikkje av same format reint teknisk, men nådde like langt i motivvariasjon og fantasirikdom. Arbeida til Embrik vitnar om ein tyngre og traustare karakter. Han var ein stillfarande, strevsam alvorsmann og djupt religiøs. I bildemålinga rådde han over eit stort repertoar av bibelske motiv, fritt omdikta etter førebilda og utan sut for anatomi og proporsjonar. Desse naive figurscenene eig ofte eit sterkt uttrykk med einfelt religiøs patos.

Den mest interessante og eksperimenterande perioden er åra frå ca. 1825 til 1850. I eldre år synest fargesansen hans å ha tapt seg noko. Eit eige trekk er den nesten overdrivne interessa for gult. To-tre gultonar i ein og same komposisjon kunne han stundom varte opp med. Og nokre av dei yngre målarane tok etter han i dette. I ein viss grad vart målinga til Embrik Bæra prega av forfallet på slutten av 1800-talet.

10

Snowshoe Thompson "Gone but not forgotten"

Mail carrying Norwegian-American hero of the Sierra Nevada Mountains

With daring and courage, John A. Thompson answered this advertisement in the *Sacramento Union* newspaper during the fall of 1855: *"People lost to the world, Uncle Sam needs a mail carrier."* The Norwegian immigrant became a one-man U.S. Postal Service on skis (called snow-shoes in the mining camps), crossing the 90-mile trek across the high Sierras from Placerville, California to Carson Valley, Nevada. For 20 years, he delivered the mail to gold miners isolated from the rest of the world, when the mountain passes were closed because of snow.

The narrow Sierra Nevada Mountain range is about 400 miles long and has over 100 peaks topping 13,000 feet, including one at 14,495 feet, the highest peak in the United States outside of Alaska. Thousands of California-bound gold-seekers and immigrants in the middle and late 1800's used Donner Pass, the principal route across the mountains. During the winter of 1846 to 1847, the infamous *"Donner Party"* became trapped in this mountain range. From 1856 to 1876, Snowshoe Thompson made his *"Snow-Shoe Express"* the counterpart of the *"Pony Express."*

Photos by Gene Estensen

25-pound skis

In 1851, then 24, John A. Thompson headed to California to stake his claim. While cutting down an oak tree on his Putah Creek, Sacramento Valley farm in the fall of 1855, it is said that Thompson hit upon the idea of making a pair of skis or snow-skates from his childhood memories in Norway.

Unlike the snowshoes of the North American Indians or Canadians, Thompson's skis were about ten feet long, four inches wide, made of green oak, and weighed 25 pounds. Only fastened by a single strap over the toe of the boot, they were the first Norwegian skis seen in California.

Standing six feet tall and weighing 180 pounds, Thompson had no problem with the heavy skis. With his blond hair and beard, fair skin, and blue eyes, he looked like a genuine Viking.

In response to the cries for mail from the people living east of the Sierra Nevada Mountains, Thompson began practicing on his skis. After a short while, he set off for Placerville and offered his service to Uncle Sam as a mail carrier. During his January 3, 1856 departure on the first trip across the mountain, an optimistic voice yelled out *"Good Luck Snow-shoe Thompson"* and the name stuck.

Traversing the high Sierra

John A. "Snowshoe" Thompson certainly was a true flesh-and-blood character, but because of the countless stories written about him, it has become impossible to completely separate fact-from-fiction and history-from-legend. Dan De Quille a.k.a. William Wright, editor of Virginia City's *Territorial Enterprise*, was a friend of Thompson's and wrote about his 90-mile trek. Under De Quille's tutelage was young Samuel Clemens a.k.a Mark Twain.

Ten years after Snowshoe Thompson died, a story about him appeared in the *Overland Monthly* of October 1886 by Dan De Quille. George Wharton James quoted De Quille's 1886 story in the 1910 book *Heroes of California*, from which I have sourced many of his adventures.

Snowshoe Thompson was one of the most remarkable and fearless of all the Pacific Coast mountaineers. By both day and night he braved the winter storms, gliding over fields of snow that were in places 30 to 50 feet deep. Due to numerous steep climbs, it took three days to ski eastward, from Placerville to Carson Valley. The return westward trip required only two days, skiing 45 miles per day.

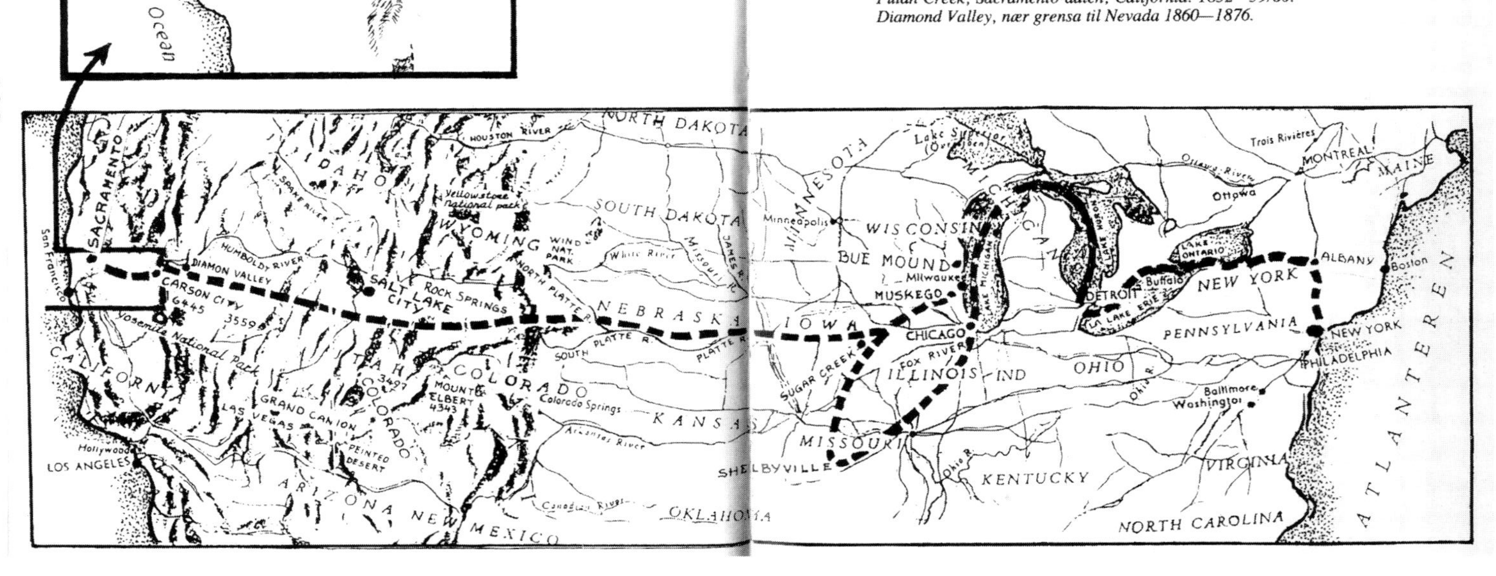

VEGEN MOT VEST

Dette er Jons opphaldsstader i Amerika:

New York: Her steig Rue-følgjet i land 15. august 1837. Truleg reiste dei opp Hudson-elva gjennom Eric kanalen til Buffalo. Derifrå over dei store sjøane til Chicago, dit kom dei i september.

Fox River, Illinois: Vinteren 1837—38 var dei i settlementet Fox River i Illinois.

Shellbyville, Missouri: Frå våren 1838 til -40.

Sugar Creek, Iowa: Frå 1840—46.

I Wisconsin 1846—51: Nær tilknytning til Blue Mound Settlement.

Til California: Våren 1851.

Putah Creek, Sacramento-dalen, California. 1852—59/60.

Diamond Valley, nær grensa til Nevada 1860—1876.

De Quille told of Thompson's unique skiing style: "With his feet firmly braced, and his balance-pole in his hands, he flew down the mountain slopes, as much at home as an eagle soaring and circling above the neighboring peaks. He did not ride astride his guide-pole, nor trail it by his side in the snow, as is the practice of other snow-shoers (skiers) when descending a steep mountain, but held it horizontally before him, after the manner of a tightrope walker."

The mailbag on Thompson's back weighed 60 to 80 pounds, but often was over 100 pounds. In addition to mail, the bag sometimes contained ore samples, medicine, and hard-to-get items for the residents on both sides of the mountain. To lighten his load he carried no gun after about the first year.

Snowshoe's exertions kept him warm while traveling in the mountains, thus he never brought along blankets. He wore a Mackinaw jacket, a wide rimmed hat, and painted his face black with charcoal to prevent snow blindness. Thompson carried only a small quantity of food consisting of jerked beef or dried sausage and a few crackers or biscuits. To quench his thirst, he caught up a handful of snow or drank from a stream.

Night camps were wherever Thompson happened to be at the moment. He always tried to find a dry stump or a dead pine tree with a decided lean to start on fire. Often the tree would burn through and fall to the ground by morning, thus it was important to know which side of the tree was safe to sleep under. He lay on a bed of tree branches with his feet towards the fire and his head on Uncle Sam's mailbag.

"I was never lost – I can't be lost," he modestly told De Quille. Then tapping his forehead with his forefinger, he continued: "There's something in here which keeps me right." Snowshoe's advice to anyone lost in the narrow Sierra mountain range was clear and simple . . . to always keep on going down hill . . . which would take one to a ravine, canyon, stream, below the snowline, and finally to a path in the valley.

Thompson needed no compass as he read his bearing from the trees and rocks, stars, moss and lichen growth, flow of streams, animal tracks, snowdrifts, and a feel for which way the wind blew. In Lutheran Pastor Erling Ylvisaker's 1934 book, *Eminent Pioneers: Norwegian-American Pioneer Sketches*, he told that Snowshoe Thompson: "Carefully watched the rock formations and the vegetation especially. To him even moss and bark could tell the points of the compass, for he knew that certain kinds of moss grew on the south side of a hill and that trees had the thickest bark on the north slope."

About Snowshoe Thompson receiving no payment from the post office De Quille concluded: "First and last, he did a vast deal of work for nothing . . . he would eventually be paid . . . but all he got was promises . . . He was the father of all the race of snow-shoers (skiers) in the Sierra Nevadas; and in those mountains he was the pioneer of the pack-train, the stage-coach and the locomotive. On the Pacific Coast his equal in his particular line will probably never again be seen."

One of Thompson's most notable, of his many rescues of people lost in the narrow mountain range, is published by the Norwegian-America Historical Association (NAHA) in a 1958 book by Kenneth O. Bjork, *West of the Great Divide: Norwegian Migration to the Pacific Coast, 1847-1893*. Bjork quoted the story of Snowshoe Thompson saving the life of a prospector found in a seemingly deserted cabin near Lake Tahoe, during Christmas week of 1856. The spectacular rescue was originally printed in the *Sacramento Union* of January 10, 1857.

"The sufferer proved to be James

Sisson . . . [who lived] about six miles above Placerville. He had been engaged in the packing business, and left for Carson Valley on snow shoes some two weeks previous. The storm overtook him on his way, and his feet becoming frozen, it was with great difficulty he reached his cabin or trading post. On arriving there he found his matches so wet that he could not strike a light, and thus he remained for four days, when he discovered a box of matches in his cabin, which furnished him a fire. He then attempted to cut his boots off his feet, but could not succeed; and nothing remained for him but to await either succor or death."

According to *Snowshoe Thompson*, published by the Carson Valley Historical Society, Sisson's legs had turned blue up to his knees. Sisson was nearly ready to amputate both of his legs at the knee with the use of his axe, when Thompson discovered him. Convincing Sisson to wait, Snowshoe skied to Genoa and brought back several men and a sled. With great labor they took Sisson down to Genoa, only to find the doctor had no chloroform to amputate the feet.

Snowshoe then skied westward back over the mountain to Placerville to get chloroform. Finding none in Placerville, he continued onward to Sacramento before returning to Genoa with the anesthetic. Sisson survived mainly because Snowshoe traveled an estimated 400 miles in ten days.

The Carson Valley Historical Society further tells of a trip through the mountains in 1857 when Snowshoe came upon the one thing he feared the most: "Directly in his path was a pack of timber wolves feeding on a deer carcass they had dug out of the snow . . . He decided the only thing he could do was keep going straight ahead and not look at the wolves. There were six wolves and they seemed quite ferocious . . . He said the wolves started coming toward him and that when the leader was about 30 yards away he wheeled around and sat down on his haunches. The other five did the same thing. Just as Snowshoe was directly across from them they threw back their heads and howled – one long, loud howl . . . They sat still and watched him as he passed by."

It was through interviews and writings by Hjalmar Rued Holand in his 1908 book *De Norske Settlementers Historie* that many Norwegian-Americans learned of Snowshoe Thompson. Holand retold the stories of Thompson and said he could "serve as a model for the god of the ski sport. It has been attested, for example, that on one occasion he sailed off a cliff 180 feet in height, and came down standing up . . . a hero, a superman who was not subject to ordinary human frailty, but disported himself over bridges of ice and avalanches of snow and made light of Nature's stern moods."

According to the 1991 book *Lost Sierra: Gold, Ghosts & Skis* by William Banks Berry, an article in the *Territorial Enterprise* May 19, 1876 told: "Snowshoe Thompson carried over the Sierra from Genoa . . . done up in the remnant of a check shirt . . . some strange black material, which was bothering the miners who were working the Gold Canyon." After the ore samples were delivered to Sacramento and analyzed, it triggered world attention to Virginia City's Comstock Lode. The vein of gold and silver discovered in 1859 was the richest known U.S. silver deposit.

History of skis

The word *"ski"* (pronounced *"shee"* in Norwegian) is an Old Norwegian word that has entered languages worldwide. It originally meant a split piece of firewood. By strapping a couple of wooden planks to their feet, Norwegians have used skis since the Stone Age, over 4000 years ago. A well-known story in Norway's Viking history occurred in 1206. In a dramatic flight over the mountains, two heroic Birkebeiners (Birchlegs) carried two-

Snowshoe Thompson Monument at Boreal Ridge, California.
Postcard reprinted with permission from Snowshoe Thompson Lodge 78, Sons of Norway, Yuba City, California.
My special thanks to Lee Olson for his assistance.

SNOWSHOE THOMPSON

A hero of the Sierra Nevada Mountains!
Probably the first skier of the west.
This Viking son of Norway exemplified the
spirit of a true pioneer: strong, daring,
faithful, and courageous.
He was the answer to California's motto,
"Bring me men to match my mountains."
For 20 years he was the winter lifeline
between the new state of California and
the east with a regular mail schedule
between Placerville, California and
Genoa, Nevada and other isolated
hamlets of the Mother Lode Country.
Mail, news of the world, medicine, supplies,
and equipment arrived on the sturdy
shoulders of this giant Snow Viking.
Over great snowdrifts, through raging
winter storms, with packs of up to
100 pounds he made his appointed
rounds. His daring rescues, errands of
mercy, and many kindnesses made him a
legend in his own time. He was born
(Jon Torsteinsson Rue)
John Tostensen at Tinn in Telemark,
Norway, April 30, 1827. He died May 15, 1876
at the age of 49. He rests at the base of
the mountains he loved, by the side of his
wife and son in the cemetery at
Genoa, Nevada. A simple headstone,
engraved with a pair of skis, marks his
grave.

May 15, 1976 - Statue dedicated at Boreal Ridge Winter Park off Interstate 80, Donner Summit. This monument is a 10-foot high steel likeness of Snowshoe, astride his skis and holding a balance pole. The statue was erected by the Sons of Norway, Snowshoe Thompson Lodge, Yuba City, California, and was designed by artist Angus Kent Lamar of Grady County, Oklahoma. It was dedicated on the 100th anniversary of Snowshoe's death.

year-old Prince Håkon Håkonsson to safety on skies. *"The Cradle of Skiing"* is Telemark, Norway, where the now internationally known word *"slalom"* originated in 1886.

Until 1850, skis were as familiar as ones shoes during wintertime in Norway, as skiing was an essential means of transportation, not a sport. Such was the life of the ten-year-old boy, Jon Torsteinsson Rue (later named John A. "Snowshoe" Thompson), who had learned skiing as a child in Tinn i Telemark. Along with his widowed mother, Gro, Jon immigrated to America in 1837.

Snowshoe Thompson's childhood

The distinctly mountainous Tinn *kommune* (township) is located in the northeastern corner of Telemark *Fylke* (county), in eastern Norway. According to *Tinns emigrasjons historie 1847-1907*, a 1968 thesis by Andres A. Svalestuen (translated by C.A. Clausen and summarized by NAHA), Tinn covered an area of about 706.4 square miles. Only 4.4 square miles or 0.6 percent was under cultivation and 99 percent consisted of mountainous terrain, upland pastures, forests, and water.

Food was scarce throughout Norway during the middle of the 18th century, when the country experienced a long period of crop failures. Documents tell of the people eating meals of moss and bark from birch, elm, and willow trees. Clergy, who became known as "potato priests," helped spread the word of one of the most important crops to be introduced, the potato. However, the resulting population explosion along with a lowered death rate created a crisis. Between 1801 and 1835, the population of Tinn increased by 37 percent to 2,481 people.

It was during this time that Torstein Olsson Gollo and Kjersti Toresdatter Lurås-Rue lived on the south Rue farm, a farm in a cluster of farms called Luråsbygde or Luråsgrende in Tinn. They had eight children: Ola, Tore, Tore, Gro, Tomas, Aslaug, Anne, and Hølje. One of their children, Tomas Torsteinsson Rue, was married in 1831 to Aslaug Torgrimsdatter Steinsrud under Dale. Aslaug was an aunt to my great-great-grandfather, Gullick Tovsson Thompson, who lived in the Big Woods of Fillmore County, Minnesota.

When Kjersti died in 1809, her cousin, Gro Jonsdatter Einungbrekke (Håkaland), was hired to take care of Torstein's children. Torstein and Gro later married in 1812 and six more children were born: Kjersti, Birgit, Jon, Torstein, Kari, and Jon. The youngest child, Jon Torsteinsson Rue (Snowshoe

Thompson), was born on April 30, 1827. In 1829 when Jon was only two years old, his father died leaving Gro with three minor children.

Norwegian farm life

Most Norwegians lived on farms until the last half of the 1800's. In the social ladder, the *bønde* or *gårdmann* were the farm owners. Those doing much of the farm work were the *husmenn* or cotters, who lived on the outer fringes of the farm in return for labor or a fee. The cotters were treated as an inferior class. Located higher up in the mountains was the seter or summer pasture for the cattle, goats, and sheep.

When Gro's husband died, her oldest stepson took over the south Rue farm, and the widow moved with her three youngest into the small cotter's farm belonging to Rue, which was called Jordeskos. Her children, like most cotters' offspring, were hired out for service. Poverty stricken, Gro and her youngest ones worked on a neighboring *seter* during the summer months.

The average size of a Tinn i Telemark farm was five to seven and one-half acres and most often was located along river valleys or steep mountain slopes. In H.H. Einung's 1953 book, *Tinn Soga* (Band II), he describes the south Rue farm (translated from Norwegian): "In 1835, on the farmstead in south Rue, there was one horse, six cows, four sheep, and two goats. They seeded two *tønne* (barrels) of barley and four *tønne* of potatoes." One Norwegian *tønne* is equivalent to about four bushels.

The Rue Party

There was much excitement in the Luràs-Rue neighborhood during 1836 and 1837, when two Nattestad brothers from nearby Veggli i Numedal brought news about immigration to America. They told of audacious plans and spread *"American fever"* to Tinn, which resulted in the first group emigration from eastern Norway, known as the Rue Party. Fundamentally, however, it was an exodus due to preconditioned social and economic conditions.

On the morning of May 17, 1837, the widow Gro and her then ten-year-old son, Jon Torsteinsson Rue, bid farewell to the rest of the family, as they joined the group of some 50 emigrants for their unprecedented departure. By rowing boats, the party crossed three lakes, Tinnsjø, Heddalsvatnet, and Norsjø, as they made their way downward toward Skien. After a few days, the Rue Party boarded a boat to Gøteborg (Gothenburg), Sweden, from where they would depart for America.

The Swedish brig Niord sailed the end of May 1837. Tightly packed into their emigrant trunks and wooden boxes was food for the voyage, consisting of *spekekjøtt* or cured dried meat, stacks of flatbread, cheese, and butter, along with cooking utensils, homespun clothes, and tools to work the new land. Crowded and terrified in the bottom of the ship, the Rue Party encountered ocean storms and seasickness, however they arrived two and one-half months later in New York City on August 15, 1837.

The New World

From New York City it is believed that the Rue Party traveled by steamboat up the Hudson River and on through the Eric Canal to Buffalo, New York. From there they took a steamer across the Great Lakes to Chicago, where they arrived in September 1837. It was only 12 years earlier, in 1825 that the first Norwegian immigration began with Cleng Peerson. He was not only considered the Father of Norwegian immigration in America, but also the pathfinder of Norwegian settlements in the West.

The Tinn i Telemark emigrants arriving in 1837 followed Cleng Peerson's paths to the Fox River settlement near Chicago, Illinois. In the spring of 1838, under the leadership of Cleng Peerson, Gro and Jon Rue left Fox River along with other Norwegians and settled in Shellbyville, Shelby County, Missouri. Due to too much wilderness, they moved about 100 miles northeast to Sugar Creek in Lee County, located in the very southeast corner of Iowa.

In the fall of 1839, a second group of immigrants arrived from Tinn i Telemark. Among them were two of Gro's children, Torstein and Kari. In 1843, Jon and Torstein's half-brother, Tore Torsteinsson Rue Røysland, immigrated. It was during this time that the three Rue men, Jon, Torstein, and Tore, all changed their last name from Rue to Thompson. Jon Torsteinsson Rue, who became known as John A. Thompson and later Snowshoe Thompson, lived for some time in Wisconsin and again in Illinois before joining the Gold Rush, in 1851.

Jon Haukaas tells in his 1993 book *Snowshoe Thompson*, published by Fjell-Ljom Ungdomslag, that Thompson's half-brother, Tore, "conceived the idea of taking along a herd of cows in order to sell milk to the miners . . . It is said they were able to sell milk 'at fabulous prices' for a short time, but perhaps it is true that the cattle died during the first winter." Tore returned to Wisconsin.

John A. Thompson stayed and worked as a miner for some time at Coon Hollow and Kelsey's Diggings near Hangtown (now Placerville), but was unsuccessful and did not care for mining life. It was during 1854 and 1855, while a rancher in Sacramento Valley, that Thompson longed for the mountains, where he would ski for the next 20 years.

U.S. postage stamp

After an illness of only a few days, John A. "Snowshoe" Thompson died at his ranch in Diamond Valley, Nevada, on May 15, 1876 at age 49. Only two years later, his wife, Agnes Singleton, buried their only child beside him. Beneath a pair of skis on Thompson's tombstone in Genoa, Nevada, the inscription reads *"Gone but not forgotten."*

Snowshoe Thompson is certainly not forgotten. He exemplified the spirit of a true pioneer and became a legend in his own time. To commemorate the 150th anniversary of Snowshoe Thompson's first trip carrying the U.S. Postal Mail, NAHA and others have written to the U.S. Postal Service and requested that a postal stamp be issued in his remembrance during 2006.

Special thanks to

• Gene Estensen, Telelaget of America Historian and Webmaster, for his assistance with genealogy and pictures. For more information about Snowshoe Thompson and Telemark visit http://www.telelaget.com
• Sons of Norway Snowshoe Thompson Lodge No. 78, Yuba City, California

Snowshoe Thompson "Borte, men ikke glemt"

Norsk-amerikansk postbud fikk heltestatus i Sierra-Nevada-fjellene

Snowshoe Thompsons barndom

Midt på 1800-tallet opplevde Norge mange feilslåtte avlinger, og det var dårlig med mat. Dokumenter forteller om at folk spiste mose og bark fra bjørk, alm og pil. Kirkens menn fikk navnet "potetprester", da de hjalp til med å spre budskapet om innførselen av den så viktige poteten. Likevel førte en befolkningseksplosjon, sammen med lavere dødelighet, til krise. Mellom 1801 og 1835 økte befolkningen i Tinn med 37 prosent til 2481 mennesker.

Det var på denne tiden at Torstein Olsson Gollo og Kjersti Toresdatter Lurås-Rue bodde på den sørlige Rue-gården, en gård som lå i en ansamling av gårder kalt Lurås-bygde eller Luråsgrende i Tinn. De hadde åtte barn: Ola, Tore, Tore, Gro, Tomas, Aslaug, Anne og Hølje. Ett av barna, Tomas Torsteinsson Rue, ble i 1831 gift med Aslaug Torgrimsdatter Steinsrud under Dale. Aslaug var tante til en av mine tipp-oldefedre, Gullick Tovsson Thompson, som bodde i Big Woods i Fillmore County, Minnesota.

Da Kjersti døde i 1809, var det hennes søskenbarn, Gro Jonsdatter Einungbrekke (Håkaland), som ble bedt om å ta seg av Torsteins barn. Torstein og Gro giftet seg senere i 1812, og det ble født seks barn til: Kjersti, Birgit, Jon, Torstein, Kari og Jon. Det yngste barnet, Jon Torsteinsson Rue, ble født 30 april 1827. I 1829, da Jon bare var to år gammel, døde faren, og Gro ble alene med tre små barn.

Telers at Snowshoe's ranch near Genoa

Ruefølget

Det hersket stor spenning i nabolaget i Luràs-Rue i 1836 og 1837, da to Nattestad-brødre fra Veggli-området i Numedal brakte nyheter om immigrasjonen i Amerika. De fortalte om dristige planer og spredte "amerikafeberen" til Tinn, hvilket førte til at den første gruppen med emigranter, også kalt Ruefølget, forlot Østlandet. Helt klart var det likevel en utvandring forårsaket av de sosiale og økonomiske forholdene.

Om morgenen 17. mai 1837 sa enken Gro og hennes ti år gamle sønn, Jon Torsteinsson Rue, farvel med resten av familien, før de slo seg sammen med en gruppe på om lag 50 emigranter som var klare for en uvanlig avreise. Selskapet rodde over tre innsjøer, Tinnsjø, Heddalsvatnet og Norsjø på sin vei nedover mot Skien. Etter noen dager gikk Ruefølget om bord i en båt i Gøteborg i Sverige, for å dra videre til Amerika derfra.

Den svenske briggen "Niord" seilte i slutten av mai 1837. I emigrantkister og trebokser var mat til reisen pakket tett sammen, den bestod av spekekjøtt eller konservert, tørket kjøtt, flatbrødstabler, ost og smør sammen med kokekar, hjemmelagede klær og verktøy for bruk i det nye landet. Skrekkslagne og tett pakket sammen i bunnen av skipet, møtte Ruefølget stormer og sjøsyke på havet, men var uansett framme i New York City 15.august 1837, to og en halv måned senere.

Den nye verden

Fra New York City mener man at selskapet reiste med dampbåt oppover Hudsonelva og gjennom Eriekanalen til Buffalo, New York. Derfra tok de en dampbåt over over de store sjøene til Chicago, hvor de ankom i september 1837. Den norske immigrasjonen hadde begynt bare 12 år tidligere i 1825 med Cleng Peerson. Han ble ikke bare betraktet som far til den norske immigrasjonen i Amerika, men var også kjentmann i de norske bebyggelsene i vest.

Da emigrantene fra Tinn i Telemark ankom i 1837, fulgte de Cleng Peersons veier til bosettingen Fox River i nærheten av Chicago, Illinois. Om våren 1838, under ledelse av Cleng Peerson, forlot Gro og Jon Rue Fox

River sammen med andre nordmenn og slo seg ned i Shellbyville, Shelby County, Missouri. Fordi der var for mye villmark, dro de om lag 160 kilometer lenger nordøst til Sugar Creek i Lee County, som lå helt inne i det sørøstlige hjørnet av Iowa.

Høsten 1839 kom det en ny gruppe med immigranter fra Tinn i Telemark. Blant dem var to av Gros barn, Torstein og Kari. I 1843 immigrerte Jons og Torsteins halvbror, Tore Torsteinsson Rue Røysland. På denne tiden forandret alle de tre Rue-mennene, Jon, Torstein og Tore, sine etternavn fra Rue til Thompson. Jon Torsteinsson Rue, som ble kjent som John A. Thompson, og senere som Snowshoe Thompson, bodde en tid i Wisconsin og dro tilbake igjen til Illinois, før han tok del i gullrushet i 1851.

Jon Haukaas forteller i sin bok *Snowshoe Thompson*, utgitt av Fjell-Ljom Ungdomslag, 1993, at Thompsons halvbror, Tore, fikk ideen å ta med seg en flokk kyr for å kunne selge melk til gullgraverne...Det er sagt at de en kort tid var i stand til å selge melk "til utrolige priser", men kanskje er det sant at kyrne døde den første vinteren. Tore dro tilbake til Wisconsin.

John A. Thompson arbeidet en tid i gruvene i Coon Hollow og Kelsey's Diggings nær Hangtown (nå Placerville), men han lykkes ikke og likte ikke livet i gruvene. Det var i løpet av 1854 og 1855, mens han drev gård i Sacramento Village, at Thompson begynte å lengte etter fjellene, hvor han skulle tilbringe de neste 20 årene på ski. Under navnet Snowshoe Thompson ble han en legendarisk postombærer i Sierra-Nevada-fjellene, og han ble etter sin død hedret med et eget minnesmerke.

"Jeg gikk meg aldri vill - jeg kan ikke gå meg vill," sa Snowshoe Thompson beskjedent til De Quille, redaktøren av Virginias Territorial Entreprise, som også var en venn av Thompson-familien. Idet han banket fingeren mot panna, fortsatte han: "Det finnes noe her inne som fører meg på rett vei."

Snowshoes råd til enhver som gikk seg bort i de trange Sierra Nevada-fjellene, var ganske enkelt alltid å gå i nedoverbakke, noe som ville føre ham til en snøløs ravine, en kløft – og et vassdrag - som til sist ville føre til en sti i dalen.

Gaustatoppen

SNOWSHOE THOMPSON
Minnesmerkets inskripsjon

En kjempe fra Sierra-Nevada-fjellene! Trolig den første skiløper i vest. Denne norske vikingsønnen viste en sann pionerånd: styrke, dristighet, trofasthet og mot.

Han var svaret på Californias motto: "Bring meg mennesker som er som fjellene." I tjue år strakte han seg gjennom vinteren mellom den nye staten California og øst. Regelmessig fraktet han posten mellom Placerville, California og Genoa, Nevada og andre isolerte bygder i Moderårens land. Brev, nyheter fra omverdenen, medisiner, forsyninger og utstyr ankom på de stødige skuldrene til denne kjempen, en fjellenes viking var han.

Over de store snøfonnene, gjennom rasende vinterstormer og med pakker opp til 45 kilo, gjorde han sine avtalte runder. Hans dristige redninger, små tjenester og gode gjerninger gjorde ham til en legende mens han levde.

Han var født John Tostensen (Jon Torsteinsson Rue) i Tinn i Telemark, Norge, 30. april 1827. Han døde 15. mai 1876, 49 år gammel. Han hviler ved foten av fjellene han elsket, ved siden av sin hustru og sønn, på kirkegården i Genoa, Nevada. En enkel gravstein som viser et par ski, markerer graven hans.

Gene Estensen brick at Genoa monument
Fjellene minnes (Mountains remember)

11

The Great Flu Epidemic of 1918

Hermanson family lost seven family members in one week

> ***I had a little bird,***
> ***its name was Enza.***
> ***I opened the window,***
> ***and in-flu-enza.***

Children skipped rope to this rhyme during the flu epidemic

The 1918 influenza virus or Spanish flu was the worst epidemic the United States has known, taking the lives of an estimated 675,000 Americans, including 43,000 servicemen. More Americans died in one year from the influenza than in World War I, World War II, the Korean War, and the Vietnam War combined. Yet, most people know very little about the epidemic or have forgotten that period of history.

Unlike any strain ever seen, the mysterious killer virus spread across the country overflowing hospitals and filling mass graves. Joe Hermanson, the nephew of my great-great-great-grand-

Char Nelson visiting with her distant cousin Leonard Hermanson. He is holding a copy of the *Fillmore County Journal* with Deb's front-page story of the Great Flu Epidemic, which devastated his family.
http://www.fillmorecountyjournal.com

Top: *Joe and Emma Hermanson are pictured with their 12 children and one son-in-law in the fall of 1919. During one week in February 1920, influenza claimed the lives of Emma and six of the children.*
Bottom: *Joe was pictured with 5 of the 6 surviving children. Gena and her husband, Christ Hanson, were missing from the picture.*
(Photos courtesy of Ann Norskog Bratland)

mother, Kari Hermanson (Nese) Ekse, lost his wife Emma (Olson), 42, and six of their twelve children in one week due to the deadly flu.

Kari Hermundsdatter Nese immigrated in 1861 from *Nese i Arnaford, Sogn* and married Nils Nilsson Ekse that same year. Her brothers, Elling and Endre; sister, Anna; and father, Hermund Johannesson Nese immigrated together in 1867. Hermund died in 1886 and was buried in the pioneer section of the Black Hammer cemetery, near Spring Grove, Houston County, Minnesota. Spring Grove is recognized as the first Norwegian settlement in Minnesota.

A newspaper clipping from February 1920 reads: *The Joe Hermanson family of Black Hammer near Spring Grove is the most severely stricken family ever known in this section of the state. The family was taken sick the first of the month. Mrs. Hermanson died Wednesday, and Saturday the two oldest boys died, and in the night a nine-year-old boy. Monday afternoon and night two more died, and Tuesday still another making seven dead, while small hopes are entertained for two more. Mr. Hermanson is recovering.*

Joe and two of the children, Evelyn and Henry, were taken to the Spring Grove Hospital. According to a family member, the children survived by the doctor draining fluid from their lungs. Emma's brother and niece assisted the remaining family members. Others left food on the porch and helped with the livestock chores.

Because of severe cold and deep snow, the seven flu fatalities were placed in the summer kitchen for a later burial in the Black Hammer Cemetery. All their names, including Joe, who died nine years later, are on one tombstone.

Only one of the children, Leonard Hermanson, now age 92 in 2004, still survives. My mother, Char Nelson, and I visited him in the Houston Nursing Home. In earlier years Leonard and his family lived in Looney Valley near Houston, where he had worked as a farmer and carpenter.

I could sense that deep down sadness that has never gone away as Leonard described *his wonderful mother, Emma.* Recalling that tragic year, 1920, he cited the names and ages of all twelve children, the six who died from the flu: Edwin, 19; Clarence, 18; Julia, 16; Johnnie, 12; Selmer, 9; Mabel, 7; and the six who survived: Gena, 20; Evelyn, 15; Mina, 13; Henry, 10; Leonard (himself), 8; and Bernice, 4.

Mina's daughter, Ann Bratland, of Laurel, Montana, relayed to me that her mother had gone to help her older pregnant sister, Gena. Gena and her husband, Chris Hanson, lived a mile down the road from the home farm. Mina found out about the family deaths in the Spring Grove paper, as the families had no phones.

Influenza Claims Seven of One Family

The family of Joe Hermanson, residing in the north part of Black Hammer, have suffered a terrible loss of death by the influenza epidemic. Seven of a family of fourteen have been called to the Great Beyond, and at this writing, two more are in a critical condition.

The death of the wife and mother Mrs. Emma Hermanson, aged 42, on last Thursday, has been followed by the death of six of the children, Edward Julius, 19 years, Clarence, 18 years, Julia, 16 years, Selmar, 9 years, Mabel, 7 years, and John.

Surely, the bereaved family have the sympathy of the entire community.

Spring Grove Herald
February 12, 1920

The First Wave

The point of origin of the influenza epidemic is thought to have been Camp Funston, part of Fort Riley, Kansas on March 9, 1918. Sandwiched between bone-chilling winters and sweltering summers were blinding dust storms. Stifling, ever-accumulating manure from the camp's thousands of horses and mules was disposed of by burning. The dust combined with the manure ashes was said to have created a *stinging, stinking, yellow haze* turning the sky black.

Two days later, over one hundred men were ill, all complaining of fever, sore throat and headache. More than five hundred were reported sick after another two days, many gravely ill with severe pneumonia. No one knew why. The elusive killer spread, striking military camps throughout the country at the very time draft call-ups and troop shipments were in high gear for a nation at war.

In March and April 1918 over 200,000 American World War I soldiers sailed across the Atlantic in overcrowded ships. By May, 1918 the flu had established itself on two continents. Little did the soldiers know they were carrying with them a virus that would kill tens of thousands by July 1918, and would be more deadly than their rifles.

The influenza had now extended beyond the U.S. and Europe, and cases were reported in Russia, North Africa, India, China, Japan, the Philippines and New Zealand. This first wave was a mere prelude of what was to come that fall.

In early 2003 I attended a lecture on the 1918 influenza at Luther College, presented by retired microbiologist, Professor John Tjostem. He explained that because the world was at war, the Americans and the Germans censored their flu statistics, while Spain, a neutral country, published their flu deaths in the newspapers. The epidemic would later be inaccurately dubbed the *Spanish flu*. Professor Tjostem further explained that the 1918 influenza pandemic took four months to make its way around the world. With today's modern transportation, it would take only four days.

The Second Wave

In the fall of 1918, the relentless flu was reintroduced from Europe with troops returning to the United States from World War I. It hit with a vengeance, as the mutated virus was now more deadly than ever. The lethal flu spread from person to person by tiny droplets produced by coughing and sneezing. It was everywhere and no one was safe, as everyone had to breathe. Unlike any other flu, almost every family lost someone.

Researchers had developed vaccines for diseases such as meningitis, diphtheria, and anthrax, which were caused by bacteria, but they had nothing, in 1918, to stop influenza. Science was powerless, as the electron microscope needed to see the virus had not yet been invented. DNA and RNA, the genetic material of viruses, had not been discovered. Americans took to wearing gauze masks, but they were as effective as *keeping out dust with chicken wire*.

Many people turned to folk remedies such as garlic, camphor balls or kerosene poured on sugar. Schools closed and laws forbade spitting on the streets. Nothing worked. As the war raged, people gathered for rallies and bond drives where they coughed and infected each other. In October 1918 alone, more than 195,000 Americans died from the epidemic. A public health disaster had been created by the time the war ended on November 11, 1918. In some places, because of a nationwide shortage, caskets had to be guarded from thieves.

So Quick, so Sudden, so Terrifying

Unlike ordinary influenza that kills mainly the very young or elderly, the 1918 flu targeted young robust adults. Professor Tjostem stated: *the fact that twenty to forty year olds were hit the hard-*

est is difficult to explain. People who had lived during a period when a major flu epidemic had previously hit were partially protected. The very young were likely more vulnerable because their immune systems were still developing.

Joe and Anna Hermanson "Home Place"
Black Hammer, Houston County, Minnesota
(Photos courtesy of Ann Norskog Bratland)

Twenty-five times more deadly than the normal flu, the 1918 flu pandemic killed an estimated 40-50 million people in the world. Within about 48 hours, most victims were dead. They had high delirious fevers, bloody noses, and coughed up blood. Eventually, their bodies turned purplish-blue, the lungs filled with reddish fluid, and they drowned in their own secretions.

The Influenza Viruses

The three types of influenza virus are A, B, and C. Influenza A viruses are found in humans and animals, including pigs, horses, chickens, ducks, and some wild birds. Influenza B and C viruses are found only in humans and appear to be more stable than Influenza A.

In 1918 influenza outbreaks appeared in humans and pigs almost simultaneously. It's unclear, however, if pigs infected the humans or if humans infected the pigs. Millions of pigs became ill with severe respiratory infection in the Midwest, decimating entire hog farms.

Influenza viruses, like a chameleon, change their coats each year. Thus, one has to be inoculated each year to have sufficient immunity. In 1918, it's believed a new kind of subtype influenza A virus emerged that was closely related to what is now known as classic swine influenza virus. Pigs are thought to be an intermediary or mixing vessel in this process, since they can be infected with both avian and human strains. The new virus was so different, that few had any kind of immunity, so it spread uncontrollably throughout the human population.

In 1998, after 80 years, scientists identified the genetic code of the 1918 virus by autopsying lung tissue samples from three cases that represented the only known sources of genetic material. Two were paraffin wax samples belonging to U.S. servicemen stationed in Fort Jackson, South Carolina, and Camp Upton, New York. The third belonged to a native Eskimo woman, buried in a mass grave and preserved in permafrost, at the Brevig Mission in Alaska.

China and Southeast Asia are believed to be the epicenter for emerging strains of influenza A virus, due to the region's enormous numbers and close proximity of humans, pigs, and aquatic birds. As a result of the 2003 outbreak of Severe Acute Respiratory Syndrome (SARS), the World Health Organization began a global surveillance of respiratory virus activity to prevent a 21st century pandemic.

Influenza in Minnesota

The *Preston Republican* in the October 25, 1918, issue reported: *In all health matters follow the advice of your doctor and obey the regulation of your local and state health officers. Cover up each cough and sneeze, if you don't you'll spread disease.*

This headline was published in *Levang's Weekly* in Lanesboro on January 29, 1920: *Influenza in Minnesota - Declared epidemic by State Board of Health, St. Paul. Health authorities throughout the state were immediately called upon to put into effect regulation for its control.*

Professor Tjostem contacted his former student, Michael T. Osterholm, PhD, MPH, on my behalf, in regards to the flu that so tragically struck the Joe and Emma Hermanson family in February 1920. Both Tjostem and Osterholm, Director of the Center for Infectious Disease Research and Policy, agreed that the Hermanson's flu could have been *a case of swine transmission back to humans in a more virulent form than that present in 1918.*

Forgotten Epidemic

The deadly 1918 influenza disappeared just as mysteriously as it started. Perhaps it ran out of people who were susceptible or the survivors developed immunity. What's known is that as soon as the dying stopped, the forgetting began.

Den store influensaepidemien i 1918

Familien Hermanson mistet sju familiemedlemmer på en uke

I had a little bird,
its name was Enza.
I opened the window,
and in-flu-enza.

Barnerim ungene hoppet tau etter under influensaepidemien

Spanskesyken i 1918 er den verste virusepidemien De forente stater har sett. Den tok livet av anslagsvis 675 000 amerikanere, 43 000 av dem militære tjenestemenn. Det døde flere amerikanere av influensa bare i løpet av ett år enn i første verdenskrig, andre verdenskrig, Koreakrigen og Vietnamkrigen til sammen. Likevel vet de fleste svært lite om epidemien, eller så har de glemt denne perioden av vår historie.

Ulik all kjent smitte, spredte det mystiske dødsviruset seg over landet og fylte hospitalene og massegravene. Nevøen til min tipp-tipp-oldemor, Kari Hermanson (Nese) Ekse, Joe Hermanson, mistet sin kone Emma (Olson), 42, og seks av deres tolv barn i løpet av en uke under den dødelige influensaepidemien.

Kari Hermunsdatter Nese immigrerte i 1861 fra Nese i Arnaford, Sogn, og giftet seg samme år med Nils Nilsson Ekse. Hennes brødre, Elling og Endre, søsteren Anna og faren, Hermund Johannesson Nese, immigrerte sammen i 1867. Hermund døde i 1886 og ble begravet på pionerseksjonen av Black Hammer-kirkegården i Minnesota, i nærheten av Spring Grove, Houston County, Minnesota. Spring Grove er kjent som den første norske bosettingen i Minnesota.

Et avisklipp fra februar 1920 forteller: *Joe Hermanson-familien fra Black Hammer ved Spring Grove er den hardest rammede familien vi kjenner fra denne delen av staten. Familien ble syk*

•	1612	1861	Kari	22	Husm.dtr.	64-0	Hermund Johanneson
	1613	1866	Marta Larsdtr.	26	Tenestejente		
	1614	1867	Anders	54	Husm.	64-0	Endre Knutson Henjum
	1615	1867	Ragnhild	42	Husm.kone	64-0	Ellend Jonson Vollevik
	1616	1867	Andreas	4	Husm.son	64-0	Anders Endreson
•	1617	1867	Hermund	64	Sjøm/husm.	64-0	Johannes Einarson
•	1618	1867	Anna	24	Husm.dtr.	64-0	Hermund Johanneson
•	1619	1867	Elling	14	Husm.son	64-0	Hermund Johanneson
	1620	1867	Karl	22	Tenar	64-4	Ola Jonson «Ness-Ola»
	1621	1867	Lars	20	Tenar	64-4	Endre Larson
•	1622	1867	Endre	32	Husm.son	64-0	Hermund Johanneson

Immigration from Nese i Arnafjord
Source: Ein Stad Skal Ein Vera - Utvandringa Frå Vik i Sogn
by Rasmus Sunde

Nils Nilsson Ekse

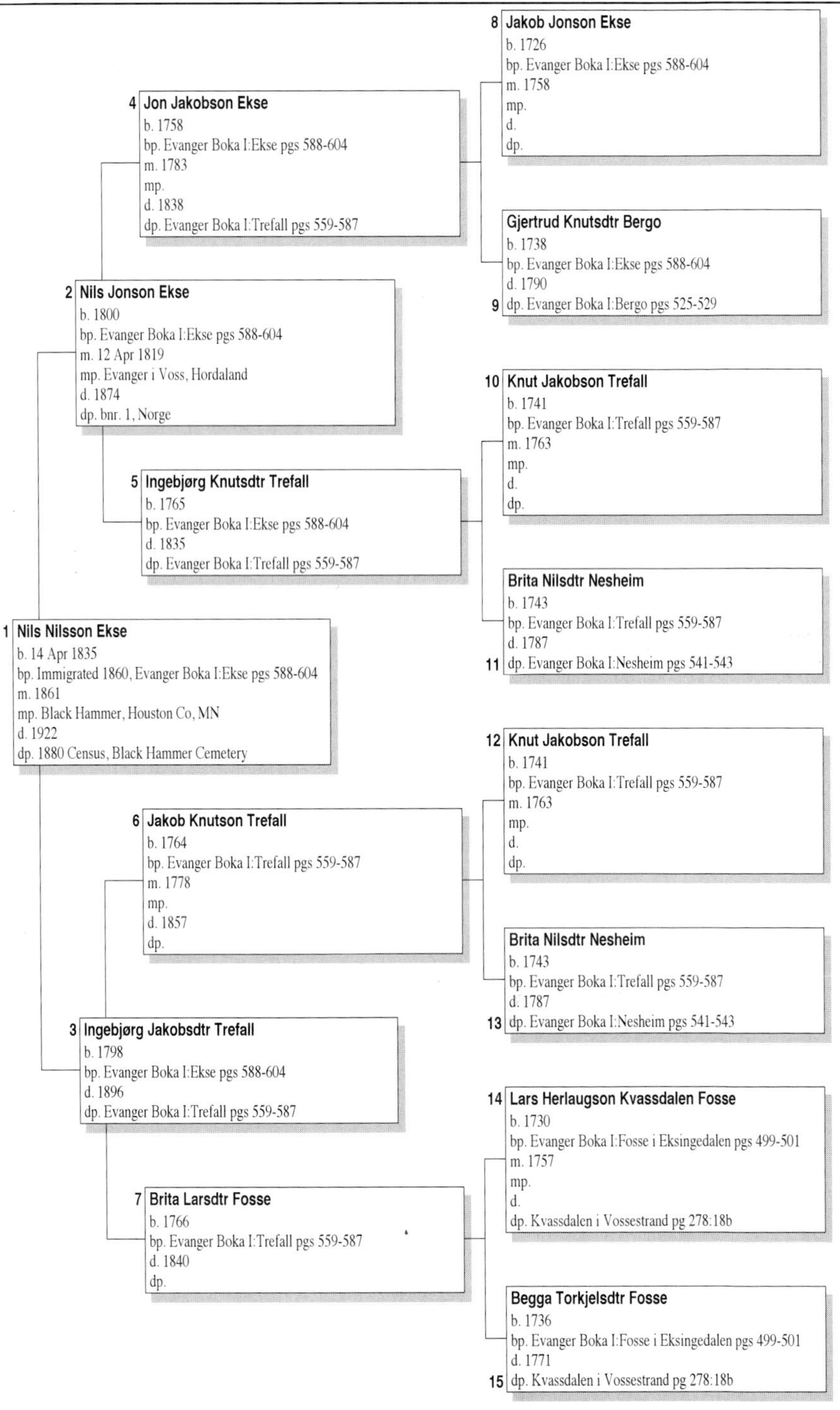

Kari Hermundsdtr (Nese) Hermanson

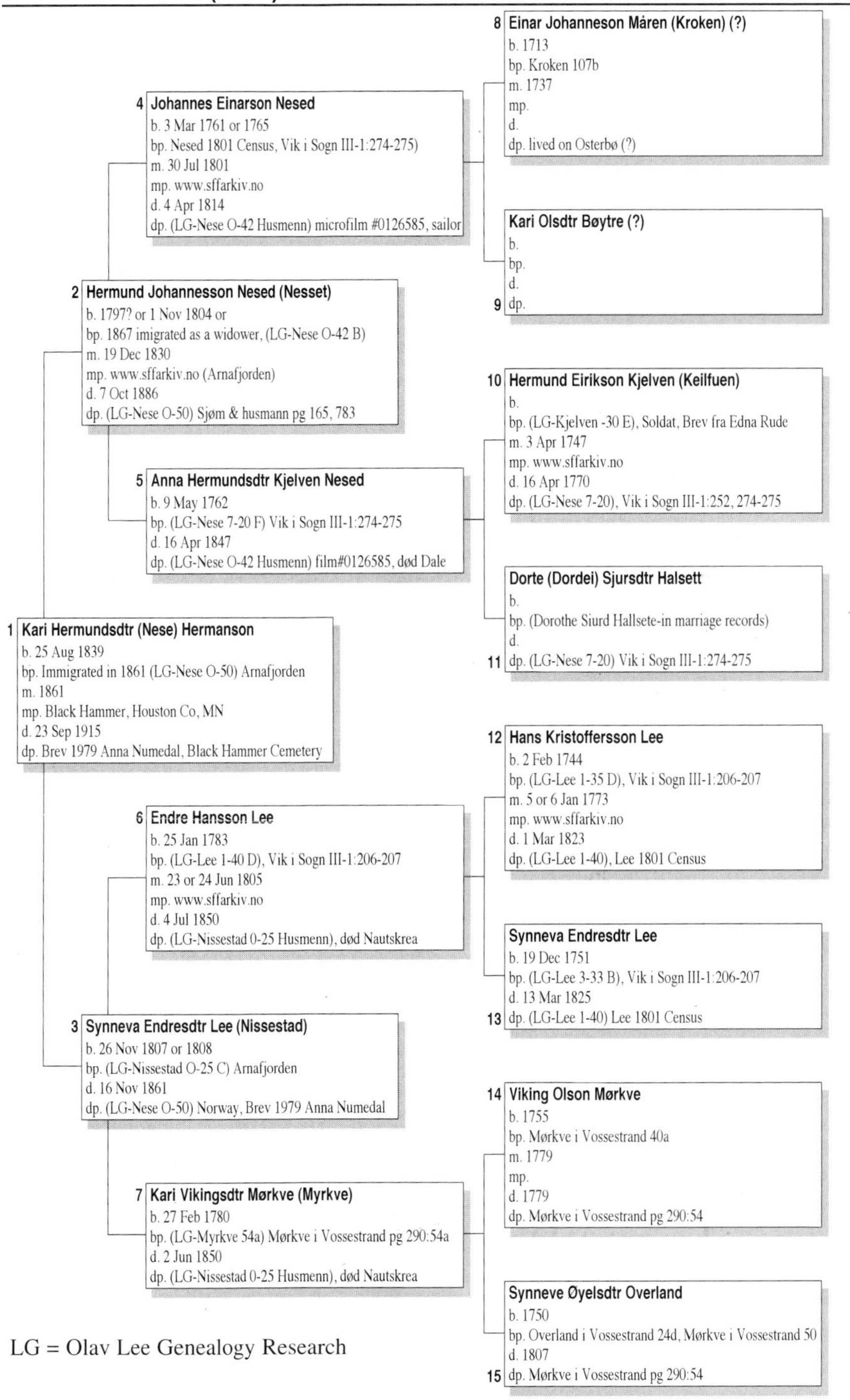

LG = Olav Lee Genealogy Research

den første i måneden. Fru Hermanson døde onsdag, lørdag døde de to eldste guttene, og om natten en ni år gammel gutt. Mandag ettermiddag og natt døde to til, og torsdag enda en, hvilket gir sju døde, mens det finnes håp for to andre. Herr Hermanson er på bedringens vei.

Joe og to av barna, Evelyn og Henry, ble brakt til Spring Grove Hospital. I følge familiemedlemmene overlevde barna ved at legen drenerte væske fra lungene deres. Emmas bror og niese hjalp de gjenlevende familiemedlemmene. Andre satte igjen mat til dem på verandaen, og hjalp til med å stelle husdyrene.

The influenza has reaped a harvest in the home of Joe Hermanson, seven of a family of twelve having died in a week's time. The mother, formerly Emma Olson, aged 39 years passed away a week ago last Wednesday night. Since that time up to last Wednesday morning, six of the children have passed away, the the cause of death in each case being influenza-pneumonia. The children who are dead are Edwin, aged 19; Clarence, 18; Julia, 17; Mabel, 10; Johnnie, 12; and Selmer, aged nine. The father and two more of the children are also seriously ill.

Mrs. Hermanson's brother, Oscar Olson of the Choice neighborhood informed a Herald reporter Wednesday that deaths in the family have occurred every night and that small hopes were entertained for the recovery of the father and two more of the children. The Hermanson home is three miles north of the Blackhammer church, near the Yucatan store. Mrs. Hermanson is well known to many of our people.

(From the Peterson Herald)
Wykoff Enterprise
February 20, 1920

På grunn av streng kulde og dyp snø, ble de sju som hadde dødd av influensa plassert i sommerkjøkkenet i påvente av en senere begravelse på Black Hammer-kirkegården. Alle deres navn, inkludert Joes, som døde ni år senere, står på gravsteinen.

Bare ett av barna, Leonard Hermanson, som nå i 2004 er 92 år gammel, lever fortsatt. Min mor, Char Nelson, og jeg besøkte ham på sykehjemmet i Houston. Tidligere bodde Leonard og familien i Looney Valley ved Houston, der han hadde vært farmer og håndverker.

Jeg kunne kjenne den dype sorgen som aldri hadde forlatt Leonard da han beskrev sin vidunderlige mor, Emma. Da han erindret det tragiske året 1920, nevnte han navnet på alle de tolv barna, de seks som døde av influensaen: Edwin, 19; Clarence, 18; Julia, 16; Johnnie, 12; Selmer, 9; Mabel, 7; og de seks som overlevde: Gena, 20; Evelyn, 15; Mina, 13; Henry,10; Leonard (han selv), 8; og Bernice, 4.

Minas datter, Ann Bratland fra Laurel, Montana, fortale i en telefonsamtale at moren hadde dratt for å hjelpe sin eldre søster, Gena, som var gravid. Gena og ektemannen, Chris Hanson, bodde halvannen kilometer nedover veien fra hjemgården. Mina fikk nyheten om familiens døde gjennom lokalavisen i Spring Grove, da familiene ikke hadde telefon.

Den første bølgen

Man mener at influensaepidemien startet 9. mars 1918 i Camp Funston, som ligger i Fort Riley i Kansas. I overgangen mellom beinkald vinter og kvelende sommer, reiste de forblindende støvstormene seg. Leirens tusener av hester og muldyr skapte en kvelende og stadig voksende mengde møkk, som ble samlet opp og brent. Støvet kombinert med asken av hestegjødslet, ble sagt å ha skapt stinkende gule skyer som stakk i øynene og gjorde himmelen svart.

To dager senere ble mer enn hundre

menn syke, alle klaget over feber, sår munn og hodepine. Mer enn fem hundre ble rapportert syke etter to nye dager, mange alvorlig syke med lungebetennelse. Ingen visste hvorfor. Den dødbringende og uhåndterlige sykdommen spredte seg og slo ned i militære leirer over hele landet, på en tid der troppeforsendelser og innkallinger til militærtjeneste preget en nasjon i krig.

I mars og april 1918 seilte mer enn 200 000 amerikanske soldater over Atlanteren i overfylte skip for å delta i første verdenskrig. I mai 1918 hadde influensaen etablert seg på to kontinenter. Lite visste soldatene at de brakte med seg et virus som skulle drepe titusener innen juli 1918, og som skulle komme til å bli mer dødelig enn geværer.

Influensaen hadde nå bredt seg ut av USA og Europa, og tilfeller ble rapportert i Russland, Nord-Afrika, India, Kina, Japan, Filippinene og New Zealand. Den første bølgen var en ren forsmak på det høsten skulle bringe.

Tidlig i 2003 overvar jeg ved Luther College en forelesning om 1918-influensaen med den pensjonerte mikrobiologen, professor John Tjostem. Han forklarte at fordi verden var i krig sensurerte amerikanerne og tyskerne sin influensastatistikk, mens Spania, som var et nøytralt land, publiserte dødstallene i sine aviser. Epidemien skulle senere upresist bli kalt *spanskesyken*. Professor Tjostem forklarte videre at influensapandemien i 1918 brukte fire måneder på å gå verden rundt. Med dagens moderne transportforhold ville det ha tatt fire dager.

Den andre bølgen

Om høsten 1918 ble influensaen ført tilbake fra første verdenskrig i Europa til De forente stater. Den rammet så det kjentes, da det muterte viruset nå var mer dødelig enn noen gang før. Den dødbringende influensaen spredte seg fra person til person gjennom små dråper når man hostet eller nøs. Den var overalt, og ingen var trygge, ettersom alle måtte puste. Ulik all annen influensa, var denne slik at enhver familie mistet noen.

Forskningen har utviklet vaksiner mot sykdommer som meningitt, difteri og miltbrann, som forårsakes av bakterier, men i 1918 hadde de ingenting å stoppe influensaen med. Vitenskapen var maktesløs, og elektronmikroskopet man trengte for å se et virus med, var ennå ikke oppfunnet. DNA og RNA, virusets genetiske materiale, var ennå ikke avslørt. Amerikanerne begynte å bære gassmasker, men de var ikke mer effektive enn om man skulle prøve å beskytte seg mot støv med hønsenetting.

Mange mennesker forsøkte folkelige råd som kvitløk, kamferdråper eller parafin på sukker. Skolene stengte og lover forbød spytting på gata. Ingenting hjalp. Mens krigen raste, samlet folk

Joe and Emma

seg til stevner og innsamlingsaksjoner for å finansiere krigen, hvor de hostet og infiserte hverandre. Bare i oktober 1918 døde mer enn 195 000 amerikanere av epidemien. En offentlig helsekatastrofe var skapt da krigen tok slutt 11. november 1918. Noen steder måtte likkistene voktes mot tyver på grunn av den landsomfattende mangelen på varer.

Så raskt, så plutselig, så skremmende

Ulik ordinær influensa, som først

Front side of Hermanson stone

og fremst dreper de svært unge og eldre, var 1918- influensaens offer unge, robuste voksne. Professor Tjosten slo fast: *det faktum at tjue- til førtiåringer var hardest rammet, er vanskelig å forklare. Mennesker som hadde levd gjennom perioder med tidligere influensaer var delvis beskyttet. De helt unge var sannsynligvis mer sårbare, fordi deres immunsystem fortsatt var under utvikling.*

Influensapandemien i 1918 var

Back side of Hermanson stone

tjuefem ganger mer dødelig enn en normal influensa, og den drepte anslagsvis 40-50 millioner mennesker i verden. I løpet av om lag 48 timer var de fleste ofrene døde. De hadde deliriske anfall under høy feber, og de blødde fra nesen og hostet opp blod. Til slutt ble kroppen purpurblå, lungene fyltes med rødlig væske og de druknet i sine egne sekreter.

Influensaviruset

De tre typene med influensavirus er A, B og C. Influensa A-viruset er funnet hos mennesker og dyr, inkludert griser, hester, kyllinger, ender og noen ville fugler. Influensa B- og C-virusene er funnet bare hos mennesker, og synes å være mer stabile enn influensa A.

I 1918 brøt influensaen ut blant mennesker og griser omtrent samtidig. Det er likevel uklart om grisene smittet menneskene, eller om det var menneskene som smittet grisene. I Midtvesten ble millioner av griser syke, med alvorlige infeksjoner i pusteorganene, noe som reduserte bestanden på grisegårdene kraftig.

Influensavirus endrer seg som kameloner skifter ham en gang om året. Derfor må man vaksineres hvert år for å være tilstrekkelig immun. Det man tror er at det i 1918 dukket opp en undertype av influensa A-viruset, som var nært beslektet med det vi nå kjenner som det klassiske svineinfluensaviruset. Man mener at griser er mellomledd eller "blandekar" i denne prosessen, ettersom både fugler og mennesker kan smitte dem. Det nye viruset var så annerledes at få hadde noen som helst motstandskraft, derfor spredte det seg ukontrollert gjennom hele befolkningen.

I 1998 identifiserte vitenskapsfolk, etter 80 år, den genetiske koden til 1918-viruset gjennom prøver av lungemateriale fra tre tilfeller som representerte de eneste kjente kildene med genetisk materiale. To var eksemplarer som hadde vært oppbevart i parafinvoks, og som tilhørte amerikanske militære, stasjonert i Fort Jackson, Sør-Carolina, og i Camp Upton, New York. Det tredje hørte til en innfødt eskimokvinne, gravlagt i en massegrav i permafrost ved Brevig Mission i Alaska.

Man tror at Kina og Sørøst-Asia utgjør det vitale senteret for økningen i antall tilfeller av influensa A-viruset, på grunn av regionens enorme antall og tette bebyggelse av mennesker, griser og vadefugler. Da det akutte respirasjonssyndromet, SARS, brøt ut i 2003, opprettet Verdens Helseorganisasjon en global overvåkning av lungevirusaktiviteten, for å forhindre en pandemi i det 21. århundre.

Influensaen i Minnesota

Avisen *Preston Republican* meldte 25. oktober 1918: *Følg legens råd i alle helsespørsmål, og godta de lokale eller statlige reguleringer som blir pålagt. Dekk til ethvert host eller nys, hvis ikke vil du spre sykdommen.*

Disse overskriftene ble 29. januar 1920 publisert i *Levang's Weekly* i Lanesboro: *Influensa i Minnesota – De statlige helsemyndighetene i St. Paul har erklært epidemi. Helsemyndighetene over hele staten ble øyeblikkelig påkalt for å sette i verk tiltak for å kontrollere epidemien.*

Professor Tjostem kontaktet sin tidligere student Michael T. Osterholm, PhD, MPH, på mine vegne angående influensaen som så tragisk rammet familien Joe og Emma Hermanson i februar 1920. Både Tjostem og Osterholm, direktør ved Center of Infectious Disease Research and Policy, var enige om at influensaen Hermanson-familien fikk, kunne ha vært *et tilfelle av smitte fra svin tilbake til mennesker, i en mer virulent form enn den varianten som opptrådte i 1918.*

Glemt epidemi

Den dødelige 1918-influensen forsvant på like mystisk vis som den startet. Kanskje opparbeidet de overlevende immunitet mot den. Det vi vet er at så snart influensaen ikke lenger tok liv, så bredte glemselen seg.

© Deb Nelson Gourley

KAUTOKEINO

Deb Nelson Gourley's 1976 travel route

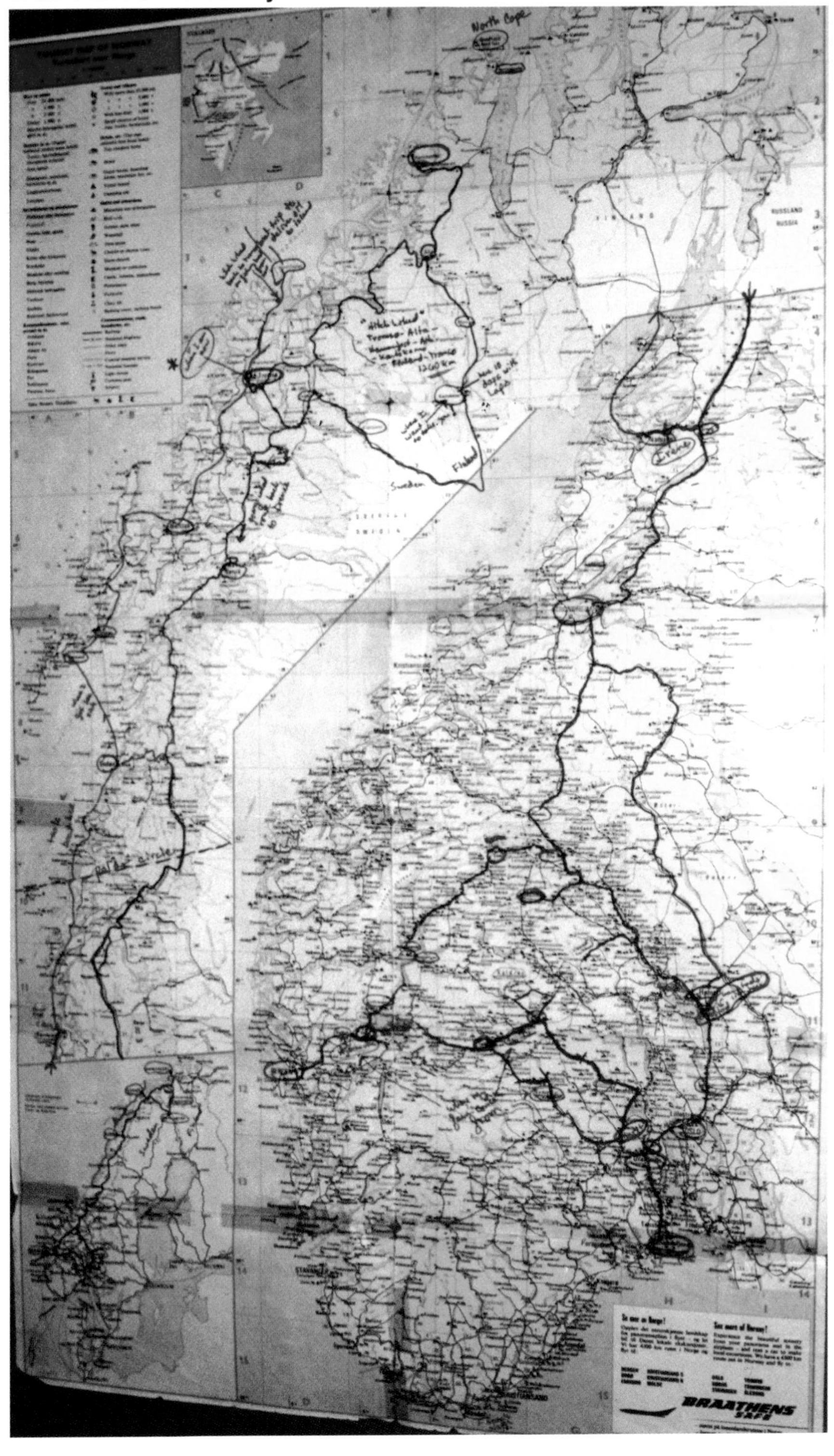

Bunadsølv

ERECTED BY THE STATE OF MINNESOTA
SETTLERS OF JACKSON COUNTY, WHOSE NAMES ARE
1857 MASSACRE
WILLIAM WOOD
GEORGE WOOD
JOSHUA STEWART
WILLIE THOMAS
TWO CHILDREN OF JOSHUA STEWART
1862 MASSACRE
OLE FORRE
JOHANES AXE
MIKKEL OLSON
LARS FURNESS
BRITA LANCELAND
ANNA LANCELAND
KNUD LANCELAND
KNUD MIDDSSAD AND WIFE
LARS GJORNEVIK AND WIFE
Photos courtesy of Steve Raska

Photos courtesy of Steve Raska

mother
OSSB

SLEKTSTEVNE ARNAFJORD
NESE
1668 2003
12.07.2003

Photo courtesy of Ingolf Kvist, Vik i Sogn

First International Rosemaling Symposium, *The Art of Rosemaling: Tradition Meets the Creative Mind*, during April 2004.
Left to right: Harley Refsal, Sigmund Aarseth, Deb Nelson Gourley, Nils Ellingsgard, and Alex Huntrods

Rosemaling by Sigmund Aarseth

Scandinavian Studies program at Telemark University College in Bø, Norway during 2003.

Photos courtesy of Krisztina László, Hungary

Alex

Picking multer (cloudberries)

JOZO
SALT

Deb's two sons, Alex and Ben Huntrods, at Russvatnet during 2003.

1971 & 1995 (24 years later)
Sylvan and Charlotte Nelson family
Left to right: Sylvan, Joe, Charlotte, Teresa, Todd, Robert, Deb (the author), and Kevin

Cutting Horse competition at the Sylvan and Charlotte Nelson arena on the 150-year-old ancestral farm in Amherst, near Canton, Minnesota
Photos courtesy of Teresa (Nelson) O'Connor

Deb Nelson Gourley holds the honors of being the first female FFA member to be pictured on the cover of the National Future Farmer magazine.

12

Sabotaging occupied Norway's heavy water

Byproduct of Vemork's chemical fertilizer production was a vital ingredient needed in Hitler's atom bomb

Sabotage, heavy water, and atom bomb are words one would not expect to hear when simply trying to find ancestral farms in Norway. Knowing only that the two farms were located in the area of Tinn i Telemark, my family and I set our course west from Oslo for the town of Rjukan, renowned for its death-defying cliffs and deep gorges. History was coming to life beneath our feet as we learned about some of the most daring sabotage acts during World War II, which not only prevented Nazi Germany from carrying out their atomic agenda, but also put Rjukan on the world map.

Town of Rjukan

Rjukan itself is situated at the bottom of the very deep Vestfjord Valley (Vestfjorddalen) surrounded by the 3,000-foot forested mountain that rises up almost vertically to the *Hardangervidda* (Hardanger Mountain Plateau), the largest and wildest mountain plateau in northern Europe. The plateau, about 3,500 square miles of barren territory with countless hills, rolling plains, rivers, lakes, marshes, and mountains, is a place where reindeer roam and humans dare not reside.

Towering majestically above the town of Rjukan, at a height of 6,178

feet, is *Gaustatoppen*, one of the most beautiful mountains in Norway. On a clear day, one can see one-sixth of Norway, all the way south to the coast and east to Sweden. Located inside *Gaustatoppen* today is a cable line. Built by NATO, the combination railway and elevator transportation system is 3,380 feet long with a 39° gradient and is used for transportation purposes.

Norway was still a poor country around 1900, with farming and fishing the primary means of subsistence. Up to 1905, there were still only about 50 farm families or 350 people that lived around Rjukan's isolated farming valley. It's therefore difficult to fathom that the population of this remote peasant society would swell to over 10,000 in only ten years and become the site of Norway's first heavy industry.

Hydroelectric power station

Engineer Sam Eyde, whom Rjukan's main street, *Sam Eydesgate*, was named after, sought to improve agriculture by finding a way of extracting nitrogen from the air in order to make artificial fertilizers. Together with physicist Kristian Birkeland, they developed the electric arc furnace for making mineral fertilizer and in 1905 founded *Norsk Hydro*.

The power of the mighty Rjukan waterfall was harnessed to produce fertilizer. It had a sheer drop of 341 feet and was located on the west side of Rjukan in Vemork. The never ending supply of water flowing from the *Hardangervidda* down into Vestfjorddalen provided Sam Eyde the basis for building *Norsk Hydro* on a shelf of rock below the waterfall. It was the largest hydroelectric power station in the world in 1911, with its generators churning out 120,000 kilowatts of electric power.

Twelve highly visible penstock pipelines, each with a diameter of 5.5 feet and about 900 feet long, were constructed to carry a constant flow of water from the reservoirs, lakes, and dams on top of the mountain. At a rate of 6,300,000 cubic feet every hour, endless tons of water plunged down the steep mountainside to the power station's massive turbines below.

Electrolysis plant

In 1928, a separate seven-story electrolysis plant was built in front of the hydroelectric power station on a broad shelf of rock blasted out of an

almost vertical mountainside. Made from blocks of stone cut out of the mountain, 800 tons of steel, and 1,700 barrels of cement, the huge electrolysis plant sat like an eagle's nest protected by nature.

The building site was deeply embedded in the gorge, and sat over 500 feet above the Måna River below. Due to the geography, only two routes gave access to the location, a single-track railway running on a narrow shelf along the mountainside, and a 75-foot long suspension bridge crossing the gorge 300 feet above the river.

At the electrolysis plant, hydrogen was used to produce artificial fertilizer, with a byproduct of this process being heavy water (deuterium oxide). It took roughly 100,000 gallons of water to end up with one gallon of 99.5 percent heavy water. No one dreamed that the byproduct from a fertilizer production process could serve as a vital ingredient for a superweapon.

Visiting the old hydroelectric power station in Vemork, site of the Norwegian Industrial Worker Museum, we learned the difference between regular water (H_2O) and heavy water (D_2O). Heavy water is water from which both hydrogen atoms have been replaced with deuterium, an isotope of hydrogen. Because deuterium also contains a neutron in addition to the proton, heavy water is about 10% heavier than regular water. Hence its name. Although heavy water tastes and looks like ordinary water, the extra weight works to concentrate the fission reactions.

"blood is thicker even than heavy water"

Krossobanen

Krossobanen, northern Europe's first cable car, was built in 1928 as a gift to the Rjukan townspeople from *Norsk Hydro*. Rjukan's mountains are so sheer that the sun's rays fail to reach the town's streets during four months of the winter. The cable car allows the inhabitants to rise high enough out of the deep gorge to enjoy the sunlight during the winter months. This past summer, as the cable car carried us to a point 2,907 feet above sea level, we could see for ourselves the heavy mountain shadows cast into Vestfjorddalen below.

Blitzkrieg comes to Norway

Nazi Germany attacked Norway on April 9, 1940 with a combined force of army, navy, and air force. Since Norway had a limited military force, all resistance was easily smashed. Bewildered and paralyzed, Norway was at war for the first time in 126 years. King Haakon VII, the royal family, and the government left for Britain on June 7, 1940 to continue their fight with help from the Allies.

The Nazi's interfered with every aspect of Norwegian daily life. They controlled the press, radio, and politics. Hitler feared an Allied invasion from the north, and therefore had as many as 430,000 soldiers in Norway at one time. Before Norway was liberated in 1945, more than 30,000 were imprisoned, 8,000 were sent to POW camps in Germany, and over 2,000 members of the resistance died.

Popular outrage escalated when it was demanded that King Haakon abdicate his throne. There was a great revival amongst the people awaking from the shock of defeat, which spread like wildfire throughout the country. With intense patriotism and love of their King and country, the Norwegian Resistance movement grew. Young Norwegian men made their way to England and Scotland to train in commando operations and sabotage. They would become legends in their homeland, demonstrating that "blood is thicker even than heavy water."

Assault preparation

Albert Einstein, whose theories were crucial to the exploitation of nuclear energy, had warned President Franklin Roosevelt as early as 1939 of the danger of a German atomic bomb.

Only one month after the Norwegian occupation, in May of 1940, the Germans ordered *Norsk Hydro* to increase production of heavy water to 3,000 pounds per year. It soon became clear that the Germans were interested in heavy water for their nuclear program. In February 1942, an increase to 10,000 pounds per year was ordered. Vemork was the only facility in the world capable of producing the quantities of heavy water the Nazis needed.

On the night of June 17, 1942, Winston Churchill left Britain and flew to Hyde Park, New York to meet with President Roosevelt. The British and American physicists both agreed that Hitler was trying to produce a uranium and heavy water pile in his atomic bomb program. The race was now on to stop Hitler's dream of possessing the ultimate weapon.

London, England and Washington, D.C. agreed that heavy water had something to do with Hitler's threat of a secret weapon. It was decided to sabotage the heavy water production at Vemork to prevent usage by the Nazis. The allies determined that the Germans would not expect a sabotage attack, since Vemork was so well protected by nature.

The first lone Norwegian parachutist was dropped above the *Hardandervidda* on March 28, 1942 and was followed on October 19, 1942 by four Norwegians just west of Rjukan. Code named "Grouse," their mission was to collect intelligence on heavy water production, maintain radio contact with the Allied Command in London, and prepare the ground for the sabotage operation.

The struggle to destroy the heavy water produced in Vemork took more than two years and involved four daring assaults.

British commando soldiers

On November 19, 1942, the first assault on the heavy water plant, code named "Freshman," ended in total tragedy. Two Halifax bombers were each to tow a Horsa glider all the way from Wick Airfield in Scotland, across 400 miles of sea over the mountain in Norway, and then release the gliders to land on the *Hardangervidda* near Rjukan. On board the two gliders would be a total of 34 specially trained British commando soldiers that would sabotage the heavy water unit at Vemork.

For the "Freshman" operation to be successful, a clear, moonlit night was needed. By the time the crew reached the Norwegian mountains, they ran into heavy clouds and ice formed on the wings. Both gliders and one bomber crashed into the mountain, and the other bomber returned to Scotland. What soldiers survived the crash were rounded up by the Germans and brutally executed. Although the commando soldiers were fully dressed in British uniforms, the Gestapo considered them saboteurs instead of POW's.

At the glider crash site, the Germans had found maps indicating that the British soldiers were en route to Rjukan to destroy the heavy water installations. To reinforce defense at Vemork, the Germans placed machine guns and searchlights on top of the heavy water plant, brightly illuminating the whole complex. The suspension bridge was patrolled 24 hours per day. More mines were planted, and floodlights were placed on the penstock pipelines. To provide protection from an aerial attack, anti-aircraft guns were installed and wires were stretched across Vestfjorddalen from mountain to mountain.

The glider disasters forced the still intact five-member Norwegian "Grouse" group, renamed "Swallow," to withdraw into the heart of the *Hardangervidda*, 3,937 feet above sea level. They survived several winter months by hunting and eating reindeer. The stomach contents were consumed, in order to obtain vitamins from the moss eaten by the reindeer. The Norwegians also scrounged oats, sugar, and dry firewood from hunters' huts.

Meanwhile, drop-by-drop, the precious heavy water collected in the electrolysis building. The gradual concentration process actually started on the fifth floor and trickled from cell-to-cell, and floor-to-floor, until it reached the 18 identical high concentration cells located in the corner room of the basement. Norwegians within the facility managed to temporarily curb production by secretly adding castor oil and cod liver oil to the electrolysis process, causing intense frothing and foaming.

Norwegian resistance saboteurs

On February 16, 1943, a new group of six Norwegian resistance saboteurs trained in explosives were dropped by parachute into a blizzard on the *Hardangervidda*, 30 miles from their intended dropping zone. After a strenuous trek on skis, they joined the "Swallow" group, making a total of 11 men. A second assault, code named operation "Gunnerside," was carried out by nine of the saboteurs, while the two wireless operators stayed in the mountains to maintain communications with London. Before infiltrating their homeland, all 11 of the Norwegians had been specially trained in England and Scotland by Special Operations Executive.

One of the most heroic sabotage acts of World War II occurred on February 27, 1943, at 8:00 P.M. The brave Norwegians set out to attach heavy explosives to the fully concentrated heavy water cells in the basement room at Vemork. To avoid German reprisals against the local civilian population should they be caught, they wore British army uniforms under their white camouflage suits. Each man also was issued a cyanide pill enclosed in a rubber capsule that could bring death in three to five seconds if needed.

The Germans, believing that no one could scale the 600-foot sheer rock face on the south side of the gorge, left it and the railroad track above unguarded. Shuffling through some aerial photographs, a startling discovery was made when one of the saboteurs noticed small trees and shrubbery sprouted from the vertical cliff. He concluded, *"Where trees grow, a man can climb."* An immediate reconnaissance mission confirmed a way to cross what was considered an impassible gorge.

The nine Norwegians slithered down the sheer north side of the canyon to Vemork, carrying their skis through the heavier forested areas along with their 50-to-65-pound backpacks. They were weighed down with explosive charges, pistols, tommy guns, ammunition, grenades, and knives. Before crossing the icy east-west Rjukan Road along the north side of the gorge, they buried their white camouflage suits, skis, poles, and extra equipment to be retrieved on their return.

Once over the ice-choked river at the bottom of the gorge, the saboteurs edged up the formidable wall on the opposite side with determination and skill. They searched for crevices, cracks, juniper bushes, and greenery, for foot-and-finger holds, as they moved from ledge-to-ledge. The Norwegians emerged by the unguarded railway track leading to the heavy water plant, avoiding other routes where they would encounter the minefields laid by the Germans and the highly protected suspension bridge.

In the wee hours of February 28, 1943, the explosive charges set by the resistance fighters destroyed all 18 of the high concentration cells that were four feet two inches high, 12 inches in diameter, and jacketed in heavy gauge stainless steel. In all, about 1,000 pounds of heavy water had suddenly "evaporated." The German guards hardly grasped that there had been an explosion, due to the powerful drone of the generators and the building's thick concrete walls.

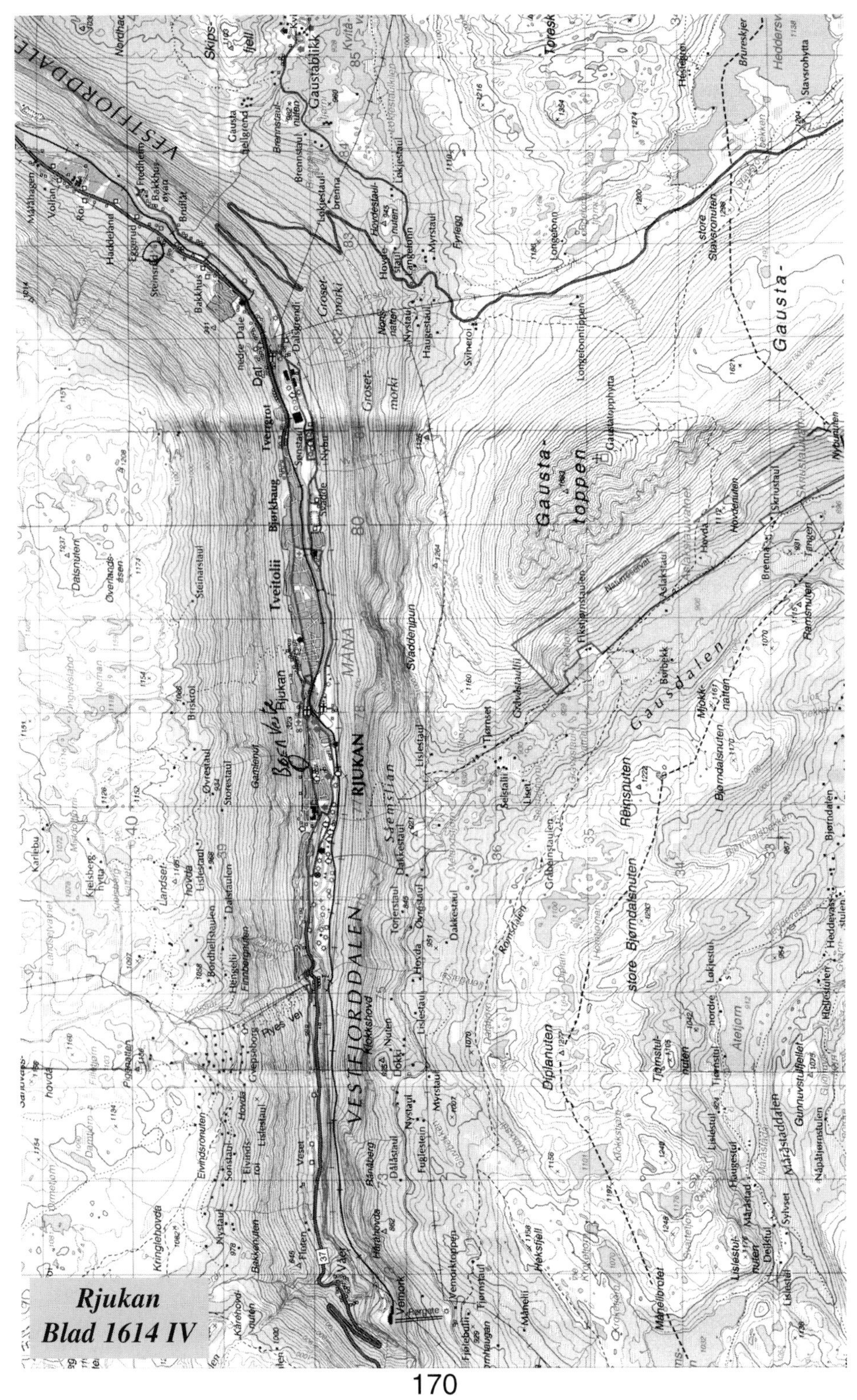
Rjukan
Blad 1614 IV
RJUKAN
VESTFJORDDALEN
Gausta-
toppen
Gausdalen
MÅNA
Tveitolii
Gaustatoppen

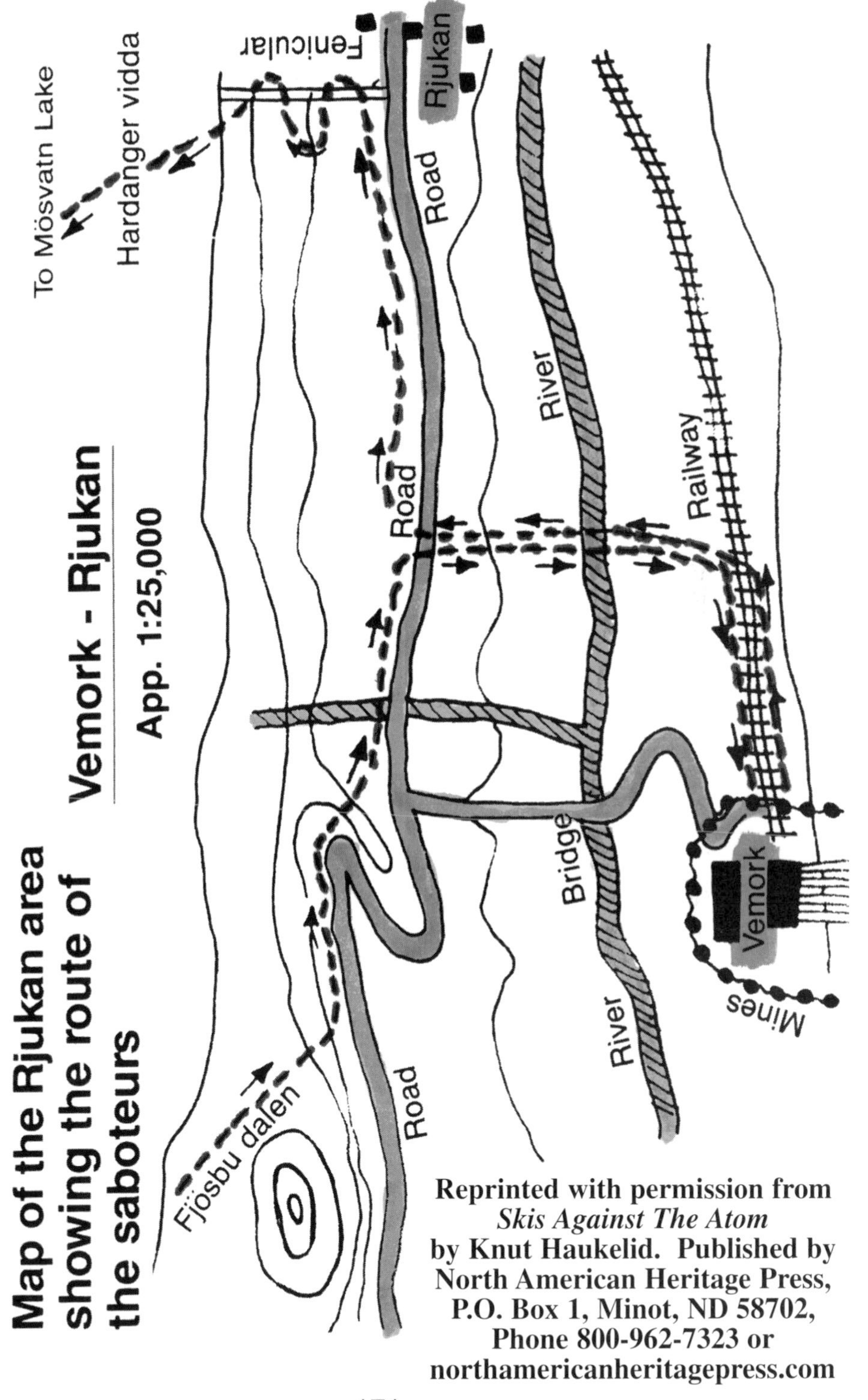

Reprinted with permission from
Skis Against The Atom
by Knut Haukelid. Published by
North American Heritage Press,
P.O. Box 1, Minot, ND 58702,
Phone 800-962-7323 or
northamericanheritagepress.com

The Norwegians had already crossed the Måna River when they heard the air-raid sirens sound for general mobilization in the Rjukan area. The saboteurs had gotten two lucky breaks. First, because of recent reassignments, the guards did not know where the switch was to the powerful illumination system, which would have revealed the location of the resistance fighters in the gorge. And second, the guard dogs were not sent out that night because of foul weather.

Germany's supreme military commander in Norway arrived at the site a few hours later. He actually marveled at the performance of the "British bandits." The General surprisingly called the sabotage the finest coup he had seen in the war.

Char Nelson and Teresa (Nelson) O'Connor

To avoid capture after retrieving their gear, the resistance fighters actually reversed directions and skied towards Rjukan. All the while, they watched the headlights of the military vehicles swarming towards Vemork on the Rjukan Road below them. It would take another three hours, until about 5:00 A.M., to climb up the mountainous Ryes Road, zigzagging under *Krossobanen*, the cable car lift. The men reached the safety of the *Hardangervidda*, only to be greeted by the full force of the North Atlantic winds.

The Norwegians, *"born with skis on their feet,"* had skiing abilities far superior to the German guards. Five of the group skied the treacherous two-week trip to safety in Sweden. The other six saboteurs not only skillfully avoided capture by over 10,000 Germans in their sweep of the *Hardangervidda*, but also maintained their radio contact with London.

It was one of the worst winters in the history of the Hardanger Mountain Plateau. Trying to avoid the German sweep and a violent westerly gale, two of the resistance fighters were forced to stay in thin sleeping bags under two mounds of snow for five days and nights. They survived by melting snow with tallow candles and chewing on raw pemmican.

In a chase that lasted for several hours on the *Hardangervidda*, one of the saboteurs outskied five Germans that were pursuing him on skis. Fatigued from covering over 100 miles in 36 hours, he accidentally fell over a 120-foot cliff and was injured. He was later captured, but managed an escape during transit to the concentration camp near Oslo. Until his arm and shoulder healed, fellow Norwegians hid him as a "dangerous lunatic" for three weeks in a solitary cell at the Lier Asylum, near Drammen.

American bombing raid

During the next six months, the electrolysis plant was rebuilt and production restarted. A third assault was made on November 16, 1943, only this time by the Americans. The Germans had an ideal location for a wartime project, difficult to bomb and easy to defend.

From the United States airfield, about 90 miles northeast of London, 174 aircraft swooped in over the narrow Rjukan Valley and dropped 828 bombs, each weighing 500 or 1,000 pounds. The bombs fell everywhere for 33 minutes. Only two hit the electrolysis plant damaging the top floors, leaving the high concentration of heavy water secured under the seven stories of concrete untouched.

Three bombs hit the penstock pipelines, but fortunately for the civilians, automatic closings at the top of the reservoir stopped the devastating flow of water. Four bombs struck the hydroelectric power station with little damage, one collapsed the suspension bridge over the gorge, and one directly hit the newly constructed air-raid shelter. The bombs killed 22 Norwegians, mostly women and children in the shelter. The attack convinced the Germans to abandon any further production at Vemork.

Sinking of the ferry

A couple of months later, the remaining group of Norwegian saboteurs discovered that the Germans planned to ship the entire semi-finished heavy water product from Vemork to the fatherland. That quantity far exceeded what had been destroyed earlier. Orders for a fourth assault came by radio from London. The plan was to destroy the heavy water during transit before it reached the ocean voyage.

The remaining heavy water was to be put into 39 drums for shipment, loaded onto the railway wagons at Vemork, and then taken by rail along the mountainside to Lake Tinnsjø. Intelligence reports revealed to the Norwegian resistance fighters that the weakest link in the transport of the heavy water was the two-hour journey by civilian ferry over Lake Tinnsjø. The third deepest lake in all of Europe, it is 1509 feet at its lowest point. On the railway ferry, the drums would be in one location versus spread out over several railway wagons.

Obviously afraid of an attack, Rjukan was packed with Germans troops. There were more Germans than Norwegians in Vestfjorddalen. While awaiting transportation on the ferry the next morning, the railway wagons were floodlighted and surrounded by armed guards.

The Germans, however, failed to place a guard at the D/F Hydro railway ferry that was to be used the following morning for the heavy water transport on Lake Tinnsjø. Three Norwegians were able to secretly board the ferry during the night and place a 19-pound charge in the hull, using two alarm clocks and a detonating mechanism.

On Sunday, February 20, 1944, as the clocks ticked away, the ferry approached the deepest part of Lake Tinnsjø. At 10:45 A.M., an explosion blew a hole in the ferry. As calculated, the bow went under taking on water, causing the stern to rise. The railway wagons, loaded with drums of heavy water, rolled forward and tumbled into the lake. In only four minutes, the heavy water went down with the ferry, where it still lies in the bottom of Lake Tinnsjø.

The resistance fighters were unable to warn the unsuspecting ferry passengers for fear the Germans would become suspicious, and as a result 26 people died. With ruthless logic, daring, and endurance, the last chapter in the battle for heavy water in Norway had finally ended, preventing Hitler from carrying out his atomic project.

In April 1945, a dismantled high concentration plant was found in Bavaria, Germany. The atomic pile with uranium and heavy water was on the brink of "going critical" or sustaining a nuclear reaction. All that was lacking was about 740 quarts of additional heavy water.

Family farms

After discovering that our ancestral farms, "Bøen Vestre" and "Steinsrud under Dale," were located on Rjukan's *Sam Eydesgate*, my teenage sons, Alex and Ben, concluded that genealogy research is really interesting.

For four generations, going back to the 1600's, our ancestors from "Bøen Vestre" owned what is now the center of Rjukan. On the east end of Rjukan was "Steinsrud under Dale" where my great-great-great-grandfather, Tov Torgrimsson, was born in 1799. It was Tov's son, Gullik Tovsson (Thompson), born in Kjosa, Imingen i Numedal who immigrated in 1876 to Black Hammer in Houston County, Minnesota. He later moved to Simley Springs in the Big Woods of Fillmore County, Minnesota.

As we stood on the Vemork suspension bridge, it seemed almost unbelievable that only 60 years earlier, events that unfolded in this remote, ancestral Vestfjorddalen, changed the outcome of the Second World War.

For further information

• Gallagher, Thomas. *Assault in Norway: Sabotaging the Nazi Nuclear Program.* Connecticut: The Lyons Press, 2002. (Available at the Vesterheim Museum in Decorah, Iowa)

• Haukelid, Knut. *Skis Against The Atom.* North American Heritage Press, 1989. (Available from North American Heritage Press, P.O. Box 1, Minot, ND 58702, phone 800-962-7323, or northamericanheritagepress.com)

• Kurzman, Dan. *Blood and Water: Sabotaging Hitler's Bomb.* New York: Henry Holt and Company, Inc., 1997.

• Columbia Pictures Video. *The Heroes of Telemark.* (Hollywood version). Filmed on location in Vemork and Rjukan. 1965.

• National Geographic Video. *Untold Stories of World War II: Three Secrets That Changed the War.* 1998. http://www.nationalgeographic.com

Norske sabotører stoppet Hitlers atombombe

Tungtvannet havnet på bunnen av Tinnsjøen

Sabotasje, tungtvann og atombomber er ord en ikke venter å høre når en bare skal forsøke å lokalisere slektsgårder i Norge. Uten å vite annet enn at de to gårdene lå i området rundt Tinn i Telemark, satte familien og jeg kursen vestover fra Oslo mot Rjukan, som er kjent for sine livsfarlige klipper og dype juv. Historien ble levende under føttene våre etter hvert som vi hørte om en av de mest vågale sabotasjeaksjonene under andre verdenskrig, en aksjon som ikke bare forhindret Nazi-Tyskland fra å gjennomføre sine planer om atomvåpen, men også satte Rjukan på verdenskartet.

Rjukan

Selve Rjukan ligger helt i bunnen av den dype Vestfjorddalen, omgitt av de vel 900 meter høye skogkledde fjellene som reiser seg nesten vertikalt opp mot Hardangervidda (Hardangerfjellplatået), det største og mest uberørte fjellplatået i Nord-Europa. Platået, med sine om lag 9000 kvadratkilometer med ødemark, med utallige åser, bølgende vidder, elver, innsjøer, myrer og fjell, er et område hvor reinsdyrene streifer omkring, og hvor mennesker ikke bosetter seg.

Over Rjukan ruver den majestetiske Gaustatoppen 1883 meter over havet, et av de vakreste fjellene i Norge. På en klar dag kan man se en sjettedel av Norge, helt til kysten i sør, og østover til Sverige. Inne i Gaustatoppen finnes det i dag en kabelbane. Den er en kombinasjon av jernbane og elevatorsystem, bygd av NATO, og brukt til transportformål, 1030 meter lang og med 39° stigning.

Norge var fortsatt et fattig land rundt 1900, med jordbruk og fiske som hovedutkomme. Fram mot 1905 var det fortsatt bare 50 bondefamilier, eller 350 mennesker, som levde langs Rjukans isolerte jordbruksdal. Det er derfor vanskelig å fatte at befolkningen i dette avsidesliggende bondesamfunnet skulle vokse til over 10 000 i løpet av bare ti år, og at dette skulle bli åsted for Norges første tungindustri.

Den hydroelektriske kraftstasjonen

Ingeniøren Sam Eyde, som har gitt navn til Rjukans hovedgate, Sam Eydesgate, forsøkte å forbedre jordbruket gjennom å finne en måte å trekke ut nitrogen fra luften på, for slik å lage kunstig gjødsel. Sammen med fysikeren Kristian Birkeland utviklet han den elektriske smelteovnen for å lage mineralgjødsel, og grunnla Norsk Hydro i

Photo by Alex Huntrods

1905.

Kraften fra den mektige Rjukanfossen ble temmet for å produsere kunstgjødsel. Den hadde et bratt fall på vel 100 meter og lå i Vemork, på vestsiden av Rjukan. Den aldri sviktende tilførselen av vann, som flommer fra Hardangervidda ned i Vestfjorddalen, sikret Sam Eyde grunnlaget for å bygge Norsk Hydro, på en fjellhylle under fossen. Med generatorer som kvernet ut 120 000 kilowatt med elektrisk kraft, var dette i 1911 den største hydroelektriske kraftsstasjonen i verden.

Tolv godt synlige 274 meter lange vannledninger, hver med en diameter på vel halvannen meter, ble konstruert for å føre en konstant vannstrøm ned fra reservoarene, innsjøene og dammene som lå på toppen av fjellet. Med en fart på 178 396 kubikkmeter per time, fosset endeløse mengder med vann nedover til kraftstasjonens massive turbiner, som lå under den bratte fjellsiden.

Elektrolyseanlegget

I 1928 ble et separat sjuetasjers elektrolyseverk bygd på en bred fjellhylle som var sprengt ut i en nesten vertikal fjellside foran den hydroelektriske kraftstasjonen. Laget av steinblokker som var hogd ut av fjellet, 800 tonn stål og 1700 tønner med sement, lå det enorme elektrolyseverket der som et ørnerede, beskyttet av naturen.

Byggestedet lå begravd dypt nede i juvet, 152 meter over elva Måna. På grunn av geografien ga bare to veier adgang til stedet, en enkelsporet jernbane, som gikk langs en smal hylle i fjellsiden, og en 23 meter lang hengebru, som krysset juvet vel 90 meter over elva.

Ved elektrolyseanlegget ble det brukt hydrogen for å produsere kunstgjødsel, og et biprodukt av prosessen var tungtvann (deuterium oksid). Det gikk med om lag 378 500 liter med vann for å ende opp med en gallon (3.7 liter) 99.5% tungtvann. Ingen drømte om at biproduktet fra kunstgjødselproduksjonen kunne tjene som vital bestanddel i et supervåpen.

Da vi besøkte den gamle hydroelektriske kraftstasjonen i Vemork ved Norsk Industriarbeidermuseum, fikk vi vite forskjellen på vanlig vann (H_2O) og tungtvann (D_2O). Tungtvann er vann der begge hydrogenatomene er erstattet med deuterium, en isotop av hydrogen. Fordi deuterium også inneholder et nøytron i tillegg til protonet, er tungtvann om lag 10% tyngre enn vanlig vann. Derav navnet. Selv om tungtvann smaker og ser ut som vanlig vann, bidrar den ekstra vekten til å konsentrere fisjonsreaksjonen.

Krossobanen

Krossobanen, Nord-Europas første kabelbane, ble bygd i 1928, og var en gave fra Norsk Hydro til beboerne i Rjukan. Rjukans fjellsider er så bratte at solen ikke når ned til byens gater i fire vintermåneder. Kabelbanen gjør det mulig for innbyggerne å dra høyt nok opp fra den dype dalen til å kunne ha glede av solen om vinteren. Da kabelbanen sist sommer bar oss opp til 886 meter over havet, kunne vi se for oss de tunge skyggene av fjellene i Vestfjorddalen under oss.

Blitzkrigen kommer til Norge

Nazi-Tyskland angrep Norge 9. april 1940 med en kombinert styrke av hær, marine og luftvåpen. Siden Norge hadde begrenset med militærmakt, ble all motstand lett smadret. Forvillet og paralysert var Norge for første gang på 126 år i krig. Kong Håkon VII, den kongelige familie og regjeringen dro til England 7. juni 1940 for å fortsette kampen derfra med hjelp fra de allierte.

Nazistene tok over alle sider ved norsk dagligliv. De kontrollerte pressen, radioen og politikken. Hitler fryktet en alliert invasjon fra nord, og hadde derfor hele 430 000 soldater i Norge på en gang. Før Norge ble frigjort i 1945 ble mer enn 30 000 tatt til fange, 8000 ble sendt til konsentrasjonsleirer i Tyskland og over 2000 medlemmer av motstandsbevegelsen døde.

Det allmenne opprøret ble sterkere da det ble krevd at kong Håkon ga fra seg tronen. Folk våknet opp fra sjokket over å være slått, og motstanden spredte seg som ild over landet. Med intens patriotisme og kjærlighet til konge og fedreland, vokste motstandsbevegelsen. Unge norske menn tok seg over til England og Skottland for å få trening til kommandooperasjoner og sabotasje. De skulle komme til å bli legender i sitt hjemland ved å vise at "blod var tykkere enn tungtvann."

Forberedelser til angrep

Albert Einstein, hvis teorier var grunnleggende for utnyttelsen av atomenergien, hadde så tidlig som i 1939 advart president Roosevelt mot faren for en tysk atombombe.

Bare en måned etter okkupasjonen av Norge, i mai 1940, gav tyskerne Norsk Hydro ordre om å øke produksjonen av tungtvann til 1362 kilo per år. Det ble fort klart at tyskernes interesse for tungtvannet hadde tilknytning til deres atomprogram. I februar 1942 ble det bestilt en økning til vel 4535 kilo per år. Vemork var den eneste innretningen i verden som var i stand til å produsere de mengdene med tungtvann som nazistene trengte.

Natten til 17. juni 1942 forlot Winston Churchill Storbritannia og fløy til Hyde Park, New York, for å møte president Roosevelt. De britiske og amerikanske fysikerne var enige om at Hitler forsøkte å produsere en reaktor av uranium og tungtvann i forbindelse med et atombombeprogram. Kappløpet om å stoppe Hitlers drøm om det ultimate våpenet var nå i gang.

London, England og Washington, D.C., var klar over at tungtvannet hadde noe å gjøre med Hitlers trussel om et hemmelig våpen. Det ble bestemt å sabotere tungtvannsenheten ved Vemork hydrogenfabrikk for å forhindre at den ble brukt av nazistene. De allierte forutsatte at tyskerne ikke ville vente noe sabotasjeangrep, siden Vemork var så godt beskyttet av naturen.

Den første norske fallskjermhopperen ble sluppet over Hardangervidda 28. mars 1942, og ble 19. oktober 1942 fulgt av fire andre vest for Rjukan. Under kodenavnet "Grouse" var oppdraget å samle hemmelig informasjon om tungtvannsproduksjonen, opprette radiokontakt med de alliertes kommando i London, og å gjøre klart for en sabotasjeaksjon.

Arbeidet med å ødelegge tungtvannsproduksjonen i Vemork tok mer enn to år og innebar fire dristige angrep.

Britiske kommandosoldater

Den 19. november 1942 endte det første angrepet på tungtvannsfabrikken under kodenavnet "Freshman", i fullstendig tragedie. To Halifax-bombefly tauet et "Horsa" glidefly hver de 400 sjømilene fra Wick Airfield i Skottland, og over fjellene i Norge, hvor de skulle slippe dem løs for å lande på Hardangervidda, nær Rjukan. Om bord på glideflyene var det 34 spesialtrente britiske kommandosoldater som skulle sabotere tungtvannsenheten i Vemork.

For at "Freshman"-operasjonen skulle lykkes, trengte man en klar, månelys natt. Da besetningen ankom de

Krossobanen

norske fjellene, fløy de rett inn i tunge skyer, og det dannet seg is på vingene. Begge gliderne og et bombefly kolliderte med fjellet, det andre bombeflyet returnerte til Skottland. De soldatene som overlevde havariet ble omringet av tyskerne og brutalt henrettet. Selv om kommandosoldatene var kledd i britiske uniformer, betraktet Gestapo dem som sabotører i stedet for som krigsfanger.

Der gliderne hadde havarert, fant tyskerne kart som viste at de britiske soldatene var på vei til Rjukan for å ødelegge tungtvannsinstallasjonen. For å forsterke forsvaret på Vemork, plasserte tyskerne maskingevær og lyskastere på toppen av tungtvannsfabrikken, og det lyste opp hele anlegget. Hengebrua ble patruljert 24 timer i døgnet. Flere miner ble plassert ut, og flomlys ble plassert på fabrikkpipene. For å sikre seg beskyttelse mot luftangrep ble antiluftskyts installert, og det ble strukket wirer tvers over Vestfjorddalen fra fjell til fjell.

Glideflykatastrofen tvang den fortsatt intakte norske "Grouse"-gruppa på fem personer å trekke seg tilbake til hjertet av Hardangervidda, 1200 meter over havet, nå under det nye navnet "Swallow". De overlevde flere vintermåneder ved å jakte og spise reinsdyr. Selv mageinnholdet ble fortært, i den hensikt å skaffe seg vitaminer fra mosen reinsdyrene spiste. Nordmennene forsynte seg også med havre, sukker og tørr ved fra jakthyttene.

I mellomtiden samlet det verdifulle tungtvannet seg dråpe for dråpe i elektrolysebygningen. Den gradvise konsentrasjonsprosessen begynte faktisk i femte etasje, og væsken dryppet fra celle til celle, etasje til etasje, inntil den nådde den attende konsentrasjonscellen som lå i et rom i hjørnet av kjelleren. Nordmennene inne i bygningen lykkes i å sinke produksjonen midlertidig ved i all hemmelighet å tilsette laksérolje eller tran under elektrolyseprosessen, noe som gjorde at det frådet og skummet intenst.

Norske sabotører

16. februar 1943 ble en ny gruppe med trente sprengningseksperter og sabotører fra den norske motstandsbevegelsen sluppet ut i fallskjerm i en snøstorm på Hardangervidda, nærmere fem mil fra det planlagte landingsstedet. Etter en strabasiøs skitur slo de seg sammen med "Svale"-gruppa, slik at de samlet var elleve menn. Et andre angrep, under kodenavnet "Gunnerside", ble gjennomført av ni av sabotørene, mens de to radiooperatørene ble igjen i fjellet for å opprettholde kontakten med London. Før de infiltrerte sitt hjemland, var alle elleve spesialtrent i England og Skottland av Special Operations Executive.

En av de mest heroiske sabotasjeaksjonene under andre verdenskrig skjedde klokken åtte om kvelden den 27. februar 1943. De modige nordmennene dro ut for å angripe den ferdig konsentrerte tungtvannscellen i kjellerrommet på Vemork. For å unngå tyske represalier mot lokalbefolkningen, skulle de bli tatt, og de bar britiske hæruniformer under de hvite kamuflasjedraktene. Hver mann fikk også tildelt en cyanidpille lukket inne i en gummikapsel, den brakte døden i løpet av tre til fem sekunder, om nødvendig.

Tyskerne som ikke trodde at noen kunne forsere den 182 meter høye fjellsiden på sørsiden av juvet, lot jernbanesporet på oversiden være ubevoktet. Idet de bladde gjennom noen flyfotografier ble det gjort en overraskende oppdagelse da en av sabotørene la merke til at det vokste små trær og busker på den vertikale klippen. *"Der det vokser trær, er det også mulig å klatre"*, slo han fast. En rask rekognoseringsferd bekreftet at det fantes en mulighet for å krysse det som ble betraktet som et ugjennomtrengelig juv.

De ni nordmennene skled ned den bratte fjellsiden på nordsiden av juvet, ned til Vemork, mens de bar både ski og 20-30 kilos ryggsekker gjennom de tyngste skogvokste områdene. De var tynget ned med eksplosiver, pistoler, maskingeværer, ammunisjon, granater og kniver. Før de krysset den isete østvestgående veien langs nordsiden av skaret, grov de ned de hvite kamuflasjedraktene, ski, staver og ekstra utstyr, med tanke på å finne det når de vendte tilbake.

Så snart de var over den ispakkede elva i bunnene av juvet, lirket de seg besluttsomt og presist oppover den formidable fjellveggen på motsatt side. De søkte etter revner og sprekker, einer og annet buskas for å få tak med føtter og fingre mens de beveget seg fra hylle til hylle. De nådde fram langs den ubevoktede jernbanelinjen som førte til tungtvannsfabrikken, idet de der unngikk både minefeltene tyskerne hadde lagt, og den strengt bevoktede hengebrua.

I de tidlige morgentimene den 28. februar 1943, ødela de eksplosive ladningene som motstandskjemperne plasserte, alle 18 containerne med tungtvann. De var halvannen meter høye, 30 centimeter i diameter, og var dekket av tungt, standardisert rustfritt stål. I alt hadde drøyt 450 kilo med tungtvann forduftet. På grunn av de sterke drønnene fra generatorene og de tykke betongveggene i bygningen, skjønte tyskerne knapt at der hadde vært en eksplosjon.

Nordmennene hadde allerede krysset Månaelva da de hørte luftvernsirenene varsle generell mobilisering i Rjukanområdet. Sabotørene hadde fått to heldige utsettelser. På grunn av nyutnevnelser, så visste ikke vaktene hvor bryteren til det kraftige lyskastersystemet var, ellers ville de ha avslørt motstandskjemperne i juvet. I tillegg til det ble ikke vakthundene sendt ut den natten på grunn av det dårlige været.

Den tyske øverstkommanderende i Norge ankom stedet få timer senere. Han undret seg faktisk over det "de britiske bandittene" hadde utrettet. Generalen kalte overraskende nok sabotasjeaksjonen for det best utførte kupp han hadde sett under krigen.

For å unngå å bli tatt etter å ha funnet igjen utstyret, snudde faktisk motstandskjemperne og gikk i motsatt retning, på ski mot Rjukan. Hele tiden betraktet de lyskasterne fra de militære kjøretøyene som myldret ned mot Vemork langs Rjukanveien lenger nede. Det ville ta enda tre timer, til om lag fem om morgenen, å klatre opp Ryes vei, i siksak oppover fjellet under Krossobanen. Mennene nådde i sikkerhet på Hardangervidda bare for å bli møtt av de nordatlantiske vindenes fulle styrke.

Nordmennene, som sies å være født med ski på beina, hadde langt bedre skiferdigheter enn de tyske vaktene. Fem fra gruppa gikk i to strabasiøse uker på ski til sikkerhet i Sverige. De andre seks sabotørene unngikk ikke bare på dyktig vis å bli tatt til fange av de mer enn 10 000 tyskerne som gjennomsøkte Hardangervidda, de opprettholdt også radiokontakten med England.

Dette var en av de verste vintrene i manns minne på Hardangerfjellplatået. For å unngå tyskernes sveip og en kraftig vestlig kulig ble to av motstandskjemperne tvunget til å oppholde seg i soveposene under to snøskavler i fem døgn. De overlevde ved å smelte snø med talglys og tygge på rå pemmikan.

I en flere timers flukt på Hardangervidda, gikk en av sabotørene fra fem tyskere som fulgte etter ham på ski. Utslitt etter å ha tilbakelagt 16 mil i løpet av 36 timer, falt han ned en 35 meter høy klippe og ble skadet. Han ble senere tatt, men greide å unnslippe i løpet av transporten til fangeleiren, som lå i nærheten av Oslo. Inntil armen og skulderen var leget, utgav en annen nordmann ham for å være "farlig sinnsyk" og skjulte ham i tre uker i et isolat ved asylet i Lier ved Drammen.

Amerikansk bomberaid

I løpet de neste seks månedene ble tungtvannsfabrikken bygd opp igjen og produksjonen gjenopptatt. Et tredje angrep ble gjort 16. november 1943, men denne gangen av amerikanerne. Tyskerne hadde funnet et ideelt sted for et krigsprosjekt, vanskelig å bombe og lett å forsvare.

Fra den amerikanske flyplassen som lå om lag 14 mil nordøst for London, sveipte 174 fly inn over den trange Rjukandalen og slapp 828 bomber, hver på mellom 220 og 450 kilo. Bombene landet overalt i 33 minutter. Bare to traff elektrolyseanlegget uten å forvolde særlig mye skade, en ødela hengebrua over juvet og en traff rett på det nybygde tilfluktsrommet. Bombene drepte 22 nordmenn, flest kvinner og barn som hadde søkt skjul i tilfluktsrommet. Angrepet overbeviste tyskerne om at de måtte avvikle all videre produksjon på Vemork.

Ferga senkes

Noen måneder senere oppdaget den gjenværende gruppa med norske sabotører at tyskerne planla å skipe ut alt det halvferdig tungtvannsproduktet fra Vemork til hjemlandet. Mengden overgikk langt det som var blitt ødelagt tidligere. Ordre om et fjerde angrep kom over radio fra London. Planen var

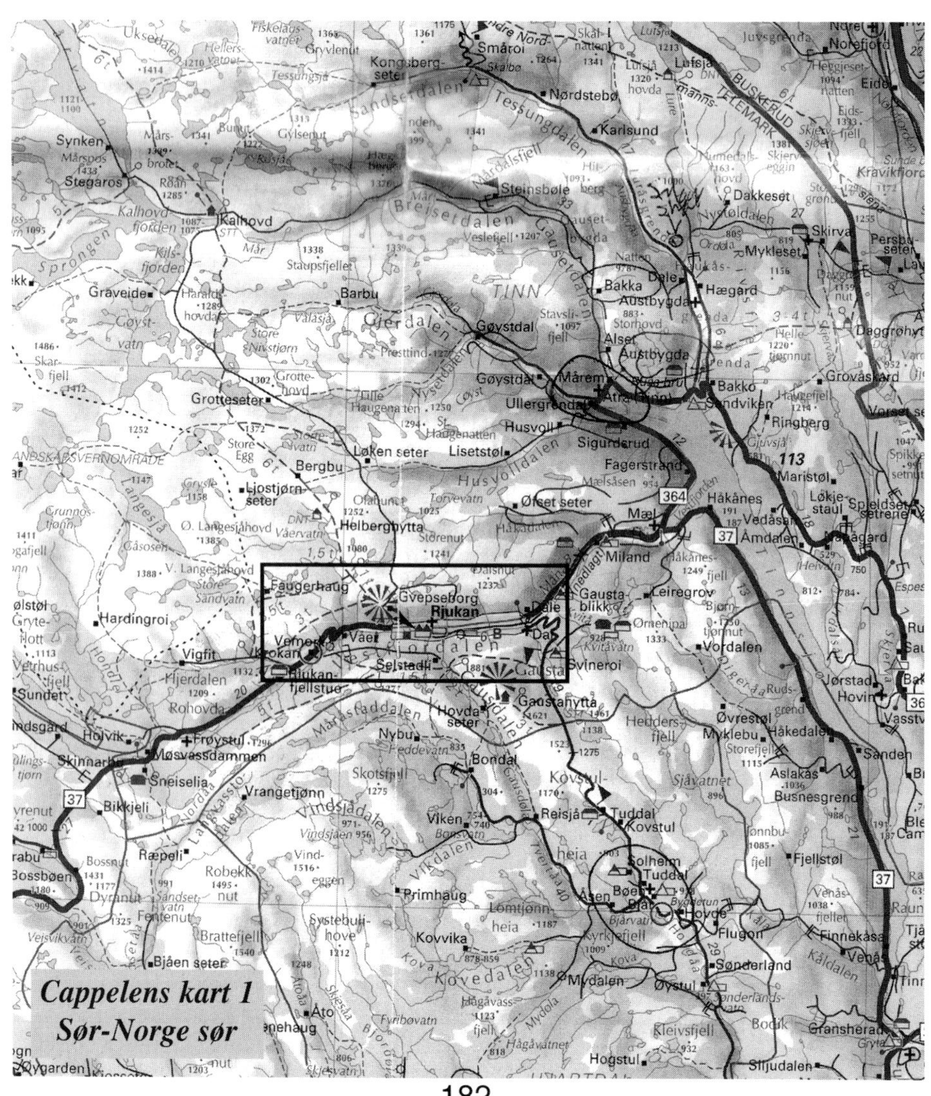

Cappelens kart 1 Sør-Norge sør

å ødelegge tungtvannet under transitten før det nådde havet.

Det gjenværende tungtvannet ble plassert i 39 tønner og lastet på jernbanevogner på Vemork for utskipning, og så brakt med tog langs fjellsiden til Tinnsjø. Etterretningsrapporter avslørte for de norske motstandskjemperne at det svakeste punktet i transporten av tungtvannet var den to timer lange turen over Tinnsjøen med den lokale ferga. Den er den tredje dypeste innsjøen i Europa, med sine 460 meter på sitt dypeste. På jernbaneferga ville tønnene være samlet på ett sted, bare spredt ut over flere jernbanevogner.

Åpenbart fordi tyskerne fryktet angrep, ble Rjukan fylt med tyske tropper. Der var flere tyskere enn nordmenn i Vestfjorddalen. Mens de ventet på at transporten med ferga skulle starte om morgenen, var jernbanevognene flombelyst og omgitt av bevæpnede vakter.

Tyskerne mislykkes likevel i å plassere en vakt på jernbanefergen "D/F Hydro", som skulle brukes den påfølgende morgenen for å transportere tungtvannet over Tinnsjøen. Tre nordmenn greide å snike seg om bord på ferga i all hemmelighet om natten og plasserte en 8.5 kilos ladning i skroget. Den var laget av to vekkerklokker og en detoneringsmekanisme.

Mens klokkene tikket, nærmet ferga seg søndag 20. februar 1944 det dypeste området av Tinnsjøen. Klokka 10.45 blåste en eksplosjon hull i ferga. Som planlagt gikk baugen under og ferga tok inn vann, noe som førte til at akterenden hevet seg. Jernbanevognene, lesset med tønner med tungtvann, rullet framover og gikk i sjøen. På bare fire minutter gikk tungtvannet ned med ferga, og det ligger fortsatt der på bunnen av Tinnsjøen.

Motstandsmennene var ute av stand til å advare de uvitende fergepassasjerene, for frykt ville gjøre tyskerne mistenksomme, og derfor omkom 26 mennesker. Med nådeløs logikk, mot og utholdenhet, var det siste kapitlet i kampen om tungtvannet avsluttet, idet det hindret Hitler i å gjennomføre sitt atomprosjekt.

Familiegårder

Etter å ha funnet ut at slektsgårdene "Bøen Vestre" og "Steinsrud under Dale" var plassert på Rjukans Sam Eydesgate, slo mine tenåringssønner, Alex og Ben, fast at slektsforskning var virkelig interessante saker.

På 1600-tallet, fire generasjoner bakover i tid, eide våre forfedre fra "Bøen Vestre" det som nå er Rjukan sentrum. Ved østenden av Rjukan var "Steinsrud under Dale", hvor min tipptipp-olderfar, Tov Torgrimsson, ble født i 1799. Det var Tovs sønn, Gullik Tovson (Thompson), født i Kjosa, Imingen i Numedal, som immigrerte i 1876 til Black Hammer i Houston County, Minnesota. Han flyttet senere til Simley Springs i Big Woods i Fillmore County, Minnesota.

Da vi stod på hengebrua på Vemork, virket det helt utrolig at våre forfedres Vestfjorddalen skulle ha vært åsted for begivenheter bare 60 år tidligere som endret utfallet av den andre verdenskrig.

For ytterligere informasjon

• Gallagher, Thomas. *Assault in Norway: Sabotaging the Nazi Nuclear Program.* Connecticut: The Lyons Press, 2002. (Tilgjengelig på Vesterheim Museum i Decorah, Iowa)
• Haukelid, Knut. *Skis Against The Atom.* North American Heritage Press, 1989. (Tilgjengelig på North American Heritage Press, P.O. Box 1, Minot, ND 58702, phone 800-962-7323, or northamericanheritagepress.com)
• Kurzman, Dan. *Blood and Water: Sabotaging Hitler's bomb.* New York: Henry Holt and Company, Inc, 1997.
• Columbia Pictures Video. *The heroes of Telemark* (Hollywood-versjonen). Filmet lokalt på Vemork og i Rjukan. 1965.
• National Geographic Video. *Untold stories of World War II: Three Secrets That Changed the War.* 1998. http://www.nationalgeographic.com

13

Amherst had Indians and wolves

200-mile-long by 40-mile-wide Neutral Ground boundary between warring Indian tribes passed through the Big Woods

Amherst, Henrytown, Lenora, Newburg, Tawney, and Highland are a few of what were once thriving but now sleeping villages in southeastern Minnesota's Fillmore County. The weathered buildings and old farmsteads along the narrow gravel roads bear silent testimony to the once prosperous communities. Learning about the early day-to-day life of Amherst, the ancestral village where I was raised, has given incredible depth to my research.

The Big Woods

Although affected by them, southeastern Minnesota is an area that was not covered by the last glaciers. The glacial melt-waters carved out hundreds of feet of limestone and sandstone creating a landscape of towering bluffs, scenic valleys, rolling hills, pastoral fields, sinkholes, spring fed creeks, and winding rivers.

The Big Woods is a unique geographical area in the southeast part of Fillmore County consisting mostly of hardwood forests and the south fork of the Root River. Encompassing roughly 25,000 acres, the Big Woods is about five miles wide by eight miles long. The present-day borders are Amherst on the west, Lenora and Newburg on the south, Tawney and Choice on the east, and Highland on the north.

The hunting and fishing grounds of

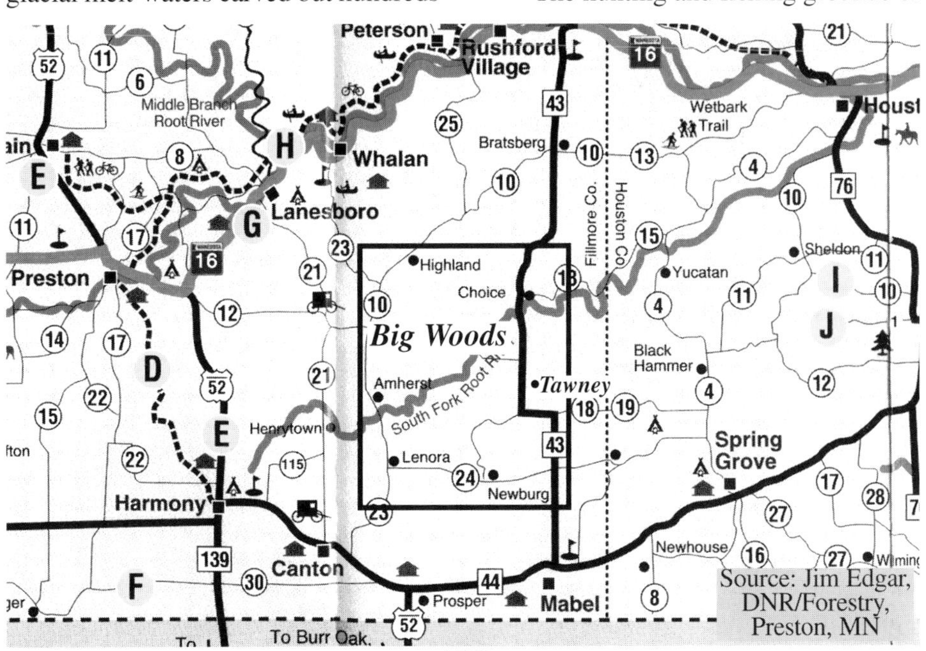

Source: Jim Edgar, DNR/Forestry, Preston, MN

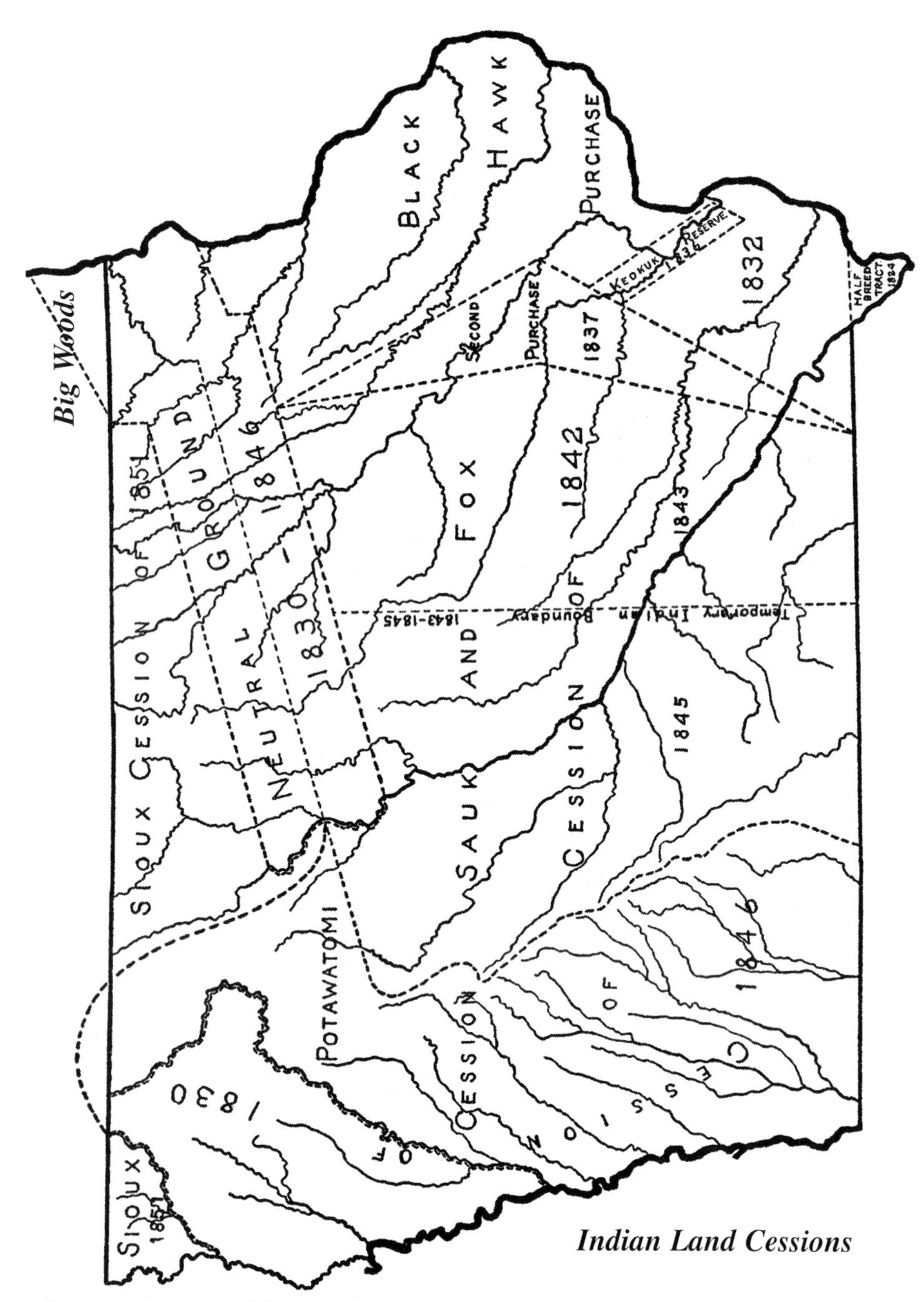

Source: Iowa Public Land Disposal by Roscoe L. Lokken, Published at Iowa City Iowa in 1942 by the State Historical Society of Iowa, page 15.

Special thanks to Lynn E. Nielsen, University of Northern Iowa, and Dorothy Schwieder, Iowa State University, for their assistance in locating the original source of this map.

"By the treaty of August 19, 1825, at Prairie du Chien, it was agreed that the United States government should run a boundary line between the Sioux, on the north, and the Sacs and Foxes, on the south, along the Upper Iowa, as follows; Commencing at the mouth of the Upper Iowa river on the west bank of the Mississippi and ascending said Iowa river to its west fork; thence up the fork to its source; thence crossing the fork of the Red Cedar river in a direct line to the second or upper fork of the Des Moines river.

"The cause which led to the establishment of this boundary line continuing to exist, namely, the frequent hostilities between these hereditary enemies, another treaty was entered into on July 15, 1830, at Prairie du Chien, by the terms of which the Sacs and Foxes ceded to the United States a strip of country lying south of the above boundary line, twenty miles in width, and extending along the line aforesaid from the Mississippi to the Des Moines river. The Sioux also ceded to the government, in the same treaty, a like strip of twenty miles on the north side of said boundary; thus making a territory forty miles wide, and in length from the Mississippi to the Des Moines, which was known as the "Neutral Ground." Within these limits both tribes were permitted to hunt and fish unmolested by each other except at the peril of the aggressor, from the government.

"In the maps of that day upon which their neutral ground was shown, there appears a little jog of perhaps six or eight miles in each of the three lines, north, south, and central, at a distance of about thirty miles west of the Mississippi, which has puzzled not a few. The key to this appears in the language of the treaty of 1825 establishing the central, or original boundary line: "ascending said Iowa river to its west fork (some texts read left fork), thence up the fork to its source," etc. This fork, judging from the maps which show it as a little short, unnamed stream, can be no other than Trout Run, near Decorah. The corresponding job in the northern line, twenty miles north, appears along the course of the "Red Cedar creek," apparently the Canoe; and a similar deflection in the southern line is along the Turkey river. No explanation is given of this break in the course of the original boundary, that we have been able to ascertain.

"The original boundary line striking the upper fork of the Des Moines river, at Dakota City in Humboldt county, the southwest corner of the Neutral Ground would be a short distance below Fort Dodge, in Webster county; and the north line being carried to the west fork would terminate in the southeast corner of Palo Alto."

Source: Chapter 3, Historical Past & Present of Allamakee County, 1913
http://www.rootsweb.com/~iaallama/history2/chap3.htm

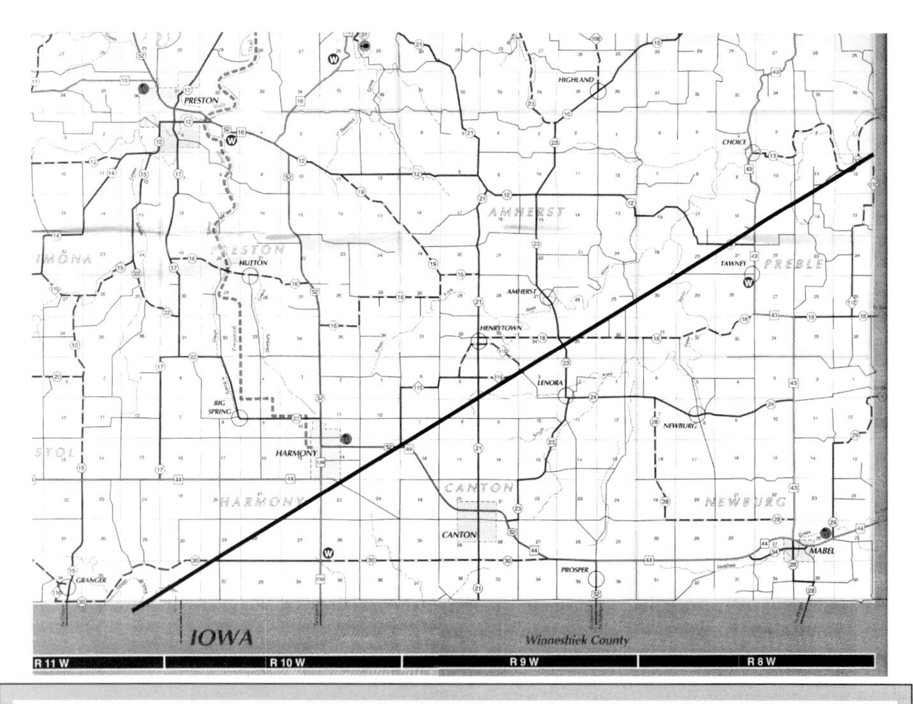

"The northern boundary of this neutral strip, according to the survey by James Craig, completed in 1833, entered Fillmore County between sections 1 and 12, Preble Township, crossed that township, then crossed a part of Amherst, Canton, and Harmony Townships, and left the county on the southern line of section 36 in Bristol township. The part of the county south of that line was in the Neutral Strip and the rest of the county in Sioux territory."

Source: History of Fillmore County, Minnesota, 1912, Vol 1. Chapter III. Indian treaties, page 26.

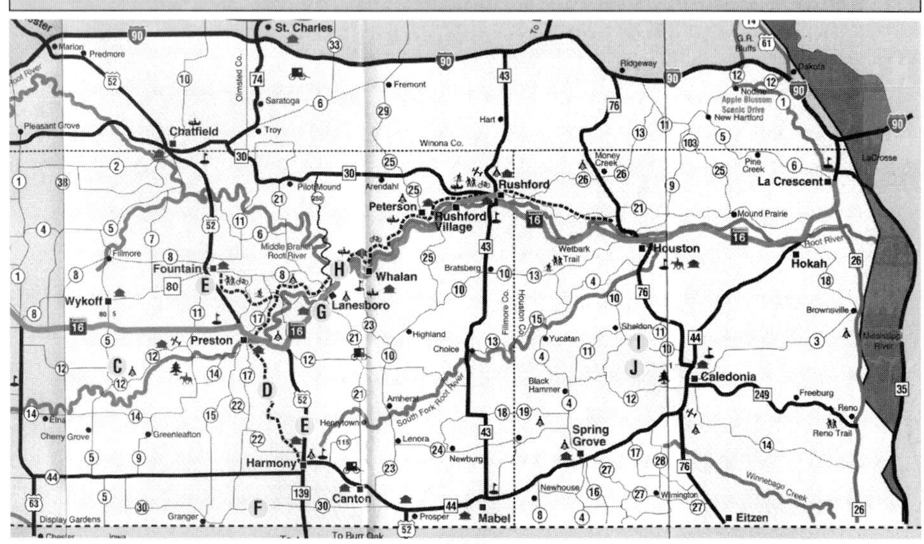

the Big Woods became a fiercely contested battleground by the Sioux, Fox, and Sauk Indian tribes that roamed over much of what would become southeast Minnesota and northeast Iowa. A treaty signed in Prairie du Chien, Wisconsin during 1825 established a Neutral Line that would keep the warring Sioux to the north, the Fox and Sauk to the south. The imaginary Neutral Line began near the very northeast corner of Iowa where the mouth of the Upper Iowa River and the Mississippi River joined and extended southwest.

After several broken treaties, the United States government negotiated a treaty that was signed on July 15, 1830, and appropriated by Congress on March 2, 1831. Two more lines were drawn parallel to the Neutral Line, one twenty miles to the north and one twenty miles to the south. The very northeast border of the 200-mile-long by 40-mile-wide Neutral Ground boundary between the warring Indian tribes passed through the Chickentown Creek valley in the midst of the Big Woods in Southeast Minnesota. In 1832, Nathan Boone, the youngest son of Kentucky frontiersman Daniel Boone, was among those who surveyed the northern or Sioux portion of the Neutral Ground.

On July 23, 1851, the United States Government signed the *Treaty of Traverse des Sioux* with the See-see-toan and Wah-pay-toan bands of Dakota or Sioux for their lands in the State of Iowa and the Territory of Minnesota. With the proclamation on February 24, 1853, this treaty opened millions of acres to land-hungry settlers.

Fillmore County in the 1800's

Iowa, Wisconsin, and Minnesota did not become states until the years 1846, 1848, and 1858, respectively. Norwegian pioneers settled in Iowa's Allamakee and Winneshiek Counties in 1850, Minnesota's Fillmore County in 1851, and Minnesota's Houston County in 1853.

Listed in *The Saga of Old Muskego*, published in 1943, are the first fifteen Norwegian settlements in America. Fillmore County, Minnesota, is not only included in the list as number fifteen, but is the oldest Norwegian settlement in Minnesota.

"This County Named for President Fillmore," an article published in the *Almanac for 1885*, tells the following: *The Minnesota Territorial Legislature approved the name 'Fillmore,' and on March 5, 1853, the county was created. Franklin Pierce had taken the oath of office as president one day previous. However,* [President] *Millard Fillmore, sturdy old character, was honored through the selection of his name for the then pioneer section of the state of Minnesota.*

The *History of Fillmore County* published in 1858 indicates that a few settlements were made in the year 1853 and that there were only fourteen families in the county in January 1854. At that time Fillmore County included the present Minnesota counties of Houston, Winona, Fillmore, and part of Olmsted counties.

The early Fillmore County immigrants, mostly Norwegian, English, Irish, and German, rapidly populated the county as per the census: *1850 - 7 people; 1860 - 8,425 people; and 1870 - 35,900 people. The Norwegian Research Guide* published in 2000 describes the Norwegian population in southeastern Minnesota as: *The triangle from Houston and Fillmore counties to Albert Lea and Blue Earth to the west and Faribault, Northfield and Red Wing to the north had more Norwegians than any other place in America.*

Knudson land title

In 1853, my great-great-grandparents, Knud Knudson Sævre and Gunhild Guttormsdatter Myhre from *Nes i Hallingdal*, were the first white people to settle in what was to become Stringtown or Amherst Village in Fillmore County. They had immigrated in 1846 and 1848, respectively, to Wisconsin, married in 1851, and had two children before pushing westward into Minnesota territory.

The land selected by Knud and Gunhild for their 160-acre farm, which has now been in our family for over 150 years, included the south fork of the Root River running through their property. They built a 12-by-14-foot log cabin and later added land to make 600 acres. In addition to opening their home to many of the pioneer families that arrived during the next few years, Knud was the first Justice of the Peace in Amherst.

The *History of Fillmore County* published in 1912 gives evidence of Amherst's early days: *In the fall of 1853 eight of the Onstine party rode over the prairie on horseback in a northeast direction from what is now Henrytown, in search for timber enough to maintain a farm . . . In going over they passed near Knut Knutson's* [Knud Knudson's], *now Stringtown.*

The first titles to land in Amherst Township were issued by the government in 1854. Knud Knudson's name was among those listed in the *Book of Abstract of Entries* at the Fillmore County Courthouse and *History of Fillmore County* published in 1912 as receiving his land title on September 7, 1854, for the following 160 acres: *The west half of the southeast quarter and the east half of the southwest quarter of section 27 in township 102 of range 9 west.*

President Abraham Lincoln signed the land patent for the Knudson farm on March 1, 1862. My Grandpa Henry Knudson was awarded the Minnesota Century Farm Ownership Certificate dated August 26, 1958: *In 1858, the year Minnesota became a state, this property was owned by Knud Knudson and it has since remained in continuous family ownership.*

Minnesota Century Farm

OWNERSHIP CERTIFICATE

HENRY KNUDSON

has/have presented proof of present ownership of a Minnesota farm

located in FILLMORE county.

In 1858, the year Minnesota became a state, this property was owned by

KNUD KNUDSON

And it has since remained in continuous family ownership.

In Recognition Hereof,

The Minneapolis Star and Tribune and the Minnesota State Fair
Award this Century Farm Ownership Certificate

Dated August 26, 1958

John Cowles
President
Minneapolis Star and Tribune

C. A. Moore
President
Minnesota State Fair

The first fifteen Norwegian settlements in America:
1. Kendall, New York, 1825
2. Fox River, Illinois, 1834
3. Chicago, Illinois, 1836
4. Beaver Creek, Illinois, 1837
5. Shelly County, Missouri, 1837
6. Jefferson Prairie, Wisconsin, 1838
7. Rock Prairie (Luther Valley), Wisconsin, 1839
8. Muskego, Wisconsin, 1839
9. Koshkonong, Wisconsin, 1840
10. Sugar Creek, Iowa, 1840
11. Wiota, Wisconsin, 1841
12. Spring Prairie and Bonnet Prairie, Wisconsin, 1845
13. Washington Prairie, Iowa, 1850
14. Saint Ansgar, Iowa, 1853
15. Fillmore County, Minnesota 1853

Source: The Saga of Old Muskego by N. N. Rønning, 1943, page 69.

Fillmore County Land Office Records in 1854
The first titles to land in Amherst Township were issued by the government in 1854. Those who obtained land that year were as follows, the date of the issuance of the warrant being given first, then the name of the owner and then the sections in which the land was largely located:
January 18, Michael Onstine, 26
August 8, Benjamin F. Tillott, 33
August 18, Francis Richardson, 34
August 29, Peter Oleson, 34
August 29, Henry Onstine, 32
August 29, Lars Pederson, 34
September 1, Annanias Lashmet 25-26
September 1, Levi M. Smith, 22
September 1, Jemima Streator, 25
September 6, Robert Gilbert, 25
September 6, Thomas Gilbert, 35
September 6, James Lynn, 26-27
September 7, Knud Knudson, 27
September 8, Heluk Christopher, 11
September 8, Lars Trulson, 1
September 8, Lars Christensen, 11
September 8, Andrew Haldersen, 2
September 8, Thomas Knudson, 11
December 23, William J. Adams, 33
December 27, Henry Hutchison, 25
December 27, Levi Manning, 24

Source: Book of Abstract of Entries, Office of County Recorder, Fillmore County Courthouse and History of Fillmore County, Minnesota, 1912, page 298.

'CENTURY FARMS' I

About 300 farms in Dodge, Fillmore, Goodhue, Houston, Mower, Olmsted, Wabasha and Winona counties have been recognized by the Minnesota State 'Fair' as century farms.

In order to qualify for the designation, the farms must have been operated by a direct descendent of the farm's operator 100 or more years ago. The state fair based its lists on applications for recognition from descendents of pioneer landowners throughout the state.

Of the eight counties, Fillmore County leads the listings with 74 farms recognized by the fair. Houston County follows close behind with 72 farms. There 20 recognized century farms in Dodge County, 28 in Goodhue County, 25 in Mower County, 33 in Olmsted County, 18 in Wabasha County and 28 in Winona County.

The names of persons currently operating farms follows with the date of the first year of farm operation by an ancestor in parentheses.

DODGE COUNTY

Klaus Alberts-Barbara Alberts, Kasson (1874); Earl D. and Esther H. Bartel, Kasson (1876); Douglas V. Dennison, Hayfield (1876); Garth Evarts, West Concord (1857); Charles E. Finn and Yvonne L. Finn, Kasson (1873); Stella Fjerstad, Hayfield, (1876); Donald R. and Selm H. Gilderhus, Hayfield (1874);

Herbert Hallaway and Myrtle Hallaway, Claremont (1865); Minnie Himle, Hayfield (1869); Helmer, Kermit, Arlen and Harris D. Peterson, Blooming Prairie (1857); Lawrence Hythecker, Claremont (1876); Henry M. Kording, Hayfield (1872); Richard A. and Alpha B. Jensen, Kasson (1868);

Martha A. Lee, Ida A. Lee and Edward T. Lee, Hayfield (1873); Harry and Ruth Mohn, Hayfield (1860); David R. Thoe and Robert E. Thoe, Hayfield (1860); Gary and Glenda Thronson, Hayfield (1869); Mr. and Mrs. Reuben Tverberg, Hayfield (1871); Spencer H. Wilson and Ellen M. Wilson, Hayfield (1864); Francis Wyatt, Kasson (1863).

FILLMORE COUNTY

...tain (1866); Mr. and Mrs. Norris M. Nagel, Preston (1865); Thomas E. O'Connor, Preston (1866);

Dennis E. and Ruth C. Peterson, Rushford (1868); Norman and Doris Peterson, Wykoff (1871); Aaron John Prinsen, Preston (1876); Vernon C. and Ione D. Rindahl, Ostrander (1876); Fred C. Rick, Spring Valley (1858); Hilbert and J. Floy Roeloffs, Preston (1866); Olaf Rustad, Lanesboro (1858);

Lawrence Sorum, Rushford (1855); Percy Steffensrud, Harmony (1856); Robert Stenogard, Rushford (1856); Clement H. Snyder Jr., Preston (1860); Theodore S. Tangen, Fountain (1854); Mr. and Mrs. Elvin O. Tuff, Rushford (1872); Dale Turner, Harmony (1855); Byron Vatland and Odis Vatland, Mabel (1854);

Joseph and Marian Walsh, Fountain (1874); Shelby and Doris Westby, Peterson (1875); Clayton Zebaugh, Spring Valley (1855); Lew and Georgia Larson, Mabel (1858); Amil Junior Cadlec, Chatfield (1871); Victor T. Asleson, Fountain (1855); Wallace D. Hutton, Harmony (1858); Kathleen Susan Michael and William Caldwell, Harmony (1855);

Mrs. L.E. Heidlebaugh, Spring Valley (1856); Alden H. Onstine, Harmony (1854); William A. Pease, Chatfield (1857); Walter Mills, Preston (1858); Bernard Lerol, Whalen (1855); Wayne Hoog, Harmony (1855); Victor Flattum and Vilda Flattum, Whalen (1857);

John and Mildred Gjerdrum, Mabel (1854); Lowell Tollefson, Preston (1857); Arnold Hogie, Lanesboro (1856); Henry Knudson and Sylvan Nelson, Canton (1854); Norman W. Grabau, Spring Valley, (1856).

GOODHUE COUNTY

David and Carol Baker, Kenyon (1868); Mr. and Mrs. Gerhard Bjugan, Pine Island (1866); Michael M. Davidson, John E. Davidson Jr., Jeffery C. Davidson, Kenyon (1874); H. Herbert Fredickson, Zumbrota (1859); Carl, Bernice and Steve Gustafson, Welch (1875); George and Mary Ann Henry, West Concord (1875);

Elmer and Wynette Hovel, Zumbrota (1869); Bertil G. Johnson, Cannon Falls (1872); Mr. and Mrs. Manley J. Langeness, Zumbrota (1873); Jerrold N. Lexvold, Zumbrota (1868); Mr. and Mrs. Ralph A. Magnuson, Cannon Falls (1873);

When I was eight years old, we moved from Lenora to Amherst after my parents purchased my mother's ancestral Knudson farm, which had been owned by her parents, Henry and Esther (Thompson) Knudson. It was there that I located the *Astri Herbrandsdatter 1812* trunk that once belonged to my great-great-great-grandmother and began my genealogy interest.

In researching my Knudson ancestral farm, I not only learned that the farmstead had remained in our family for over 150 years, but that it was one of the oldest Norwegian farms in Minnesota.

Amherst Village and Township

The Village of Amherst and Amherst Township were organized in 1858. Amherst was one of the early and wealthy villages of Fillmore County. The dark loam mixed with clay soil and its generally rolling prairie with timber made the land valuable.

Even the early names of Amherst, *Strung out town* and *Stringtown*, were indicative of its early growth. The name Stringtown came from the fact that all the settlers built their houses along the road in the ravine where the village is located. The name *Amherst* was given by Ethan P. Eddy in honor of his wife Julia Onstine, who was born in Amherst, Ohio.

In 1860, W. Winch started the Stringtown Store. Other owners included Ole Olson, Ward, Langley, Halvorson, J. D. Elliot, and lastly Babcock. Amherst had one store, a blacksmith shop, a schoolhouse, and in 1864, a post office. W. Winch was the first postmaster of the Amherst Post Office, which was located in the Winch Store.

In the early 1900s a cooperative creamery was built in Amherst. Its patrons cut firewood and ice for the creamery. Grandpa Henry used to haul cream from as far away as Kendallville, Iowa. Butter was hauled to nearby Canton to be shipped by railroad. Down the creek from the creamery was a pond from which Grandpa Henry helped cut squares of ice during the winter.

July 4th celebrations were held behind the creamery or on the Knudson land. Ball games were a popular event as there were very few fireworks in those days. Dances were held for special occasions on a wooden floor with a local band. An old newspaper clipping entitled "Amherst Celebrates 4th of July," reads: *The people generally are invited to join the Amherst Creamery Association in celebrating the great day of Independence on the grounds surrounding their new creamery at Amherst, Minn. Bring your lunch basket and enjoy a regular picnic dinner in the shade of the lusty oaks surrounding our beautiful creamery where you can breath the pure atmosphere and smell the fragrance of flowers and listen to the beautiful songs of the birds and the rippling of the brook.*

The Amherst school was organized in 1857. In 1858 a frame building was erected, but afterwards sold and used for a blacksmith shop. In 1867, a 20-foot by 30-foot school was built which was kept open until 1947. In the early 1900s there were approximately twenty pupils in grades one to eight.

In 1854, there were about 100 Indians in the South Fork Valley, located a few miles from Amherst. There was a big Indian scare in Fillmore County during 1862. Although there were no hostile Indians within 140 miles, the village of Preston was jammed full of people and teams of horses. All houses, shops, mills, and every available shelter were crowded with people; however, no shots were fired during this panic. Grandpa Henry remembered seeing a few Indians about 1900.

There were also horse thieves and murders in the early days. In 1874 a vigilante committee was organized in Fillmore County against horse thieves. According to the auditor's books, there were 104 wolves captured in Fillmore County during April 1881. Bounty was $7.00 for each wolf.

Weisel Flood

On the 6th of August 1866 there was a flash flood in the normally placid Weisel Creek, on the south branch of the Root River about three miles from the Amherst Store. The home of Mr. and Mrs. David Weisel was swept from its foundation and crushed into fragments. Five people, including family and friends, drowned. Mrs. Weisel was found alive the following morning, still clinging to her bed on which she had floated down stream. By the time the flood subsided, sixteen lives were lost.

Lilly's Store

All that now remains in the village of Amherst is Lilly's Store, opened by Lillian Haagenson and her husband, Griffen, April 1, 1954, in the old creamery building. Lilly and I share this special date, as it was also the day I was born. Lilly recently celebrated her 50th year of owning and operating the Amherst Store, one of the last country stores in the area still open.

I distinctly remember the many times we six kids made the long trip down the snowy, bitterly cold driveway only to find that school had been canceled. It was Lilly who would yell across the road and give us the word to go back home, so we wouldn't stand there and freeze. On days when we got off the school bus during the pouring rain, Lilly's Store was always a warm shelter until the rain subsided.

During my years of growing up in Amherst, Lilly was in the store the majority of the day, seven days a week. Although she might have just walked up the steep sidewalk to her house, she was, and still is, always willing to reopen the store even if all you need is a half-gallon of milk, a loaf of Wonder Bread, a round of Hormel Thuringer, a local Spring Grove soda pop, or a few gallons of gas from the single gas pump. However, Lilly's store rule still holds that you can only take one of a particular item if only two remain, as she saves the last one for the next customer. Thanks to Lilly, many have been fortunate to experience the enchantment of an old country store.

Fillmore County today

As picturesque today as it was to the Indians and early settlers is the scenic landscape in Fillmore County. Minnesota Highway 16, which crosses the full width of the county from Spring Valley to Rushford, was designated a National Scenic Byway on June 13, 2002. Horse-drawn Amish buggies are often seen in the *buggy lane* along Highway 52's Amish Byway connecting Preston and Prosper. The Amish community that began in the 1970s near Canton and Harmony is now estimated at about 700 residents.

The winding Root River, trout streams, fish hatchery, state park, paved bike trails, and the only caves in Minnesota are just a few of the places to explore in Fillmore County. The natural resources along with the ethnic culture and hospitality of the people is what gives such charm to the small towns and villages found in America's rural Midwest.

For further information

- *Forestville/Mystery Cave State Park, Route 2 Box 128, Preston, MN 55965, http://www.dnr.state.mn.us*
- *Niagara Cave, PO Box 444, Harmony, MN 55939 http://www.niagaracave.com*
- *Southeastern Minnesota Historic Bluff Country Inc., 15 Second St NW, PO Box 609, Harmony, MN 55939, http://www.bluffcountry.com*
- *Iowa History Project, Iowa Journal of History and Politics, Vol.VIII July, 1915 No. 3, http://iagenweb.org/history/journal/july1915.htm*

My brother, Joe Nelson, originally wrote a portion of this story as part of a historical project while in high school. It was first printed in The Mabel Record on August 3, 1978 and is being reprinted with his permission.

Amherst hadde indianere og ulver

Et nøytralt belte mellom krigende indianerstammer gikk gjennom Big Woods

Amherst, Henrytown, Lenora, Newburg, Tawney og Highland er bare noen av de blomstrende landsbyene i det sørøstlige Minnesotas Fillmore County som nå har falt i søvn. De værslitte bygningene og gamle gårdene langs de smale grusveiene vitner stille om tidligere tiders velstand. Det jeg har lært om fortidens dagligliv i Amherst, landsbyen hvor jeg vokste opp, har gitt utrolige dybder til min slektsforskning.

De store skogene

Sørøstlige Minnesota var ikke dekket av de siste isbreene, men var likevel påvirket av dem. Smeltevannet grov ut mengder med kalkstein og sandstein, og skapte et landskap av høye skrenter, naturskjønne daler, bølgene bakker, idylliske marker, jettegryter, bekker med grunnvann og buktende elver.

Big Woods er et særegent geografisk område i den sørøstlige delen av Fillmore County. Det består mest av løvskog, og en sørlig forgreining av Root River. Big Woods omfatter rundt 100 000 mål, og er om lag åtte kilometer bredt og nærmere tretten kilometer langt. Dagens grenser dannes av Amherst i vest, Lenora og Newburg i sør, Tawney og Choice i øst og Highland i nord.

Jakt- og fiskeområdene i Big Woods ble årsak til heftig strid mellom sioux-, fox- og saukindianerne, som streifet omkring i store deler av det som skulle bli sørøstlige Minnesota og nordlige Iowa. En traktat som ble signert i 1825 i Prairie du Chien, Wisconsin, etablerte en nøytral linje som skulle holde de krigende siouxene i ro i nord, fox- og sauk-indianerne i sør.

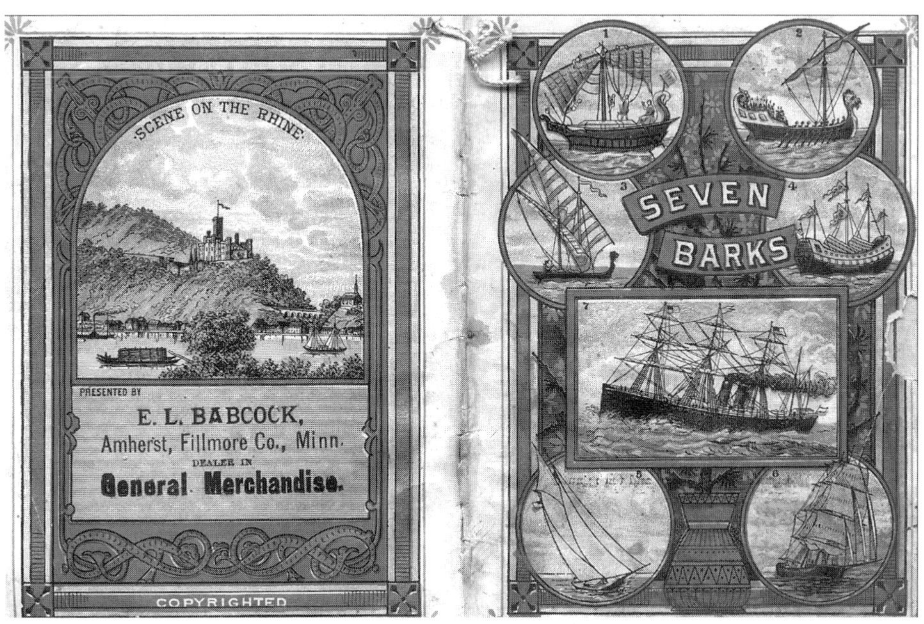

Amherst photos courtesy of Fillmore County History Center and Genealogy Library

Den imaginære nøytrale linjen begynte i nærheten av det nordøstlige hjørnet av Iowa, hvor munningen av Upper Iowa River og Mississippi River fløt sammen og strakte seg sørvestover.

Etter flere brutte avtaler, forhandlet USAs regjering fram en avtale som ble signert den 5. juli 1830, og som ble vedtatt av kongressen 2. mars 1831. To linjer til ble tegnet parallelt med den nøytrale linjen, den ene tre mil lenger nord og en annen tre mil lenger sør. Den nordøstlige grensen av den 32 mil lange og 6.4 mil brede nøytrale beltet mellom de krigende indianerstammene gikk gjennom Chickentown Creek Valley, midt i Big Woods i det sørøstlige Minnesota. I 1832 var Nathan Boone en av dem som overvåket den nordlige sioux-delen av den nøytrale området. Han var yngste sønn av Daniel Boone, som levde ved grensen i Kentucky.

23 juli 1851 signerte USAs regjering *Treaty of Travers des Sioux*, som var en avtale med see-see-toan og wah-pay-toan-gruppene av dakotaindianerne, eller sioux, om landområder i staten Iowa og territoriet Minnesota. Med proklamasjonen fra 24. februar 1853, gjorde denne avtalen millioner av mål tilgjengelige for landhungrige settlere.

Fillmore County på 1800-tallet

Iowa, Wisconsin og Minnesota ble ikke egne stater før i henholdsvis 1846, 1848 og 1858. Norske nybyggere bosatte seg i Allamakee og Winnishiek i Iowa i 1850, i Minnesotas Fillmore County i 1851, og i Minnesotas Houston County i 1853.

De første femten norske bosettingene i Amerika er nevnt i *The Saga of Old Muskego*, utgitt i 1943. Minnesotas Fillmore County er ikke bare det femtende navnet på listen, men var også den eldste av de norske bosettingene i Minnesota.

Artikkelen "This County Named for President Fillmore," som ble trykket i *Almanac for 1885*, forteller følgende: *Minnesota Territorial Legislature godkjente navnet Fillmore, og 5. mars 1853 var fylket etablert. Franklin Pierce var tatt i ed som president dagen før.*

Amherst school picnic about 1894

Likevel ble [president] *Millard Fillmore, en stødig type av den gamle sorten, æret gjennom valget av navnet på det som da var et nybyggerområde i staten Minnesota.*

History of Fillmore County, som kom ut i 1858, tyder på at noen få bosettinger ble etablert i 1853, og at det bare var fjorten familier i fylket i januar 1854. På den tiden omfattet Fillmore County de nåværende fylkene i Minnesota: Houston, Winona, Fillmore og en del av Olmstead.

De første Fillmore County-immigrantene, flest norske, engelske, irske og tyske, befolket raskt området. Folketellingene viser: *1850 – 7 mennesker; 1860 – 8 425 mennesker; og i 1870 – 35 900 mennesker. The Norwegian Research Guide*, 2000, beskriver den norske befolkningen i det sørøstlige Minnesota slik: *Triangelet fra Houston og Fillmore Counties til Albert Lea og Blue Earth i vest og Faribault, Northfield og Red Wing i nord, hadde flere nordmenn enn noe annet sted i Amerika.*

Knudsons landeierskap

I 1853 var mine tipp-oldeforeldre, Knud Knudson Sævre og Gunhild Guttormsdatter Myhre fra Nes i Hallingdal, de første hvite som slo seg ned i det som skulle bli Stringtown eller Amherst Village i Fillmore County. De hadde immigrert til Wisconsin i henholdsvis 1846 og 1848, giftet seg i 1851, og hadde to barn før de dro videre vestover til Minnesota.

Landet Knud og Gunhild valgte til den gården som nå har vært familiens eie i mer enn 150 år, inkluderer den sørlige forgreiningen av Root River, som renner over eiendommen. De bygde en 15 kvadratmeter stor hytte og utvidet etter hvert gården til 2400 mål. I tillegg til at de åpnet sine hjem for mange pionerfamilier som ankom i løpet av de første årene, var Knud den første fredsdommeren i Amherst.

History of Fillmore County,1912, beretter om Amhersts spede begynnelse: *Høsten 1853 red åtte fra Onstinefølget nordøstover over prærien i retning av det som nå er Henrytown. De lette etter tømmer nok til å bygge en gård... De krysset området nær familien Knut Knutsons gård* [Knud Knudson], *nå Stringtown.*

De første skjøtene i Amherst Township ble tildelt av regjeringen i

Babcock house and store

1854. Knud Knudsons navn er blant de nevnte i *Book of Abstract of Entries* ved Fillmore Countys tinghus, og i *History of Fillmore County*, 1912. Han mottok skjøte for de følgende 640 målene den 7. september 1854: *Den vestlige halvpart av det sørøstlige kvartal, og den østlige halvpart av det sørvestlige kvartal av seksjon 27 'in township 102 of range 9 west.'*

President Abraham Lincoln signerte skjøtet for Knudson-gården 1. mars 1862. Min bestefar Henry Knudson ble gitt Minnesota Century Farm Ownership Certificate 26. august 1958: *I 1858, samme år som Minnesota ble en stat, ble eiendommen overdratt til Knud Knudson, og den har siden vært i familiens eie.*

In memory of days spent together in the school room this token is presented with the compliments of
Your Teacher

Pupils

Henry Knudson	Celia Griffith
Roy Tiffany	Eddie Knudson
Clarence Knudson	Agnes Knudson
Dorthea Peterson	Alma Peterson
George Bersal	Roy Stensgard
Laura Stensgard	Roy Anderson
Ella Anderson	Cora Torgenrud
Agnes Presather	Herbrand Simley
Inga Simley	Emma Anderson
Leonard Haugan	Manda Haugan
Clara Haugan	
Mattie Blagsvedt	Bennie Knudson
William Blagsvedt	Joseph Knudson
Alma Blagsvedt	Severina Simley
Ole Simley	Florence Vickerman
Ida Vickerman	Oscar Knutson

List of Amherst school students about the year 1900

Da jeg var åtte år gammel, flyttet vi fra Lenora til Amherst, da foreldrene mine overtok min mors slektsgård etter foreldrene Henry og Esther (Thompson) Knudson. Det var der at jeg fant Astri Herbrandsdatter 1812-kisten, som hadde tilhørt min tipp-tipp-oldemor, og der min interesse for slektsforskning startet.

Da jeg forsket på slektsgården til familien Knudson fikk jeg ikke bare vite at stedet hadde vært eid av familien i over 150 år, men at den også var den eldste norske farmen i Minnesota.

Amherst - tettsted og kommune

Landsbyen Amherst og Amherst Township [kommune] ble etablert i 1858. Amherst var en av de eldste og mest velstående småbyene i Fillmore County. Den mørke leirholdige jorda, og den bølgende prærien med alt sitt tømmer, gjorde landet rikt.

Selv de tidlige navnene på Amherst, *Strung out town* og *Stringtown*, var tegn på byens tidlige vekst. Navnet Stringtown kom fra det

Knudson children

faktum at alle nybyggerne bygde husene langs veien som gikk gjennom kløfta hvor byen ligger. Navnet *Amherst* var det Ethan P. Eddy som ga byen, til ære for sin kone Julia Onstine, som var født i Amherst, Ohio.

I 1860 startet W.Winch Stringtowns landhandel. Andre eiere var Ole Olson, Ward, Langley, Halvorson, J.D.Elliot og endelig Babcock. Amherst hadde butikk, smie, skolehus og i 1864 også postkontor. W. Winch var den første postmesteren ved Amherst postkontor, som hadde sine lokaler i "Winch Store."

Tidlig på 1900-tallet ble det bygd et fellesmeieri i Amherst. Eierne hogg ved og is til meieriet. Bestefar Henry brukte å frakte fløte fra så langt unna som Kendallville, Iowa. Smør ble fraktet til et sted i nærheten av Canton for å bli lastet på jernbanen. Langs bekken som gikk fra meieriet, lå det en dam hvor bestefar Henry hjalp til med å kutte isblokker om vinteren.

4. julifeiringen foregikk bak meieriet på Knudsons eiendom. Balleker var populære begivenheter, da det ikke var så vanlig med fyrverkeri i de dager. På tregulv og med lokalt band, ble det arrangert dans ved spesielle anledninger. Et gammelt avisutklipp med overskriften "Amherst feirer 4. juli" forteller: *Innbyggerne inviteres til å delta sammen med Amherst Creamery Association i feiringen av den store uavhengighetsdagen på jordene som ligger rundt det nye meieriet i Amherst, Minn. Ta med lunsjkurv og gled deg over et måltid i det grønne, i skyggen av de frodige eiketrærne rundt det vakre meieriet. Der kan du trekke inn frisk luft og kjenne duften av blomster, lytte til den vakre fuglesangen og sildringen fra bekken.*

Amherst skole ble etablert i 1857. I 1858 ble det reist en trebygning, men etterpå ble den solgt og brukt som smie. I 1867 ble det bygd en 55 kvadratmeter stor skole, som var i bruk til 1947. Tidlig på 1900-tallet var der om lag tjue elever fra første til åttende klasse.

I 1854 var det rundt 100 indianere i South Fork Valley, som lå bare noen kilometer fra Amherst. Frykten for indianerne skapte sterk panikk i Fillmore County i 1862. Selv om det ikke fantes fiendtlige indianere i 225 kilometers omkrets, ble landsbyen Preston fylt til randen av mennesker og hester. Alle hus, butikker, møller og ethvert tilgjengelig skjul var overfylt av folk; imidlertid ble det ikke avfyrt skudd under denne panikken. Bestefar Henry husket å ha sett noen få indianere rundt 1900.

Der fantes også hestetyver og mordere den første tiden. I 1874 ble det organisert et borgervern mot hestetyver i Fillmore County. I følge revisjonsboken ble det fanget 104 ulver i Fillmore County i april 1881. Skuddpremien var på sju dollar for hver ulv.

Weisel-flommen

6. august 1866 kom der en overraskende oversvømmelse i det normalt så uforstyrrede Weisel Creek, på den søndre greien av Root River – nesten fem mil fra Amherst Store. Hjemmet til herr og fru David Weisel ble feid av fundamentet og slått til pinneved. Fem mennesker, alle familie og venner, druknet. Fru Weisel ble funnet i live morgenen etter, der hun fortsatt klamret

seg til senga som hadde ført henne nedover strømmen. Da elva hadde trukket seg tilbake, var seksten liv gått tapt.

Lillys landhandel

Alt som nå er igjen av landsbyen Amherst er "Lilly's Store", åpnet 1. april 1954 i den gamle meieribygningen av Lillian Haagenson og ektemannen Griffen. Lilly og jeg deler denne spesielle datoen, da jeg ble født denne dagen. Lilly feiret nylig butikkens femtiårsjubileum, en av de siste butikkene i området som fortsatt er åpen.

Jeg husker så klart de mange gangene vi seks barna gjorde den lange turen ned den snødekte og bitende kalde landeveien bare for å finne ut at skoledagen var avlyst. Da var det Lilly som ropte til oss over veien og gav oss beskjed om å gå hjem igjen, slik at vi skulle slippe å stå der og fryse. På dager da vi gikk av skolebussen i øsende regnvær, var "Lilly's Store" et tørt sted å varme seg inntil regnet stoppet.

Amherst Creamery is now Lilly's Amherst Store – also pictured is Lilly's house

Amherst school

Mens jeg vokste opp i Amherst, var Lilly i butikken det meste av dagen sju dager i uka. Selv om hun nettopp hadde gått opp den bratte gangveien til huset sitt, var hun og er hun fortsatt alltid villig til å åpne butikken når man trenger en kartong melk, et "Wonder Bread", en pakke "Hormel Thuringer," en flaske "Spring Grove soda pop" eller noen liter med bensin fra den enslige bensinpumpa. Likevel er Lillys helt spesielle butikkregel fortsatt at du ikke får kjøpt mer enn en vare om det bare finnes to igjen, for hun sparer den siste til neste kunde. Takket være Lilly har mange vært så heldige å få oppleve den fortryllende, gamle landhandelen.

Fillmore County i dag

Det naturskjønne landskapet i Fillmore County fortoner seg like idyllisk for oss i dag som det må ha gjort for indianerne og de tidlige settlerne. "Minnesota Highway 16", som strekker seg gjennom landet fra Spring Valley til Rushford, ble utpekt som "National Scenic Byway" 13. juni 2002. Amish-vogner, trukket av hester, er ofte å se i "buggy lane" langs "Highway 52's Amish Byway", som forbinder Preston med Prosper. Amish-samfunnet, som ble etablert i 1970 nær Canton og Harmony, rommer nå rundt 700 fastboende.

Den buktende Root River, ørretstrømmer, fiskeoppdrett, statspark, brolagte sykkelstier og de eneste grottene i Minnesota, er bare noe av det en kan utforske i Fillmore County. Naturressursene sammen med den særegne kulturen og folkets gjestfrihet er slikt som gir sjarm til sånne små byer og landsbyer som man kan finne ute på landet i Midtvesten.

To the Fillmore County Journal and the Fillmore County History Center and Genealogy Library, I give my special thanks for assistance with the Amherst pictures.

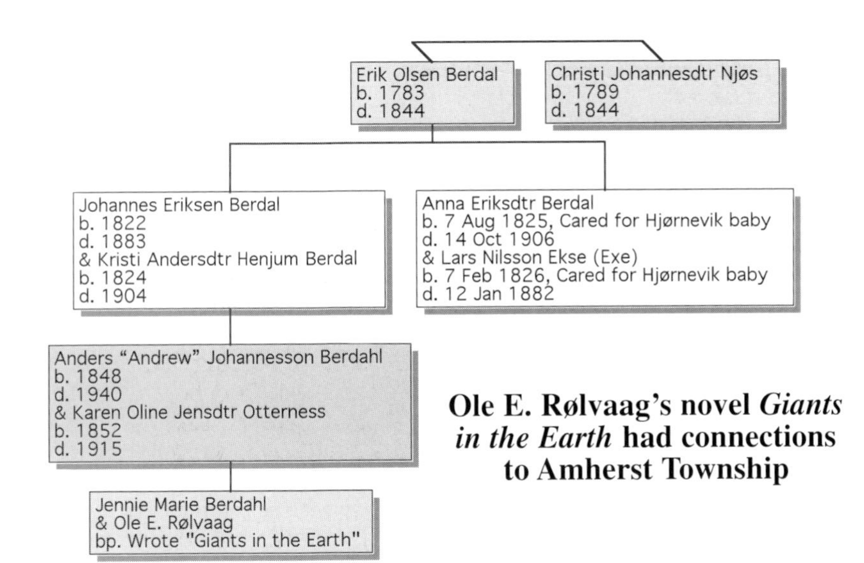

Ole E. Rølvaag's novel *Giants in the Earth* had connections to Amherst Township

Before writing *Giants in the Earth*, Ole E. Rølvaag many times discussed his plans with his wife's Berdal (Berdahl) family that lived in both Black Hammer and Amherst Township before they moved to the Dakota Territory. This information was used in Rølvaag's novel.

According to *Reminiscences* by Erick J. Berdahl, the Berdal name apparently originated from the fact that the valley, which in Norwegian is "dal," was covered with different kinds of berries, which in Norwegian is "ber." Hence the name Berdal. The "h" was added to the Berdal surname early after their arrival.

Ole E. Rølvaag's wife was Jennie Marie Berdahl and Jennie's grandfather was Johannes Eriksen Berdal. In my story, *You are a Hjørnevik, but who are you?*, it tells of the Hjørnevik baby being raised in Black Hammer by Anna Eriksdtr Berdal and her husband, Lars Nilsson Ekse (Exe). Anna Eriksdtr Berdal was a sister to Johannes Eriksen Berdal.

Three of Johannes Berdal's children were married into the Jens O. Otternes and Martha Larsdtr Ytre Lie Otternes family of Black Hammer. It was the grandmother to Gordon Eddy, Olga Maria Otterness Staven and her sister Sarah E. Otterness that told Gordon who had raised the Hjørnevik baby. I am most grateful to Gordon for this information.

The following is reprinted from the Aurland Newsletter Past and Present, Volume IV, Issue I, (January, February, March 2003), with permission from the author, Gordon Eddy, Cresco, Iowa.

"Johannes Eriksen Berdal and Kristi Andersdtr Henjum immigrated in 1856 from the Leikanger kommune i Sogn. Also in their company were Johannes Berdal's two sisters, Trine and Anna Berdal. After reaching New York, they continued on to Winneshiek County, Iowa and located in the northern part of the Big Canoe Norwegian settlement north of Decorah. They lived there for four years and worked for local farmers.

"The Berdals came to Black Hammer in 1860. By this time most of the farm land in Black Hammer had been taken by earlier settlers and land speculators who held several farms.

"In 1866 Johannes and Kristi moved to Amherst Township in Fillmore County and bought a farm consisting of 160 acres. Here in Amherst the growing family was content until they left to homestead in Dakota Territory in 1873. The oldest son, Anders J. Berdahl, who would be known as 'Andrew,' was educated as a schoolteacher and served many years as a teacher in Black Hammer. He also taught in 1871 at North Prairie, Arendahl Township in Fillmore County.

"A growing family required more land so in 1872, Johannes and two sons, Andrew and Erick, filed for homestead land in Dakota Territory recently formed in 1861. The spring of 1873 a group of relatives and neighbors in 11 covered wagons left Fillmore County for Dakota Territory. In the party were Johannes and Kristi and their seven sons and two daughters . . .

"The group entered the Slip Up Creek Valley located ten miles northeast of Sioux Falls in Minnehaha County and settled on the claims filed for earlier in what would later be rural Baltic in Edison Township. Johannes and Kristi had all their children in the same neighborhood with them. The first dwellings were sod houses. Son Andrew Berdahl returned to Black Hammer and brought his wife, Karen O. Otterness Berdahl, back in 1874."

James O. Berdahl
1881-1979
Sioux Falls lawyer and author of above Centennial brochure

Published for the descendants of the Eleven Covered Wagons Caravan that left Fillmore Co., MN in 1873. Centennial reunion held summer of 1973 at Garretson, SD. At a later date in the 1870's, a few young families from Black Hammer joined relatives & friends in this group settling in Minnehaha & Brookings counties. The booklet dealt with the "Beginnings of the Slip Up Creek Settlement" at Baltic, Dakota Territory, in what later became Edison township, Minnehaha Co., South Dak. Many of those pioneering from Black Hammer sold out after experiencing hardships and returned to Houston County.

For more information visit
http://www.aurlandnewsletter.com

Corn husking on the Lerol farm north of Highland

14

Norway's national costume

The bunad is rooted in heritage and tradition

Never out of style, the *bunad*, Norway's National costume, is worn for various events including *Syttende Mai* (17th of May), baptisms, confirmations, weddings, folk dancing, and other national holidays. It's not just a *female thing* to wear the bunad, as men of all ages are leaving behind the boring black tuxedo for the handsome, comfortable, and colorful bunad.

There are over 300 designs of bunader in Norway, indicative of one's home locality or place of ancestral birth. Much of the bunad variation was due to parish boundaries, fjords, or the isolation and remoteness of the Norwegian districts. Some areas were almost inaccessible with steep and narrow valleys surrounded by high mountains.

Among those stepping out in high style and wearing authentic, handmade Norwegian bunader at various events throughout the year are my son, Alex, and I. Alex's *Vågå i Gudbrandsdalen* bunad was ordered while we were in Norway during the summer of 2001. My *Nes i Hallingdal* bunad was made in Norway over twenty years ago by an eighty-year-old relative, Marta Sevre, and used as my wedding dress.

The author with her son Alex

Bunad origin

Norway's Constitution was signed on the 17 May 1814 in Eidsvold, marking both the country's declaration of independence from Denmark and the triumph of a constitutional government. Just as America celebrates the fourth of July as Independence Day, Norway celebrates the seventeenth of May as Constitution Day. Norway, in 1814, was not yet independent as it was joined in union with Sweden from 1815-1905.

The liberation from Denmark and then from Sweden sparked a national romantic movement. Norway was searching for its own national identity, and the people had a desire to take care of everything genuinely Norwegian.

Traditional folk costumes, which varied from district to district, were commonly worn in the Norwegian rural areas. Although the costume differences are found mostly in the cut and ornamentation of the clothes, one's ancestral heritage can be identified based on the geographic area where it originated. The people living in towns wore clothes much like that in other European and American towns. Interest in folk costumes increased as the culture and traditions of rural Norway were looked upon with nostalgia.

Two pioneers who encouraged people to revive and preserve their genuine folk costume traditions were Hulda Garborg and her folk dancing student Klara Semb. In 1947, the National Council for Folk Costumes was founded to give guidance in registering and reconstructing historic folk costumes.

Adding elegance and color to any event, the bunad is officially recognized as having the status of full formal dress. Since it is complete attire from head to toe, it thus includes a headdress and shoes. An authentic bunad, a lifetime investment, ranges in price from about $1,500 to $5,000. In Norway, many teenagers start receiving their bunader at confirmation.

The power of silver

Silver was an important part of early Norwegian life as it was functional as the only fastener on a shirt or blouse, protection against the evil forces, and ornamental to show prosperity. In Norway, silver had its roots with the farmers, as it was their only status symbol. Many farmers supplemented their small farm incomes by becoming craftsmen.

Considered magical, silver is a part of many superstitions and legends. It has been credited with healing both people and animals, protecting them against storms, improving crops, and even making beer work. People believed that supernatural creatures, *huldrefolk*, lived under the mountains. Since the silver was mined in the mountains, it was believed to have strong ties to the huldrefolk.

Sølvets makt

Før i tiden var sølvet en viktig del av livet i Norge, da det også tjente som eneste spenne på en skjorte eller bluse, som det også beskyttet mot onde makter og var en form for utsmykning som viste velstand. I Norge hadde sølvet røtter blant bøndene, hvor det var eneste statussymbol. Mange gårdbrukere spedde på de knappe inntektene fra gården ved å arbeide som håndverkere.

Knyttet til overtro og sagn som sølvet var, ble det betraktet som magisk. Det ble tillagt legende kraft både overfor mennesker og dyr, det beskyttet mot storm, forbedret avlingene og fikk til og med ølet til å gjære. Folk trodde at det overnaturlige huldrefolket levde i fjell. Siden sølv ble tatt ut av berget, mente de at det hadde sterke forbindelser til de underjordiske.

I jordbruksdistriktene i Norge bar man sølv til daglig for å beskytte seg mot huldrefolket. Man visste aldri når man kunne møte huldrer, da de prøvde å styrke ætten ved å gifte seg med mennesker og stjele barn. For å forhindre at huldrefolket byttet ut et underjordisk barn med et menneskebarn, festet mødrene sølv på klærne til sine nyfødte barn.

På grunn av dette ble sølvsmykker en nødvendig del av bunaden, og de omfattet nåler, brosjer, lenker, belter, klips, knapper, mansjettknapper, spenner, ringer og brudekroner. Den dinglende pynten ga beskyttelse ved å sende det onde vekk fra den som bar den. Metallet selv var sterkt, men ble ytterligere styrket hver gang smykket ble båret i kirken eller overlevert til neste generasjon.

Da de norske immigrantene byttet ut sine tradisjonelle klær med amerikanske, førte de bare bruken av smykkene videre. Sølvbrosjen eller *sølja* ble til en brystnål. Dagens sølv blir båret som et symbol på etnisk avstamming, selv om mange ikke er bevisst denne funksjonen, som ikke var så viktig i fortiden.

Rural Norwegians daily wore some amount of silver as protection from the huldrefolk. One never knew when huldre might be encountered, as they tried to strengthen their gene pool by marrying humans and stealing children. Mothers pinned silver on their newborn baby's clothes to prevent the huldrefolk from swapping huldre babies for human babies.

Consequently, silver jewelry became a necessary part of the bunad that included pins, brooches, chains, belts, clasps, buttons, cufflinks, buckles, rings, and the bridal crown. The dangling ornaments added protection by reflecting evil away from the wearer. The metal itself was strong, but became more powerful each time the jewelry was worn in church or handed down to the next generation.

When the Norwegian immigrants changed from their native dress to American clothing, only the use of the jewelry was retained. The silver brooch or *sølje* was turned into a breastpin. Today, silver is worn as a symbol of one's ethnic ancestry; however most wearers are not aware of the function, which was so important in the past.

Min bunad fra Nes i Hallingdal er med sitt høye liv og lange skjørt helt spesiell. Den såkalte langstakken er laget av dobbeltvevd ull, og originalene som tjener som modell for dagens bunad, ble funnet i Telemark, Hallingdal og Setesdal.

• • • • •

Den profesjonelle knivmakeren, Peer Kleiven, har håndlaget Alex' bunadkniv og -slire. Knivbladet er laget av damascenserstål, som ble utviklet i middelalderen og består av mer enn hundre lag med to forskjellige ståltyper som er smidd sammen. Bladets design kalles *Odins øye*, fra vikingtiden. Peer brukte bjørk til knivhåndtaket. Den svarte sliren med sølvkant henger fra en spesiell knapp som er plassert på høyre side av knebuksens bånd.

• • • • •

Da Alex i 2003 oppholdt seg i Norge i seks måneder, skaffet han seg en Jo Gjende-lue for å komplettere bunaden. Den røde, strikkede lua med sine svarte og hvite striper er en kopi av den lua Jo Gjende fra Kleppe i Vågå brukte. Jo Gjende var jegeren over alle jegere, en vidsynt mann alle som er kjent i Jotunheimen har hørt om, og det var trolig han som tjente som modell for Ibsens skikkelse *Peer Gynt*. Å bære Jo Gjende-lua er blitt en lokal tradisjon i Vågåområdet.

Crown Prince Haakon and his now wife Mette-Marit

Men's Gudbrandsdalen bunad

During the summer of 2001, Alex and my sister, Teresa O'Connor, represented the USA *Valdres Samband Bygdelag* (those of Valdres ancestry) in the Valdres Folkemuseum 100-year Anniversary Parade in Fagernes, Norway. Honored guests leading the parade were Norway's Crown Prince Haakon and his now wife Mette-Marit wearing their bunader.

While in Norway, Alex was measured for his very own bunad. He selected a bunad from *Vågå i Gudbrandsdalen*. *Vågå* is the home of Thor Ekre, an exchange student who lived with my parents. After Alex and I arrived in Norway, Thor's father-in-law, Erik Bjørndal took us to his family's bunad seamstress for Alex's long anticipated measuring. Alex then selected his bunad from several *Gudbrandsdalen* variations: short or long coat, knee-breeches or long pants, vest color, stocking color, tatting on the shirt collar and cuffs, design of the buttons, and quality of the wool.

Alex's bunad is made from the same high quality wool from England that has been used in the *Vågå* bunader for over 150 years. His short black woolen coat has a standing collar and lapels. Even through the hand-stitched front has two rows of silver buttons, the coat does not button up. The knee breeches are made of the same material and have a flap in the front, along with a row of buttons and a buckle at the knee.

The red, green and black double-breasted plaid vest has lapels and two rows of buttons. The back of the vest is the color of unbleached linen. Tatting is on the collar and the cuffs of the white cotton shirt. Thor's wife, Anne-Marit, helped Alex select a traditional *Vågå* silver neck pin and cufflinks for his shirt.

Alex, inspired by Thor's story of Henrik Ibsen's legendary character *Peer Gynt* riding a reindeer in *Gudbrandsdalen*, chose a special button design by that name. Alex's bunad has a total of 40 *Peer Gynt* buttons.

An accomplished knifemaker, Peer Kleiven, Thor's brother-in-law, handmade Alex's bunad knife and case. The knife's blade is damasteel, which was developed during the Middle Ages and consists of over one hundred layers of two different steel grades forged together. The blade's design is called *Odin's Eye* from the Viking Era. Peer used birch burl for the knife handle. The black leather case with silver trim hangs from a special button located on the right side of the knee breeches' waistband.

Hand-knitted ribbed stockings are also part of Alex's bunad. A decorative finger-braided or *fletting* band matching the vest color is used to hold up the stockings. The leather shoes are black with silver buckles.

New to Alex's bunad, from his six-month stay in Norway during 2003, is his *Jo Gjende lue*. The knitted red stocking cap with the black and white striped turn-up is a replica of that worn by *Jo Gjende*, most probably the character Peer Gynt was based after, from *Kleppe i Vågå*. Wearing of the *Jo Gjende* lue is a local tradition from the *Vågå* area.

Women's Hallingdal bunad

My *Nes i Hallingdal* bunad with its high bodice and long skirt is unique. This so-called long skirt is found only in the Telemark, Hallingdal, and Setesdal areas of Norway. I've found it to be a very practical bunad as it always fits.

The pleated long skirt is made of double shuttle weave wool. Woolen yarn embroidery of a floral design is on the front and back of the bodice, top of the apron, purse, cap, and all the way around the wide hem, which measures 7 inches high and 9 1/2 feet long. A fine wool apron adorned with a rose pattern is attached to the bunad. The white cotton shirt has colored embroidery around the collar and cuffs. My matching flora cap ties in a bow under the chin.

Silver is also a part of my bunad including button cufflinks, earrings, top of the purse, and shoe buckles. Two silver ornaments are attached to the bodice witch are joined with a chain. The shirt is held together with only a ring brooch at the neck and a large brooch below it.

Although I've worn my bunad for over twenty years to countless events, I still feel a sense of pride every time I put it on. I am not only keeping up tradition but keeping connected to my Norwegian heritage.

• *To learn more about Norway's National Costume and view photographs of more than 80 bunader from all parts of Norway, visit http://www.husfliden.no*

Handmade knife and case by Peer Kleiven–The blade's design is called Odin's Eye from the Viking Era.

Jo Gjende

Jo Gjende is reprinted from *Turist i Vågå* with permission from Vågå Reiseliv AS http://www.visitvaga.no and Vågå Historielag

Jo Gjende – a name familiar to all who know Jotunheimen. Jo was the hunter of all hunters, the toughest of all hill-men, bad-tempered and uncontrollable, sulphurous of speech, the undisputed authority in the mountains. But he was also a humble respecter of nature, and a wide-thinking person with views on politics, philosophy and deep issues of life.

His real name was Jo Tjøstolsson Kleppe, and he lived from 1794 to 1884. The hut he built in about 1840 still stands today at Gjendeosen, directly opposite to Gjendesheim. Jo was an orphan at an early age, and grew up with various relatives in Vågå and Heidal. The longest period was spent at Heringstad, with his mother's sister Minste-Marit Horgje. In 1850 he bought Bruruste, a farm in Heidal. The mountain played a dominant role in Jo's life, and he was known as Gjende after the name of the mountain lake which he frequented for so many years.

Jo Gjende was a man of contrasts. As well as being a great hunter and hill-man, he was interested in European intellectual life, and waded through the writings of philosophers such as Voltaire, Paine and Volney, as well as Ludvig Holberg. He was a rationalist and Enlightenment man, and a committed free-thinker and priest-hater. Although Jo Tjøstolsson came at an early age into conflict with received Christianity, he was not godless. He found his god in nature, which he could study for hours on end.

Jo was in many ways a loner, and he said himself that he did not have a wide circle of friends. But the few friends which he had were good ones. The English heirs Eardley John Blackwell and Theodore Woolman Rathbone, together with the Swiss, Balmat, visited Jo in his hut at Gjende one summer's day in 1855. The 22-year-olds remained there through the autumn, and lived the outdoor life together with the 61-year-old Jo Gjende.

We know that Henrik Ibsen heard about Jo Gjende when in the summer of 1862 he stayed with Aars, the priest in Lom. It is by no means impossible that the idea of Peer Gynt's reindeer buck ride over the Gjendin Ridge had its origins here. Perhaps we can also speculate whether the name of Peer Gynt's father, Jon Gynt, has a symbolic connection with Jo. Or indeed, what about the name Gynt- and Gjende?

Jo was very interested in guns, and spent much time handling them. Having felled his first reindeer at the age of 18, Jo Gjende developed into a hunter of unusual character. For Jo Gjende it was the leather and antlers, which were the most important prize. Therefore, the largest stags gave the largest reward. He made trousers and other mountain clothing from the leather. He had, surprisingly, little or no interest in the meat, and gave most of it away. It is estimated that Jo Gjende shot the best part of 600 reindeer. Of larger animals, it is known that he also shot bears - - probably five.

Jo Gjende is buried at Vågå churchyard, with a steatite headstone engraved after a drawing by Gerhard Munthe. The inscription is from Vinje: *I am, as you well know, a man of the mountains and am therefore off to the mountains as often as I can.*

• • • • •

Jo Gjende – det gustar jotunheimvindar av namnet. Jo var jegeren over alle, han var den seigaste av alle fjellmenn, den tråaste blant dei tråe, illsint og ustyrleg, ein svovelosande

Jo Gjende, fotografert i slutten av 1850-åra.
The photo was taken in the 1850s - photographer is unknown
Photo courtesy of Vågå Reiseliv AS and Vågå Historielag

Above: Jo Gjende's lue - Alex Huntrods and Erik Bjørndal
Below: The picture of Jo Gjende was taken at Gjendeosen

språkbrukar, den sjølsagde autoriteten i fjellet. Men han var også ein audmjuk naturvenn og eit vidsynt menneske med tanke for politikk, idelære, filosofi og djupe livssynsspørsmål.

Han heitte eigentleg Jo Tjøstolsson Kleppe, og levde frå 1794 til 1884. Bua han bygde rundt 1840, står ved Gjendeosen den dag i dag, rett overfor Gjendesheim. Jo vart tidleg foreldrelaus, og voks opp hos slektningar fleire plassar både i Vågå og Heidal. Lengst var han på Heringstad hos morsøstra Minste-Marit Horgje. I 1850 kjøpte han gardsbruket Bruruste i Heidal. Det vart for det meste fjellet som skulle bli livet til Jo, og han fekk tilnamnet Gjende etter fjellsjøen der han heldt til i mange år.

Jo gjende var ein mann av kontrastar. Samtidig som han var storjeger og fjellmann, interesserte seg for europeisk åndsliv, og streva seg gjennom skrifter etter filosofar som Voltaire,

Paine og Volney, i tellegg til Ludvig Holberg. Han var rasjonalist og opplysningsmann, og framstod som fritenkjar og prestehatar. Om Jo Tjøstolsson tidleg kom på kant med bokkristendommen, var han ingen gudlaus mann. Han fann sin gud i naturen, der han kunne studere detaljar i timevis.

Jo var på mange måtar ein einstøing, og det seier seg sjøl at han ikkje hadde nokon stor vennekrets. Men dei få han heldt seg med, var gode venner. Dei engelske rikmannsønnene Eardley John Blackwell og Theodore Woolman Rathbone oppsøkte saman med sveitsaren Balmat Jo i bua ved Gjende ein seinsommardag i 1855. 22-åringan vart verande der ut over hausten, og levde villmarksliv saman med 61-åringen Jo Gjende.

Vi veit at Henrik Ibsen fekk høyre om Jo Gjende da han sommaren 1862 stana på hos presten Aars i Lom. Det er slett ikkje usannsynleg at ideen til bukkerittet hans Peer Gynt over Gjendineggen hadde sitt utspring i samband med dette. Kanskje kan ein også spørja seg om namnet på far til Peer, Jon Gynt, har symbolsamanheng med Jo. Eller kva med namnet Gynt – og Gjende?

Jo hadde ei veldig interesse for børser. Stadig streva han med å stelle dei. Etter at han felte den første reinen i 18-årsalderen, utvikla Jo Gjende seg til å bli jeger av uvanleg format. For Jo Gjende var det i første rekke skinn og gevir som var jaktutbyttet. Såleis var det dei største bukkane han la seg etter. Av skinna gjorde han seg bukser og andre fjellklede. Kjøttet hadde han merkeleg nok lita og inga interesse av, og ga bort det meste. Det er rekna med at Jo Gjende skaut bortimot 600 reinsdyr. Av større dyr er det kjent at han også skaut bjørn-sannsynlegvis fem.

Jo Gjende er gravlagd på kyrkjegarden i Vågå, med minnestein i kleber, skoren etter originalteikning av Gerhard Munthe, Inskripsjonen er frå Vinje: *Eg er som vel du veit ein fjellets mann og derfor dreg til fjells so tidt eg kann.*

Jo Gjende 1794 - 1884

"Eg er som vel du veit ein fjellets mann og derfor dreg til fjells so tidt eg kann."

• • • • •

"I am, as you well know, a man of the mountains and am therefore off to the mountains as often as I can."

15

Youth finds his niche in studying Norwegian and woodcarving

Author's son thrives on Norsk heritage studies 150 years after ancestral immigration

What is so interesting about Norwegian heritage and culture that a teenage boy would spend five summers submerged in studies at Concordia College's Skogfjorden Norwegian Language Village and, in addition to high school, drive to Decorah's Luther College throughout eleventh grade and part of twelfth grade to study Norwegian. Furthermore, to spend whole weekends in woodcarving classes at Vesterheim Museum with adults more than twice his age and study at Bø University College in Telemark, Norway, during half of his twelfth grade?

My oldest son, Alexander Knud Huntrods, who graduated from high school in May 2004 with almost two years of college already completed, had this to say:

Skogfjorden Language Village

"I attended Skogfjorden for five summers to learn more about my heritage and have fun. I am one-half Norwegian and very proud of it, so I wanted to learn more about the people, language, culture, and customs of Norway. My reasons for attending Skogfjorden over the years never changed, I've just added more of them along the way. I enjoyed Skogfjorden's counselors, villagers, location, and educational agenda, but most of all I loved the food!

"I've had some tremendous experiences as a villager. The programs at Skogfjorden, located on the shores of

SKOGFJORDEN
Paix
Heiwa
Paz
Frieden
peace
SKOGFJORDEN
LES VOYAGEURS

Skigard in Hallingdal

Skigard built by Alex and friends at Skogfjorden

Skigard - A Norwegian rustic fence of diagonal design

Turtle River Lake, northeast of Bemidji, Minnesota, were outstanding. One experience that made a lasting impression was hiking in the woods, listening to Tove Dahl, the Dean of Skogfjorden, tell stories. It made me think about my life and all of the great reasons for being me. I also thought of things I didn't like about myself and wanted to change.

"I was one of approximately 9,500 young people ages 7 to 18 from all 50 states, Canada, and over 25 countries who attend the Villages each year. I received three years of high school Norwegian language credit at Waukon for the summer sessions spent at Skogfjorden. The sessions offered varied from one, two, and four weeks in length.

Language Villages mission:
to prepare young people for responsible citizenship in our global community

"The mission of the Language Villages is *to prepare young people for responsible citizenship in our global community*. Each day at Skogfjorden begins with the flag raising and throughout the day there are lots of tasty Norwegian foods. The villagers are immersed in the culture and language, which includes reading, writing, and speaking Norwegian. Later in the day there are arts and crafts, sports, free time, dancing, evening programs and nightly singing around the campfire.

"If I could give something back to Skogfjorden, it would be some of the knowledge and skills gained. I would like to be a counselor someday and also try to encourage others to attend Skogfjorden. As an adult, I hope to donate money for scholarships to make it possible for more youth to attend.

"In 2001 I went on a three-week trip to Norway with my grandmother, aunt, and mom. We drove throughout Hallingdal, Valdres, Numedal, Voss, and Vik doing genealogy research. The trip was a great opportunity to visit ancestral farms and practice the Norwegian I had learned at Skogfjorden.

"While touring, I became especially interested in the *skigard*, a Norwegian rustic fence of diagonal design. After photographing numerous *skigard* I visited the Hallingdal Folkemuseum, where I was provided with instructions in Norwegian for building one. For my project at Skogfjorden during the summer of 2001 and with help from camp friends, I built a 22-foot *skigard*. The following summer my friends and I added another 28 feet."

Flat-Plane Figure Carving

"I became interested in woodcarving after my mom and grandmother returned from Finland with a small woodcarving knife for me. I asked my mom to find some wood for me to carve, and she came home from the lumberyard with what was the hardest wood I've encountered.

"Hearing about a class in Scandinavian-style figure carving at Vesterheim Norwegian-American Museum in Decorah, Iowa, I decided to go for it. My first class, in which I carved a Santa Claus figure, was with Gerald Ekern. Even though I was easily half the age of every other person in the room, I was quickly accepted and had an awesome time learning to carve.

"Since then, I've carved six more figures during six classes with Harley Refsal. The particular Scandinavian style of woodcarving I do is called *flat-plane*. It tries to duplicate what a Norwegian farmer did with a large flat all-purpose knife. The farmer's knives were too thick to make smooth, rounded carvings; thus the carvings were left with large *flat-plane* surfaces.

"During February 2004 in a class taught by visiting instructor Urban Gunnarsson from Sweden, I carved a Winston Churchill figure complete with his oversized stogy."

Norwegian at Luther College

"Although I completed the highest level of Norwegian language at Skogfjorden, I wanted to gain more language skills. While taking woodcarving classes from Harley Refsal at Vesterheim, I found out that he was an Associate Professor at Luther College in Decorah, where he taught Norwegian. Needless to say, I enrolled.

"All the Norwegian speaking, writing, and reading I learned at camp was taken to a much higher level in Harley's Norwegian Level I class. It was a great opportunity to meet other students interested in Norwegian heritage and culture. During one of Harley's classes, I was greatly inspired by a guest speaker, Lisa Hjelmeland, from Telemark University College in Bø, Norway. By the end of class I knew that I wanted to study the following year in Norway.

"My instructor for Norwegian Level II was a visiting instructor, Kari Grønningsæter, from Bø. As luck would have it, Kari was also my Norwegian instructor the following year in Norway.

"I also have a strong interest in computers, so during my eleventh and twelfth grades I designed several websites and completed four computer courses at Luther College: Introduction to Computer Science levels I and II, E-Commerce/Web Design, and Management Information Systems."

Bø i Telemark, Norway

"During the first-half of my senior year in high school I was enrolled in the Scandinavian Studies program at Telemark University College in Bø, Norway. I took four classes and lived in the dormitory.

"In *Telemark Culture, Yesterday*

Harley Refsal and Alex

and Today, I learned about art, music, politics, education, health and welfare, literature, and folklore that typify Telemark culture. The class, taught by Øyvind T. Gulliksen, included numerous fun-filled study trips throughout Telemark. My *Outdoor Recreation Studies* was hands-on experience in hiking Gaustatoppen and Lifjell mountains, tenting, canoeing, sailing, and open-air cooking. In *Intermediate Norwegian Language*, I increased my skills in reading, writing, and discussing current issues. During *Communication and Bilingualism*, I studied the Norwegian and English language cultures.

"In addition to studying, I also had an opportunity to teach. I was hired by the music department to give saxophone lessons to non-English speaking students and found this to be one of my most rewarding experiences. *Lære* in Norwegian is the same word for both "teach" and "learn" in English. From my teaching experience I now understand why the same word means both."

Finding one's self

From Skogfjorden Language Village, to Vesterheim Museum woodcarving, and to Norwegian classes at Luther College and Bø, Alex's culture and heritage has become an important part of his life. In Alex's words, "it's helped me to find myself in the world, show me how I fit in, and define where I'm going."

In the fall of 2004, Alex will begin a double major in Scandinavian Studies and Computer Engineering at the University of Wisconsin in Madison, which will include studying in Norway for one year. Although it has been over 150 years since his ancestors began immigrating, Alex has found his niche in Norwegian heritage.

For further information

• Concordia Language Villages, 901 8th St South, Moorhead, Minnesota 56562, phone 800-222-4750, http://www.concordialanguagevillages.org

• Vesterheim Norwegian-American Museum, 523 West Water St, Decorah, Iowa 52101, phone 563-382-9681, http://www.vesterheim.org

• Luther College, 700 College Drive, Decorah, Iowa 52101, phone 800-258-8437, http://www.luther.edu

• Telemark University College, Scandinavian Studies, Høgskolen i Telemark, Hallvard Eikas plass, 3800 Bø, Norway, phone 011-47-35-95-25-00, http://fag.hit.no/af

• University of Wisconsin - Madison, Department of Scandinavian Studies, 1306 Van Hise Hall, 1220 Linden Drive, Madison, Wisconsin 53706, phone 608-262-2090, http://www.scandinavian.wisc.edu

Unge Alex finner et ståsted gjennom norskstudier og treskjæring

Author's son thrives on Norsk heritage studies 150 years after ancestral immigration

Forfatterens sønn, Alexander Knud Huntrods, oppholdt seg fem somre i språklandsbyen Skogfjorden ved Turtle River Lake i det nordøstlige Minnesota. Der er 9 500 barn og unge fra 25 land, og hele USA og Canada, samlet hvert år. Sommerleirens formål er å gi unge mennesker en ansvarlig holdning i et globalt samfunn. I den engelske teksten foran forteller Alex om livet ved Skogfjorden, hvor deltakerne er dette samfunnets innbyggere: "Hver dag begynte med at vi heiste flagget, og i løpet av dagen vanket det massevis av velsmakende norsk mat. Innbyggerne fordyper seg i kulturen og språket gjennom å lese, skrive og snakke norsk. Senere på dagen er det kunst og håndverk, sport, fritid, dans, kveldsprogram og nattlig sang rundt leirbålet."

"Om jeg skulle gi noe tilbake til Skogfjorden, måtte det være noe av den kunnskapen og de ferdighetene jeg tilegnet meg. Jeg vil gjerne bli rådgiver en dag og prøve å oppmuntre andre til et opphold ved Skogfjorden. Som voksen håper jeg å kunne gi penger til stipend, slik at flere unge kan delta.

"I 2001 dro jeg på en treukers tur til Norge sammen med min bestemor, tante og mor. Vi kjørte gjennom Hallingdal, Valdres, Numedal, Voss og Vik mens vi drev slektsforskning. Turen var en flott mulighet til å besøke slektsgårder og praktisere norsken jeg hadde lært ved Skogfjorden.

"Mens vi reiste ble jeg særlig interessert i *skigardene*, disse landsens gjerdene med diagonaltliggende skier.

Etter å ha fotografert utallige skigarder, besøkte jeg Hallingdal Folkemuseum, hvor de utstyrte meg med en byggeanvisning på norsk. Mitt prosjekt ved Skogfjorden sommeren 2001 ble, med hjelp fra venner, å bygge en 6.7 meter lang skigard. Sommeren etter føyde mine venner og jeg til ytterligere 8.5 meter."

Figurskjæring

"Jeg ble interessert i treskjæring etter at min mor og bestemor kom tilbake fra Finland med en liten treskjærerkniv til meg. Jeg spurte mor om hun kunne finne et treemne til meg som jeg kunne skjære i, og hun kom tilbake fra trelasthandleren med noe av det hardeste treet jeg har støtt på.

"Jeg hørte om et kurs i skandinavisk treskjæring ved Vesterheim Norwegian-American Museum i Decorah, Iowa, og bestemte meg for å melde meg på. Mitt første kurs, der jeg skar ut en julenisse, var ledet av Gerard Ekern. Selv om jeg bare var halvparten så gammel som de andre i rommet, ble jeg raskt akseptert, og hadde en fin og lærerik tid.

"Siden den gang har jeg skåret ut seks figurer til i løpet av seks kurs med Harley Refsal. Den spesielle skandinaviske treskjæringsteknikken kalles flatskurd. Den forsøker å kopiere det de norske bøndene gjorde med en stor, flat kniv som ble brukt til alt mulig. Bøndenes kniver var for tykke til å lage glatte, buede innskjæringer; derfor ble treskjæringen preget av store, rette overflater.

"På et kurs med den besøkende instruktøren Urban Gunnarsson i februar 2004, laget jeg Winston Churchill i helfigur med overdimensjonert sigar."

Norskstudier i Decorah og i Telemark

"Selv om jeg tok det avsluttende kurset i norsk ved Skogfjorden, ønsket jeg bedre språkferdigheter. Mens jeg tok treskjæringstimer med Harley Refsal i Vesterheim, fant jeg ut at han var "Associate Professor" ved Luther College i Decorah, hvor han underviste i norsk. Det er unødvendig å si det; jeg meldte meg på.

"Alt jeg hadde lært om å snakke, skrive og lese norsk på leiren, ble hevet til et mye høyere nivå i Harleys klasse på nivå I. Det var en utmerket mulighet til å møte andre studenter som var interessert i norsk kulturarv. I en av Harleys timer ble jeg svært inspirert av en gjesteforeleser, Lisa Hjelmeland fra Høgskolen i Bø i Telemark. Mot slutten av forelesningen visste jeg at jeg ville studere norsk i Norge det kommende året.

"Min lærer i norsk på nivå II var en gjesteforeleser fra Bø, Kari Grønningsæter. Tilfeldigvis ble Kari også min norsklærer det påfølgende året i Norge."

Urban Gunnarsson and Alex

16

The turning out of the horses in Sikkilsdalen

Author experiences a time-honored tradition

Having been raised myself on a farm with as many as 22 horses at one time and having won at the National level in horseback riding during 1972, I was thrilled when Mads and Anna Gaustad invited me to attend the *Hesteslepp i Sikkilsdalen.*

The *hesteslepp* is a time-honored tradition of releasing selected stallions, including one that belonged to the Gaustads in 1976, with the mares into various mountain pastures in Norway. *Sikkilsdalen*, located about half way between *Vågåmo* and *Fagernes*, is the most well known of Norway's mountain grazing areas.

I give my heartfelt thanks to the Gaustad family for taking me along to *Sikkilsdalen* several times during the summer of 1976 and for giving me the two newspaper articles that appeared shortly thereafter. The articles were both written by Kåre Prytz, whom I was most fortunate to meet while hiking up in the mountains at *Sikkilsdalen*.

One article about me, *Møte med fyrverkeri i Jotunheimen – Debra fra Midt-Vesten studerer inseminasjon*, appeared in the *Hamar Arbeiderblad* on July 3, 1976.

Photo by Kåre Prytz

- Nå får du være flink gutt i sommer da, for nå kommer Barlunds-blessen.

«Gammeldags» og fin stemning i Sikkilsdalen:

Sol, sommer og 2000 tilskuere da tre hingster og 115 hopper begynte somm

Kåre Prytz

Det er ikke greit å være mor med et lite føll når en plutselig blir sloppet inn i en innhegning med 60-70 andre mødre, pluss en flokk våryre og halvgærne unghopper uten avkom. For mange hopper ble det derfor en søvnløs natt før hingsteslippene i Sikkilsdalen. De lureste tok med seg småen og trakk seg helt ned i utkanten av den store setervollen i fred og ro. Men de fleste samlet seg på vollen like nedenfor Sikkilsdals-setra - alltid parat til å knegge illevarslende og lange ut med et spark om det ble for voldsomt i nærheten av føllet. For litt voldsomt ble det: Ikke alle liker hverandre i hesteverdenen heller, og noen streifet frem og tilbake og holdt leven. En unghoppe så ut til å være nokså fortvilet over dette sosiale samvær. Den jaget hvileløst frem og tilbake hele tiden, avviste ethvert forsøk på kontakt fra de andre, og røpet en tydelig hjemlengsel ved å ta oppstilling ved grinda den var kommet inn igjennom.

«Gammeldags» i Sikkilsdalen igjen.

Det ble nesten «gammeldags» kvelden før slippet i år. Allerede dagen før slippet ble vegen inn til hestehavna sperret, slik at bare de som hadde noe å gjøre der kom inn gjennom bommen før slippdagen. Ungdomsgjengene som har preget denne begivenheten kvelden og natta i forvegen var borte. Både den gamle generasjonen av hestekarer og den nye av både hestekarer og -jenter kunne i fred og ro samle seg rundt kvea og inne i kvea for å se til at deres dyr befant seg vel før møtet med hingstene og sommeren i Jotunheimen. Hele natta igjennom var det folk ute sammen med dyrene. Det ble forresten ingen natt, det ble bare et blekt slør fra en klar himmel en liten stund ved midnatt. Det nyutsprungne løvet som hadde trengt seg helt inn til snøfonnene ble blekere. Men tross et par kuldegrader midt på natta, var det leven av vadefugler på myrene og en litt melankolsk galing av gauk som var i ferd med å bebyrde andre med fødsel og barneoppdragelse utover sommeren.

Nå må det i sannhetens navn sies at hestefolket ikke bare ruslet sindige og snerpete rundt på vollen. Lommelerkene var på lommene, og de ble sendt rundt og tørket med håndflaten før de gikk til nestemann. I hytter og på rommene ble verdensproblemene enklere og enklere etter som klokka gikk. De store historiefortellere dør tydeligvis ikke ut sammen med vår generasjon, og noen oppdaget plutselig at det var blitt morran akkurat da de hadde tenkt på å legge seg nedpå litt før den store dagen.

To tusen så slippene.

Og forsommerens store festdag i fjellet opprant med strålende sol og varme. Det ble utendørs frokost i varm sol som nøytraliserte det lille kjølige draget fra snøfjellene omkring. Bommen for tilskuere ble åpnet klokken seks om morgenen, og i løpet av formiddagstimene ble det i alt et par tusen. Et par dyktige politifolk sørget for at det ikke ble noe parkeringskaos - tross fem hundre biler.

I alt ble det sloppet 115 hopper, og noen kommer til senere. Et par hopper fikk kolikk den første natta. Enten det er godt beite eller uvanlig kosthold skal være usagt, men beitet ser alminnelig bra ut. Og begge hoppene kom seg igjen.

Det første slippet ble foretatt i

Portions of the newspaper article on pages 224 and 225 are reprinted below.

Norwegian written by Kåre Prytz

Translated into English by James Skurdall

Sun, summer, and 2,000 spectators when three stallions and 115 mares opened the summer

It isn't pleasant being the mother of a foal when you are suddenly led into an enclosure with 60-70 other mothers, plus a band of frolicking, half-wild young mares with no offspring. Many had a sleepless night before this year's turning out of the horses for mountain pasture in Sikkilsdalen. The smarter ones took their foals down to the edge of the enclosure to find peace and quiet. But most of the others gathered in a meadow right below Sikkilsdalsetra—always ready to neigh threateningly and let go a kick whenever things got too intense around their foals. And things did get intense. Not everyone likes everyone else in the horse world either. One young mare seemed to lose heart from all the socializing. She raced restlessly back and forth, rejecting all offers to make contact and clearly showing how homesick she was by standing at the gate through which she had been led.

"Like the old days" in Sikkilsdalen

It was almost "like the old days" on the evening before the horses were turned out. The road to the pastures had been closed the previous day and only those involved in the event were

hingster og 115 hopper begynte sommeren

Kåre Prytz

Det er ikke greit å være mor med et lite føll når en plutselig blir sloppet inn i en innhegning med 60-70 andre mødre, pluss en flokk våryre og halvgærne unghopper uten avkom. For mange hopper ble det derfor en søvnløs natt før hingsteslippene i Sikkilsdalen. De lureste tok med seg småen og trakk seg helt ned i utkanten av den store setervollen i fred og ro. Men de fleste samlet seg på vollen like nedenfor Sikkilsdals-setra - alltid parat til å knegge illevarslende og lange ut med et spark om det ble for voldsomt i nærheten av føllet. For litt voldsomt ble det: Ikke alle liker hverandre i hesteverdenen heller, og noen streifet frem og tilbake og holdt leven. En unghoppe så ut til å være nokså fortvilet over dette sosiale samvær. Den jaget hvileløst frem og tilbake hele tiden, avviste ethvert forsøk på kontakt fra de andre, og røpet en tydelig hjemlengsel ved å ta oppstilling ved grinda den var kommet inn igjennom.

«Gammeldags» i Sikkilsdalen igjen.

Det ble nesten «gammeldags» kvelden før slippet i år. Allerede dagen før slippet ble vegen inn til hestehavna sperret, slik at bare de som hadde noe å gjøre der kom inn gjennom bommen før slippdagen. Ungdomsgjengene som har preget denne begivenheten kvelden og natta i forvegen var borte. Både den gamle generasjonen av hestekarer og den nye av både hestekarer og -jenter kunne i fred og ro samle seg rundt kvea og inne i kvea for å se til at deres dyr befant seg vel før møtet med hingstene og sommeren i Jotunheimen. Hele natta igjennom var det folk ute sammen med dyrene. Det ble forresten ingen natt, det ble bare et blekt slør fra en klar himmel en liten stund ved midnatt. Det nvutsprungne løvet som hadde trengt seg helt inn til snøfonnene ble blekere. Men tross et par kuldegrader midt på natta, var det leven av vadefugler på myrene og en litt melankolsk galing av gauk som var i ferd med å bebyrde andre med fødsel og barneoppdragelse utover sommeren.

Nå må det i sannhetens navn sies at hestefolket ikke bare ruslet sindige og snerpete rundt på vollen. Lommelerkene var på lommene, og de ble sendt rundt og tørket med håndflaten før de gikk til nestemann. I hytter og på rommene ble verdensproblemene enklere og enklere etter som klokka gikk. De store historiefortellere dør tydeligvis ikke ut sammen med vår generasjon, og noen oppdaget plutselig at det var blitt morran akkurat da de hadde tenkt på å legge seg nedpå litt før den store dagen.

To tusen så slippene.

Og forsommerens store festdag i fjellet opprant med strålende sol og varme. Det ble utendørs frokost i varm sol som nøytraliserte det lille kjølige draget fra snøfjellene omkring. Bommen for tilskuere ble åpnet klokken seks om morgenen, og i løpet av formiddagstimene ble det i alt et par tusen. Et par dyktige politifolk sørget for at det ikke ble noe parkeringskaos - tross fem hundre biler.

I alt ble det sloppet 115 hopper, og noen kommer til senere. Et par hopper fikk kolikk den første natta. Enten det er godt beite eller uvanlig kosthold skal være usagt, men beitet ser alminnelig bra ut. Og begge hoppene kom seg igjen.

Det første slippet ble foretatt i Bristol-havna, der traveren Barlund-blessen og hans 41 hopper ble satt fri med relativt lite publikum, på grunn av den lange vegen. Fireåringen var en rolig gjeter, som innledet sommerens mange oppgaver med å bedekke et par hopper. Det var litt sus av tradisjon over dette slippet, idet Asmund Stenseng for 39. gang møtte opp som gjeter.

En amatørhingst og en god gjeter.

Det store «publikums-slippet» i Prinsehavna, der det er nærmest amfi, var da tre år gamle «Skagesvarten» - den eneste typiske dølahesten i år, tok over ansvaret for 30 hopper. Selv om gjeterinstinktet er medfødt, hadde ikke Skagesvarten noen stor debut. Hoppene fikk streife litt som de ville til å begynne med, men etter en times tid begynte den å innringe dem litt - og etter å ha tatt imot mye knubs fra damene begynte den å ta igjen. Et par timer senere var det i hvert fall ingen tvil om hvem som var sjefen, selv om den var litt overbærende.

Publikumsfavoritten dette året ble nok Mads Gaustads ti år gamle Petter Best som ble sloppet i den fremste hamningen. Det er en merkelig hest - ypperlig gjeter, men med en tålmodighet som ga den en slitsom dag. Ustanselig måtte den ut for å hente flyktende og streifende som den brakte tilbake til haremet uten voldsomheter. Men all tålmodighet har en grense, og den ble nådd da to hopper stakk av helt til Sikkilsdals-setra. Den satte etter, og det endte med at de alle tre ble fanget inn og leid tilbake til havna, der det imens var uorden. Da en hoppe igjen flyktet mot Sikkilsdals-setra ble den og hingsten stoppet av møtende folk.

«Petter Best» fant seg i det utrolige av utbrudd uten å miste tålmodigheten. Men en grense var det, og nå er den småsint.

allowed past the barrier. The older generation of horsemen and the mixed-gender younger generation were able to gather undisturbed in and around the corrals to look after their mares prior to the encounter with the stallions and their summer in the pastures of Jotunheimen. Folks were out with their animals all night, although there was not much night to speak of, just a faint veil of darkness across a clear sky briefly around midnight.

For the sake of accuracy it must be said that these horse lovers were not by any means a soberminded, straitlaced bunch. Hip flasks were pulled from pockets and the top wiped off with the palm of the hand before being passed on to the next man. In cabins and rooms the problems of the world became simpler with the passing of each hour. Gifted storytellers clearly will not all die out with our generation, and some who had just lain down to catch a little sleep before the big day discovered quite suddenly that it was time to get up.

Two thousand at the event

Early summer's gala day in the mountains dawned with radiant sunshine and warmth. The gate was opened for spectators at six o'clock and a couple of thousand arrived during the morning hours.

A total of 115 mares were turned out. At Bristolhavna the trotter Barlundblessen and his 41 mares were let loose first with relatively few onlookers due to the remoteness of the corral. Calmly keeping his charges under his control, the four-year-old initiated a busy season by covering two mares. Asmund Stenseng served as herdsman for the 39th year, adding a touch of tradition to this event.

Amateur stallion and good herder

The favorite event was at Prinsehavna, where Skagesvarten, a three-year-old and the only typical "dølahest" (a sturdy horse of Eastern Norway) was given charge of 30 mares, and even though stallions are born with the herder instinct, he did not have an impressive debut. At first the mares roamed at will. Then he began to encircle them, and after some jostling by the ladies he started fighting back. Several hours later, although he was still somewhat indulgent, it was clear who the boss was.

The popular favorite this year was Mads Gaustad's ten-year-old stallion, Petter Best, which was turned out in the front enclosure. He is an unusual horse, a first-class herder, but with a patience that made his day a strenuous one. He repeatedly had to fetch stray mares and lead them back to his harem.

Hesteslepp i Sikkilsdalen

Forfatteren overværer en gammel tradisjon

Sol, sommer og 2000 tilskuere da tre hingster og 115 hopper begynte sommeren – Av Kåre Prytz

Det er ikke greit å være mor med et lite føll når en plutselig blir sluppet inn i en innhegning med 60-70 andre mødre, pluss en flokk våryre og halvgærne unghopper uten avkom. For mange hopper ble det derfor en søvnløs natt før hingsteslippene i Sikkilsdalen. De lureste tok med seg småen og trakk seg helt ned i utkanten av den store setervollen i fred og ro. Men de fleste samlet seg på vollen like nedenfor Sikkilsdals-setra, alltid parat til å knegge illevarslende og lange ut med et spark om det ble for voldsomt i nærheten av føllet. For litt voldsomt ble det. Ikke alle liker hverandre i hesteverdenen heller. En unghoppe så ut til å være nokså fortvilet over dette sosiale samvær. Den jaget hvileløst frem og tilbake hele tiden, avviste ethvert forsøk på kontakt fra de andre, og røpet en tydelig hjemlengsel ved å ta oppstilling ved grinda den var kommet inn igjennom.

"Gammeldags" i Sikkilsdalen igjen

Det ble nesten "gammeldags" kvelden før slippet. Allerede dagen før slippet ble vegen inn til hestehavna sperret, slik at bare de som hadde noe å gjøre der kom inn gjennom bommen før slippdagen. Både den gamle generasjonen av hestekarer og den nye av både karer og jenter kunne i fred og ro samle

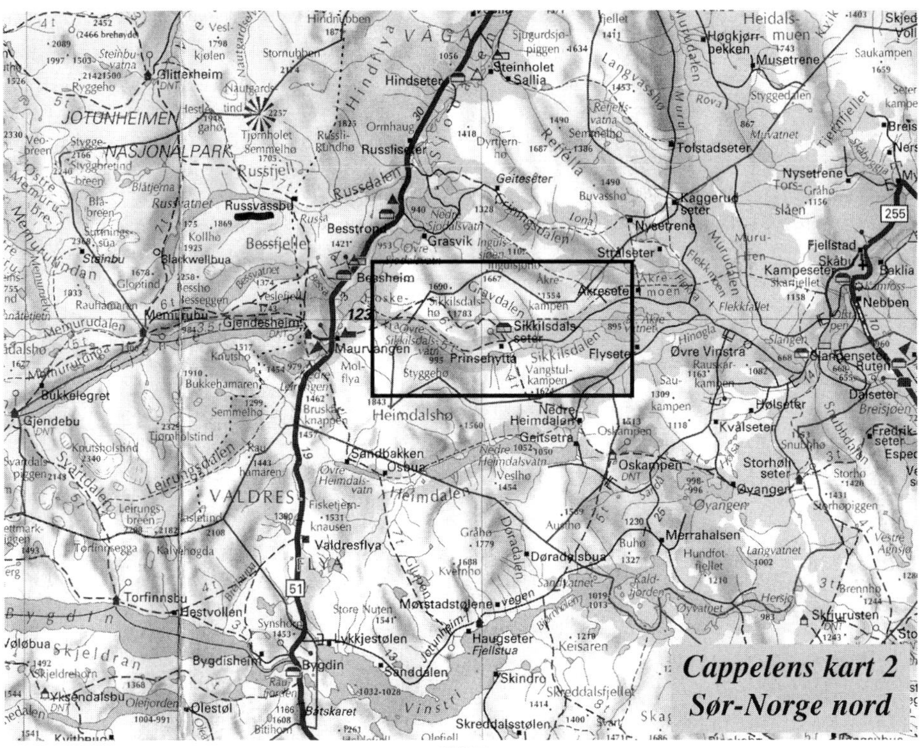

Cappelens kart 2 Sør-Norge nord

seg rundt kvea og inne i kvea for å se til at deres dyr befant seg vel før møtet med hingstene og sommeren i Jotunheimen. Hele natta igjennom var det folk ute sammen med dyrene. Det ble forresten ingen natt, det ble bare et blekt slør fra en klar himmel en liten stund ved midnatt

Nå må det i sannhetens navn sies at hestefolket ikke bare ruslet sindige og snerpete rundt på vollen. Lommelerkene var på lommene, og de ble sendt rundt og tørket med håndflaten før de gikk til nestemann. I hytter og på rommene ble verdensproblemene enklere og enklere etter som klokka gikk. De store historiefortellere dør tydeligvis ikke ut sammen med vår generasjon, og noen oppdaget plutselig at det var blitt morran akkurat da de hadde tenkt på å legge seg nedpå litt før den store dagen.

To tusen så slippene

Og forsommerens store festdag i fjellet opprant med strålende sol og varme. Bommen for tilskuere ble åpnet klokken seks om morgenen, og i løpet av formiddagstimene ble det et par tusen.

I alt ble det sluppet 115 hopper. Det første slippet ble foretatt i Bristolhavna, der traveren Barlund-blessen og hans 41 hopper ble satt fri med relativt lite publikum på grunn av den lange vegen. Fireåringen var en rolig gjeter som innledet sommerens mange oppgaver med å bedekke et par hopper. Det var litt sus av tradisjon over dette slippet, idet Asmund Stenseng for 39. gang møtte opp som gjeter.

En amatørhingst

Det store publikums-slippet i Prinsehavna var da tre år gamle Skagesvarten, den eneste typiske dølahesten i år, tok over ansvaret for 30 hopper. Selv om gjeterinstinktet er medfødt, hadde ikke Skagesvarten noen stor debut. Hoppene fikk streife som de ville til å begynne med, men så begynte den å innringe dem, og etter å ha tatt imot mye knubs fra damene begynte den å ta igjen. Et par timer senere var det i hvert fall ingen tvil om hvem som var sjefen, selv om den var litt overbærende.

Publikumsfavoritten dette året ble nok Mads Gaustads ti år gamle Petter Best som ble sluppet i den fremste hamningen. Det er en merkelig hest, en ypperlig gjeter, men med en tålmodighet som ga den en slitsom dag. Ustanselig måtte den ut for å hente flyktende og streifende som den brakte tilbake til haremet.

LØRDAG 3. juli 1976 15

Møte med fyrverkeri i Jotunheimen

Debra fra Midt-Vesten studerer inseminasjon

Kåre Prytz

Stedet var en varde langt inne i Jotunheimen – det var sol og fred, sjo fra en flomdiger elv. Fugler jublet, gjøken gol og en enslig heilo varslet vemodsfylt en regnskur, enda det ikke var en sky på himmelen.

Det var da Debra S. Nelson rykket inn i vårt liv. Hun kom på tvers av alle stier, et ganglag som røpet en blanding av optimisme, pågangsmot og henrykkelse over panoramaet. Men innen hun satt på reinmosen var henrykkelsesområdet utvidet til å gjelde Norge generelt. Vi prøvde å dempe ned litt med å minne om novembertåke, tykk stillongs og isete veger, men det var med i hennes kalkulasjon:

By Kåre Prytz: "The place was a watch-tower, far into *Jotunheimen* – there was sunshine and peace, a sea from an overflowing river. Birds sang, *gjøken* crowed, and only a halo gave warning of a rain shower approaching soon. Although there was not a cloud in the sky, it was there that Debra S. Nelson entered into our lives. She came with a spirit that displayed a mixture of optimism, determination, and courage and with a delight and enthusiasm for the scenery and panorama in *Jotunheimen*. Soon the delight and enthusiasm included all of Norway. We tried to dampen her enthusiasm a little by reminding her of the November fog, winter, and icy roads, but she had calculated that." (Translated by friends of my parents during 1976).

In pursuit of
Lars G. Hjørnevik and wife research

Since writing *You are a Hjørnevik, but who are you?*, the question still lingers as to *Who am I?*, due to my unknown Hjørnevik genealogy. After exhausting records since 1976, I am now turning to my readers for help. My hope is that, as with my Astri trunk story, new research materials will be found by sharing what I have accumulated. Therefore, I am enclosing my ongoing *"raw research notes"* with hopes that it will also help others in the search for their families.

What I do know: My great-great-grandfather, Johannes Larson (son of Lars), was the two-year-old baby that survived the August 24, 1862 Belmont Massacre, Jackson County, MN. His parents, *"Lars G. Jornevik [Gjornevik/Hjørnevik] and wife,"* were both killed. Johannes was taken back to Black Hammer, Houston County, MN and raised by Lars Nilsson Ekse (first cousin to Johannes Knutson Ekse that was killed in the massacre) and his wife, Anne Eriksdatter Berdal (Berdahl). Johannes Larson was born June 15, 1860 and is buried in the Black Hammer cemetery near Spring Grove, MN.

What I don't know: Why the *"parents"* of Johannes Larson, the two-year-old baby, are listed two different ways in the research materials – *"Lars G. Jornevik and wife"* and sometimes *"Lars and Anna Furnes."* Are these perhaps all the same people? The various documents include:

• Map of the Norwegian Settlements in Jackson, MN – note location of Jornevik & that there is no Furnes on the map (Pgs 104-105 of History of Jackson County, 1910, by Arthur P. Rose) - - see pg 19.

• Lars Furnes is documented as having NW1/4, 16, Belmont, (Pg 94 of History of Jackson County). Lars G. Jornevik and family are documented as settling in Belmont (Pg 98 of History of Jackson County). However, when a plat map is used – Lars Furnes NW1/4, 16, Belmont is the *"same location"* as Jornevik on the settlement map.

• Plaque erected by the State of MN in Jackson, MN. Those killed in August 24, 1862 included both Lars Furness and Lars Gjornevik (Hjørnevik) and wife - - see pg 21. Is Lars Gjornevik perhaps an Americanized spelling of Hjørnevik (Gjor = Hjør)? If so, the use of the middle initial "G." as in "Lars G." in the History of Jackson county text would be an error. Thus, the name of Lar's father in Norway would not begin with a "G."

• Documentation of Lars Furnes, Lars G. Jornevik, and Mrs. Lars G. Jornevik deaths as well as two-year-old child (my great-great-grandfather) being unharmed (Pgs 101-106 of Chapter VIII, The Belmont Massacre 1862, History of Jackson County).

• *Nordmændene i Amerika* (Norwegians in America), 1907, by Martin Ulvestad, pgs 99-100. List of those killed does not have Jornevik, but lists:
– Lars Larsen Førenes and Anna Larsen (his wife), from Stilelandet, born 1834

• *De Norske Settlementers Historie* (The Norwegian Settlers History), 1912 (reprint of 1908), by Hjalmar Rued Holand, pages 519-521. List of those killed does not have Jornevik, but lists:
– Lars L. Furunes
– Anna Furunes

• Letter addressed to Deb, a.k.a Debra S. Nelson, on July 9, 1976, from Gerhard B. Naeseth sighting pages 12-22 references to Førenes and Furunes names - - see pg 5

• Historie om Undvandringen fra Voss (History of Emigration from Voss), 1930, The First Effort to settle in Jackson County, MN translation by Stanley J. Nuland, M.D., pages 641-644. List of those that went to Belmont Settlement includes Hjørnevik and Lars Furunæs. Lists Anna Furunæs as being the mother to the baby.

• Map showing location of farms near Evanger i Voss (near Bergen), Norway including: Langeland, Mæstad, Fadnes, Hærnes, Jørnevik, and Furnes - - see pgs 15 & 30

• Article by Lew Hudson about cabin possibly built by Lars G. Jornevik

• • • • •

Norwegian settlement during 1860 and 1861 in what would become Belmont, Christiania, and Des Moines Townships in Jackson County, Minnesota. Thirteen of these settlers (names in bold) were killed in the 24 August 1862 Belmont Massacre

The following list contains my research data. Both Norwegian and Americanized spellings used by these individuals have been included. The list also contains birth dates, where they immigrated from in Norway, and where they first settled in America. The brackets contain dates and land descriptions of where they settled in Jackson, MN.

• Matthias Aasved from Stod, [1860] via Winneshiek County
• Rev. Peter Baker, [1860]
• Lars Bradvold and family, [1860, SE1/4, 3, Des Moines]
• Bottolf and Nils Peterson Brugjeld from Sogn, [1860] via Winneshiek County
• Ole and Jonas Børreson from Holtaalen i Guldalen, [1860] via Winneshiek County
• Pastor Clausen from St Ansgar – name only mentioned in text
• Ole Pederson Eide from Røros, [1860] via Winneshiek County
• **Johannes Knutson Ekse** (Axe/Exe), born 26 August 1833, Evanger, from Bergenstist, [1861] via Winneshiek County, died 24 August 1862
• Mrs. Ekse (Axe/Exe) or Brytteva Jonsdatter Mestad, born 1826 Evanger, from Bergenstist, [1861] via Winneshiek County
• Ole Estenson, Anne Pedersdatter, Ingeborg, born March 6, 1860, Spring Grove, MN [1861, 6, Belmont or 31, Christiania (east of river)]
• Ole Fladland from Telemark, [1860] via Winneshiek County
• **Lars Larson Furunes**, born 1834, from Strilelandet/Bergenstist, [1860 or 1861] via Winneshiek County (Furnes/Furness/Furunæs/Førenes), died 24 August 1862, [NW1/4, 16, Belmont]
• Anna Furunes, born 1834, from Strilelandet/Bergenstist, 1861 via Winneshiek County (Furnes, Furness, Furunæs, Førenes)
• **Ole Olson Frye** (Fohre/Førde/Forde), born 18 Jan 1822 Evanger, immigrated 1859, 1860 via Winneshiek County, died 24 August 1862, [NW1/4, 22, Belmont]

• Mrs. Fyre (Fohre/Førde/Forde) or Kari Nilsdtr Horvei, born 1823 Evanger, immigrated 1859, [1860] via Winneshiek County
• Ole (child) Olson Fyre (went by Ole F. Forde), born 27 January 1851, Evanger, immigrated 1859, [1860] via Winneshiek County
• Ole (child) Olson Fyre, born 1852, Evanger, immigrated 1859
• Martha (child) Olsdatter Fyre, born 1857 Jørnevik i Evanger, immigrated 1859, [1860] via Winneshiek County
• Anna (child) Olsdatter Fyre, born 1859 Jørnevik i Evanger, immigrated 1859, [1860] via Winneshiek County
• Guro (child) Olsdatter Fyre, born in America, [1860] via Winneshiek County
• Nils (child) Olson Fyre, born in Jackson County, MN
• Tarald Halstensen, Marit Halvorsdatter, Ingeborg Anna, born at St. Ansgar, February 25, 1861
• Lars Halverson and family, immigrated 1859, [1861, SE, 25, Des Moines]
• **Lars G. Hjørnevik**, died 24 August 1862, [1861, Belmont]
• **Mrs. Lars G. Hjørnevik**, died 24 August 1862
• Lars Hærnes (Hernes)
• Hans Kjøstelsen (Kjøstolfson/Kiøstolfson/Kgostolson/Chesterson), son of Sigur, Marit Syversdatter; Jan Theodor, born April 9, 1862, Rushford, MN; Sofie Marie, born March 28, 1864, Rushford, MN [1861, SW, 15, Des Moines]
• Sigur Kjøstelsen (Kjøstolfson/Kiøstolfson/Kgostolson/Chesterson)
• Anders O Kirkevoldsmoen and three children (Ole Anderson, Christina, and Bertha), [1861, NW, 3, Des Moines]
• Knud Nilsson Langeland, born 1825 Evanger, 1858 to Big Canoe, 1861 via Winneshiek County, [SE, 16, Belmont]
• **Anna (wife) Knutsdatter (Bjørgo) Langeland**, born 1824 Evanger, 1858 to Big Canoe, 1861 via Winneshiek County, died 24 August 1862
• **Anna (child) Langeland**, born 1853 Evanger, 1858 to Big Canoe, 1861 via Winneshiek County, died 24 August 1862
• Martha (child) Langeland, born 1854 Evanger, 1858 to Big Canoe, 1861 via Winneshiek County
• **Aagaata (child) Langeland**, born at Koshkonong, January 2, 1857, 1858 to Big Canoe, 1861 via Winneshiek County, died 24 August 1862
• Julia (child) Langeland, born 29 Oct 1858, baptized 2 Jan 1859 at Big Canoe, 1861 via Winneshiek County
• **Nicolai Johan (child) Langeland**, born 28 March 1860 and baptized 17 May 1860 at Big Canoe, 1861 via Winneshiek County, died 24 August 1862
• **Knud (child) Langeland**, born at St. Ansgar, IA, July 26, 1861, 1861 via Winneshiek County, died 24 August 1862
• Lars Askjelson Lid (Askelson, Askerson, Lee, Li, Lie), born 1825 Evanger i Voss, immigrated 1860, [SW1/4, 21, Belmont]
• Mrs. Lars Askjelson Lid (Ingeborg Olsdatter Fyre), born 1827 Evanger i Voss, immigrated 1860. Children born at Jørnevik near Evanger include: Askjel, born 1853; Ole, born 1854; Marjo, born 1856
• Hans Johanson Lien and family from Røros (wife Gjertrud Børresdatter was daughter of Børre Olson), Johannes born 1858 in Big Canoe, [1860 via Winneshiek County, SW1/4, 15, Des Moines]
• **Knud (Knut/Knute) Mestad** (Midtstad/Mæstad/Midstad/Middssad) from Voss, 1860 via Winneshiek County, died 24 August 1862, [NE1/4, 28, Belmont (west of river)]
• **Brita Mestad** (Midtstad/Mæstad/Midstad/Middssad) from Voss, 1860 via Winneshiek County, died 24 August 1862

• Anders Monson, Berit Johnsdatter, Berith Maria, born at Big Canoe, August 1, 1857; Anton, born April 4, 1859, Spring Grove; Anne, born August 28, 1861, Spring Grove, [1861, SE, 13, Des Moines]
• Børre (Burre) and Julia Olson, 3 sons (Bersvend, Ole & Johan) & 1 daughter (wife to Hans Lien), from Holtdaalen, 1860 via Big Canoe, Winneshiek County, [SW1/4, 11, Des Moines] (Other notes show: Børre Olsen, Anne Olsdatter, Anton, born April 23, 1859 Washington Prairie, Winneshiek Co., IA; Olaus, born at St. Ansgar, IA, September 2, 1864)
• Holsten (Halsten) Olson immigrated in 1833, married Ingeborg Olsdatter (Slaabakken), members of the Hauge Lutheran Church, early immigrants to Boone Co., Illinois. Children: Olaves, born in Boone Co., February 25, 1860; Cannelius (Cornelius), born October 25, 1861, Boone Co.; Hellena, born in Jackson Co., MN, March 3, 1868 [1861 NW, 34, Belmont]
• Lars Olson and family, [1861, NE, 30, Christiania]
• Ole Olsen, Kari Nielsdatter, Niels, born April 15, 1861, Jackson Co., born at St. Ansgar, IA
• Simon Olsen, Inga Torine Helgesdatter, Karen, born at Silver Lake, Winnebago Co., IA, December 25, 1862, born at St. Ansgar, IA
• Lars Paulson from Hallingdal, 1860 via Winneshiek County
• Ole Peterson and family from Røros, [1860, SW1/4, 2, Des Moines]
• Taral Ramlo and family, [1860, section 15, Belmont]
• Ole Ranum from Valdres, 1860 via Winneshiek County
• Anders Olson Slaabakken from Tolgen i Østerdalen, Hedmark, via Rock Prairie in 1858, first Norwegian to settle along Des Moines River in Jackson County, [SW1/4, 34, Belmont (east of river)]
• Anders (child) Olson Slaabakken, 13-year-old son of Englebret, from Tolgen i Østerdalen, Hedmark
• Englebret Olson Slaabakken and family from Tolgen i Østerdalen, Hedmark, 1860 or 1861, [SE1/4, 22 Belmont]
• John Olson Slaabakken from Tolgen i Østerdalen, Hedmark, [1861, Belmont]
• **Mikkel Olson Slaabakken**, born 1 March 1822, from Tolgen i Østerdalen, Hedmark, 1861 via Winneshiek County, died 24 August 1862, [NE, 28, Belmont (west of river)]
• Ole Olson Slaabakken from Tolgen i Østerdalen, Hedmark, 1860 via Winneshiek County
• Peter Olson Slaabakken, from Tolgen i Østerdalen, Hedmark, [1861, NW, 23, Des Moines]
• Simon Olson Slaabakken, from Tolgen i Østerdalen, Hedmark, [1861, Belmont]
• Tollef Olson Slaabakken, from Tolgen i Østerdalen, Hedmark, [1861, Belmont]
• Ole Torgenson (Torgeson), 1861, [6, Belmont or 31, Christiania (east of river)]
• K Torreson and family – (possible Kolbein Torrison pg 346 De Norske Settlementer Historie), 1861, [NW, 14, Des Moines]

Sources:
• Blaine Hedberg, Vesterheim Genealogical Center and Naeseth Library, Madison, WI
• *De Norske Settlementers Historie*, 1912, by Hjalmar Rued Holand, pages 519-521.
• *Historie om Udvandringen fra Voss*, 1930, by K. A. Rene, pages 641-644.
• *History of Jackson County*, 1910, by Arthur P. Rose, Chapter VII The Norwegian Settlement 1860-1862 and Chapter VIII The Belmont Massacre 1862.
• *Nordmændene i Amerika*, 1907, by Martin Ulvestad, pages 99-100.

Additional information about the Norwegian settlement families:

Lars Askjelson Lid (Li, Lee, Lie) and Ingeborg Olsdatter Fyre left for America in 1860 with three small children: Askjel, 1853; Ole, 1854; and Marjo, 1856. (Reference: Evanger Boka II:403, Jørnevik). Ingeborg was a sister to Ole Olson Fyre. The family survived by walking back to Decorah, Iowa, which took eight days. Other children included Nils, 1860; Anna, 1862; and Olina, 1865. Spouses of the six children include: Askjel (Cecelia Grindeland), Ole (Kari Dale), Marjo or Mary Louise (Andrew A. Holtan), Nils (unknown), Anna (Ole Olson Gordon), and Olina (unknown).

An account of the Knut N. Langeland family is found in *Historie om Udvandringen fra Voss og Vossingerne i Amerika*, 1930, by K. A. Rene and translated by Stanley J. Nuland, M.D., page 417-418: "They came to America in 1856 and stayed in Koshkonong for two years . . . in 1858 they moved to Big Canoe . . . in 1861 they went in the wagon train with several other Norwegians and Vossings to Jackson County, Minnesota and settled in by the Des Moines River on pioneer land . . . Knut Langeland went back to Big Canoe with his two surviving daughters. In the 1870 years [1872], he went to Watonwan County, Minnesota, where he lived the rest of his life at his daughter Julia's, the one he had carried to Spirit Lake. His daughter Martha married a Sivertson [George P.] and lives in Westbrook, Minnesota. She has six children [Knute, John, Peter, Gertrude, Anna, and Mabel]."

K. A. Rene, page 643, further tells of the two oldest Fyre children: "Ole Olson the older, who took on the name Ole F. Forde, . . . was treated by a doctor in Spirit Lake, but the doctor wanted to amputate the arm. This, the mother would not allow. After this he was treated by Dr. Billington of Decorah, Iowa and he recovered. In 1873 he entered matrimony with Betsie Nilsdatter Gilderhus, daughter of Koshkonong's first pioneer, Nils Sjurson Gilderhus. First, they claimed a homestead, but sold this, and Ole has worked for the Great Northern Railway since. He lived in Wyndmere, North Dakota, in 1919 – has seven children: Martha, Ragnild, Nellie, Albert, Seward, Oscar, and Albin. Ole Olson the younger was . . . in the cellar and was saved. He was one of the first pioneers in Sogn, Nelson County, ND.

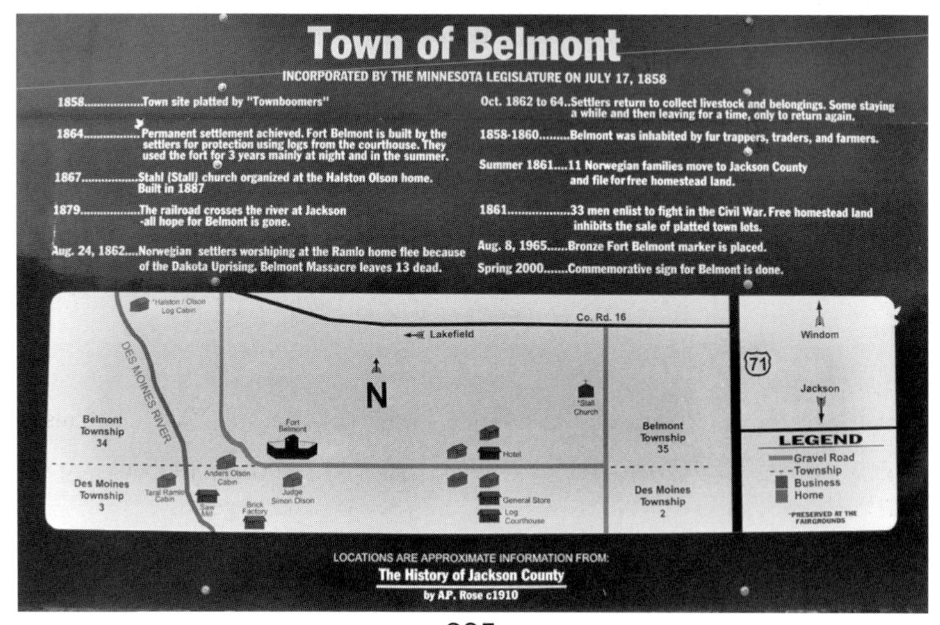

Historic log cabin stands near Jackson

Daily Globe
October 20, 1979

Mystery, Indian lore surround it

By LEW HUDSON
Daily Globe Regional Editor

JACKSON — There's nothing too unusual about a log cabin. Just about every major community in the region has moved one in from the country and set it up in a city park as a reminder to present-day citizens of how life on the frontier was lived a century and more ago.

Somehow or other, though, the sterile surroundings of a city park don't do them justice. To really feel the isolation, the self reliance and the courage of those who braved the wilds one must see a cabin as it originally was.

There is one. It sits in a small clearing among the twisted burr oaks on the east bluff of the Des Moines river in Belmont township on land owned by Mr. and Mrs. Don Holthe. Passersby on the gravel road sometimes miss it entirely but those who do spot it and stop are rewarded with a 118-year step backward into time.

There's a bit of mystery about the cabin and a wealth of history encased mutely within its walls. Originally it stood across the road on land owned by Holthe's parents, Mr. and Mrs. Ole Holthe and before them his grandparents Mr. and Mrs. Odin Holthe. When they first came to the valley in 1910 it was already old but they utilized it for a home until 1918 when they built a farmhouse nearby.

As years went by it deteriorated and in 1963 the Holthe's offered it to the Jackson County Historical Society along with an acre of land on the west side of the road providing the society would restore and preserve the structure. It did and the cabin is today in good shape. It is kept securely locked and nothing is kept inside. Holthe's family keeps the yard mowed, and an occasional passerby stops to wander around looking. Otherwise the site is as quiet as it was in 1861 when an early settler took his axe to the trees to get the logs from which it was built.

No one really knows who that settler was. Early Jackson county land records were lost in the Indian massacre that swirled around the then new cabin. The best guess is the builder was a Norwegian immigrant named Lars G. Jornevik. His was one of 23 poverty stricken Norwegian families which came to the Des Moines river valley in 1861 seeking new homes. They scattered cabins up and down the valley in what was to become Belmont, Des Moines and Christiania townships.

A witness of an Indian massacre

While just about everything else has changed, this old log cabin and the trees in which it stands are pretty much the same as they were 118 years ago when settlers were just moving into the Des Moines river valley above Jackson. No one knows for sure who built it but it is thought to have been a witness to the tragic Belmont massacre of Aug. 24, 1862 when 13 Norwegian settlers fell to the knives, axes and guns of rampaging Indians. (Photo by Lew Hudson)

man from New Ulm who, despite the language barrier, managed to tell them the Indians were on the war path. For protection the Jackson county families began spending nights gathered in the stronger cabins but continued to work their claims during the daytime. They had decided to start building a fort on Monday, Aug. 25, but the Indians did not wait.

At 10 a.m. on Sunday a party of about 50 came down river. Splitting into smaller groups they began attacks on the isolated Des Moines river valley cabins. First to be hit was the Ole Fohre cabin in Section 22 of Belmont township where several persons had gathered for mutual support. Jornevik and his wife were among them. Also present were Mrs. Fohre, her son, 12-year-old Ole Olson Fohre, Johannes Axe and his wife, Lars Furnes, and eight small children.

The women and eight children hid in the cellar while the men and one boy barricaded the doors. They had no firearms. Several days earlier, Jornevik, described as a man with a violent temper and somewhat deficient in judgment, filled his pockets with stones saying he would defend himself with them "any time the Indians want to come."

Log cabin
Continued on Page 4

"No one really knows who that settler was. Early Jackson county land records were lost in the Indian massacre that swirled around the then new cabin. The best guess is the builder was a Norwegian immigrant named **Lars G. Jornevik**. His was one of 23 poverty stricken Norwegian families, which came to the Des Moines river valley in 1861 seeking new homes. They scattered cabins up and down the valley in what was to become Belmont, Des Moines, and Christiania townships."

Latest discovery – a photocopy of an old newspaper article – cabin possibly built by my great-great-great-grandfather, Lars G. Hjørnevik

In pursuit of Astri research

Since writing *Astri Herbrandsdatter 1812* and *Astri, my Astri, where art thou?*, I have continued my research in pursuit of where Astri lived and is buried. My special thanks to Jerry Henke and the staff at the Fillmore County History Center and Genealogy Library, Fountain, Minnesota for their research assistance.

Astri's three daughters lived within a few miles of each other:
1. Knud and Gunhild #1 (Astri's daughter–1st husband, Guttorm) Knudson lived on the Amherst farm
2. Nels and Gunhild #2 (Astri's daughter–2nd husband, Tosten) Evans lived nearby
3. Hans and Ingeborg (Astri's daughter–2nd husband, Tosten) lived nearby

I have come to the conclusion that Astri lived with Knud and Gunhild Knudson on the ancestral farm in Amherst since she is documented as living in the same household during the 1865, 1870, and 1875 census records. This is the same farm where I found my Astri trunk. As to which one, Gunhild in 1848 or Astri in 1857, that brought the trunk to America I will perhaps never know.

As to where Astri is buried, I know that Gunhild (#1) immigrated to Wisconsin in 1848 and married Knud Knudson. Knud and Gunhild (#1) came to Amherst, Minnesota in 1853 and they are both buried in the Elstad Lutheran Church cemetery. Astri's other two daughters, Gunhild (#2) and Ingeborg, are buried with their husbands in the Highland Lutheran Church cemetery nearby. I can only speculate that both Astri and her husband, Tosten, are also buried in one of these two cemeteries.

• • • • •

Data compiled from the 1860, 1865, 1870, 1875, 1880, and 1885 Amherst Township census microfilms with the *"actual spelling of the various names"* the individuals used throughout the years plus death records

• • • • •

Astri:
- *Ann Tosten* (no age) 1865 Amherst Township census with Knud and Gunel G. Knudson
- *Astra Gulbranson* (age 80) 1870 Amherst Township census with Knud and Gunnell Knudson
- *Astra Tostenson* (age 85 from Norway) 1875 Amherst Township census with Knud & Gunnell Knudson
- *Astri Larson* (age 88 years, 11 months, 14 days) May 13, 1878 Death Certificate listing father as Herbran and mother as Ragne
- Unknown where Astri is buried

• • • • •

Tosten (Astri's 2nd husband):
(Perhaps Tosten lived with his daughters to assist them while their husbands were in the Civil War and after the early death of his son-in-law)
- *Thorson Larson* (#54) 1865 Amherst Township census next to Hans and Ingeborg Gunvalson
- *Tosten Larson* 1870 Amherst Township census with Nels and Caroline Evenson
- *Thomas Larson* 1875 Amherst Township census with Jane Evans
- *Tosten Larson* (age 82 years) January 16, 1877 Death Certificate listing father as Lars and mother as Gunild
- Unknown where Tosten is buried

• • • • •

Knud:
• *Knud Knutson* 1860 Amherst Township census
• *Knud Knudson* (#173) 1865 Amherst Township census
• *Knud Knudson* 1870 Amherst Township census
• *Knud Knudson* (#185) 1875 Amherst Township census
• *Knudt Knudtson* 1880 Amherst Township census
• Knud Knudson Sævre died November 8, 1882, buried in the Elstad cemetery

• • • • •

Gunhild (#1):
• *Eunice Knutson* 1860 Amherst Township census
• *Gunel G. Knudson* (#173) 1865 Amherst Township census
• *Gunnell Knudson* 1870 Amherst Township census
• *Unis Knudson* (#185) 1875 Amherst Township census
• *Eunice Knudtson* 1880 Amherst Township census
• *Gunild* (rest unreadable), died July 1880, buried in the Elstad cemetery

• • • • •

Nels: (also by Neils Evensen, Nelson Evans)
• *Nelson Evans* (#51) 1865 Amherst Township census
• *Nels Evenson* (#35) 1870 Amherst Township census
• *Nelson Evans* 1872 Death Certificate
• *Nels Evans* died August 6, 1872, buried in the Highland cemetery

• • • • •

Gunhild (#2):
• *(Unreadable) N Evans* (#51) 1865 Amherst Township census
• *Caroline Evenson* (#35) 1870 Amherst Township census
• *Jane Evans* (#14) 1875 Amherst Township census
• *Jane Evans* 1880 Amherst Township census
• *Jane Evans* (#120) 1885 Amherst Township census
• *Gunniel Evans* 1923 Death Certificate listing father as Tosten Larson and mother as unknown
• Gunhild Evans died June 14, 1923, buried in the Highland cemetery

• • • • •

Hans:
• *Hans Gunvalson* (#55) 1865 Amherst Township census
• *Hans Gunvalson* 1870 Amherst Township census
• *Hans Gunvalson* (#18) 1875 Amherst Township census
• *Hans Gunvalson* 1880 Amherst Township census
• *Hans Gunvalson* 1885 Amherst Township census
• *Hans Gunvalson* died August 11, 1909, buried in the Highland cemetery

• • • • •

Ingeborg:
• *Ingeborg Gunvalson* (#55) 1865 Amherst Township census
• *Isabell Gunvalson* 1870 Amherst Township census
• *Isabell Gunvalson* (#18) 1875 Amherst Township census
• *Issabel Gunvalson* 1880 Amherst Township census
• *Isabelle Gunvalson* 1885 Amherst Township census
• *Ingeborg L. Gunvalson* (age 66) Death Certificate, listing father as Tosten Larson and mother as Astris Larson
• *Mrs. Gundvaldson* in 1903 obituary
• *Ingeborg Gunvalson* died December 8, 1903, buried in the Highland cemetery

Postscript/Etterord

The Story of an Immigrant Chest

By Øyvind T. Gulliksen

Norwegian-American literature is not being written any more. As a small branch of American literature it died out shortly before World War II. But Norwegian-American stories are still written; new stories about what once was. Deb Nelson Gourley has written such a story. Even though her book is primarily a collection of stories about her own cultural heritage and her family history, it should—and it will—attract readers outside her own family circle. Like most Norwegian-American stories of the Midwest, her stories begin in a culture of farms and farming. She tells about the Indian rebellion of 1862, about epidemics, about letters and packages and visits to Norway after years of Nazi occupation. Her family and its history is thereby linked to a larger historical framework. Most fascinating of all her stories is the title story, the saga of Astri, one of the author's foremothers, and her family trunk.

The trunk, made by an unknown Norwegian local artist, becomes an immigrant chest and finally ends up as a cherished heirloom in a modern American home. It develops into the central symbol in the story. Yet, it is not a symbol but the real thing; real people have lived their real lives around it for generations. The discovery of the old wooden trunk initiates a search for family roots and cultural identity. It was the author herself who by some miracle saved it from death by fire. In 1962, when she was just a little girl, the trunk was tossed on a farm wagon, discarded and ready to be dumped. This is the starting point of her story, and from there on the author takes us back and forth in the exciting history of the trunk and the people whose hands must have touched it—a time span of more than two hundred years!

Back in 1962 no one could remember who Astri was, and the trunk had no useful function. To Americans then it was not even a museum piece, but a fairly useless and impractical item, gnawed by mice, a remnant from immigrant days long past. To the child, however, who caught sight of the trunk on the wagon, it was a thing of wonder, of flowers and strange letters. So she asked for it. And got it! The child's imagination saved the trunk from perdition. Thus the story begins with a child's victory over what was then adult lack of interest.

As an adult herself, the rescuer of the trunk starts searching for clues to the trunk's past and to her own past as well. She begins by collecting pieces of stories she has heard about the trunk, even if it is not much to start with. Eventually the trunk will lead her to a twofold identity, binding the old and the new world. More than forty years will pass from the time the trunk is saved and stored till the day when the story is about to be completed. The result is a typical American immigrant story. People, both in Norway and in the Midwest, dead and forgotten a long time ago, but who had once lived with this particular trunk in their midst, come alive through stories told about them. A wooden chest has a considerably longer lifespan than a human being—if saved from the flames.

At the same time, the trunk links the author's family to the larger American story of mass immigration from the Scandinavian countries during the mid -1800s. It served as a suitcase, a table, and a chair during the transatlantic voyage, which the author takes time to reconstruct. The trunk, as it appears on recent pictures, has a name on the front and a mouse hole on one side. Astri's name, painted on the trunk, remained a mystery for a long time. The mouse hole is an American addition. Mice left their marks when it was stored in a barn in Fillmore County. For them it turned out to be an enormous grain bin and a welcome gift. Both Norwegian *rosemaler* and American mice have left their marks. The immigrant chest, a cherished gift in the old country, was for a time turned into a seed-saving container in Minnesota. The wooden trunk was used by humans and other smaller creatures. But a person is needed to see and to write about this. That is what Deb Nelson Gourley does.

In Astri's trunk there is room for a hymnal, a Bible, and bed linen. It contained the sacred and the everyday. It is elegantly furnished with heart patterns in wrought iron. That makes sense because in Norway such trunks were often used as bridal gifts. The author now searches from trunk to church records to archives of local history to tombstones—endlessly. And finally, her work is rewarded: during a stay in Norway she solves the puzzle. The trunk's first owner is identified. From an anonymous name Astri emerges as a real woman!

It turns out that the trunk once belonged to one of the author's great-great-great-grandmothers. Her full farm name was not included on the trunk, so that had to be researched through other sources. Her name now appears as Astri Herbrandsdatter Børtnes Syversrud from Nes in Hallingdal, Norway. She was born in 1792. In all likelihood she must have given her trunk, a possession most dear to her, to her daughter Gunhild, when she emigrated to the Midwest in 1848. The trunk has the year 1812. Did Astri perhaps receive the trunk a year before she married in 1813? Or is it maybe even older than that?

Gunhild, her daughter, probably took the trunk with her across the Atlantic to New York, and through the Erie Canal and over the Great Lakes to Milwaukee. If so, it remained Gunhild's link to her mother and the old country. It traveled on bumpy roads to Koshkonong (or *Kaskeland* as the Norwegian immigrants named it) and to Luther Valley, where Gunhild married Knud Knudson Sævre in 1851. The trunk is therefore witness to the early growth of Norwegian-American Lutheranism and farm culture in the Midwest. And it traveled with Gunhild and Knud as they moved to Fillmore County to claim land west of the Mississippi River, where their great-great-grandchild, Deb, rescued the trunk from death by fire. It is indeed a fascinating story!

The trunk becomes a central focus of a true American story, a story that includes two parts, leaving and arriving. It must have been given a place of honor in the home of Gunhild and Knud, yet as its history was forgotten, its status diminished. It came to be regarded as useless trash, but was later restored to a new status, the binding element in a story of up until then six generations.

One problem remains. What happened to Astri? For a long time the author looked for her grave in Norway, but to no avail. Then all of a sudden someone reveals that in fact Astri immigrated to the United States—in 1857! Indeed, immigration records show that Astri left Norway with two daughters and her second husband in 1857, when she was 65 years old. That is fairly late for a person to immigrate. It is almost unbelievable that this information was not family knowledge a hundred years later. But such things happen. Quite unexpectedly a daughter of hers appears on a photo taken in Lanesboro, Minnesota, in 1916. The author then starts on a new search for Astri's grave in the Midwest, narrowing it down to two cemeteries in Minnesota where she is certain she must be buried. But she is unable to find the exact spot. The marker is gone.

The reader may then ask if it could have been Astri who brought the Norwegian trunk with her when she arrived nine years after her daughter, Gunhild, had left Norway. Be that as it may, she did in fact live with Knud and Gunhild in Fillmore County in the southeastern part of Minnesota and saw her trunk that had been transferred to her American home. That leaves ample room for meditation.

The story of "Astri Herbrandsdatter 1812" is a typical and at the same time a unique Norwegian-American story. Moreover, it is a local story about women, about the immigration of women, and about objects of special importance to immigrant women at the time. The story about the search for Astri Herbrandsdatter's grave in Minnesota, although told on a different level, has in fact the same drive as does Alice Walker's story about trying (also unsuccessfully) to find Zora Neale Hurston's grave, as related in her famous essay in *In Search of Our Mothers' Gardens* (1983). Hurston is well known; Astri is not and never will be, but that is of lesser importance. Astri's trunk, touched by women's hands over generations, serves a similar purpose as the accordion in E. Annie Proulx's important novel *Accordion Crimes* (1996). The accordion is in a sense the main character in the novel, as is the wooden trunk in the story about Astri. Owned by various American immigrants of different nationalities, Proulx's accordion is also ready for the dump, but miraculously saved in the end.

Finally, we know the immigrant chest as a symbol in Ole E. Rølvaag's *Giants in the Earth* (1927), where it is linked to the fate of the immigrant woman, Beret, who—when we meet her—is on her way west from Fillmore County in the early 1870s, at a time when Astri's trunk was placed on a very real farm in the very same county. On the prairie Beret's Norwegian trunk becomes not only the central piece of family furniture, but an altar table and a hiding place.

The writing of Walker, Proulx, and Rølvaag belongs to world literature. The story of Astri does not. The saga of Astri and her wooden trunk is splendid local history with a personal touch. The interest behind the story and its central symbol remind us of the great tales we read, as well as our own stories.

A closing note. My maternal grandmother's sister left with *her* Norwegian trunk as a young girl to Brooklyn shortly after 1900. Her mother, my great-grandmother, had just died in Norway. From Brooklyn the young immigrant went to Lyle, Minnesota. She married a blacksmith and they did not make much money. Later, her one son was murdered while serving as an American missionary in the Far East. Her little Norwegian trunk remains. It is now painted red and placed underneath a staircase in a good American home in a suburb of Minneapolis. What dreams did she put into that trunk and what does it tell us today? What will it mean to future generations? I am left contemplating these and similar questions after reading Deb Nelson Gourley's story of the old immigrant trunk that once belonged to Astri Herbrandsdatter.

Fortellingen om ei immigrantkiste

Av Øyvind T. Gulliksen

Det skrives ikke lenger norskamerikansk litteratur. Det var en liten grein av amerikansk litteratur som døde ut i tida før andre verdenskrig. Men det skrives stadig nye norskamerikanske fortellinger. Nye fortellinger om det som engang var. Deb Nelson Gourley har laget en slik fortelling. Det er først og fremst en slektshistorie eller en familiefortelling, men den har interesse ut over fortellerens egen slekt. Som de fleste norskamerikanske fortellingene i Midtvesten, begynner hennes historie i en jordbrukskultur. Boka er satt sammen av mange historier. Hun forteller om indianeropprøret i 1862, om epidemier, om brev og pakker og besøk etter verdenskrigen. I disse tekstene knyttes familien til et større historisk bilde. Men soga om Astri, en av fortellerens formødre, og om kista hennes er avgjort den beste.

Det sentrale bilde i fortellingen er immigrantkista og de personene som har vært knytta til den gjennom generasjoner. Kista setter fortelleren i gang med å nøste fram sin egen identitet og kulturelle arv. Det var fortelleren sjøl som – ved et under – fikk bevart gamle Astris kiste. I 1962 ble kista nemlig lempa på et lass med skrot som skulle brennes opp i forbindelse med flytting. Fortellingen om kista begynner der, men går deretter fram og tilbake i tid og sted, gjennom en periode på godt over to hundre år. I 1962 var det ingen som huska lenger hvem denne Astri var, og kista hadde ingen praktisk funksjon. For amerikanere var den da redusert til en musegnagd ting fra fortida, et unødvendig minne om et land og ei tid de ikke lenger hadde noe særlig forhold til. Men for det barnet som fikk øye på kista på lasset, var det en spennende sak med blomster og rare bokstaver. Barnet og dets fantasi redda skatten fra utslettelse. Historien begynner derfor med et barn som vinner over de voksnes manglende interesse og tidstypiske tankeløshet.

Da den jenta som redda kista blir voksen, begynner hun å leite tilbake til kistas fortid. Hun samler biter til fortellingen om kista, og dermed også om seg sjøl. Hun ender opp med en tosidig identitet. Mer enn førti år går det fra kista blir redda fra bålet og til fortellingen om den gjøres ferdig. Resultatet er en typisk amerikansk immigrantfortelling. Personer som var døde og glømt, både i det gamle og det nye landet, og som i perioder hadde vært knytta til kista, får igjen nytt liv ved at det dukker opp historier om dem. Ei kiste lever atskillig lenger enn et menneske. Om den kan unngå å fortæres av ild.

Samtidig blir kista i fortellingen det punktet som knytter slekta til en større amerikansk innvandrerhistorie. Kista har vært reisekasse, og den har tjent som stol og bord på ei reise over Atlanteren, ei reise som forfatteren etter hvert får mer kunnskap om. Kista har et navn på framsida og et musehull i bunnen. Astri, navnet på kista var lenge glømt, men familien veit sjølsagt at det er et norsk navn. Musehullet i bunnen av kista er et amerikansk tillegg. Musa har tilført kista enda et minne mens den sto i et uthus i Fillmore County, Minnesota. For musa har kista vært et gedigent kornkammer. Både norsk rosemaler og amerikansk mus har altså satt sine spor. Immigrantkista, ei forseggjort gave i gamlelandet, ble i en periode brukt til å oppbevare såkorn på en gard i Midtvesten. Kista har altså vært brukt av mennesker og anna småkryp, og har tydelige spor etter det. Men det trengs en person til å skrive dette ned, legge bitene sammen, og leite opp nye spor. Det er det fortelleren gjør.

I Astris kiste er det plass til salmebok og sengetøy. Den er forsynt med hjerter i smijern. Det er ikke så underlig, for i Norge var kister vanlige som brudegave. Fortelleren går på leiting fra kiste, til kirkebøker, til lokalhistorie, til gravsteiner. Og endelig, etter et opphold i Norge, løser hun gåta med navnet på kista. Kista har fått sitt opphav forklart. Astri dukker opp av historien som ei virkelig kvinne.

Det viser seg nemlig at det er mor til ei av fortellernes tippoldemødre som har hatt kista. Gårdsnavnet hennes sto ikke på, så det måtte forfatteren leite seg fram til fra andre kilder. Hun het Astri Herbrandsdatter Børtnes Syversrud og var fra Nes i Hallingdal. Astri, som var født i 1792, får fra det øyeblikk et nytt liv for fortelleren. Etter all sannsynlighet har Astri gitt kista til sin 19-årige datter, Gunhild, da hun utvandra i 1848. Det står 1812 på kista, så Astri kan ha fått den året før hun ble gift i 1813? Kanskje er kista enda eldre og går tilbake til 1700-tallet? Puslespillet blir langsomt lagt sammen.

Astris datter Gunhild har etter all sannsynlighet tatt kista med seg over Atlanteren til New York, opp Erie kanalen, over de store innsjøene og fram til Milwaukee. For henne var moras kiste reisekasse om bord på immigrantskuta, samtidig som den var et konkret tegn på kontakt med mora og med slekta bakover. Med Gunhild kommer den, skranglende på et kjerrelass, til Koshkonong (eller *Kaskeland*, som de sa på norsk) og til Luther Valley. Den blir altså et taust vitne til at norskamerikansk lutherdom og jordbruk vokser fram i Wisconsin. Kista er i Gunhilds eie da hun gifter seg med Knud Knudson Sævre i Luther Valley, Wisconsin, i 1851. Den flytta med henne da hun og Knud reiste til Fillmore County og tok ut land der. Og endelig er det altså et tippoldebarn til disse som i 1962 redder kassa fra å bli brent opp.

Kista blir dermed del av en amerikansk fortelling. Som alle amerikanske immigrantfortellinger er den todelt. Den handler om å si farvel og om å komme fram. Fortelleren måtte tilbake til Norge for å få dette klart. På gården i Fillmore hadde kista sikkert en hedersplass hos tippoldeforeldra, men med nye generasjoner ble kunnskapen om den borte, den sank i verdi, og til ble den satt i uthuset med såkorn, for deretter å skulle kastes som skrot. Den blir redda i siste sekund, får en ny æresplass, og blir slik et virkelig symbol i en fortelling som strekker seg fra 1700-tallet til vår egen tid, nedarva i seks ledd fram til da.

Fortelleren står igjen med et problem. Hva skjedde med Astri, hun som fikk navnet sitt malt på kista? I lang tid leita fortelleren naturlig nok etter Astris grav i Norge. Men så viser det seg plutselig at Astri utvandra til U.S.A., i 1857! Immigrantlister viser at Astri kom til Minnesota med to nye barn og sin nye mann da hun var 65 år gammel. Det er ganske ubegripelig at dette ikke var en del av familiekunnskapen et hundre år etter, men slikt skjer. Plutselig dukker en annen av Astris døtre opp på et gammelt fotografi fra Lanesboro i 1916. Fortelleren drar på ny leiting etter Astris grav, og konsentrerer seg til slutt om to kirkegårder, der hun regner med at Astri er gravlagt, men må til slutt gi opp å finne sjølve grava.

Leseren spør seg sjøl om ikke det kunne ha vært Astri som tok kista med seg da hun kom ni år etter datteren. Hun busatte seg i Fillmore County, Minnesota, og bodde faktisk noen år sammen med Knud og Gunhild. Hun har altså kunnet se kista si igjen i Minnesota. Det gir grobunn for mange refleksjoner!

Fortellingen om Astris kiste er en typisk norskamerikansk fortelling. Det er også en fortelling om kvinner, om kvinners utvandring, og om gjenstander som i hovedsak hørte kvinneverden til. I grunnen er det den samme spenning som driver fortelleren ut for å finne gamle Astris grav i Minnesota, som den Alice Walker beskriver når hun forsøker å finne Zora Neale Hurstons grav (også uten å lykkes) i boka *In Search of Our Mothers' Gardens* (1983). Hurston er kjent, Astri er ikke det og vil heller aldri bli det, men det spiller mindre rolle. Det er noe av samme drivkraft i fortellingen om Astris kiste, slik kista er berørt av kvinners hender i mange generasjoner, som den vi finner i E. Annie Proulx store roman, *Accordion Crimes* (1996), om trekkspillet som etter tur eies av ulike amerikanske innvandrere. I den romanen er trekkspillet hoved personen, slik kista er det i *Astri, My Astri*. Trekkspillet blir symbolet for ulike immigrantkulturer. Det reddes til slutt fra søppelhaugen, slik som Astris kiste reddes fra flammene.

Endelig kjenner vi immigrantkista som et hovedsymbol i Ole E. Rølvaags store romanserie, *Giants in the Earth* (1927). Der er kista også knytta til immigrantkvinna. På prærien blir kista en samlingsplass for familien, alterbord, og gjømmested. På de første sidene i romanen møter vi Rølvaags hovedperson, Beret, på vei vestover fra Fillmore County i begynnelsen av 1870-åra, altså på et tidspunkt da Astris virkelige kiste sto på en virkelig gard i samme county!

Walker, Proulx og Rølvaag, hører til verdenslitteraturen. Fortellingen om Astris kiste gjør sjølsagt ikke det. *Astri, My Astri* er en fin lokalhistorisk fortelling. Men den interessa som driver fortellingen og det sentrale symbolet i den, minner en del om det vi møter i de virkelig store fortellingene vi leser. Slik blir den vesle fortellingen om å leite etter hemmeligheten og historien til Astris kiste en del av en større fortelling og samtidig en del av vår egen.

Til slutt. Søster til mi bestemor reiste med si vesle immigrantkiste som ung jente til Brooklyn etter 1900, og derfra videre til Lyle, Minnesota. Hennes mor, min oldemor, var nettopp død i heimlandet. Den unge immigrantkvinna ble gift med en smed. De hadde lite å rutte med. Hennes sønn ble mange år seinere drept mens han virka som amerikansk misjonær i Asia. Hennes vesle immigrantkiste finnes ennå. Den er rødmalt, og står under ei stuetrapp i et solid amerikansk hjem i en forstad til Minneapolis. Skal tro hva slags drømmer hun en gang la ned i den? Og hva kan den fortelle oss i dag? Vil neste slektsledd syns noe om den? Det er slike meditasjoner jeg går med etter å ha lest Deb Nelsons Gourleys fortelling om den gamle immigrantkista som engang tilhørte Astri Herbrandsdatter.